Communications and Networking for the IBM PC and Compatibles

Third Edition

Larry Jordan
and
Bruce Churchill

Brady
New York   London   Toronto   Sydney   Tokyo   Singapore

 **BRADY**

Simon & Schuster, Inc.
15 Columbus Circle
New York, NY 10023

DISTRIBUTED BY PRENTICE HALL TRADE

Manufactured in the United States of America

10 9 8 7 6 5 4 3 2 1

Library of Congress Cataloging-in-Publication Data

Jordan, Larry E., 1947–
    Communications and networking for the IBM PC / Larry Jordan and
Bruce Churchhill. —3rd ed.
        p. cm.
    1. Data transmission systems. 2. Computer networks. 3. IBM
Personal computer. I. Churchill, Bruce, 1939– . II. Title.
TK5105.J67   1989
004.6—dc20   89-25391
                                                      CIP

ISBN 0-13-153933-7

TRADEMARKS

IBM, AT, Personal Computer AT, Personal System/2, PS/2, ROLM, PROFS, and RT are registered trademarks of the International Business Machines Corporation.

Personal Computer XT, XT, Micro Channel, 2400 bps Modem, Modem 1200, Token-Ring Network, PC Network, RT, Series 1, System/36, System/38, Application System/400, AS/400, System/370, 3090, Operating System/2, OS/2, OS/2 Extended Editor, OS/2 EE, OS/2 Extended Edition Communications Manager, OS/2 Extended Edition Database Manager, System Network Architecture, SNA, APPC/PC LU 6.2, PU 2.0, PU 2.1, MVS VM/CMS IBM PC Network, IBM Token-Ring Network, IBM PC LAN Program, IBM PC LAN Support Program, IBM PC DOS, RTIC Multiport, RTIC Multiport/2 LAN Asynchronous Communications Server, LANACS, NETBEUI, NETBIOS, Presentation Manager, OfficeVision, Operating System/400, Netbios, System Network Architecture, AIX, and NetView are trademarks of the International Business Machines Corporation.

ProComm is a trademark of Datastorm, Inc.

Carbon Copy is a trademark of Meridian Technology.

Close-Up is a trademark of Norton-Lambert Corporation.

The Major BBS is a trademark of Galacticomm, Inc.

Crosstalk XVI, Crosstalk Mark 4, Remote, and Crosstalk Network are trademarks of Digital Communications Associates, Inc.

BLAST is a trademark of Communications Research Group, Inc.

DESQview is a trademark of Quarterdeck Software.

The Greenleaf Functions and The Greenleaf Comm Library are trademarks of Greenleaf Software Inc.

Asynch Manager is a trademark of Blaise Computing Inc.

Prodigy is a registered trademark of Prodigy Services Company.

EAASY SABRE is a service mark of Sabre Travel Information Network.

UNIX and Starlan are registered trademarks of AT&T Corporation.

Disk Optimizer is a trademark of Mathtec.

Qmodem is a trademark of The Forbin Project Inc.

SoftermPC is a trademark of Softronics.

CP/M is a trademark of Digital Research, Inc.

WordStar is a trademark of WordStar, Inc.

dBASE is a trademark of Ashton-Tate.

PC-TALK and Freeware are trademarks of The Headlines Press, Inc.

Hayes is a registered trademark, and Smartmodem 9600, V-series, and Smartcom are trademarks of Hayes Microcomputer Products, Inc.

Grammatik is a trademark of Reference Software, Inc.

TCOMM and TCOMMnet are trademarks of The CommSoft Group.

TELENET is a trademark of GTE Telenet Communications Corporation.

TYMNET is a trademark of Tymnet, Inc.

Intel and Connection CoProcessor are trademarks of Intel Corporation.

DEC is a registered trademark of Digital Equipment Corporation.

DNA, Digital Network Architecture, DECNet, and VAX are trademarks of Digital Equipment Corporation.

CONTENTS

Preface

This book introduces the personal computer novice to the full spectrum of data communications and networking capabilities of the IBM Personal Computer and Personal System/2 families of personal computers. The development of the IBM Personal Computer was a significant event in the short history of microcomputers, and the communications and networking capabilities of the machine have made a major contribution to the revolution that is taking place today in computer applications.

As the data communications and networking power of the PC increase, the power of data processing moves closer to you, the end user. This technology is becoming your window into a world driven more every day by information and the transfer of that information. The PC provides a flexible and powerful microscope for researching the meaning of data and a telescope for researching the breadth of data. Data communications and networking provide the tools you will need to do both of these researching functions.

Part I

The purpose of Part I of this book is to introduce the reader to both the fundamentals and the applications of data communications with the IBM Personal Computer. We explore the reasons for selecting data communications over other forms of data transfer. We also review typical communications needs, along with the specific hardware and software components required to meet these needs.

In Part I we cover the full spectrum of communications, from PC-to-PC to PC-to-Mainframe. In the initial introductory chapters, we tell you where in both Part I and Part II you can find more technical details on each communications element. These initial chapters prepare you for the greater levels of detail that follow.

We assume you know very little about data communications when you start reading this book. Each subject begins with an introduction and a definition of terms that will help you understand the concepts related to that subject. Each chapter builds upon the knowledge you have gained from previous chapters. If you use this book as a reference and read only the portions you need to solve a specific communications problem, you will want to make use of the extensive index we provide. It provides all the significant references for the technical terms you will encounter.

The sequence of the chapters in Part I takes you from communications fundamentals to the hardware and software that make communications a reality. Chapters 1 and 2 provide the background and fundamentals. Chapter 3 provides the technical details for hardware. Chapters 4 and 5 provide the full communications software story.

Later chapters in Part I provide the intermediate level reader with detailed discussions about error correction and wide area networking with minicomputer and mainframe computers. Chapter 6 provides a complete tutorial on data communications error detection and the techniques vendors use to correct these errors. Chapter 7 provides information about systems that conform with international, open-system standards, along with details of IBM's System Network Architecture (SNA).

Part I ends with a chapter that tells you how to solve some typical data communications problems. These problems and solutions were taken from real situations. The solutions we present may help you solve one of your most pressing communications problem.

Part II

Local area networks have become intensely popular with personal computers during the past five years. Expensive hardware, such as hard disks and laser printers, can be shared by several microcomputers, thereby reducing the effective cost per work station for network configurations. Part II of this book explores this topic in both its fundamental concept and in practical application as it applies to the IBM Personal Computer. This information should prove useful for businesses that need network power, but not the computing power of a minicomputer or mainframe system.

The future of communications and networking is exciting and new. Applications of the techniques are developing that will allow the user to reach out to information banks and to services never before available. Information that improves business performance and provides individual entertainment is available now and new horizons are developing rapidly.

Larry Jordan
Germantown, MD

Bruce Churchill
San Diego, CA

ACKNOWLEDGMENTS

This book, like most other books, owes its existence to the efforts of many people. Our wives, Betsy and Kathy, showed great patience during its original development, during the development of the second edition, and now with this latest edition. Our thanks also go to Laura McKenna, formerly of Brady, for her coordination and assistance in getting this project started and for its initial reviews. Others at Brady who kept the process moving were Burt Gabriel, Tom Dillon, and Geraldine Ivins. Thanks also goes to Joe Wolken for his tireless reviews and helpful comments during several iterations of some of the chapters. Finally, we acknowledge contributors from the LAN industry who were so generous in providing product information and technical assistance, including Patty Heisser of Novell, Margaret Lewis of Novell Development Services, Rita Parker of Banyan, and Jay Misra, Jim Lima, and Paul White of 3Com.

LIMITS OF LIABILITY AND DISCLAIMER OF WARRANTY

PART I

Data Communications

1

Introduction to Data Communications

The introduction of the IBM Personal Computer revolutionized data communications throughout the United States and many other parts of the world. Before IBM's entry into the personal computer market in August 1981, most data communications took place between terminals and large host computers. Business, government, or research groups used or managed most of these communication links. Hobbyists or computer programmers executed the data communications between personal computers because they were tenacious enough to forge through the murky electronic waters. They had little to guide them except a sense of adventure. Things have changed a great deal since those days.

The introduction of the IBM PC stabilized the home computer market and provided a flexible communications tool that took several years for full exploitation. At the time IBM announced what has now become known as the PC-1, there were few personal computer hardware vendors and few business applications for microcomputers. The predominant personal computer brands before August 1981 were Apple Computer, Radio Shack, and Commodore. Although there were many entertainment software packages for these machines, there were only a few good word processing, database, and spreadsheet packages available. There were also few communications software packages at the time. The features and power of today's communications packages dwarf the capabilities in the communications packages of the early 1980s. One example of these limitations is that most of the communications software available had a maximum operating speed of 300 bits per second. Typical communications software for personal computers today can operate 32 times that fast!

The original IBM PC had several limitations compared with subsequent system units released by IBM, but communications was not one of them. The PC-1 (IBM Model

5150) had memory and diskette capacity of 640 and 160 Kbytes, respectively, compared with 16 Mbytes and 628 Mbytes, respectively, for IBM's most powerful Personal System/2 today. The communications adapter available for the PC-1, on the other hand, had all the same capabilities that exist with the most recently announced IBM PS/2 system unit, except for speed. The maximum data rate of the most powerful PS/2 is twice that of the original PC-1. All other built-in communications capabilities of the PC-1 and the PS/2 are the same.

Although IBM provided a powerful and flexible communications adapter with its original personal computer offering, it took over two years for communications software to push the limits of the hardware. Now communications software packages are stretching hardware limits at every turn. Because of the difficulty in designing communications software, especially the human interface, it took some of the best software developers several years to put together packages that were powerful, yet easy to use. Since the end of 1982, many companies have succeeded in this marriage of science and art. The personal computer user today has a wide choice of excellent software and hardware that allow connection to a whole new world of communications. Gone are the days that an office worker has to play telephone tag for hours to get through to a colleague in another building, office, or city. Gone are the days that an office worker has to wait for days to receive a memo, report, or software program from a distant city. Through data communications with the IBM PC, these tasks can be accomplished in minutes.

To take full advantage of the IBM Personal Computer's communications capabilities, the user needs a good understanding of the techniques of communications. This book provides information on these techniques without assuming a high level of user knowledge of computers. The technical details provided apply to the full range of currently available IBM Personal Computers. The chapters discuss specific differences in the system units where appropriate. Part I begins with an introduction to data communications and provides information on all aspects, including the hardware and software required to meet specific communications needs. Part II provides information on another form of communication between personal computers called local area networking (LAN). Part II parallels Part I by providing an introduction to the technology and information on LAN hardware and software. Before delving into the details of these technologies, Part I begins with a discussion of the roles and current applications of data communications. This section describes what the end user can expect to receive from this powerful capability.

Current Roles of Communications

Personal Computers provide both personal and business communications features and functions. Personal Computers in the home allow users to obtain information, shop from home, and reach forms of entertainment only a computer can provide. Personal Computers in small businesses allow users to communicate in order to share expensive hardware and to access time-sharing information and business systems. Personal Computers in large business enterprises allow users to communicate with mini- and mainframe computers to execute a variety of functions, including database access, intensive computing, and electronic mail communications.

There are also many computer buffs thrilled by the idea of conversing or communicating with another computer or service system. They will delve into communications frequently, whether or not they achieve anything worthwhile. This type of communication often results in useful information and software moving from one part of the country to another. For example, a PC programmer in Dallas, Texas may produce a database analysis program and communicate the software to a friend. The friend may, in turn, communicate it to a national electronic bulletin board, which then communicates it to thousands of PC users. This process can take place in a matter of days. It would take two or three months for this same software to reach users through listings in computer magazines and journals.

Advantages of Electronic Data Transfer

There are four primary advantages of electronic information transfer. First, it can be done any time of the day or night. Second, it can be done rapidly. Third, it can be done with high reliability. Finally, because of the standardization of communication codes, it can be done between equipment made by different vendors.

Almost all transmission errors can be eliminated with the electronic transfer of data. Text can be transmitted at 240 characters per second (2400 bits per second) over most standard telephone lines, which means that an entire 200-page book can be transmitted in about 20 minutes. This may sound like a long transmission time, but when you stop to consider that the book can be completely reformatted or printed in a variety of styles on the receiving end without rekeying the text, it may be well worth the time.

Hobbyists and home users of microcomputers sometimes want up-to-the-minute information on stock prices, news on world events, or information about their computers. Access through communications to time-sharing information sources or local electronic bulletin boards allows these users to obtain that information. IBM PC owners who do not want to program computers will be most interested in communications because it allows them access to software in the public domain. Data communications allow them to transfer programs from time-sharing systems and personal computer bulletin boards to their own disk storage units. Access to these public domain programs might not be possible without an active user group in the area willing to make the data communications transfers and distribute the programs on public-domain diskettes.

Businesses often require information to be transmitted rapidly and accurately across town or across the country to stay one step ahead of the competition. Data communications help make that possible. Documents and files generated electronically by the firm may be transmitted to other offices of the firm or to other firms using data communications. Thus, the documents and files remain in *soft copy* throughout the process. Users may also transmit documents and files generated by others and available only in *hard copy*, but the users must first scan the material into electronic form using an image-scanning device or an optical character reader.

Express-delivery and facsimile (FAX) services are two other options available for transferring information, but these services have limitations. Express-delivery services usually take at least 24 hours for delivery coast-to-coast and packages usually have to be sent on a scheduled basis. FAX allows immediate transfer of information, but the quality of the end product is not always satisfactory for business use, and the process can be time consuming. Sending large volumes of information by FAX is usually impractical because of the time required to scan the documents.

The FAX option is improving for PC owners as vendors introduce FAX capabilities that operate from the PC. The techniques used by these vendors require improvement, however, before this option becomes more attractive than data communications. Intel Corporation, for example, produces a FAX hardware and software package for the PC called the *Connection CoProcessor*. This package allows you to send documents or images to remote FAX machines or PCs in a background mode while you perform other tasks in the foreground. Hayes Microcomputer Products produces a package called the *JT Fax* that has similar capabilities. Many PC product reviewers feel, however, that these packages contain limitations that depend upon the operating system. Developers must migrate to a true multitasking environment such as Operating System/2 (OS/2) to overcome these limitations.

In spite of the technological advances made in data communications and FAX during the past ten years, some people still insist on moving information and data the old fashioned way: They mail it. They send information physically stored on electronic disk or tape so that further processing can take place on the receiving end. This physical transfer of information, however, requires transport time. The transport medium is also subject to electromagnetic, environmental, and handling damage. Incompatibility between disk storage formats used by the computers on the sending and receiving ends may also make the physical transfer of information impractical.

Electronic transfer is fast, powerful, and flexible, but it is not always the best method of getting data from one place to another. If time is not a critical constraint or if the information will not require further development on the receiving end, other methods of transfer may be more cost efficient. Copy protection provided with some software may also require the physical transport of the electronic media.

Many other considerations must be made before you decide to go with the electronic transfer of information. This book does not present all these considerations. This book does present some common uses of PC communications to give your imagination a starting point. The pros and cons of electronic transfer can be better assessed with a good understanding of data communications.

Business Applications

One prevalent business application of computer communications is the collection of data from several sources. For example, a host computer can be set up to receive portions of software from several authors. A central user can link the portions together to form a volume of text or a computer program. Another example is the development of a bid proposal. Proposal writers can send their sections of the proposal to a centralized host after preparing the text off line with a word processor. A central user can combine these sections to form a complete proposal, ready for final editing.

Aside from the development of text and software using a team approach, there are many other advantages in the electronic transfer of data between the PC and another computer. The technique can be used to put together expertise from different parts of the country and can allow work to be performed at home. The portability of laptop computers lends them to this type of environment, because they can be easily transported between home and the office as phases of a project change. Businesses are always looking for ways to reduce overhead costs. Combining remotely produced portions of a project and portions produced by participants who work at home could produce a deciding competitive edge for some companies. This type of development work does often present problems, such as: quality control of contributions from several individuals; elimination of duplicated efforts caused by improper communications; and the scheduling of remote tasks that require special project management talents. The advantages of electronic data transfer may, however, make such development attractive.

Information Service Applications

Data communications can provide more timely distribution of information than is possible through traditional magazines and journals. By the time a magazine or newsletter reaches its audience, it may contain information that is no longer current. Because of the three-month lead time required to publish most of these periodicals, publishers are unable to provide you with up-to-the-minute changes. To get this kind of information, you have to rely on word-of-mouth transfer of facts or tune in to a source that changes as rapidly as the IBM PC world changes. Other than local users' groups, the best sources of such information are the electronic information services, sometimes called *information utilities*.

Electronic sources of information take many forms. Users normally classified them as either profit-making businesses information systems or private, nonprofit bulletin boards. Some examples of business information services are *Prodigy*, *The SOURCE*, *CompuServe*, the *Dow Jones News Retrieval Service*, and *NewsNet*. These services provide individuals and businesses with a wealth of information ranging from stock quotations to current news. Users can access these services by dialing local telephone numbers in most major metropolitan areas. Each information utility provides a good communications software package for the PC to enhance the ease of use of their particular system. Prodigy, however, provides the only Videotex-like package that lets you navigate around using a cursor or mouse. It provides colors and menus that make the system easy to use.

Information utilities provide value by functioning as *information brokers*. These services buy information from a variety of sources, store the information, reformat the information to match the needs of users, and provide user access to the information. The sources of information are responsible for updating the data, and the information utilities are responsible for maintaining the hardware and software needed for storage and access. Because of this division of responsibility, the user gets reliable access to well-maintained information. Tables 1-1 through 1-5 provide summaries of typical services available from the major information utilities.

Table 1-1. Prodigy Interactive Personal Service typical services.

- Extra Extra—Prodigy poll results and people news.
- Consumer—Product ratings and recommendations.
- Weather—Weather maps and forecasts in full color.
- Sports—Sports scores, headlines, and statistics.
- Business—Business news and stock market results.
- Newsroom—Local and national news.
- Eaasy Sabre—Airline reservation system.

Table 1-2. The SOURCE typical services.

- News, weather, and sports—The hour's top news and sports and 24-hour weather service are continually updated and allow key word search.
- Business and Investing—Provides timely information on stocks, bonds, commodities, precious metals, futures, and so on.
- Communications—Provides electronic mail, bulletin boards with file downloading, on-line chatting with other subscribers, computer conferencing, specific topics, and member publishing.
- Travel Services—Provides airline schedules and allows you to make airline and hotel reservations.
- Shopping, Games, and Leisure—Allows you to shop from home, play on-line games, read movie reviews, and determine your horoscope.
- Files and Features—Allows you to produce text using a powerful editor as well as upload text to The SOURCE's computer disks for later retrieval.

Table 1-3. CompuServe Information Service typical services.

- News, weather, and sports from major newspaper and international news services.
- Financial information with updates and historical information on stocks, bonds, and mutual funds.
- Entertainment—Theater, book, movie, and restaurant reviews, plus information on opera, symphony, ballet, dance, museums, and galleries.
- Electronic Mail—Allows you to create, edit, send, and receive messages from other users.
- Home Information—Government publications and articles from home magazines.
- Personal Computing Services:

Software exchange	Line printer art gallery
Word processing	Programming languages
Business software	Educational software
Computer games	IBM Personal Computer area

- Simulation of citizens band radio.
- National Bulletin Board system and special-interest bulletin boards.
- Feedback to CompuServe—Comments, suggestions, and questions.
- CompuServe System News on new or modified services.

Table 1-4. Dow Jones News Retrieval Service typical services.

- Financial News—As recent as 90 seconds or as dated as 90 days; from the pages of the *Wall Street Journal, Barron's*, and the *Dow Jones News Service*.
- Current market quotes:
    1. Stocks and warrants, corporate bonds, and options updated continuously.
    2. Nasdaq OTC stocks updated hourly.
    3. Selected U.S. Treasury Notes, bonds, and mutual funds updated daily.
- Detailed financial statistics, including stock price, volume, and financial indicators, are available for all New York and American Stock Exchange traded companies plus 800 over-the-counter traded companies.
- Wall Street Week—Transcripts of the PBS television program discussing the latest economic developments.

Table 1-5. NewsNet typical services.

NewsNet offers electronic newsletter editions of many national newsletters. The service provides key word searches, archival indexing, and publisher contact covering the following topics:

Advertising and marketing	Government and regulatory
Aerospace	Health and hospitals
Automotive	International
Building and construction	Investment
Chemical	Management
Education	Office
Electronics and computer	Politics
Energy	Publishing and broadcasting
Entertainment and leisure	Real estate
Environment	Research and development
Farming and food	Social sciences taxation
Finance and accounting	Telecommunications
General business	

The major advantage of these electronic information services is the timeliness of the information they provide. Stock quotations can be updated continuously, as can other items, such as the news and local area activities. Magazines and published periodicals cannot match such timeliness, although television, radio, and newspapers can come close. These sources of information do not, however, allow you to do selective searching for information based on subject matter or key words, which is possible using the electronic alternatives.

For the IBM PC owner, both The SOURCE and CompuServe have special areas set aside for exchanging information on IBM Personal Computer products. By gaining access to these areas, you are apprised of the latest news and developments associated with the Personal Computer. You will also have access to tips and utilities provided by other PC owners. In addition, you will have access to public-domain software, some of which is better than commercial software packages that perform the same tasks. Because of the lack of quality control of the software placed in the files of these services, however, you may also find software there that does not perform as advertised by the authors. You or someone you know who has the expertise, will have to test the software you obtain from these services to be sure it performs properly.

Finally, the major advantage these services provide is access to thousands of other IBM Personal Computer owners, one of whom may have a solution to your most pressing problem. An uncanny phenomenon of the microcomputer world is the abundance of users who are more than happy to share solutions to problems just for the sake of helping. If you ask for solutions in an open request (as an unprotected message to anyone who calls in), you are likely to get several suggested solutions within a short time. If your problem is legitimate and no one can come up with a solution, the problem may become a major issue among IBM PC owners. The visibility of the complaint produces results. In any event, you are more likely to get sound suggestions from the myriad of service users than you are from some local retailers. Dealers do not always maintain technical staffs to handle owner problems.

Local Area Information Exchange

Another category of communication that has become popular with owners of the entire family of IBM Personal Computers is *local area information exchange*. This includes both public *bulletin board systems* (*BBS*) and private host systems set up by individuals and users' groups for exchanging tips, software, and information.

To give you some perspective on the demand for this type of service, the Washington, D.C. area's Capital PC User Group bulletin board logged over 30,000 calls during its first two years of operation. The average call resulted in a connect time of 35 minutes. Callers read messages and tips on various operational characteristics and anomalies associated with the PC and PS/2. Users also downloaded programs and software patches.

The Capital PC User Group now has a multiuser bulletin board system that allows simultaneous access by as many as eight callers. This multiuser system allows callers to join conferences dedicated to specific topics and exchange ideas and information related to that topic. Smart personal computer owners in Washington, D.C. check the information on this system before making a new hardware purchase.

Local area bulletin boards can be entertaining and informative. Some offer games that can be played either by individuals or by simultaneous correspondence with other users. Some bulletin boards also provoke controversy by offering a forum for the discussion of such issues as ethics and religion. Others allow local user groups to post notices for upcoming meetings and products that will be available for purchase at the meeting. Many bulletin boards also allow callers to leave messages for specific callers or to leave general messages (such as comments on products) for all callers to read.

Table 1-6. Typical bulletin board features.

Write Message—Allows you to leave a private message for one individual or a public message for anyone who calls in (directed to "ALL").
Scan Messages—Allows you to scan brief summaries of all messages and mark ones of interest for later retrieval.
Retrieve Message—Allows you to retrieve either marked messages or messages identified by specific numbers.
Delete Message—Allows you to delete a message you left earlier.
Userlog—Allows you to see a list of recent callers' names and locations.
Bulletins—Allows you to read text files left by the system operator.
Information—Gives you information on the bulletin board hardware and software.
Help—Gives novice users help in using the bulletin board.
Download—Allows you to copy public domain software to your computer over the telephone.
Upload—Allows you to copy public domain software to the bulletin board for other users to download.
Chat—Allows you to page the system operator for an on-line, electronic chat from keyboard to keyboard.
Expert Mode—Allows you to change the detailed menu to a brief, abbreviated menu or allows you to eliminate menus completely.
Merchandise—Allows you to order equipment or software while on line.
Terminate—Allows you to terminate the communications session and log off the bulletin board.

The introduction of software that allows you to turn your personal computer into an unattended communications manager is a revolutionary use of communications. One of these packages is the Remote Bulletin Board System for the IBM PC (RBBS-PC). This package is in the public domain and can be downloaded from many public bulletin board systems. The RBBS-PC BASIC source code that comes with the package provides a good education in unattended communications. Table 1-6 shows a summary of the characteristics and capabilities of RBBS-PC.

As you can see from this array of capabilities, unattended communications software allows individuals, groups, and companies to set up personal computers to do much work for them. Messages and software can be exchanged between friends, among members of a group, or among the employees of a company. This type of software also allows companies to advertise their wares and take electronic orders for hardware and software 24 hours a day.

These local-area information exchange items illustrate two points. First, communication with local area information services is an important part of IBM PC communications. Second, the hobbyist and home user is also going to be a significant user of the PC's communication capabilities. As private host and public bulletin board software becomes more readily available, more users are going to be "coming on line" with communications.

Communication Network Systems

After discussing the reasons for using PC communications and the various applications of communications, it is appropriate to discuss communication network systems. Network systems pertain to the services available to the public for communicating between an IBM PC and the various information sources discussed earlier in the chapter.

The oldest and most commonly used network is the public telephone system. At one time, AT&T provided this service exclusively. Deregulation by the Federal Communication Commission in the early 1980s, however, has resulted in the addition of MCI and US Sprint as providers of public dial service. Subscribers to these services have a choice of the provider they wish to use. Competition between them has resulted in better quality of service and lower prices for many users over the years.

Because of the widespread availability of the public telephone system, it often provides the wide area network for microcomputer communications. For local area communication or infrequent long-distance communication, this network is a good choice for PC owners. For frequent long-distance communication, however, the user should consider other *common carrier services*.

Two commonly used alternatives to the public telephone system are *value-added networks* and *private telephone systems*. The value-added systems, such as *Tymnet* and *Telenet*, use special hardware and software to route data between connections in a network. The network includes leased, public-telephone circuits and hardware, and the service rates are less than those charged for public telephone services. Besides routing data, these services provide *backup equipment*, *alternative data routing* and *error-checking* of transmitted data. Because of the redundancy of equipment used and the error-checking performed, these services provide more reliable and accurate data transfer than that achieved using the public telephone system.

Growing Excitement

People are excited about data communications because of the communication applications now available. They are also getting excited about the trend in data communications. To take advantage of all these opportunities, however, it is necessary to have a basic understanding of the mechanics of data communications. Much that you will learn about communications will come from trial and error on the PC, but a good background in the subject improves the learning process. The following chapters give you the background you need to get into this exciting field of microcomputer application.

Part I provides all the information you will need to get started in the exciting application of data communications with the IBM PC. Part II of this book provides all the information you will need to get started in the equally exciting application of local area networking with the IBM PC. Chapter 2 explains all the basic technical aspects of data communications you need to understand in order to use this technology. This chapter helps you get started immediately with data communications. Chapter 2 also provides a road map into the remaining chapters in Part I that provide more technical details on each aspect of data communications hardware and software. Part II gives you the same kind of introduction and road map into the technical details of LAN applications and technology.

Data communications will allow you to tap into a new and intriguing world. The world of data communications lets you keep track of information as fast as computer systems record its changes, regardless of where in the world the changes take place. We wish you good luck with your plunge into this paperless universe. As you move into this electronic medium, you will find that you can do more than watch the flow of information. You will become a part of the flow, contributing to an ever-changing collection of information that is becoming the most valuable resource a country can own.

2

Taking the Mystery Out of Communications

There are many buzz words associated with microcomputer data communications, and this chapter takes some of the mystery out of these terms. In addition, the following paragraphs provide a basis for our discussions of communications hardware and software that appear in later chapters. You will also find this chapter a handy reference when terms and concepts in communications articles are not clear.

Data Communications Overview

The phrase *data communications* covers everything from the transfer of data between a disk drive and memory to the transfer of data from the IBM PC to a mainframe system in another country. Obviously, that scope is much too large to cover in a single book. Since many good books are already available that explain the concepts and the details of microcomputer input/output with peripherals, we concentrate on the aspect of data communications between the IBM PC and other computers in this book. We discuss some aspects of internal communication and communication with attached devices (peripherals), but the emphasis in Part I is communications with remote computers through the public telephone system. We also provide examples of communications through use of the BASIC and C language.

The IBM PC, like all other digital computers, stores and processes data as signals that represent 1s and 0s. Each of these 1s and 0s represents a *BInary digiT* (*bit*) of information. The IBM PC stores these bits in 8-bit groups called *bytes*. The PC also stores pairs of bytes (16 total bits) called *words*. The top of the line PS/2 models can store information in groups of four bytes (32 total bits) called *double words*. Although information may occupy two or more bytes of total storage space in the PC's memory, data movement between components in the PC may not match this capability.

As shown in Table 2.1, the original IBM PC's *central processor* (*CPU*) can handle data in groups of 16 bits, but that same data moves through the *data bus* in groups of 8 bits. Later model IBM PC ATs and PS/2s can both store and move data in groups of at least 16 bits. However, this data cannot be sent out to the rest of the world in groups that large. The PC hardware must break the internal data streams into eight-bit bytes before it is transmitted to the outside world. This chapter describes this process in detail.

Table 2-1. IBM PS/2 and PC Micro Channel and bus.

System Unit	CPU Size	Data Bus 8-bit	16-bit	Micro Channel 16-bit	32-bit
IBM PC	16	x			
IBM PC XT	16	x			
IBM PC AT	16	x	x		
IBM PS/2 Model 30	16	x	x		
IBM PS/2 Model 50	16			x	
IBM PS/2 Model 60	16			x	
IBM PS/2 Model 70	32			x	x
IBM PS/2 Model 80	32			x	x

Although the IBM PC stores and communicates data as bits, the internal hardware must follow specific rules during the storage and transfer of the data. The CPU and all its peripherals must "speak the same language," otherwise data transferred and stored will not be useful. Internal devices must follow certain rules and *conventions* to be compatible. Devices that provide the communications between the Personal Computer and other external computer systems must also follow these same rules. Table 2-2 shows the organizations that develop many of the computer rules and conventions. Figure 2.1 shows a simplified diagram of the major data flow paths within a typical IBM PC. Many of the standards and recommendations that define these flow paths come from these same organizations shown in Table 2-1.

Table 2-2. Standards organizations.

IEEE: The Institute of Electrical and Electronic Engineers (IEEE) is an American professional group that establishes electrical standards. The organization has a microprocessor standards committee that sets electrical and electronic standards for the design of microcomputer components and systems.

EIA: The Electronics Industries Association (EIA) represents American manufacturers. The EIA publishes standards, such as RS-232C and RS-449, that govern the electrical characteristics of connections between the personal computer and external peripherals such as printers and modems.

CCITT: The Consultive Committee in International Telegraphy and Telephony (CCITT) is an International Telecommunications Union (ITU) committee. Two study groups within the CCITT develop data communications standards. The standards produced by the CCITT study groups are international versions of the standards produced by the EIA.

ISO: The International Standards Organization (ISO) is a worldwide group composed of representatives from member nations. The American National Standards Institute (ANSI) represents the United States. The ISO develops international standards for data communications. A seven-layer Open Systems Interconnection (OSI) model was developed by this organization to define a universal architecture for interconnecting different types of computer systems.

The remainder of this chapter describes how the rules and standards developed by IBM and other organizations are implemented to support data communications with the IBM PC. A thorough understanding of these concepts is not necessary to perform data communications, but the information will help you solve whatever communication prob-

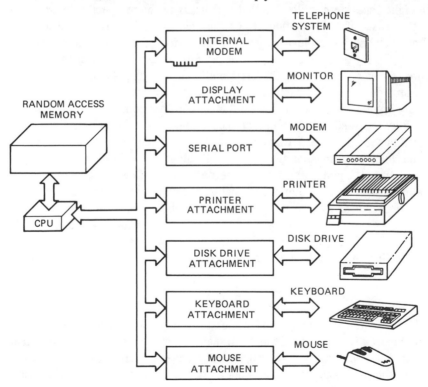

Figure 2.1 Typical PS/2 data flow paths.

lems may arise. The information also provides a foundation for the hardware and software discussions we provide in later chapters.

Data Transfer Modes

The IBM PC uses two modes of data transfer, depending on how close the computer is to the device with which it is communicating. For distances less than 100 feet, data can be transferred using *parallel communications*. For distances over 100 feet, data are transferred from the PC to another device through *serial communications*. Although both methods fall under the heading of *input/output* (*I/O*), there are many differences in these two types of communication. The following paragraphs explore both modes of communication. They explore serial communication in more detail because of its relevance to other data communications topics contained in this book.

Parallel I/O

In parallel data transfer, at least eight data bits move simultaneously from one device to another. As illustrated in Figure 2.2, the sending device transmits eight data bits through eight separate data lines called a *data bus* or, more specifically, an 8-bit data bus in this case. The destination device receives the data through these same eight data lines. The receiving devices uses the data without modification or translation. Figure 2.3 shows a simplified diagram of the 8-bit data bus used in the original IBM PC. More recent vintage IBM PC system units, such as the AT, contain a 16-bit data bus that provide 16 parallel data lines for communication with internal devices. In the same sense, system units such as the PS/2 Model 70 that contain a 32-bit data bus have the capability to send data between devices through 32 parallel data lines.

Parallel data buses used in the transfer of parallel data may take several physical forms, but each form accomplishes the same result. Most of the Personal Computer's data buses are circuit boards, and tracing the path of the flow of data may prove difficult for a hardware novice. Other buses, such as the cable connecting the disk drive controller board to the disk drive in a PC, are flat ribbon cables and can be easily traced. Data buses external to the PC system unit, on the other hand, are often round, shielded cables. This latter form of cable traps extraneous radio-frequency signals while communicating the data from source to destination.

Serial I/O

In serial data transfer, data bits transfer one at a time between the source and the destination. Compared with the simultaneous transfer of groups of bits that takes place in parallel communication, this type of communication does not appear to be a fast way of moving data, and in actual practice it is not as fast as parallel transfer. Why, then, does anyone choose that alternative over parallel transfer? The answer is the same as the answer to many other questions about the design of hardware. Users chose serial

Place
First Class
Postage
Here
Post Office
Will Not
Deliver Without
Postage

Brady Books
15 Columbus Circle
New York, NY 10023

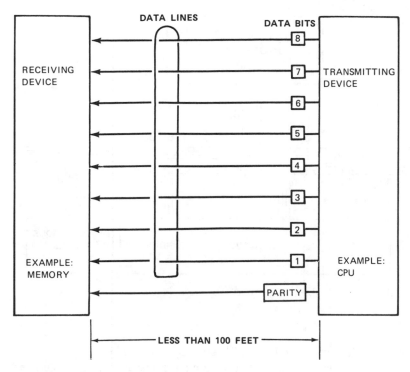

Figure 2.2 Parallel data transfer

data transfer when the economics and practicality of hardware implementation dictate that choice.

Parallel data transfer between computers requires the installation of a cable containing at least eight data lines between the two machines. For short-distance communications (less than 100 feet), this method of connectivity is available at a reasonable cost. For long-distance communications, however, it is more economical to use existing telephone equipment than to install parallel cables and signal amplifiers.

Because of the design of public telephone lines and equipment, computers must communicate through this system using *serial data communications* techniques. The telephone system was originally designed for voice communications through a pair of wires. The simple analog signals used to transmit and receive voice signals did not require parallel signal paths. Now that tremendous sums of money are invested in voice communications equipment, it makes good sense to convert data communications into signals compatible with that equipment. With only a single pair of wires available, or two pairs in more sophisticated systems, the telephone system can only transmit data serially, one bit at a time, using analog techniques that work well for voice communications.

The future direction for voice communications networks is a gradual conversion to digital signal transmission, but the conversion process will be slow. Tests are underway in several major cities to determine the feasibility of transmitting both voice and

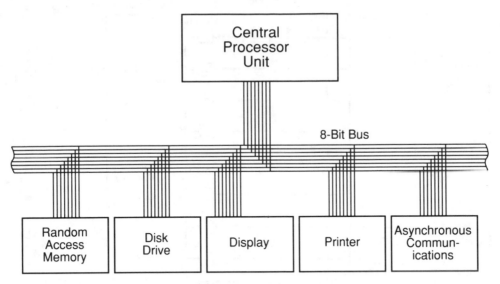

Figure 2.3 The IBM PC 8-bit data bus.

data signals through high-speed digital lines. These *Integrated Services Digital Network (ISDN)* lines provide two voice and one packet data circuit over lines previously used for only one voice circuit or one voice-grade data circuit. So far these tests have been successful. However, it will take many years for telephone companies throughout the United States to convert to the hardware and software necessary to support this capability. If vendors implement these services on a large scale throughout the United States, ISDN will allow users to transmit or receive telegraph, telex, music, telephone, facsimile, data, or slow-scan video over the same pair of wires. Access to large public and private data networks will also be possible from business or residential locations.

As illustrated in Figure 2.4, the sending device in a personal computer with an 8-bit bus transmits eight simultaneous bits of data to the serial conversion hardware. The data bits move sequentially, one bit at a time, from that equipment to the receiving station. PC hardware must convert the parallel data stream to a serial stream at the transmitting end. PC hardware must also transformed that stream back to a parallel stream at the receiving end. The process is not, however, as easy as it looks. Serial communications requires a high-quality combination of hardware and software in order to achieve acceptable data transfers between one computer and another computer or device.

Serial Duplex Configurations

Figure 2.5 shows the three commonly used conventions for serial communications through telephone connections. The *simplex* configuration shown in Figure 2.5a allows

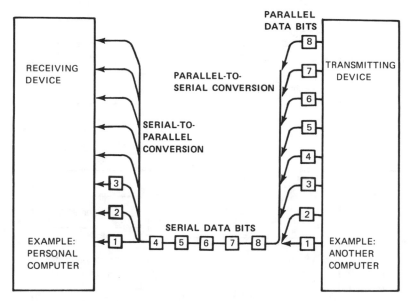

Figure 2.4 Serial data transfer.

data to flow in only one direction and is sometimes called a *unidirectional data bus*. The *half-duplex* configuration shown in Figure 2.5b, on the other hand, allows data to flow in either direction and is called a *bidirectional data bus*. The half-duplex configuration surpasses the simplex mode in that data can flow both ways, but the half-duplex design permits data to flow in only one direction at a time. So, half-duplex is simplex that switches directions. The third configuration, shown in Figure 2.5c, is the *full-duplex* interface (sometimes just called *duplex*). It allows data to move in both directions simultaneously. Thus, full-duplex is a dual-simplex configuration that requires both communicating devices to have full and independent transmit and receive capabilities.

Half-duplex and full-duplex operations are independent of the number of wires in the communication line. The terms *two-wire* and *four-wire* are sometimes confused with half-duplex and full-duplex. The public telephone system uses two wires, whereas leased telephone lines may have four wires. Either communications system will support both half-and full-duplex.

The term *local echo* is also often confused with duplex mode. The confusion arises from the capability of communications software to produce a local echo of characters when a duplex mode mismatch exists between the host and the PC. If the host computer is communicating in full-duplex, it will echo characters back to the PC immediately after receiving them. This immediate echo, called *echo-plex*, allows the PC user to verify proper transmission of characters to the host. When the host computer is operating in half-duplex, it will not echo received characters back to the PC. The communications link must provide another technique for displaying the input.

A PC user can correct a mismatch in duplex modes in one of two ways. First, the PC user can switch the local modem, the device used to communicate through the tele-

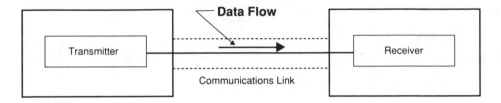

(a) The Simplex Connection

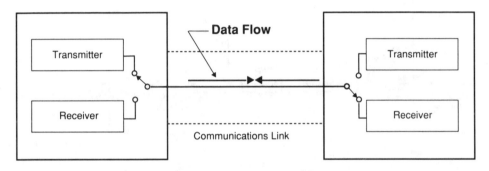

(b) The Half-Duplex Connection

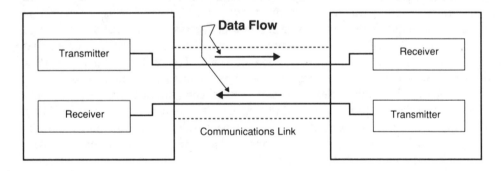

(c) The Full-Duplex Connection

Figure 2.5 Direction of data flow.

phone system, to the half-duplex mode. This causes the modem to echo transmitted characters to the PC's monitor. Second, the PC user can instruct the communications software to print transmitted characters on the PC screen. The term to describe the latter of these two options is *local echo*. This local software echo is a substitute for switching the local modem to half-duplex. Figure 2.6 shows a simple BASIC communications program that illustrates full-and half-duplex. Figure 2.7 shows a flow diagram of this program.

```
100 ' SIMPLE COMMUNICATIONS PROGRAM
110 '
120 ' SET HALFDUPLEX = -1 FOR HALF-DUPLEX OPERATION
130 ' SET HALFDUPLEX = 0 FOR FULL-DUPLEX OPERATION
140 HALFDUPLEX = -1
150 CLOSE #1
160 OPEN ""COM1:300,E,7,1,DS,CD"" AS #1
170 PCKEY$=INKEY$:IF PCKEY$="" THEN 200
180 PRINT #1,PCKEY$;
190 IF HALFDUPLEX THEN PRINT PCKEY$;
200 IF EOF(1) THEN 170
210 HOSTCHAR$=INPUT$(LOC(1),#1)
220 PRINT HOSTCHAR$;
230 GOTO 170
```

Figure 2.6 BASIC communications program.

Another important factor in serial data transfer is the timing of data transmission and the timing of data receipt. In parallel data transfer, eight or more data bits move simultaneously from source to destination, leaving no doubt about the association of bits with bytes. In serial data transfer, on the other hand, each data bit moves sequentially from source to destination. This technique requires *synchronization* between the data source and data destination to segregate bits, characters (bytes), and messages. Without synchronization, the receiving device will receive a series of signals that have no meaning. Synchronization that signals the start of data transmission is necessary for the received signals to be interpreted as meaningful information.

Data link control (*DLC*) governs the synchronization between two communicating stations. Data link control requires the transmission of bits, characters, or messages along with data as the data go from one station to another. Communications hardware or software adds or deletes this information, and their operation is transparent to the user. The information synchronizes the clocks contained in the hardware of both the sending and receiving stations. This ensures that the signals transmitted by the sending station are properly recognized by the receiving station. The pattern of ones and zeros must not become distorted through the communications process.

The two DLC methods that computer vendors use to synchronize and control data communications between computers are *asynchronous* (also called *start-stop*) and *synchronous*. The asynchronous method of data link control is prevalent in several protocols. The PC's asynchronous communications port uses this protocol to transmit and receive a data stream compatible with the *teletypewriter* (*TTY*) terminals used in the 1950s and 1960s. The synchronous method of data link control, on the other hand, supports three protocols that define the rules for message exchange. These protocols are *binary synchronous communications* (also called *BSC* or *bisync*), *synchronous data link control* (*SDLC*), and *high-level data link control* (*HDLC*).

Asynchronous data, as their name implies, are not a continuous flow of synchronized bits. The communications hardware adds synchronizing information to every byte it transmits. As illustrated in Figure 2.8, each asynchronous byte begins with a *start bit*

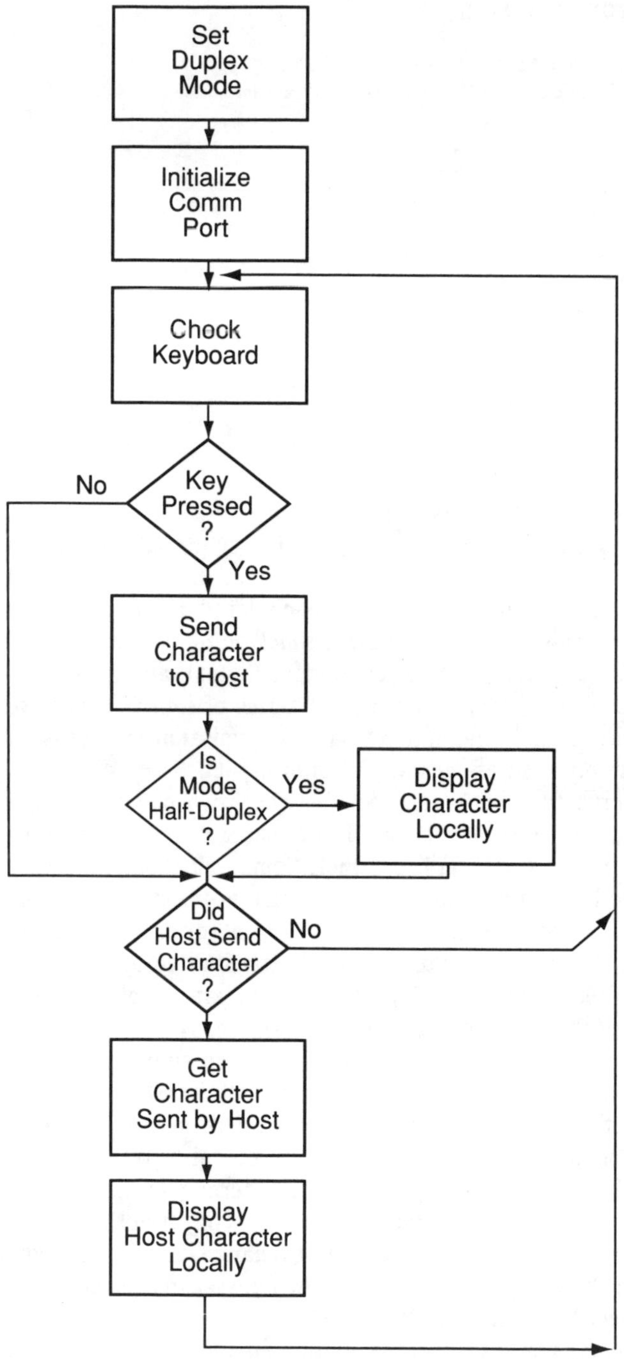

Figure 2.7 BASIC communication program flow chart.

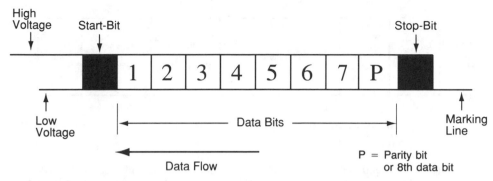

Figure 2.8 Asychronous data byte and framing bits.

that tells the receiving device to begin measuring the subsequent data for the presence of 1s and 0s. A low-voltage signal on the data line always precedes the start bit. This *marking line* or *marking state* provides a clear contrast for the start bit and allows the receiving device to detect the beginning of a new start bit. At the end of every "train" of eight data bits is a "caboose" called a *stop bit*. (There may be one, one and one-half, or two stop bits at the end of each character, but most IBM PC communications use one stop bit.) The stop bit is a low-voltage marker that shows the receiving device the end of a byte of data. It returns the data line to the marking state in preparation for the next byte of data. These start and stop bits *frame* the 1s and 0s in each transmitted byte to clearly segregate them from the byte of data that will follow.

In contrast with the individually framed asynchronous bytes, synchronous data move in *blocks*, and synchronization information is either contained in the blocks for long-distance transmission or provided on a separate data line for local transmission. Figure 2.9 shows the SDLC protocol data structure. This protocol provides clear marks at the beginning and end of each block of data. The protocol does not frame the individual 8-bit groups of 1s and 0s. In fact, synchronous communications may not be character-oriented at all. The data link control of synchronous protocols may be either character-oriented or bit-oriented. *Character-oriented protocols* recognize bytes of data as specific characters, whereas *bit-oriented protocols* do not impose character assignments to transmitted data bits.

Synchronous communications has three advantages when compared with asynchronous communications. The elimination of character *synchronizing bits* with synchronous communications results in a greater ratio of data bits to total bits in a communications stream compared with asynchronous communications. The synchronous method also allows a user to transmit binary data that have no character meaning. The greatest advantage in using the synchronous method, however, is that it allows the PC user to communicate with mainframe computers through synchronous communications networks.

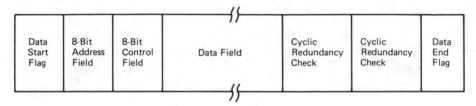

Figure 2.9 Synchronous data-link control (SDLC).

Although synchronous communications provides several advantages for the IBM PC user, vendors normally use this protocol for communications between the PC and an IBM host or between sophisticated error-correcting modems. The hardware and software required to support this method of data link control is prohibitively expensive for personal use. A business that already has a synchronous network installed can justify the cost of synchronous support, but many home-computer owners will have difficulty justifying the difference in cost. With new introductions of products that use increasingly larger-scale chip integration, this cost difference should grow smaller with time.

Serial Data Transfer Speeds

In serial communications, data transfer rates are measured in *bits per second* (*bps*). *Modem* signaling rates, on the other hand, are measured in baud. The baud rate of a modem describes the total number of *binary signal events* it produces every second to transmit binary data through a telephone line in the form of sounds. This baud rate defines the duration of the voltage signal the modem uses to represent a binary signal event. The following formula is an exact mathematical definition of the term:

$$\text{Baud rate} = \frac{1}{\text{Bit signal duration}}$$

By decreasing the duration of the binary signal event, sometimes called *bit time*, you can increase the baud rate. Conversely, by increasing the duration of the binary signal event, you can decrease the baud rate.

The relationship between baud and bits per second depend upon the technique a data communications device uses to encode data. For low-speed communications, the baud rate will equal the data transfer *bit rate*. High-speed communications, on the other hand, require devices that superimpose several binary data signals on each binary signal event. This allows the data transfer bit rate to exceed the baud rate. For communications below 600 baud, the baud rate and bit rate are the same. For communications at 600 baud and higher, the baud rate and bit rate are different. For the remainder of this book, we will use the term *bit rate* or *bits per second* (*bps*) when referring to data transfer rates to eliminate any confusion between baud and bit rate.

This description of baud and bit rate ends the introduction to data communications. The previous paragraphs provided a brief overview of data communications and an introduction to the remaining sections of this chapter. If you are interested in the details of serial communications, you will want to continue reading this chapter. If you are interested in specific hardware or software components that support data communications, you may want to go directly to the chapters that provide that information. The following paragraphs will, however, provide you with technical details that will help you understand these other chapters.

Details of Serial Communications

Although most internal PC data communications takes place in the parallel mode, communications with other computers and remote devices normally takes place in the serial mode. For data communications over distances greater than 100 feet, there are only two alternatives that provide economic connectivity. Personal computers can communicate over long distances through local area networks. This connectivity option is explored in detail in Part II of this book. Personal computers can also communicate in the serial mode either through direct connections or through telephone connections. This serial mode of communications is explored in detail in the following paragraphs.

Asynchronous Communication

We use the term *asynchronous communication* throughout this book to describe the *TTY* data communications protocol provided by the IBM PC serial port. This "plain vanilla" protocol duplicates most of the characteristics of a hard-copy, teletypewriter terminal. This TTY protocol also provides access to any computer or word processor that has a communications port configured for TTY data communications. Most devices configured for asynchronous ASCII communications are compatible with the TTY protocol.

To communicate properly with a host computer or word processors that do not support the TTY protocol, the IBM PC must use one of two techniques. First, the PC can communicate through a *protocol converter*, which translates between the TTY protocol and the host or word processor's native terminal data stream. Second, the PC can *emulate* the native host or word processor's terminal through a combination of hardware and software.

Asynchronous communications, as explained earlier, refers to serial data transfer characterized by irregular transmission of data segments. This form of data link control is character-oriented. Each set of transmitted data bits constitutes one character and each character has its own *framing data*. A start bit and a stop bit frame the character's data bits and act as *synchronizing flags* for the receiving device. After receiving a start bit, the receiving device must be able to measure accurately a total of nine bits (eight data bits and a stop bit) to determine whether each is a logical 1 or 0. Because of this *character-by-character resynchronization*, asynchronous communication allows some tolerance for inaccuracies between the clocks of the transmitter and receiver. As you might expect, this helps keep the cost of this synchronizing method low. The following paragraphs provide more details on the framing, parity, and data bits used in asynchronous data transfer.

Start Bit

As shown in Figure 2.8, an idle asynchronous data line remains in a *marking state* until data begin to move through the line. A logical 1 line voltage represents this marking signal. A change in data line voltage to a logical 0 for one bit time period indicates a *start bit*. This start bit is the signal that tells the receiver to "wake up" and start measuring data bits. This signal simply signifies the start of a character; it contains no information on the length or type of data to follow. All the receiver knows is that it should keep counting bits until told to stop by another signal.

Noise on a telephone line can cause problems with the start bit that asynchronous hardware must trap and eliminate. Line noise caused by electrical storms or faulty telephone equipment can appear to a communications receiver as a logical 0 and the start of a character. A noise misinterpretation of this type causes a communications error because no data bits follow the *false start bit*. Asynchronous communications hardware eliminates this type of error by trapping faulty start bits. The communications hardware frequently checks the data line voltage while it is in a marking state. This voltage checking allows the hardware to accurately measure the duration of bit signals and ignore signals that have the line voltage but not the duration of a start bit.

Data Bits

After the communications hardware transmits a start bit, it begins to transmit *data bits*. Figure 2.10 shows the five-, six-, seven-, and eight-data-bit configurations supported by asynchronous data link control. This figure also shows the maximum number of characters that each data format can represent. Almost all asynchronous communications performed with the IBM PC is done using seven or eight data bits, principally because of the larger number of characters these formats can produce and the requirements of file transfer protocols.

The number of required data bits may be dictated by the capabilities of the remote computer or the type of data you wish to move from one computer to another. The *American Standard Code for Information Interchange (ASCII)*, discussed briefly in the following paragraph and in detail in Appendix A, is by far the most commonly used character code for computers. Most PC information services use this code, and it will display properly on the PC screen using either seven or eight data bits. The IBM and Microsoft extensions to this code will not, however, display properly on the PC screen unless the PC communicates using eight data bits. Bulletin board systems often transmit these *8-bit* or *high-bit* ASCII characters (characters whose ASCII value exceeds 127) to create graphic or color images on the receiving computer's display. To properly receive these data, the PC must operate using eight data bits and no parity.

Number of Data Bits	Serial Data Configuration*	Maximum No. Bit Patterns	Maximum No. Characters	8-bit ASCII Supported
5	OxxxxxP1	2^5	32	No
6	OxxxxxxP1	2^6	64	No
7	OxxxxxxxP1	2^7	128	No
8	Oxxxxxxxx1	2^8	256	Yes

*Data configuration legend:

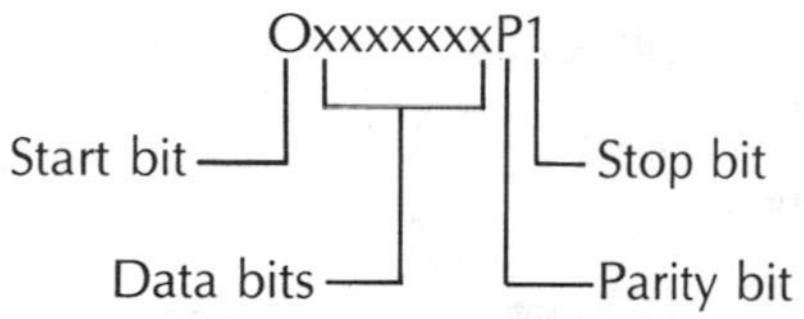

OxxxxxxxP1

Start bit ──┐ ┌── Stop bit

Data bits ──┘ └── Parity bit

Figure 2.10　Data bit alternatives.

A PC must use a special file transfer protocol to transmit or receive a file containing 8-bit characters or binary data if the PC is using a data format of seven data bits. The protocol must convert the data to a 7-bit format on the transmitting end and reconstruct the data to an 8-bit format on the receiving end. The Kermit file transfer protocol performs this type of operation. If two computers are communicating using seven data bits, the Kermit on the transmitting end translates data from 8-bit groups into 7-bit groups that have the same bit patterns as printable text. The Kermit on the receiving computer converts the data stream back to the original 8-bit groups before storing the data on disk.

A process called *stripping off the high bit* will convert files produced by some word processors into 7-bit files that can be transferred using seven or eight data bits. Figure 2.11 shows an interpretive BASIC program that will perform this operation for text files created by the WordStar word processor. After conversion, a WordStar file can be transferred using seven data bits without problems. The file does not have to be converted back to 8-bit data on the receiving end.

```
10 'This program converts a Wordstar ver 3.3 file to a
20 'standard text file that can be transmitted using 7 data bits.
100 DEFINT A:CLS:KEY OFF
110 LOCATE 9,25:INPUT "Wordstar file to convert";OLDFILE$
120 LOCATE 11,25:INPUT "Write conversion to what file";NEWFILE$
130 OPEN OLDFILE$ FOR INPUT AS #1
140 OPEN NEWFILE$ FOR OUTPUT AS #2
150 LOCATE 18,25:PRINT "Working on character: ";
160 WHILE NOT EOF(1)
170     A1=ASC(INPUT$(1,1))
180     IF A1<27 THEN 210
190     LOCATE 18,48:PRINT CHR$(A1)
200     A1=A1-128
210     A$=CHR$(A1):PRINT #2,A$;
220     IF A1=26 THEN 999
230 WEND
900 CLOSE:LOCATE 20,25:PRINT "Conversion completed...." :BEEP
990 END
```

Figure 2.11 Wordstar text file conversion program.

ASCII Data

ASCII is the character code format chosen by IBM for its line of personal computers. The PC stores files created with text editors in the 8-bit ASCII format and only files stored in that format can be edited using PC text editors. On the other hand, the PC stores BASIC programs as non-ASCII binary files unless they are saved using the following save command format:

SAVE "filename.ext",A

BASIC files stored without the A option are in a *tokenized (compressed)* format. The user cannot edit these files with a text editor, list them using the PC-DOS TYPE command, or transmit them using the 7-bit ASCII data bit format. The PC uses the tokenized format as the default storage method for BASIC files because files stored in that format are about 20 percent smaller and load much faster than the same files stored in the ASCII format. A data format of eight data bits and no parity is required to transmit these files.

Users should be cautious when transferring BASIC program files that contain the PC's special ASCII characters. The first 128 IBM ASCII characters are *standard 7-bit ASCII code*, and files that contain only those characters will transmit properly using seven data bits. Files containing the IBM *special extension characters* with ASCII values greater than 127 will contain errors when transmitted using seven data bits. The ASCII values of these characters will be reduced to values in the range 0–127. In order to transmit these ASCII extension characters while communicating in the seven-data-bit mode, the user has to convert the characters to their string equivalents using the

BASIC CHR$*(*n*) and *STRING$(*n*) functions. The following example shows the conversion from 8-bit characters to 7-bit string functions:

Before conversion:

```
100 PRINT "————————————"
```

After conversion:

```
100 PRINT STRING$(14,205)
```

Modifications such as the one shown can be done quickly using either the BASIC editor or a text editor. The user must store the file in an ASCII format, however, before transmitting it to another computer while using seven data bits.

Users should also be cautious when transferring ASCII files because the PC's ASCII code is not necessarily the same as the ASCII code vendors use in other microcomputers. The ASCII characters with values from 0 to 127 are the same as those used by most other computers, but characters with ASCII values above 127 are not. Only IBM Personal Computers and IBM-compatible personal computers use the same characters with ASCII values greater than 127. Appendix A shows a complete listing of the IBM Personal Computer character set.

Other Communication Codes

As mentioned earlier, the other two data communication codes are the *EBCDIC* and *Baudot*. IBM and a few other vendors use the EBCDIC code to store text files on mini- and mainframe computers and to communicate data between these same computers. Other vendors use the Baudot code in special-purpose networks. Of the two, the EBCDIC code is by far the most popular.

When equipped with the proper terminal emulation adapter and software, the IBM PC can store ASCII files in a larger computer in an EBCDIC format. The emulator translates the files from ASCII to EBCDIC as they move from the PC to the host. The same emulation package can translate EBCDIC files to ASCII as they move from the host to the PC. This translation allows the user to edit text files on either the PC or the host using editors that are native to each environment.

The EBCDIC character set requires eight data bits and provides a wide array of characters. The ASCII and EBCDIC codes are listed in Appendices A and C, respectively. From these listings, you can see that most of the 7-bit ASCII characters have equivalent 8-bit EBCDIC characters. Some of the 8-bit ASCII extension characters also have equivalent EBCDIC characters. The ASCII extension characters that do not have EBCDIC equivalent representations will not translate properly when a file is moved from a PC to an IBM host with ASCII-to-EBCDIC translation.

The *Baudot code* is an older 5-bit character code. Networks established several years ago for the handicapped still use this code. There are some special applications for this code, but it ranks a distant third to the other two. Appendix D shows the complete Baudot character set. You can see from that listing that the code supports a smaller number of characters than ASCII and EBCDIC. The 5-bit code can support only 32 characters (two to the fifth power), but two of the characters shift the code between uppercase and lowercase, resulting in a full alphabet of letters and a limited set of numbers and figures.

Binary Data

ASCII files containing special 8-bit ASCII characters are sometimes called *binary files*, a term that causes confusion among data communications novices. Binary files are not word-processing files that contain special 8-bit ASCII characters. They are files produced by assemblers or compilers (for example, files with COM and EXE file name extensions), and transferring these files is more complicated than transferring word-processing files.

Some data communications software packages provide an ASCII file transfer mode that allows the transfer of text or word-processing files. You may successfully use these packages to transmit and receive 8-bit text files, but you may not be able to use the same programs to transmit and receive binary files. A communications program will not properly transmit or receive binary files if it uses the ASCII *end-of-file marker* (a *control-Z*) to identify the end of a file transfer. If a bit pattern in the binary data matches the control-Z pattern, the communications software on the receiving end will terminate the file transfer before all data are received.

To transfer binary files (for example, files with EXE and COM extensions) properly, you should use a communications software package that contains a *file transfer protocol* designed to transfer files in blocks of bits. Most communications packages include one or more of these protocols that allow you to automatically transfer binary files. These protocols, including Xmodem and Ymodem, provide near error-free transfer of any kind of data by retransmitting data blocks that contain errors.

You can transmit binary data without a file transfer protocol, but the process requires extra steps on the sending and receiving ends of the link. The sender must use special software to convert the files into a special hexadecimal format before the transfer, and the receiver must convert the hexadecimal ASCII data back to its original form after the file transfer. Several conversion programs are also available that will convert binary files into ASCII BASIC programs. These BASIC programs recreate the original binary files when you run them on the receiving end.

Parity Bit

Errors invariably occur during serial data transmission regardless of the type of data line used. Good data communications, therefore, requires a method of detecting these errors. The asynchronous data link control allows the use of a *parity bit* to perform this *error detection*. Asynchronous communication supports the intermittent transmission of characters, and the parity bit supports error detection on a character-by-character basis that matches well with this protocol.

Instead of sending the same character twice to detect transmission errors, the parity bit provides information in a single bit that describes the character sent. Asynchronous communications hardware counts the total number of logical 1s in the character's data bits, then determines the value of the parity bit based on whether the total number of data bits is even or odd. If the hardware is operating using *even parity*, the same hardware sets the parity bit at 0 if the number of 1s in the character data bits is even, or it sets parity at 1 if the number of 1s in the character data bits is odd. If the hardware is operating using *odd parity*, it sets the parity bit at 1 if the number of 1s in the character data bits is even, or it sets parity at 0 if the number of 1s in the data bits is odd. Figure 2.12 shows examples of parity bit determinations.

ASCII Character	Character Data Bits	Parity Bit for Even Parity	Parity Bit for Odd Parity
A	1000001	0	1
D	1000100	0	1
F	1000110	1	0
DEL	1111111	1	0

Figure 2.12 Parity bit determination.

The parity error detection method is an easy way to check for *single-bit errors*, but it is also subject to failure. Although the hardware flags single-bit errors, it may not flag *multibit errors*—the type of noise-generated errors most often found on data communication lines. For example, a PC could transmit an "A", but noise on the telephone line could cause the PC at the other end of the link to receive a "D". In our examples of how to calculate parity bits, the transmission error is not detected because the resulting number of logical 1s is still even for even parity or odd for odd parity. The error-detection limitations of the parity bit can be overcome in asynchronous communications, as discussed earlier, by using a *protocol file transfer* that contains a more sophisticated scheme for error detection. Chapter 6 provides more detailed information regarding protocol transfers.

Parity error detection also fails to detect *data bit truncation* when transmitting 8-bit ASCII characters. If the PC is using seven data bits for data transmission, all characters with ASCII values higher than 127 (the DEL character shown in the previous example) are transmitted as other characters, but the parity calculated by the sender and receiver are the same. Table 2-3 shows examples of this type of transmission.

Table 2-3. Character translation from truncation of data bits.

IBM PC Character	IBM PC Character Code	7-bit Code Transmitted	Character Received	Error Detected
		10110011	0110011	3	No
=	11001101	1001101	M	No
Σ	11100100	1100100	d	No
β	11100001	1100001	a	No

The only way to avoid this type of error is to use eight data bits for all data transfers. Unfortunately, there are circumstances that preclude the use of eight data bits. Some information services and bulletin boards operate with seven data bits and even parity. Communicating with this latter type of system still requires that you use seven data bits and parity, or communications will not take place properly. Most services, particularly personal host systems, do not check for parity errors, even though they require the use of parity.

The parity bit is also set to off, space, or mark by some communications systems. *Off* or *no parity* simply means that the parity bit is not checked for transmission errors. No parity is required when using eight data bits with PC serial ports. *Mark parity* means that the parity bit is always set at 1, and *space parity* means that the parity bit is always set at 0. Some mainframe systems that use the mark or space parity will not communicate properly with another computer or a terminal unless the same parity bit mode is operating on both ends of the communication link. Other systems transmit in the mark or space parity mode but do not check received parity. The PC can access these systems by using a communications package that transmits either even or odd parity, but does no parity error detection. This applies to many IBM PC communications packages.

Stop Bits

The final binary signals associated with asynchronous communication are *stop bits*. Stop bits follow the data bits and the parity bit (if parity detection is activated) and constitute the end of transmission of a character. The start bit constitutes the *starting frame* of a character and the stop bits constitute the *ending frame* for that same character. Stop bits are software selectable and are either 1-, 1.5-, or 2-bit times in length. They are simply logical 1s that ensure that the data line is at the marking state before the next start bit (logical 0) begins. This marking state, which precedes the start of each new character, is necessary to support the accurate detection of the start of each character. Without accurate detection of start bits, there is no way to detect and eliminate false start bits and no way to synchronize and measure data bits.

Although the number of stop bits is software selectable, most PC communications use a value of 1. Stop bits do not contain useful data, so the user should set their duration to the minimum allowable value to maximize data throughput. Table 2-4 provides a good guideline for selecting stop bits.

Table 2-4. Stop bit selection.

Bit Rate Range	Stop Bits Required
Less than 110	2
110	2
300	1
Above 300	1

Putting It All Together

Now that you understand the meaning of start, data, parity, and stop bits, you may wonder how you are going to keep track of when to use which combination. Fortunately, the selection and use of these parameters is not as confusing as it sounds. Table 2-5 shows the two most common sets of default communication parameters used in communication software. (The two sets have arbitrary numbers for reference only.)

Table 2-5. Communication parameters alternatives.

Parameter Set	Data Bits	Parity	Stop Bits	IBM BASIC Communications File Open Command
1	7	Even	1	OPEN "COM1:300,E,7,1" AS #1
2	8	None	1	OPEN "COM1:300,N,8,1" AS #1

The first parameter set will work with most of the information services listed in Table 2-6, but you may find the second set useful for communications with some microcomputers. The second set will also allow you to transfer the special IBM ASCII characters if the receiving computer is also using eight data bits. The key to proper communication for any of these applications is to use the same parameters for both sending and receiving computers.

Table 2-6. Information utility communication parameters.

Parameter	The Source	CompuServe	NewsNet	Dow Jones
Data Bits	8	7/8	8	8
Parity	None	Even/None	None	None
Stop Bits	1	1	1	1

If you do not know the communication parameters a particular host uses, you can call the host and experiment until you select parameters that work. Until you find the right combination, you will probably receive characters from the host that look like an executable program displayed on a monitor using the PC-DOS TYPE command. Figure 2.13 shows an example of a screen display caused by mismatched parameters.

Asynchronous Communication Speed-matching

The previous discussions of serial data transfer assumed that data move directly from one computer to another where they are stored or displayed, but this is not always true. If data could be routed to another computer and immediately printed, displayed, or saved, there would be no delays or interruption in serial data transfer. Differences in

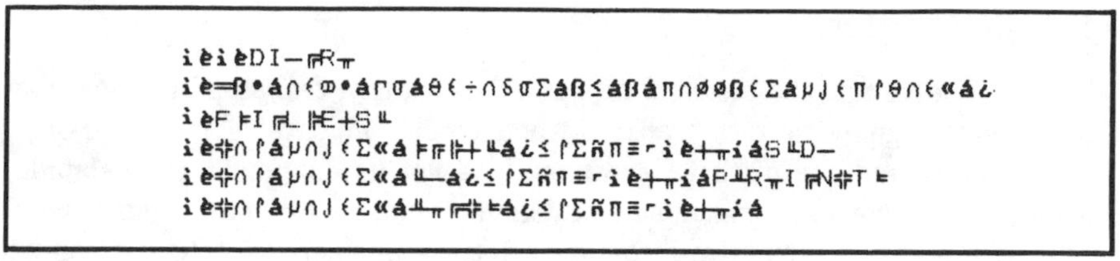

```
i è i è D I — ⌐R┳
i è=ß•å∩∈⊙•årσåθ∈÷∩δσΣåß≤åßå∩∅∅ß∈Σåμ∫∈∏∫θ∩∈«å¿
i èF╞I ⌐L╟E+S ╙
i è╫∩ ∫åμ∩∫∈Σ«å╞╥╟+╙å¿≤ ∫Σñ∏≡ríè+┬íåS╙D—
i è╫∩ ∫åμ∩∫∈Σ«å╙—å¿≤ ∫Σñ∏≡ríè+┬íåP╨R┳I ⌐N╪T ╘
i è╫∩ ∫åμ∩∫∈Σ«å╨┬⌐╫╙å¿≤ ∫Σñ∏≡ríè+┬íå
```

Figure 2.13 Communication parameter mismatch screen display.

the speed of some of these operations, however, result in the need for communications *flow controls*.

The need for data flow depends a great deal upon the IBM PC system unit chosen for communications and the speed of communications. The ill-fated IBM PCjr needed data-transfer flow control to keep from losing communications data received during disk I/O operation. Unlike other IBM Personal Computers, the PCjr did not have a *direct memory address* (*DMA*) device to move information from memory to the disk drive. Without this device, the PCjr's central processor had to be involved in moving data to and from disk. This also meant that the PCjr could not receive data during diskette activity. Data received by either an internal modem or the serial port while the CPU was working with the diskette drive could overrun the communications hardware; the PCjr would never see these data. They were lost. To avoid this problem, communications software for the PCjr had to provide data flow control to pace the rate of incoming data.

The PC system units sold today contain the necessary hardware and operate fast enough to reduce the need for data flow control. With DMA devices in these units, the CPU can continue accepting new data from a remote computer while simultaneously writing accumulated data to disk. The latest vintage PC system units operate at or above 10 MHz. This clock rate allows them to handle data at a much faster pace than the original IBM PC, which operated at 4.77 MHz. Yet some applications require sophisticated speed-matching because of the type of task or because of the number of tasks the PC is performing.

Data flow *speed-matching* techniques come in a variety of forms, but most of them can be categorized as either *on-off* data flow toggles or temporary *data storage* mechanisms. The next section of this chapter describes IBM PC asynchronous communication applications using both of these techniques.

Communication Buffers

A *communication buffer* is random access memory set aside to store data temporarily to compensate for the differences in rates data are received and processed. Communications software provides buffers on both the transmitting and receiving ends of a communication link, but the term communication buffer is often associated with the buffer on the receiving end only. The following paragraphs describe the flow of data, starting from a disk file in one microcomputer and ending with the saving of a copy of that file on a disk in a remote microcomputer. This scenario provides you with an insight into the operation of transmit and receive buffers.

When a PC transmits a file to a remote computer, it first reads that file from a local disk. During the transfer, the PC copies data in blocks from the file to a *transmit buffer*. The PC copies data from the file sequentially until it fills the transmit buffer, then it temporarily halts the copying while an interrupt-driven process sends the contents of the buffer out through the serial port to a remote computer.

Data transfers from the transmit buffer on a *first-in, first-out* basis; they transmit in the same sequence they were copied from the file. When the interrupt process has reduced the transmit buffer contents to a predetermined low point, the PC reads more data from the disk file and copies the data into the transmit buffer. The new data are placed immediately behind the data remaining in the buffer in order to preserve the correct sequential order of data as they are sent out of the serial port. This process continues until the entire file is copied to the transmit buffer and sent out.

The communications software design determines the size of the transmit buffer. A typical transmit buffer size is 512 bytes (about 6.5 lines of 80-column text). Some packages do allow the user to alter the buffer sizes to optimize certain operations. If the transmit buffer is reduced to the point that it is too small, however, it will reduce the file transfer throughput capability of the PC. When the transmit buffer is too small, data are transmitted to the remote computer in bursts rather than a continuous stream. The bursty display of text as it transmits or the slow performance of a file transfer may annoy the user, but the integrity of the communications is not affected unless the software designer provides no mechanism to control the flow of data to the transmit buffer. If the communications software simply copies data from the disk to the buffer without checking the amount of free space in the buffer each time it performs a copy operation, the transmit buffer can overflow. The data that overflow the buffer never get transmitted to the remote computer.

Although the size of both the transmit and receive buffers are important in the design of a package, the size of the *receive buffer* is the most crucial. If the receive buffer is too small and fills up with data during a communications session, the PC will lose data. When new data arrive, the PC will have no place to put them.

The operation of a receive is similar to the operation of the transmit buffer. The process is somewhat more complicated than the reverse of a transmit buffer, however. A transmit buffer can be sized to match the operation of a fast computer, and it will still work fine on a slow computer. A receive buffer, on the other hand, must be designed to work on a slow computer. If the computer turns out to operate faster than the design basis of the software, the receive buffer will still handle the task. It will simply have more free space in its receive buffer than planned.

A receive buffer accepts data coming in from the communication line and stores them temporarily until the communication software can process them. The terminal emulation software normally displays, prints, or stores the data in a disk file or memory space. Displaying and storing the data are fast operations and may not result in a heavy loading of the receive buffer. Simultaneous display and printing of received data are time consuming, however, and can result in a buffer *overflow*. When the receive buffer overflows and causes the PC to miss incoming data, the lost data are said to have gone "into the bit bucket" or "onto the floor."

A communication package written in C or assembly language is capable of handling data quickly and may not need a large communication buffer. A communication program written in interpreter BASIC may, however, operate at a slower speed and require 1,024 bytes or more of receive buffer. Compiled BASIC communications programs also need a receive buffer, but the size of the buffer can be smaller because of the faster operation of compiled code.

A user can set the size of the receive buffer for an interpretive BASIC communication programs with the /C: option. The user must execute this option when the BASIC interpreter is loaded and before the communications program starts. This option follows the name of the communications program on the command line if the interpreter and the communications program are loaded and executed simultaneously. The default buffer size is 256 bytes (256 text characters), but the /C: option allows you to change that value to any size from 0 to 32,767 bytes.

IBM recommends 1,024 for high-speed communications, but you may find that a value of 4,096 or higher helps to ensure no data are lost during transfers of large files. If the BASIC program does much filtering of control characters, a value of 1,024 will almost always be too small. The following is the PC-DOS command used to set up a receive buffer with 4,096 bytes for the original BASIC version of the PC-Talk communications program:

```
BASIC PC-TALK /C:4096
```

Interrupt Handlers

Communication buffers in DOS-based terminal software requires *interrupt handlers* as an interface between the PC hardware and the communications software. The communication buffers are places in random access memory where data are kept on a temporary basis. The transmit and receive buffers each have interrupt handlers that very quickly move data between these buffers and the asynchronous hardware. After the communications software loads these interrupt handlers into memory and starts their operation, they operate as support functions independent of the communications software. They become extensions to PC-DOS and the Basic Input/Output System (BIOS).

Communications interrupt handlers are the traffic cops for data traffic to and from the asynchronous communications adapter or the internal modem adapter. They are engines that have no other role to play but to move data from random access memory to the asynchronous hardware or vice versa. They are closely linked to the hardware to maximize their performance. They may also contain special handshake signaling techniques to protect buffers from overflowing.

The transmit buffer and send-interrupt handler are closely linked to the transmit portion of the asynchronous communications hardware. When the communications software has a byte of data ready for transmission, it places the byte into the transmit buffer located at a fixed position in memory. If the proper signals are present at the communications hardware, the send-interrupt handler takes the byte out of the send buffer and moves it to the asynchronous adapter. The asynchronous adapter converts the byte from parallel data to serial data and sends it out the port. The send-interrupt handler must coordinate between the send buffer and the receiving device to keep the transmit buffer from overflowing.

The receive buffer and receive-interrupt handler are likewise closely linked to the receive portion of the asynchronous communications hardware. When a byte of data arrives at the asynchronous hardware's receive register, the hardware converts the byte of data into a format compatible with the computer's internal parallel data bus and issues an interrupt signal. The receive-interrupt handler immediately moves the byte to the receive buffer located at a fixed position in memory. The communications software watches the receive buffer and processes any data it finds there. The receive-interrupt handler must operate fast enough to get data from the asynchronous hardware before new data over writes it. The interrupt handler must also coordinate between the sending device and the receive buffer to keep the buffer from overflowing.

Because of the independent operation of the transmit and receive interrupt handlers, communications software has to properly start and stop them based on user input. Once started, the interrupt handlers will create problems if they are not properly terminated. One of the first things a communications package does when it starts up is to define the interrupts and turn them on. One of the last things the software does when the user elects to terminate the software is to turn off the communications interrupt handlers and release the communications buffers so other software can use them. If a communications software package terminates without first turning off the interrupt handlers, they will continue to operate after the communications software is replaced in memory by another application. If the buffers are not released, they will reduce the amount of available memory for other software.

A communications interrupt handler will try to do its job even if the communications software is not there to help. If another application places executable code or data in the location the transmit handler knows as the transmit buffer, the interrupt handler will try to move the data out of memory and to the asynchronous hardware. The loss of code or data can cause the PC to stop operating. If a byte of data, such as a ring indication at the modem, arrives at the asynchronous hardware, the receive interrupt handler will move the data to the memory location it knows as the receive buffer. This data can corrupt an application or its data and also cause the PC to stop operating.

Software vendors design their software to properly terminate communications interrupt handlers when the user terminates the software, but some environments may defeat these designs. Terminate and stay ready (TSR) utilities that contain communications modules can, for example, take over the interrupts that should belong to another communications application. DOS-based multitasking environments may also perform task-swapping operations that create problems for the user.

Multitasking Software

Communication buffers provide a necessary function in speed-matching with remote computers, but the interrupt handlers that work with these buffers can create limitations for DOS-based multitasking software. DOS-based *multitasking* systems, such as Windows/386 or DESQview, cannot swap communications software out of memory to disk while the buffers are active. If a multitasking environment swaps a communications package to disk without halting its interrupt handlers, the next software it loads may have a problem.

Even if communications software is not swapped out to disk, the multitasking environment may slow the PC down enough to cause problems with the communications interrupt handlers. If the PC is busy performing multitasking operations and does not provide the receive interrupt handler with enough time to keep pace with data received at the asynchronous port, the handler will lose data. If the send handler is not given enough time to move data from memory to the port, the PC may lose its connection with a remote host because of timeouts.

Properly designed multitasking software can prevent problems with interrupt handlers. Most multitasking environments either preclude the operation of communications software or require a profile for the software indicating it performs communications and cannot be swapped out of memory. IBM provides an *Asynchronous Communications Device Interface* (*ACDI*) that provides multitasking asynchronous communications support for the Operating System/2 Extended Edition. A vendor can write software that maintains several concurrent communications session with one or more hosts while other software runs in both the background or foreground. The DOS Compatibility window under OS/2, however, has many of the same multitasking limitations for asynchronous communications found in other DOS-based multitasking environments.

Practical limits sometimes prevent communications software vendors from providing the proper communications buffers or interrupt handlers to handle all speed-matching requirements. To get around this problem, vendors use another speed-matching technique called *data flow throttling*. Vendors use a variety of these flow control techniques to keep data from arriving faster than they can be processed instead of providing temporary storage for data after they arrive. The most frequently used flow throttle is the XON/XOFF transmission protocol.

XON/XOFF Control

The XON/XOFF data flow control protocol is a more positive mechanism for controlling the flow of data than the communications buffer. It is an *active* rather than a *passive* technique. The capacity of a communications buffer can be exceeded if the mismatch in flow of data is significant and the PC is transmitting a large data file, but the XON/XOFF flow control toggles the flow of data on and off to prevent buffer overflow.

When communications software or hardware provide the XON/XOFF protocol at both the host and the PC ends of a communications link, the protocol controls the speed-matching of data flow without user knowledge or assistance. When the volume of data temporarily stored in the communications receive buffer begins to reach the capacity of the buffer, the software sends an XOFF to the host. (The XOFF character is ASCII Device Control 3 and is equivalent to Control S.) On receipt of the XOFF, the host temporarily halts data transmission, allowing the PC to process the data contained in its receive buffer. When the buffer empties to a predetermined low level, the PC software sends the host an XON character. This character is ASCII Device Control 1 (equivalent to Control Q), and signals the host to resume data transmission. This cycle may automatically repeat many times during the transfer of a data file.

Although most host computers support the XON/XOFF speed-matching technique, not all communication software for the IBM PC or other microcomputers provide that capability. Almost all assembly language and C language communications software uses XON/XOFF control, but some software packages written in the BASIC language do not support the protocol. Assembly language software operates fast enough to watch for and react to XOFF characters. The BASIC interpreter does operate fast enough to send XOFF and XON characters while transmitting a file, but may not operate fast enough to search received characters for the presence of an XOFF while receiving a file. The skill of the communications software programmer often determines how well the software will support the XON/XOFF protocol.

The XON/XOFF speed-matching protocol can also be included in communications hardware or executed by the user. If it is included in a modem, the protocol executes the same way it does in communications software. If the protocol is not implemented in software or hardware, the user can still execute the protocol manually from the keyboard. If a host computer supports the protocol, the PC user can control the flow of information by sending the host the XON/XOFF characters. The PC user can stop the receipt of information by sending the host a Control-S (XOFF). The user can restart the flow of information by sending the host a Control-Q (XON). The user can use this technique to match his or her reading speed with the data transfer speed of the host computer.

RTS/CTS Control

Another speed-matching technique similar to the XON/XOFF flow control is the *Request to Send* (*RTS*) and *Clear to Send* (*CTS*) protocol. This protocol uses electrical signals and a flow control logic between a system unit and a modem or other communications device. Value-added networks—such as Telenet and data networks in countries outside the United States—often support this protocol.

The RTS/CTS control is an active technique that keeps the IBM PC system unit from over-running its attached communications hardware. When properly implemented in both hardware and software, the IBM PC system unit activates the RTS signal when it is ready to send data to the receiving device. When the receiving device is ready to receive data, it activates the CTS signal. The sender will not transmit data until it receives the CTS signal. Thus, the receiving device actively controls the receipt of data, thereby preventing a device over-run condition.

Protocol Transfer

Another data flow control technique is the *protocol transfer*. The communication software at both ends of the communication link must recognize and respond to the same set of *ASCII control characters* to facilitate the transfer of *fixed-length blocks of data*. A lack of standard control characters for implementing this technique often requires that two microcomputers use communication software from the same vendor to perform protocol file transfers. Most of the software vendors who offer this transfer option for use with the IBM PC also have the software available for other types of microcomputers.

File transfer protocols divide text or binary files into fixed-length blocks and use special characters to control the flow of these data blocks between two computers. These protocols often use the following ASCII characters to perform the *handshaking* required for both flow control and file movement:

ETB—End of Transmission Block
ETX—End of Text
ENQ—Enquiry
ACK—Acknowledge
NAK—Negative Acknowledge
CAN—Cancel
SOH—Start of Heading
EOT—End of Transmission

Appendix B provides a detailed review of these control characters.

By dividing data into *blocks* of a specific length and transmitting one block at a time, protocols accomplish data flow control. If the protocol block length is smaller than the receive buffer on the receiving computer, the file transfer cannot possibly over-run the receive buffer. Each successive block is sent only after the receiving computer has processed the previous block and is ready to accept the next one. This technique, which is similar to the XON/XOFF flow control method, offers other error detection and correction features as discussed in Chapter 6.

Print Spoolers

Another data transfer speed-matching technique is the print spooler. A *print spooler* is nothing more than a *buffer* between the IBM PC and a printer that allows files to be printed while the PC is executing other tasks. This mechanism facilitates data communication speed-matching because incoming data may be printed without slowing down operation of the communications program. Without such a device, the communications program cannot process newly received data until all previously received data are printed. A typical printer buffer is less than 512 bytes (the equivalent of one quarter of a page of text). Software or hardware print spoolers, on the other hand, can add 64,000 bytes or more to that buffer. With the application of these spoolers, printing of received data may go on long after the completion of a communications session. This could happen often when communicating at 240 characters per second (2400 bits per second) and printing at less than 80 characters per second.

A software print spooler is a program that uses part of the PC's random access memory as a buffer. The buffer provides speed-matching between an application that sends output to the printer and the printer itself. When the application directs output to the printer, the spooler routes the output to the temporary buffer, then sends the output to the printer from the buffer. The application program may be completely unaware of the software print spooler. The portion of memory set aside as a print spooler is not usable by application programs for any other purpose, and reduces the total available random access memory unless the spooler is off-loaded into expansion memory.

A hardware print spooler, on the other hand, is external to the computer's system unit and is independent of the computer's random access memory. A hardware spooler is a memory buffer placed between the computer's printer port and the printer with cable connections to both. The spooler requires its own power supply, and its operation is independent of the system unit operation. Hardware print spoolers usually start with 8,000 bytes of internal memory and are expandable to either 256 KB or 512 KB. Some spoolers allow you to reprint a document several times, independent of the system unit operation—a great help for printing notices while performing communications or word-processing with the system unit.

Creating large print buffers may not always solve speed-matching problems. When a communications program is transferring large or multiple files, a large print spooler may not be sufficient to handle the work load. These instances require the use of an active speed-matching technique, such as the XON/XOFF method described earlier. The other speed-matching techniques described in the following paragraphs may also help eliminate communications bottlenecks.

Disk Emulators

A *disk emulator* is a portion of unused random access memory set up to operate as an *electronic* or *virtual disk*. Communications software can transfer data from a communications port to an electronic disk file many times faster than it can transfer the same data to a diskette or hard disk file. The electronic disk file has a much shorter access time and a much greater data transfer rate than a physical disk. This faster transfer of data results in a faster emptying of the receive buffer, thereby reducing the chances of the receive buffer overflowing.

The disadvantages of disk emulators are the volatility of stored files and the extra steps required to transfer files from the emulator to a diskette. Files stored on an electronic disk are lost if a power outage occurs before the user transfers the files to a nonvolatile disk or diskette. Some disk emulators are also destroyed when a system reset (warm boot) is required to recover from a software crash.

Some Personal Computer software packages offer a combination of electronic disk and print spooler that can be used with systems configured with more than 512 KB of random access memory. A 640 KB system could provide a 32 KB print spooler and a 160 KB electronic disk, leaving 448 KB for DOS and communications software. This combination would allow you to capture files in an electronic disk file and spool the text to a printer at the same time. The more random access memory you have in the system unit the more memory you can allocate to each function, thereby increasing both disk emulation storage and printer spooler capacity.

With the advent of *Expanded Memory* that meets the Lotus/Intel/Microsoft (LIM) specifications, a great deal of memory can be set aside as a disk emulator. PC-DOS provides support for electronic disks in the form of a device driver called VDISK.SYS. By installing a call to this device driver in the CONFIG.SYS file located in the root directory of the boot disk or diskette, normal PC random access memory can be used as virtual disks. Extended memory (memory starting at the 1M Byte address) in a 80286-based PC can be set up as one or more virtual disks, but the use of extended memory for this type of service can cause the loss of data during high-speed communications. The PC-DOS Technical Reference provides information on the use and limitations of VDISK.

Hard Disks

The fixed or *hard disk* is a speed-matching device that can be used with asynchronous communications. The data transfer rate from random access memory to a hard disk is much greater than the data transfer rate to a diskette. The typical transfer rate of a hard disk is 5–10 Mbps, compared to 250 Kbps for a diskette drive. This higher data transfer speed allows communications software to move data to and from storage much faster in a hard disk system. This translates to a greater overall data communications rate in such a system.

The data transfer rate to hard disk is less than the transfer rate to an electronic disk. However, a hard disk can normally store more data than an electronic disk. Data stored on a hard disk are also nonvolatile. A power outage immediately following the receipt of a file will not result in a loss of transferred data on a hard disk, unless the event damages the disk. The PC will lose data stored on an electronic disk, on the other hand, when a power surge or outage occurs. The probability of this type of data loss can be minimized by equipping the PC with an *uninterruptable power source* and power *surge protection*.

In addition to using a hard disk to reduce or eliminate the disk I/O bottleneck during communications, you can use disk caching to obtain even better performance. A disk cache is a portion of random access memory that is set up as a buffer between the communications software and the disk. The cache allows more data to be written to disk or read from disk with each disk I/O operation than the standard DOS provides, thereby reducing the total time required for these operations. This I/O reduction translates into faster communications software execution during file transfers.

PC-DOS allows the configuration of a small cache with the BUFFERS command. By adding the following command to the CONFIG.SYS located in the hard disk's root directory, you can improve disk performance:

```
BUFFERS = 20
```

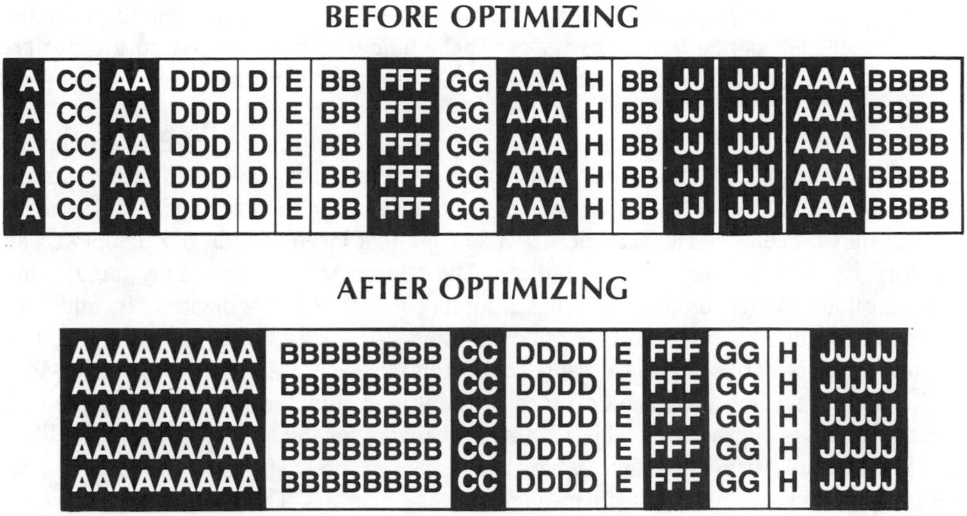

BEFORE OPTIMIZING

A	CC	AA	DDD	D	E	BB	FFF	GG	AAA	H	BB	JJ	JJJ	AAA	BBBB
A	CC	AA	DDD	D	E	BB	FFF	GG	AAA	H	BB	JJ	JJJ	AAA	BBBB
A	CC	AA	DDD	D	E	BB	FFF	GG	AAA	H	BB	JJ	JJJ	AAA	BBBB
A	CC	AA	DDD	D	E	BB	FFF	GG	AAA	H	BB	JJ	JJJ	AAA	BBBB
A	CC	AA	DDD	D	E	BB	FFF	GG	AAA	H	BB	JJ	JJJ	AAA	BBBB

AFTER OPTIMIZING

AAAAAAAAA	BBBBBBBB	CC	DDDD	E	FFF	GG	H	JJJJJ
AAAAAAAAA	BBBBBBBB	CC	DDDD	E	FFF	GG	H	JJJJJ
AAAAAAAAA	BBBBBBBB	CC	DDDD	E	FFF	GG	H	JJJJJ
AAAAAAAAA	BBBBBBBB	CC	DDDD	E	FFF	GG	H	JJJJJ
AAAAAAAAA	BBBBBBBB	CC	DDDD	E	FFF	GG	H	JJJJJ

Figure 2.14 Disk optimization.

Software vendors offer products that allow the user to set up large cache buffers that take advantage of extended or expanded memory. This technique can improve disk I/O performance by a factor of 10, under some circumstances. The *Lightning* software package, published by the Personal Computer Software Group, provides this capability.

The organization of files on a disk can also affect communications performance. Files on a hard disk can become fragmented if the disk has been in use for a long period of time. File fragmentation causes the hard disk read/write head to work harder during file transfers because the head has to move from one file fragment to another during the transfer. This head movement slows down the effective data transfer to and from the disk, thereby reducing overall system performance. You can improve file transfer performance somewhat by periodically executing a software package such as the *Disk Optimizer*, published by SoftLogic Solutions. This defragmentation software reorganizes the disk files to make all sectors of a file contiguous, thereby improving disk file access. Figure 2.14 shows the before-and-after effect of this disk organization technique.

Coprocessor Adapters

Communication *coprocessors*, devices with a long history of application in minicomputer and mainframe computer environments, became a popular data flow control technique with the IBM PC in 1985. In typical single-processor applications, communications software interrupts the IBM PC's CPU frequently to send and receive data. This constant interruption can become an unreasonable burden in high-speed communications or in multiuser applications where each terminal attached to the system unit acts as a communications device. To reduce this burden on the system unit processor, several vendors now make Personal Computer adapters that off-load communications tasks. These adapters are coprocessors that perform one or more communications task while the system unit processor performs another task.

Communications coprocessors are special-purpose adapters designed to handle all data flow to and from one or more attached devices. These adapters often contain microprocessors that operate at speeds equal to or greater than the speed of the main system unit processor. The adapter may also contain a large amount of random access memory for transmit and receive buffers. The coprocessor adapter may handle one asynchronous device or a series of multidropped synchronous devices. In addition, coprocessor vendors often provide optional connectors to facilitate the connection of various types of cabling—typical cable connections are RS-232C, RS-423, and RS-449.

The IBM Realtime Interface Co-Processor Multiport adapter is a good example of a communications coprocessor. This adapter is available for the IBM PC AT and the PS/2 and provides powerful communications capabilities. An on-board Intel 80186 microprocessor operates at 7.37 MHz to manage the coprocessor. This additional processor allows you to write multitasking applications to perform up to 253 concurrent tasks. Software available with the adapter allows you to move data in large blocks through DMA control. You can move the data between the main system unit memory and the random access memory on the adapter at high speeds. The coprocessor can be programmed to provide front-end communications processing functions and supports asynchronous, Bisync, and SDLC communications. Each adapter can provide four or eight RS-232C or RS-422A communication ports; you can use up to four adapters in a single system unit to provide up to 32 total communication ports. This type of configuration is often required to support asynchronous communications from a local area network to outside services or host computers or real-time process control.

Synchronous Communications

As stated earlier in this chapter, a major difference between asynchronous and synchronous serial data transfer is the continuity of data transmitted. Asynchronous data communications originated from character-by-character communications with random time intervals between characters. Synchronous data communications originated from the need for high transaction, continuous movement of data. Because of the differences between the protocols necessary to support asynchronous and synchronous communications, however, there are few similarities between these two categories of serial communications. Synchronous communication protocols are more complex than asynchronous communication protocols. The following paragraphs review the two synchronous protocols most frequently used with the IBM PC.

Bisync Protocol

The *Binary Synchronous Communication*(*BSC* or *bisync*) protocol, a product of IBM Corporation, is still used in many terminal implementations. The bisync is character-oriented, meaning that each character has a specified boundary. Characters are not individually framed with synchronizing bits as they are in asynchronous communications. Instead, bisync synchronization takes place at the beginning of each data message. The transmitting station sends two or more leading *pad characters* to a receiving station before transmitting data. The leading pad character is an alternating 1 and 0 bit pattern that allows the receiving station clock to *synchronize* with the transmitting station's clock.

The bisync protocol requires the transmission of a data bit during every bit interval. Before data transmission can begin, however, *character synchronization* must take place. The sender must provide the receiver with the length of individual data units and a mark that identifies the start of a data unit boundary. The *synchronous idle* (*SYN*) character provides this *handshaking*, and two or more of these characters indicate the start of each bisync data stream.

The bisync protocol SYN character is similar to the asynchronous start bit in that it is the "wake up" signal for the receiver. While waiting for a data stream to start arriving, the receiver is in a "hunt" mode. The receiver searches all incoming bits for the presence of the SYN character. After the receiver detects a SYN character, the device starts to count incoming bits so that it can identify the first bit of a character. To reduce the probability of interpreting data erroneously, most applications of the bisync protocol use the *SYN pair* instead of a single SYN character at the start of a data message. Table 2-7 shows the data-link control characters used in the bisync protocol. Figure 2.15 shows typical bisync data streams using these control characters.

Table 2-7. Bisync control characters.

Bisync Character	Hex Value	ASCII Value *	Character Description
SYN	32	22	Synchronous idle
PAD	55	85	Start of frame pad
PAD	FF	255	End of frame pad
DLE	10	16	Data link escape
ENQ	2D	5	Enquiry
SOH	01	1	Start of heading
STX	02	2	Start of text
ITB	1F	15	End of intermediate block
ETB	26	23	End of transmission (block)
ETX	03	3	End of text

* ASCII decimal value as described in the IBM Personal Computer BASIC Manual appendices.

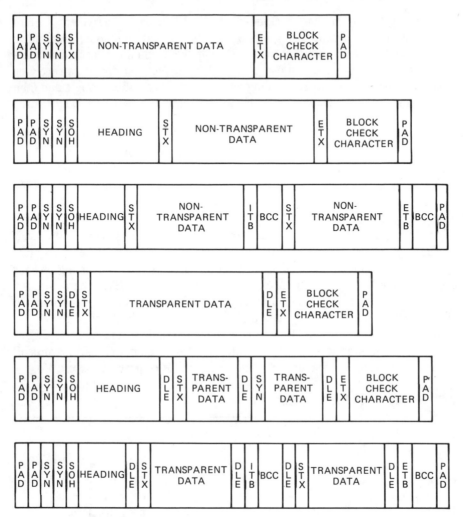

Figure 2.15 Bisync data structure.

There is no limit to the number of blocks of data that may be contained in a stream of bisync data. The data stream may also include a special block of data called a *heading*. The heading describes the data to be transmitted, but the receiver does not retain the heading as useful data.

The data units in a bisync data stream follow the same rules as asynchronous data. Each character may contain five, six, seven, or eight data bits. Each character may also be followed by an optional even or odd parity bit. The 7-bit ASCII code is normally transmitted with seven data bits and a parity bit, but it can also be transmitted using eight data bits and a parity bit. Most bisync implementations use the 8-bit *EBCDIC communications code* described in Appendix C.

When using bisync protocol, the sender can transmit data in either the *transparent* or *non-transparent mode*, but data headings always require the non-transparent mode. The transparent mode allows the user to transmit all characters, including *data link control characters*, as text. In this mode, a data link control character becomes effective only when it follows a *data link escape (DLE)* character. All other data link control characters are treated as text. The DLE-STX character sequence initiates the transparent mode as shown in Figure 2.15. A DLE followed by an ETB, ETX, or ITB character ends the transparent mode; all subsequent data link control characters perform their assigned control functions.

When data bits are not being transmitted, the bisync protocol requires some form of continuous signal transmission to maintain transmission synchronization. During these pauses, which typically occur in terminal conversation between blocks of data transfer, the transmitting device sends a stream of SYN characters while in the nontransparent mode. It sends a stream of DLE SYN characters while in the transparent mode. The receiving device ignores these "padding characters" as it waits for meaningful data.

Bisync data headings vary with applications, but some typical information contained in a heading are:

- Identification of originating device
- Identification of receiving device
- Priority of data
- Data security class
- Destination routing for data
- Control or information nature of data

The receiver checks each block of bisync data for errors in one of three ways, depending on the functions or code used. These error-checking techniques are *vertical redundancy checking (VRC)*, *longitudinal redundancy checking (LRC)*, or *cyclic redundancy checking (CRC)*. The VRC is an odd parity error-check and is the same as odd parity error checking described for asynchronous communications. The LRC uses all character bits to form a check character at both the transmitting and receiving ends of the communication link called a *block check character (BCC)*. At the completion of a transmission, the receiving station sends its BCC to the transmitting station to check the accuracy of received data.

The CRC is a more accurate method of detecting errors than the LRC and may take two forms. Vendors use the *CRC-12* with older 6-bit transmission codes and the *CRC-16* with modern 8-bit transmission codes. The CRC uses a mathematical algorithm to divide a constant (derived from a polynomial) into the numeric binary value of all character bits contained in a block of data. The receiver discards the resulting quotient and retains the remainder as a block check character. A receiving station compares the transmitted BCC to its own computed BCC and accepts the data if the two BCCs are equal. Both the LRC and CRC methods of detecting errors are more accurate than the VRC because they are just as effective at detecting multibit errors as they are at detecting single-bit errors.

Figure 2.15 shows both the non-transparent and transparent modes of bisync communication. From these examples, you can see that the longer the blocks of data, the faster the transfer of data because the ratio of data characters to control characters is higher. This observation is only valid, however, for good data line connections. When the noise on a data line is high, the sender uses smaller data blocks to reduce data retransmissions required to correct errors.

The bisync protocol provides a significant advantage over asynchronous protocols because of the ratio of data information to control information. Larger blocks of data are transmitted with few start, stop, and error-checking characters in the bisync protocol. The ratio of start, stop, and error-checking characters to data is always the same in asynchronous communication. This translates into a greater transfer rate for bisync data when the data volumes are large.

Many business mainframe networks use the bisync protocol; adding bisync to an IBM PC allows the PC to communicate in such a network without a protocol converter. Several bisync hardware/software packages are available for the IBM PC that allow them to emulate (perform almost exactly as) an IBM bisync terminal. By adding a bisync emulation package to the PC, it can access mainframe databases and computing power just like any other mainframe terminal. Several vendors offer these packages for the PC.

SDLC and HDLC Protocols

The *Synchronous Data Link Control (SDLC)* and *High-Level Data Link Control (HDLC)* synchronous data communications protocols are becoming world standards for business communications between the IBM PC and larger computers. Because of the business interest in SDLC and HDLC protocols, the following paragraphs provide a review of these protocols. Also, because of the common elements of SDLC and HDLC, they are discussed together. The protocols are discussed individually when there are differences between them.

The actual data transmitted under SDLC/HDLC is an *information field*, and that field is simply a serial stream of binary numbers. The field may be any length from zero data bits to a maximum determined by memory size and the protocol implementation. The data stream is *bit-oriented*, meaning that the data contain no character boundaries. If the data contain characters, the receiving device must segregate them after receipt of the data.

The continuity of data for SDLC/HDLC is different from that allowed under the bisync protocol. Pauses are allowed in bisync data streams; pauses are not allowed in SDLC/HDLC. There is no SDLC/HDLC equivalent of the bisync SYN character. Both SDLC and HDLC require continuous data transmission of the entire information field. If a pause or break occurs in the data transmission before transmission of the entire information field is completed, the transmitting device assumes an error occurred and aborts the transmission.

SDLC and HDLC information fields are serial data streams created from parallel data streams by an SDLC/HDLC adapter. The adapter converts the parallel data stream into

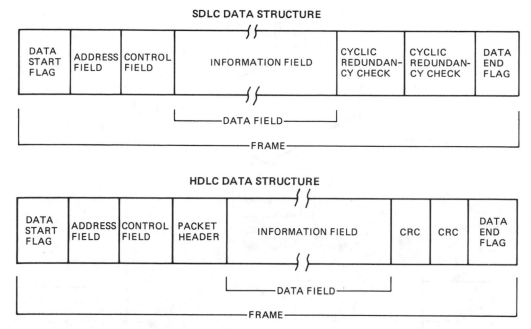

Figure 2.16 SDLC and HDLC protocols.

a serial data stream in much the same way as the asynchronous conversion described earlier. SDLC/HDLC data, like bisync data, contain only one set of framing data for the entire stream—compared to the framing provided with each character in asynchronous communication. This reduction in framing overhead makes SDLC and HDLC communications more efficient than asynchronous communications under most circumstances.

As shown in Figure 2.16, several data fields frame the SDLC and HDLC information fields. Each information unit begins with a *beginning flag* and ends with an *ending flag*. These flags are 01111110 bit patterns and serve as the outside boundaries of each frame of data. Two fields, called the *address field* and the *control field* follow a beginning flag. Both of these fields are eight bits long for SDLC and HDLC. The HDLC frame has one additional address field called a *packet header* that routes the frame through a *packet-switched network* to its proper destination.

The SDLC/HDLC information fields end with a *frame check* that is similar to a block check character. The sender and receiver calculates the cyclic redundancy check from the bit patterns of the address, control, and information fields. SDLC/HDLC uses this CRC to check for data-transmission errors. All SDLC/HDLC fields must exist to fulfill the requirements of an SDLC/HDLC frame of data. Otherwise, the protocols assume a *framing error* has occurred and demand retransmission of the data. Between frame transmissions, a transmitter may send either a sequence of *flag characters* or a *continuous high-idle signal* to maintain contact with the receiver.

The structure of SDLC/HDLC data frames allows the use of this protocol in mainframe network systems, which is the basis for the popularity of this protocol in busi-

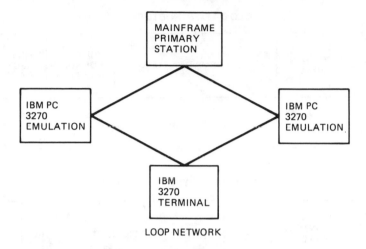

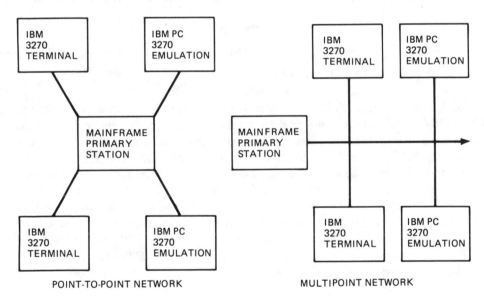

Figure 2.17 Mainframe network.

ness applications. The IBM *System Network Architecture* (*SNA*) used to control the communications between most IBM computer products requires the SDLC protocol as discussed in detail in Chapter 7. A PC with the proper SDLC hardware and software can emulate an IBM 3274 Control Unit and a 3270 terminal in such a network in addition to providing local, stand-alone processing to support spreadsheet and word-processing applications. Combining these two capabilities in one set of hardware makes the PC a powerful workstation for business applications. A PC equipped with an SDLC adapter and the proper gateway software can also provide the link between a remote local area network (LAN) and an IBM host. Thus, the SDLC protocol enables several more PCs attached to the LAN to act as host terminals in addition to the resource sharing they perform on the LAN.

As shown in Figure 2.17, the SDLC/HDLC protocols support one primary station and one or more secondary stations in IBM host networks. The address field in an SDLC/HDLC frame identifies the secondary stations that are the intended recipients of data. The address field of the primary station's frame contains a secondary station's address. The address field of a secondary station contains its own source address in addition to the address of the intended recipient—the primary station.

The presence of destination addresses in the SDLC/HDLC protocol allows the set up of networks that have *point-to-point* communications between a primary station and a secondary station, as well as networks that have *multipoint* communications between the primary and secondary stations. Multipoint networks allow more than one secondary station to be *multidropped* from the same communications cable or telephone system. Point-to-point communications can take place through either leased (*nonswitched*) or public (*switched*) telephone lines. Multipoint communications, on the other hand, require nonswitched telephone lines or network cable loops that provide continuous communications service between all active stations.

Remote Synchronous Communications

Data communications from a remote PC to a mainframe computer using a synchronous protocol such as SDLC requires the use of a device called a *modem*. The modem must translate the synchronous data signals that come from the SDLC adapter to a set of signals that can be transmitted properly through a telephone system. The receiving end requires a compatible synchronous modem to translate the analog signals back into a synchronous, digital data stream the receiving computer can understand. The next chapter provides the details on communications hardware, including the modem.

3

Communications Hardware

To be completely satisfied with your implementation of IBM PC communications, you will have to become somewhat familiar with communications-related hardware. The selection of that equipment will depend on the serial communications protocol and the physical configuration you choose. The selection will also depend upon the features and functions you wish to include in your communications. Finally, the selection will depend upon the budget you establish for this endeavor.

This chapter concentrates on asynchronous communications hardware, although we provide some details regarding synchronous communications. The chapter also describes the internal and external modem options available with the PC. Chapter 8 presents some typical hardware problems communications novices experience when setting up this type of application for the first time.

Modems

When a communications link must be established between a PC and another distant computer, the most economical method of doing so is usually through the *public telephone system*. To do this, a device called a *modem* must be installed between the PC's system board and the telephone system. This device is the final link between the digital-based PC and the analog-based telephone system. The modem is required for all data communications configurations except direct computer-to-computer connections, which are described later in this chapter. Eventually, the implementation of an all-digital communications system throughout the world, called the *Integrated Services Data*

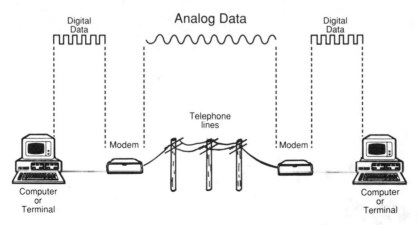

Figure 3.1 Modem signal conversion between digital and analog.

Network (*ISDN*), will eliminate the need for modems. Until that time, you must have one.

Without the modem, the data communications business would not be the booming industry it is today. The PC owner would also be deprived of one of the best personal computer applications. Modem capabilities are increasing and their costs are decreasing, making modem selection and purchase a complicated matter. The following discussion of the characteristics and capabilities of modems, including the pros and cons of internal and external modem configurations, may make that choice easier.

How Modems Work

In the simplest terms, a modem converts the *binary* electrical signals it receives into *analog* signals the telephone system can transmit. These modems modulate digital signals (square wave signals) into analog signals (oscillating signals) and demodulate analog signals into digital signals. Figure 3.1 shows this process. The name modem comes from this *MO*dulate-*DEM*odulate function.

The nature of the signal conversion process depends upon the source and destination of the signal the modem receives. As shown in Figure 3.2, the modem receives the binary signals from a terminal or computer and converts them into *voice-frequency* signals (*tones*). The modem then transmits these sounds through the public telephone system. On the receiving end, another compatible modem converts these sounds back into binary electrical signals. The modem sends these binary signals to a terminal or computer. In special cases, a modem may also receive signals that it converts and sends to a serial printer.

Digital signals must be converted into analog signals for transmission over telephone lines because of the equipment used in the telephone system. Many pieces of public telephone equipment provide *amplifying* and *filtering* functions that will alter square wave signals into unrecognizable garbage by the time they reach the other end of a communications link. To get around this problem, modems convert digital signals into analog signals that are compatible with telephone equipment.

Another limitation imposed by the quality of public telephone equipment is the rate at which data can be transferred. PC hobbyists usually find that modems that fall within their budgets operate at 2400 *bits per second* (*bps*) or less. Users can, however, communicate at data rates as high as 19,200 bps using the same telephone equipment. Modems that now provide that capability are significantly more complex and expensive than the ones that operate at lower rates.

There are several ways of categorizing modems. They can be differentiated by their speed, protocols, features, intelligence, and physical housing. Figure 3.3 shows typical methods used to categorize modems. Before delving into the details of modem features and capabilities, however, we should review some of the limitations imposed by the telephone system that affect their design. The following paragraphs discuss these limitations.

Telephone System Bandwidth

The *bandwidth* of the telephone system is the most difficult obstacle for data communications. Bandwidth is the difference between the lowest and highest *frequency* a medium can properly transmit and receive. The *data throughput* a medium will support is proportional to its bandwidth—the wider the bandwidth, the greater the potential data throughput. The bandwidth of the public telephone system is not very wide by today's standards, and is a significant *bottleneck* in data communications.

The public telephone system provides a bandwidth that covers the range of sounds produced by the human voice. That range restricts data communications. Human

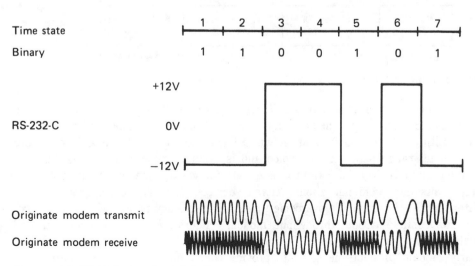

Figure 3.2 Digital signal modulation.

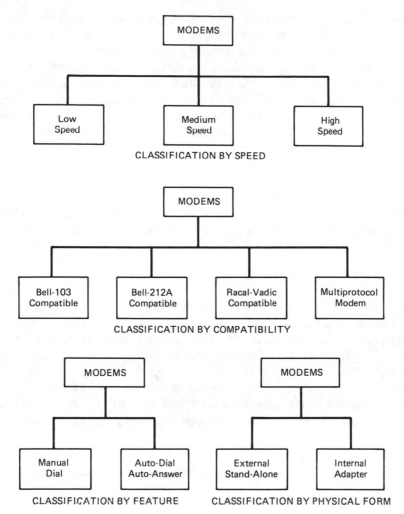

Figure 3.3 Modem classifications.

speech ranges between 20 and 20,000 *Hz* (*cycles per second*), with most voice sounds in the 100 to 3,500 Hz range. The original designers of the public telephone system chose a bandwidth of 300 to 3,000 Hz as shown in Figure 3.4. This range is a little smaller than the full range of the human voice and is a compromise between cost and full frequency support. The bandwidth is adequate for voice communications, but it severely limits data communications between devices that can be designed with far greater frequency ranges. To overcome this small frequency range and produce maximum data communications throughput, modem vendors had to develop sophisticated signaling technology.

Early modem products designed to provide communications speeds greater than 1,200 bps operated in a *half-duplex* mode. These modems used the same frequency

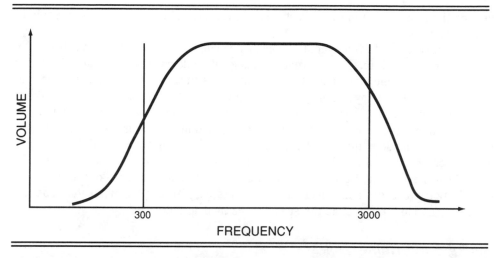

Figure 3.4 The bandwidth of a public, switched telephone line.

range for both transmitting and receiving data. The transmit and receive modes consumed the entire bandwidth. A *Request to Send* (*RTS*) and *Clear to Send* (*CTS*) *protocol* controlled the direction of data flow for these modems. To overcome the time delays required for this protocol, vendors installed *four-wire*, leased telephone lines in place of the less-expensive, public telephone lines. The four-wire lines provided double the bandwidth of *two-wire* public telephone lines, allowing simultaneous transmission and receiving of data, or full-duplex operation. Newer technology has allowed modem vendors to overcome this half-duplex limit at speeds above 1200 bps, as discussed later.

Echo Suppression

Another limitation for data communications through the public telephone system is *echo suppression*. The public telephone system uses echo cancelers to reduce low-power signal reflections produced by signal-switching stations. These devices eliminate echoes by allowing signals to transfer in only one direction at a time. When a person is talking into the telephone, the signals that carry the speaker's voice transmit to the distant listener. However, *electronic filters* eliminate return signals received while the speaker is talking. When the speaker stops talking and begins to listen, the telephone system senses the change and switches the echo filter direction. The turnaround in filter direction is approximately 300 milliseconds and is not normally noticeable during voice communications. The directional filtering and turnaround time delay is, however, a significant impediment to data communications.

Directional filters provide good, clean connections for voice communications but limit data communications to half-duplex operation when they are operating. At a data communications speed of 1200 bps, the 300-millisecond *line turnaround* delay is equivalent to the transfer time for 36 text characters. For long communications sessions that include the flow of data in both directions, this turnaround delay can produce a significant bottleneck.

To improve the data throughput of modems, vendors devised a way to electronically disable directional filters. These vendors designed modems that transmit a 2,100 Hz tone through the telephone line at specific intervals to turn off the echo suppression. By eliminating this suppression and the line turnaround protocol required to make it work, modem vendors significantly increased the rate of flow of data through the telephone line. Unfortunately, echo cancelers installed in the 1960s are not as sophisticated as later models and do not always obey the disabling tone signal. These older echo cancelers are a formidable problem for modems that operate at speeds above 1200 bps. When the *disabling signal* does work properly, the modem must take over the echo cancellation process. Taking over that process is easy at low communication speeds, but becomes more difficult as the speed of the modem increases.

Background Noise

Background noise is the final limitation on data communication imposed by the public telephone system. Modems convert digital signals into tones of approximately -10 *dBm* (dBm is a relative measure of signal strength equivalent to 1 milliwatt into a 600 ohm load). The magnitude of these modem signals, however, drops to the -30 to -40 dBm range by the time they reach a remote modem. A background noise of approximately -50 dBm also exists on the line. As the ratio of signal strength to background noise decreases, it becomes more difficult for the modem to separate the received signal from the normal line noise.

Vendors also found that increasing the complexity of modems to increase their data throughput increased the signal and noise separation problem as well. Signal and noise separation limitations prevented modem vendors from producing modems that operated above 4800 bps over public telephone lines until 1984. After the development and perfection of *automatic signal equalization* hardware, modem vendors were better able to separate noise from data. These vendors were able to design 4800 and 9600 bps modems for public telephone lines and sell them at reasonable prices.

Modem Speeds and Protocols

The jargon associated with modem speeds has created more confusion than most people can deal with when it comes time to select a particular make and model. Most of this confusion comes from the misuse of the terms baud and bits per second (bps). The following paragraphs eliminate some of this confusion by defining these terms and translating them into rates and measures you may better recognize.

Baud

Baud is the number of *signal events* transmitted per second. However, users frequently confuse baud with bits per second. Signal events are changes in the frequency, phase angle, or voltage transmitted between two or more communication devices. One baud equals one such signal event per second, but the event may communicate more than one bit to the receiver. For communications below 600 bps, the baud rate and bps transmitted between devices will be the same. In other words, a 300 baud modem is the same as a 300 bps modem. The rates differ at 600 bps and above because digital signals are superimposed onto analog signals, resulting in each signal event carrying two or more binary bit indications.

Bits per Second

The maximum rate a modem can transmit or receive data as measured in *bits per second* determines its *throughput*. Bits per second are the number of binary digits transferred per second, sometimes called *bit rate* or, simply, bps.

Table 3-1 shows the relationship between baud and bps for typical modems manufactured in the United States today. As you can see from this table, modem manufacturers have been able to improve the speeds of modems dramatically. These vendors have increased modem throughput by a factor of 32, while only increasing modem signal rates by a factor of 4. This feat of imposing multiple-bit indications upon each individual signal change has allowed these manufactures to work within the limited signaling capabilities of the public telephone system. Vendors used this technique to provide much faster modems at reasonable costs to meet the needs for faster data traffic.

Table 3-1. Modem speeds and signals.

Modem Speed (bps)	Modem Signal Rate (baud)	Speed/Signal Ratio (bits/baud)
300	300	1
1200	300	4
2400	600	4
9600	1200	4

The following paragraphs provide more details of the specific signaling techniques and characteristics of modems. Table 3-2 shows the conventional classifications and the ones used in this book. Table 3-3 shows the CCITT specifications that apply to these modem classifications.

Table 3-2. Modem speed classifications.

Modem Class	Bits Per Second
Low speed	600 or less
Medium speed	1200–9600
High speed	Over 9600

Table 3-3. CCITT dial-up modem standards.

CCITT Specification	Bit Rate (bps)	Fallback Data Rate (bps)	Full Duplex Over Dial-up
V.21	300	0-300	Yes
V.22	1200	600	Yes
V.22 bis	2400	1200	Yes
V.26 bis	2400	1200	No
V.26 tcr	2400	1200	Yes
V.27 ter	4800	2400	No
V.32	9600	4800	Yes
V.42	9600/2400	4800/1200	Yes

Low-speed Modems

Although popular with Personal Computers through 1982, the *low-speed* modem has either taken a back seat to its faster brothers in recent time or migrated to the kid's computer. Almost all modem manufacturers continue to produce *Bell-103* modems, however, because there are situations that require this modem speed. The less expensive models do not support auto-dial and auto-answer and cannot be used to store telephone numbers. Expensive models can be used for auto-dial of telephone numbers stored in disk files or stored in the modem's own memory. You can also use these sophisticated Bell-103 modems with host software for unattended auto-answer operation. The Hayes Smartmodem 300 is a good example of this type.

The distinguishing characteristic of the Bell-103 modem is the way it handles data. These modems use specific audio-frequency ranges to differentiate between transmitted and received data. Figure 3.5 shows these ranges. Table 3-4 shows the Bell-103 *originate-mode frequencies* for transmitted and received data and the binary logic associated with these frequencies. Figure 3.6 shows the relationship between the space and mark signals used in the Bell-103 protocol.

Table 3-4. Bell-103 originate-mode frequencies.

Direction	Signal Logic	Name	Frequency (Hz)
Transmit	0	Space	1,070
Transmit	1	Mark	1,270
Receive	0	Space	2,025
Receive	1	Mark	2,225

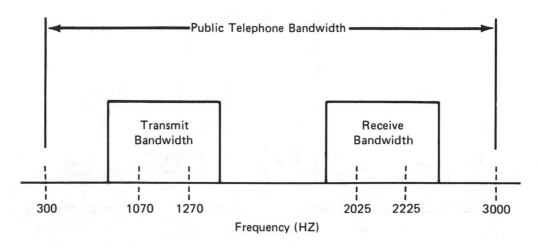

**LOW—SPEED MODEM
ORIGINATE—MODE FREQUENCY DIAGRAM**

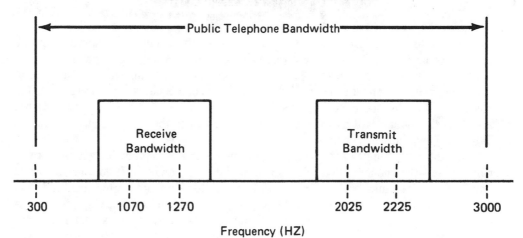

**LOW—SPEED MODEM
ANSWER—MODE FREQUENCY DIAGRAM**

Figure 3.5 Low-speed modem frequency diagrams.

Frequency shift keying (*FSK*) provides the *originate* and *answer modes* for Bell-103 modems. The modem that initiates a communications link is in the originate mode and the remote modem that responds to the initiation and completes the communications link is in the answer mode. The receive frequencies for the answer mode are the same as the transmit frequencies for the originate mode. By the same token, the receive

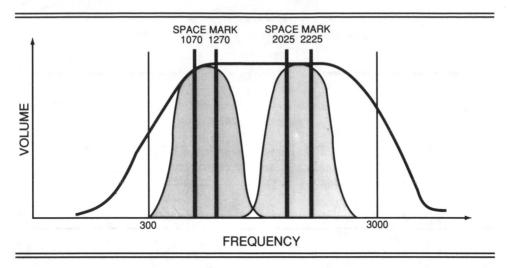

Figure 3.6 Frequency assignments for a Bell 103 modem.

frequencies for the originate mode are the same as the transmit frequencies for the answer mode. Figure 3.5 shows the relationship between these frequencies.

Bell-103 modems require matching modes for proper communications. Because of the difference in transmit and receive frequencies, one modem must operate in the answer mode. The other modem must be in the originate mode. If the modes do not match, both modems will try to transmit and receive using the same frequencies and no data will move between them.

The important thing to know regarding originate/answer modem designs is that you can get Bell-103 modems that will do one or the other, or both. If you never plan to have your modem answer an incoming call from another computer or terminal, then you do not need the answer-mode capability. Originate-only modems are generally less expensive than modems that support both modes, but most modems available today provide both modes.

Low-speed modems are good for applications that require communications in the *conversation mode* or the transfer of small files. The maximum continuous transfer rate at 300 bps is 30 characters per second (cps), which translates into about 300 words per minute (wpm), as shown in Table 3-5. An outstanding typist would have difficulty taxing such a configuration. Another advantage of 300-bps communications is that many people can comfortably read text at that speed. Listing a file on your monitor can be done if you want to read the information, but have no need to store it for later use.

Table 3-5. Data transfer rates of modems.

Modem Speed	Characters per Second	Average Words per Minute	Average Pages per Minute*
300	30	300	1.1
1200	120	1200	4.4
2400	240	2400	8.9
9600	960	9600	35.6

* Assuming 2,000 characters per page.

Time-sharing information services generally charge less for low-speed connection time that can also result in cost savings for interacting in the conversation mode. CompuServe, for example, at one time charged $6.00 per hour for a 300-bps connection or $12.50 per hour for a 1200-bps connection during evenings and weekends. At these rates, a person would have to transfer over 78 kilobytes of files for every 20 minutes of communications in the conversation mode to have a break-even cost in going from a 300-bps to a 1200-bps connection. Based on these figures, you would not want to connect at 1200 bps unless you planned to transfer a lot of data.

The following formula allows you to calculate the number of bytes that you have to transfer to reach the break-even point in going from 300 bps to 1200 bps:

$$X = \frac{6{,}984 \ (BD - AC)}{4A - B}$$

where

A = cost per hour for 300-bps connection
B = cost per hour for 1200 bps connection
C = 300-bps interactive time in minutes
D = 1200-bps interactive time in minutes
X = break-even point in file-transfer bytes
file transfer protocol = Xmodem (128 data bytes plus
    4 overhead bytes per packet)
bits per byte = 10 (8 data bits plus 1 start bit
    and 1 stop bit for each byte)

Use the following formula to calculate the number of bytes that have to be transferred to reach the break-even point in going from 1200 bps to 2400 bps:

$$Y = \frac{13{,}967 \ (HF - GE)}{E - 2F}$$

where

E = cost per hour for 2400-bps connection
F = cost per hour for 1200-bps connection
G = 2400-bps interactive time in minutes
H = 1200-bps interactive time in minutes
Y = break-even point in file-transfer bytes
file transfer protocol = Xmodem (128 data bytes plus
                                   4 overhead bytes per packet)
bits per byte = 10 (8 data bits plus 1 start bit
                         and 1 stop bit for each byte)

For applications that involve the frequent transfer of large files or the clustering of input from several terminals, low-speed modems are not a good choice. It takes about one minute to transfer 2,000 bytes of text at 300 bps. This translates into 30 minutes of connect time to transfer a 60 KB file. To transfer several 60 KB files means you have to dedicate the computer to communications for a significant period of time. You must provide operator support for the entire session if your communications software does not provide the option to transfer multiple files. For applications of that type, most businesses and hobbyists choose medium-speed modems.

Medium-speed Modems

Most of the *medium-speed modems* available to the Personal Computer owner operate at 1200 or 2400 bps. These modems achieve a higher data throughput than low-speed modems by using more sophisticated signaling techniques. Instead of shifting frequencies to signal a change from a one bit to a zero bit, these modems use *phase* and *amplitude modulation* to create more bit patterns on the telephone line at a faster rate than low-speed modems. Figure 3.7 illustrate these techniques.

At the low end of the medium-speed spectrum, *Phase Shift Keying* (*PSK*) provides 1200-bps communications. Unfortunately, modem vendors can implement three different 1200 bps PSK techniques in modems. In the United States, the two prevalent techniques are *Bell 212A* and *Racal-Vadic*. All the most popular Personal Computer modems, including the Hayes Smartmodem 1200, provide Bell 212A communications. For international communications, the most popular 1200-bps signaling scheme is the *CCITT recommendation V.22*. For proper 1200-bps communications, the modems at both ends of the communications link must use one of these signaling schemes.

Compatibility of 1200-bps modems is often an issue with PC owners because compatibility varies with the make and model of the modem at each end of a communications link. Some 1200-bps modems operate in half-duplex only. This can limit the information systems you can access. Other modems offer compatibility with either Bell-212A or Racal-Vadic systems. The more expensive medium-speed modems are compatible with both Bell-212A and Racal-Vadic, and some so-called *triple modems* support Bell-103, Bell-212A, and Racal-Vadic protocols.

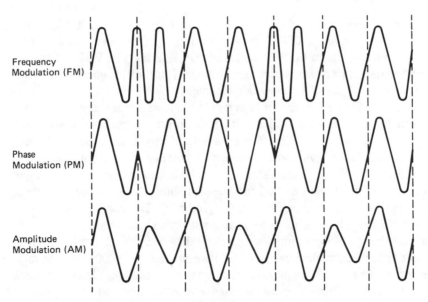

Figure 3.7 Digital modulation methods.

Generally, you get what you pay for in a 1200 bps modem—the more features it has and the higher the quality, the more it will cost. Inexpensive modems, even though they contain all the necessary electronics to match a specific protocol, may not be compatible with other modems that contain the same protocol. Low-quality electronic parts used in their construction can keep them from communicating properly.

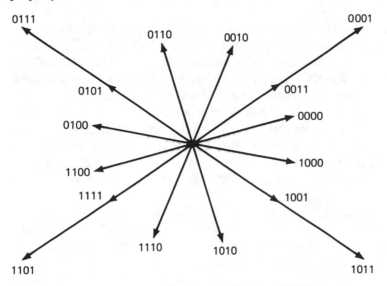

Figure 3.8 Quadrature amplitude modulation (QAM).

Fortunately for all parties involved in medium-speed communications, manufacturers of 2400-bps modems followed a CCITT recommendation, rather than create a new twist. These modems conform to *CCITT recommendation V.22 bis*. The V.22 bis specification calls for a variation on *phase amplitude modulation* (*PAM*) called *quadrature amplitude modulation* (*QAM*). Figure 3.8 shows this technique.

As you can see from Figure 3.8, the QAM signal combines 12 phase angles and four phases with amplitude modulation and results in a 16-point signal structure. This provides 16 possible *carrier states*. The four phases that have modulated amplitudes have two possible amplitude levels and provide two possible bit patterns per point. Many people call this QAM signal the "star" or "constellation" because of its shape. The V.22 bis specification contains a 600-baud line-signalling rate. Each phase angle of the QAM star represents four consecutive bits (*quad bits*). The combination of 600 signal changes with four bit patterns per signal change produces 2400 bps.

Going from 1200 bps to 2400 bps often means more than just changing the technique used to transmit bits. When modem vendors first implemented the 2400 bps data rate, they experienced an increase in error rates that was not acceptable. Many of these vendors added to their modems a continuous *error detection and correction* protocol called the *Microcom Networking Protocol* (*MNP*). MNP compensates for the increased error rate by retransmitting bad data.

MNP provides greater than 99 percent error-free communications between two modems equipped with this protocol. The protocol forces the retransmission of corrupted data until the data contain no errors. Although powerful, this reliable form of data communications requires little protocol overhead and is automatic. The modem user is normally not aware the error checking is taking place. Chapter 6 covers the MNP protocol and other hardware and software implementations of error detection and correction techniques.

One advantage many medium-speed modems have is the variety of speeds and signalling techniques they provide. For example, the IBM 5853, 2400-bps modem provides both *asynchronous* and *synchronous* communications at 2400 and 1200 bps and Bell 103 compatibility at 300 bps. When equipped with the proper software, a PC and a single IBM 5853, 2400-bps modem can support asynchronous communications between two Personal Computers. This same combination can support synchronous communications between a PC and an IBM host computer. An Operating System/2 Extended Edition software package can communicate through the 5853 modem in one mode, stop that communications session, then begin a communications session with another computer in the second mode. The user does not have to get involved in the switch between the two modes.

The Hayes Smartmodem 2400 also provides compatibility with many CCITT recommendation in one unit. It provides V.22 at 1200 bps, V.22 bis at 1200 and 2400 bps, Bell 212A at 1200 bps, and Bell 103 between 0 and 300 bps. The Smartmodem 2400 V-series also provides *data compression* and *local flow control* that can provide the equivalent of 4800 bps communications when it communicates with another compatible modem.

High-speed Modems

The next leap in speed for Personal Computer modems is from 2400 bps to at least 9600 bps. The CCITT produced the *V series* definition of the characteristics of 9600 bps data communications in a recommendation called *V.32*. This recommendation defines a family of two-wire, full-duplex modems to be used with voice-grade, switched, or leased telephone lines. Table 3-6 shows the principal characteristics of this family of modems. Vendors began to release modems in this class for the first time in 1986. This modem class raised the previous 4800 bps limit of voice-grade telephone lines by a factor of two by using new, sophisticated hardware to execute telephone-line *echo cancellation*.

Table 3-6. V.32 modem characteristics.

- Full duplex operation on general switch telephone lines and two-wire point-to-point leased lines.
- Channel separation by echo cancellation.
- Quadrature amplitude modulation for each channel with synchronous transmission at 2400 baud.
- Any combination of the following data signal rates: 9600 bps, 4800 bps, or 2400 bps.
- At 9600 bps two modulation schemes, one using 16 carrier states and one using extended coding with 32 carrier states.
- Support for the following modes of operation:

      mode 1   9600 bps synchronous
      mode 2   9600 bps asynchronous
      mode 3   4800 bps synchronous
      mode 4   4800 bps asynchronous

The V.32 specification incorporates an advanced version of the QAM technique defined for V.22 bis modems discussed earlier. V.32 requires the transmission of five data bits with each baud signal change and a signal rate of 2400 bps. The total bit throughput is 12,000 bps, but the effective data bit throughput is 9600 bps. One out of five of the transferred bits provides an error-correction technique called *Trellis coding*.

Trellis coding, called *forward error correction*, allows error detection and correction without retransmission of data. The receiving modem uses *Viterbi decoding* to detect and correct data transmission errors before it passes the data to the receiving computer or device. This scheme effectively separates the data signal from the high background noise caused by high-speed communications. It also eliminates the sporadic noise that can be generated by faulty or old telephone equipment. This technique allows two V.32 modems to communicate effectively and accurately even across noisy telephone connections.

Another unique feature of the V.32 standard is the technique it recommends for the separation of transmitted and received signals. Instead of consuming a wide bandwidth by using separate frequencies for sending and receiving data, a V.32 modem uses a special echo canceling process to calculate the received signal. It subtracts the transmitted signal and echoes from the total line signal. *Frequency-division* signal separation limits full-duplex modem speeds to 2400 bps, but this special echo canceling allows 9600-bps operation on public telephone lines.

The V.32 specification sounds too good to be true, and the first modem vendors to develop one of these modems found that to be the case. These vendors discovered three problems with the implementation of the V.32 specification. First, the echo cancellation requirements were expensive and difficult to turn into hardware. This made the initial cost of V.32 modems high. Second, telephone line noise sometimes precluded V.32 modems from operating at 9600 bps. The modems had to instead operate at the fallback speed of 4800 bps when line noise was high. Third, V.32 modems caused timeout problems for error-correcting protocols because of the time required for the modem to recover from telephone line noise.

Some early tests of V.32 modems with poor-quality telephone lines showed a 25 percent loss in data throughput with continuous error-correcting protocols such as X.PC. Vendors have overcome most of these problems with the application of different hardware technology and with modifications made in error-correcting protocols. V.32 modems may not come into widespread use, however, until telephone companies upgrade the public-telephone echo cancelers.

Because of the difficulties of implementing the V.32 specification, some modem vendors developed special techniques for dial-up communications at speeds of 9600 bps and higher. Some of these vendors chose to use variations of the techniques prescribed in the V.32 recommendations and others chose to use completely proprietary techniques. For example, Hayes Microcomputer Products uses V.32 techniques in the Smartmodem 9600, whereas the Telebit Corporation uses proprietary technology in the Trailblazer modem.

Hayes developed a special synchronizing technique that allows fast line turnaround that makes a half-duplex modem simulate the operation of a full-duplex modem. This *ping pong* protocol uses standard CCITT V.32 signal modulation techniques, along with special flow control procedures to make data appear to flow in both directions concurrently. The protocol automatically switches the direction of data flow based on the volumes going in each direction to optimize the total throughput of the communications connection. The modem provides this rapid-fire technique of switching the direction of flow at the normal 9600 bps data rate. It also provides the same technique at the 4800 bps fallback rate the modem uses when the error rate is too high for the higher speed of communications.

The Trailblazer modem has two unique design features that enable it to achieve high communications speeds while retaining near error-free data transfers. First, the Trailblazer uses synchronous communications techniques to communicate faster over dialup connections than V.32 modems. Second, this modem uses a *packet-switching*, error detection, and correction technique similar to the MNP protocol. The technique eliminates the bad side affects of high-speed data communications and corrects errors detected during communications.

The Trailblazer also uses a unique method of overcoming the bandwidth limitations of the telephone line. Instead of using one or two carrier signals, the Trailblazer uses between 400 and 500 *frequency-divided carriers*. By dividing the telephone bandwidth into many carrier signals, this modem can achieve high data throughput over good telephone lines. The modem has to only reduce throughput in 100-bps decrements when line conditions degrade. This gradual *fall-back* is automatic and is less of a penalty for poor line conditions than the factor of two fall-back contained in the V.32 modem specification. Actual tests of the Trailblazer show a throughput in the 10,000-to-12,000-bps range for long distance data communications. This is a better rate than the V.32 modem can achieve under the best conditions. As with other proprietary products, however, the modems at both ends of the link must be Trailblazer modems or Trailblazer compatible before you can achieve these data rates.

Modem Features

Level of *intelligence* is another method of classifying modems. As the costs of memory and microprocessors decrease, the power and flexibility of modems increase, making last year's model almost obsolete. This has been the trend over the past several years, and the trend will probably continue into the future.

Table 3-7 shows a list of features available in modems. Most hobbyists find that a modem offering only a few of these features meets their needs. Some business applications, on the other hand, require a full-feature modem that supports most of the listed features. It should be noted, however, that the term "full feature" differs from one modem manufacturer to another. If you need several capabilities in a single modem, you should investigate the actual features provided by available models before purchasing one.

Table 3-7. Modem features.

Help command	Command modes
Command recognition	Command abort
Quit command	Manual dial
Dialing directory	Dial tones
Name selection dialing	Last number redial
Repeat dialing	Number linking
Directory modification	Auto-answer
Busy mode	Protocol switch
Error control	Data compression
Flow control	Break handling
Set answerback string	Set backspace character
Set attention character	Set disconnect character
Modem register contents	Modem switches
Built-in self-test	Line monitor

The following paragraphs describe the most important features and functions you should look for in a modem. Unless otherwise specified, discussions of the IBM modem features pertain to the IBM Command set mode. IBM modems designed for the PC also contain an AT Command set that closely emulates the Hayes Smartmodem commands and registers. References to the AT command set in the following paragraphs include the one in the IBM modems.

Command Modes

Because of the dominance of the Hayes Smartmodem in the personal-computer community, many intelligent modems provide a Hayes Smartmodem-compatible command mode. This *AT command mode* allows the user to use software designed specifically for the Smartmodem. Aside from the Hayes mode, some modems also have a mode specifically designed by the modem manufacturer. The manufacturer's own mode often duplicates the Hayes mode, and provides additional capabilities beyond those found in a Hayes Smartmodem. You issue a short command sequence to the modem to switch modes. The Hayes mode provides an "OK" response to commands (when the verbal or verbose response mode is in effect). Some other character prompt, such as a "$" or a ">" symbol, indicates the vendor-specific mode. The Hayes mode requires a carriage return at the end of a command to initiate execution of the command. Some vendor-specific command mode commands begin execution after you type the first letter of the command word.

Some modems require specific communication software speed and parity settings before they will recognize commands, whereas others will accept commands regardless of the communication parameters used. Some experimentation may be required to determine the parameters that work. Modems that require a specific set of communication parameters often have to be reset through software commands. Some also have to go into a dormant mode before they will accept a new set of parameters. Others provide an external reset button or an off/on switch that will reset most or all the modem's parameters. Stand-alone modems can be easily switched off and back on, but internal modems require that you turn the computer off for a power-off reset. For that reason, some internal modems can be reset through software controls.

The Hayes Smartmodem family and Hayes compatible modems automatically switch parameters to match the received parity and data bits. When one of these modems receive the "AT" *attention code*, it determines the transmission data rate (bits per second) of the PC serial port from the "A" and the number of data bits and parity from the "T". The modem switches parameters to match the incoming command string and retain these parameters until it receives another command string preceded by the "AT" attention code. The modem must be in the *command mode* in order to change parameters.

Dial Tones

Modem dialing commands usually include a selection of *pulse* or *touch-tone dialing*. The dialing signals transmitted to the telephone system are the type specified by the dialing prefix command. Some modems allow the dial type to change during the dialing sequence to match in-house telephone equipment; this feature may also include a *secondary dial-tone* wait command. Dial-tone wait commands cause the dialing sequence to pause until the modem detects a secondary dial tone. These are better than a simple time delay during the dialing sequence.

A good intelligent modem not only waits for a secondary dial tone during a dialing sequence, it will sense and switch between touch-tone and pulse dialing. This type of modem will usually provide a *blind dialing* mode also. Blind dialing allows the modem to dial even when it does not detect a dial tone. Some PBX telephone systems use non-standard tones, and a regular tone-sensing modem will not be able to detect them. This type of telephone system will result in a "dead line" appearance to a modem, and blind dialing is the only way to get around the problem.

The Hayes Smartmodem series and Hayes compatible modems support both touch and pulse dialing. The vendors for these modems use the "AT" command followed by a "T" for touch tone and a "P" for pulse dialing. These modems also allow the insertion of a comma that causes a pause in the dialing sequence. Programmable registers specify the length of the pause. When in the IBM command set, the IBM can wait for a dial tone or execute blind dialing. The Hayes modems and most Hayes-compatible modems only support blind dialing.

Line Monitor

Another characteristic of modems is the method used to communicate dialing information to the IBM PC user. Some modems use a speaker to help the user understand the dialing process. After initiating a call, the user can hear the dialing sounds and the results of the call—or a busy signal. Other modems use screen messages to tell the caller the results of a call. After you initiate a call, the message may read "Call in progress..." and a busy signal may result in a message that reads "Line busy." Both methods work, but the sounds of a telephone dialing and modems synchronizing are somehow more comforting and natural.

Auto-Answer

Many intelligent modems not only operate in an automatic answer mode, they allow you to specify how many rings should occur before the modem answers the telephone. For example, the command "ATS0 = 5" will cause a Hayes Smartmodem to answer a call on the fifth ring. You can also force the modem to answer the telephone. It is necessary to perform a forced answer, for example, when you directly connect two computers with modems without going through the telephone system. You can place a short length of telephone cable between two Smartmodems and execute a force-to-answer "ATA" command on one modem and a force-to-dial "ATD" command on the other modem to establish a link between the two modems. The force-to-answer feature also allows you to use the same telephone line for voice and data communications.

Busy Mode

Some modems include a busy command that allows a user to make the telephone line look "off hook" to an incoming call. This command is useful for bulletin-board operators who want to use the system temporarily for other applications but want the system to appear busy to callers. You can use the busy command on a voice line to keep calls from coming in. Through software control, the modem can create a busy signal for certain periods of the day every day of the week.

. IBM modems use the TALK command to take the phone off the hook and place it in the voice state. Hayes Smartmodems and compatibles use the "ATH0" command to take the telephone off the hook.

Protocol Detect and Switch

The auto-answer mode of some modems will automatically detect the protocol of an incoming call and switch protocols to match that of the caller. Protocol detection includes such things as signal modulation frequency and phase angle determination. Typical protocols are Bell-103, Bell-113, and Bell-212A, but some expensive modems also include Racal-Vadic. The switch between Bell-103/113 and Bell-212A or Racal-Vadic is also a switch between 300 bps and 1200 bps. Most of the V.22 bis compatible modems, such as the Hayes Smartmodem 2400, automatically detect and match protocols and speeds from 300 bps to 2400 bps. If a modem does not provide this capability, you can usually execute a detect and switch through software controls.

Error Control

Some modems implement additional protocols in hardware to detect and control errors that occur during data communications. The MNP protocol discussed earlier is by far the most popular, but other protocols recommended by the *International Standards Organization (ISO)* are beginning to emerge. Table 3-8 shows a list of the protocols that vendors now chose from when they design and build modems.

Table 3-8. Modem error-control protocols.

Microcom Networking Protocol (MNP)
Link Access Protocol-Balanced (LAP-B)
Link Access Procedure for Modems (LAP-M)

Modems equipped with error-control protocols must also contain standard techniques to *negotiate* the use of these protocols with other modems. When one modem dials another modem through the telephone system, the two modems must exchange a series of signals or handshakes. They do this as soon as they make a connection. They must determine the form of *error control* that will prevail during the communications session. The modems must select a common error-control protocol or agree to use no error control if no common protocol exists between them. These error-control negotiations are done automatically and often without the knowledge of the user. Because of the transparent nature of these negotiations and the possibility that two modems may decide to use no protocol, many users execute the file transfer protocols described in Chapter 6 when transferring blocks of text or data.

The latest model modems produced by Hayes Microcomputer Products provide two new forms of error control. First, the V-series 2400 and 9600 bps modems contain a protocol based on CCITT *LAP-B* that can function at 1200 and 2400 bps. The LAP-B protocol provides near error-free data communications between two modems that contain that protocol. The V-series modems use an extension of the LAP-B protocol at 4800 and 9600 bps to provide the same error-free communications in a half-duplex mode. Second, the V-series V.42 versions of these same modems contain two additional protocols that can ensure near error-free communications. These are the *LAP-M* and the MNP protocols. Hayes also produces V-series and V-series V.42 modem enhancers that allow you to upgrade existing Smartmodem 1200s and 2400s to V-series and V-series V.42 functional levels.

When two Hayes Smartmodems begin a communications session, they negotiate the best form of error control to use throughout that session. The negotiations are a two step *bidding process*. The two modems first exchange a rapid sequence of characters to verify that both modems support *feature negotiations*. If this bidding is successful, the two modems compare features and select the most advanced error control common to both modems. For example, two V-series V.42 modems will elect to use the LAP-M protocol. A V-series V.42 modem will, however, elect to use the MNP protocol when it is communicating with a modem that contains only that protocol. If the V-series V.42 modem dials into an older Hayes Smartmodem that contains no error-control protocol, the two modems will communicate without error detection and correction.

Data Flow Control

Modems that provide error control often provide data *flow control* also. This method of speed-matching, described in Chapter 2, ensures that data are not lost during the retransmission process that corrects blocks of bad data. The retransmission process takes time, and the communications between the modem and the PC must be temporarily halted during this retransmission time delay. Without data flow control, the PC could send more data to the modem than the modem could store during the retransmission period, and the *data overrun* would be lost.

Modems with data flow control often provide more than one technique to accomplish this task. They also require communications software that matches their technique to ensure proper data flow control. The two flow control methods recommended in CCITT V.42 and the two most often used by modem vendors are the RTS/CTS and the XON/XOFF protocols. The *RTS/CTS* requires the PC to send an electrical Request to Send signal to the modem when it wants to transmit data. The PC cannot send data until it receives an electrical Clear to Send response from the modem. The *XON/XOFF* requires the modem to send the PC an XOFF character to stop the transmission of data and an XON character to resume the transmission of data. Both techniques accomplish the same objective and are *local handshaking* between the modem and the PC.

Data Compression

Another feature that vendors provide with modems that requires modem-to-modem negotiations to enable is *data compression*. Data compression can be executed in hardware or software to reduce the total data throughput required to transfer information or data. This technique uses encoding to eliminate redundant bit patterns on the transmitting end and requires a matching decoding technique on the receiving end. The receiver must reconstitute the data to their original form. Modems that contain data compression algorithms, however, must also contain techniques to negotiate this operation with another modem.

The Hayes V-series modems contain a feature called *adaptive compression* that comes on automatically when the modems operate in one of their error-control modes. Hayes went one step beyond data compression by providing a technique that adapts to the type of data flowing through the modem to optimize the flow of data. Two Hayes V-series modems perform data transfer at twice the rate of data communications between the two modems because of the data compression. For example, PCs connected to V-series Smartmodem 9600 V.42 modems can communicate with the modems at 19,200 while the modems communicate with each other at 9600 bps, thereby moving data at twice the rate that would be possible without data compression.

Break Handling

Modems must properly transmit *break signals* generated when a user presses specific PC keys to interrupt a host process. When no error-control protocol is in use, modems have no problem transmitting this signal because it is generated under software control in the PC and transmitted "as is." When an error-control protocol is in operation at the modem hardware level, the protocol can damage the interrupt signal by making it shorter or longer than the signal generated by the communications software. The modem must be able to recognize a break signal received from the PC and preserve the duration of this signal across the communications link. If the break signal is not properly maintained, it will not have the desired effect on the host process.

Modem Registers

It is often necessary for a communications software package to query the contents of a modem's internal *registers*. This technique is used to automatically detect and modify the contents of the registers or to detect register content changes as signals for software function initiation. A modem should provide commands that allow a software package to both query and modify the contents of its registers. The list of Hayes Smartmodem 1200 registers and the parameters they control are shown in Table 3-9. Most Hayes compatible modems implement these registers in the same sequence and use the same command syntax to change register contents. Incompatibility between communications software and a Hayes-compatible modem is often traced to incomplete or incorrect implementation of these registers.

Table 3-9. Sample of Hayes Smartmodem S registers.

Register	Range	Units	Function
S0	0-255	rings	Ring to answer on
S1	0-255	rings	Count number of rings
S2	0-127	ASCII	Escape code character
S3	0-127	ASCII	Carriage return character
S4	0-127	ASCII	Line feed character
S5	0-32, 127	ASCII	Backspace character
S6	2-255	seconds	Wait time for dial tone
S7	1-255	seconds	Wait time for carrier
S8	0-255	seconds	Pause time for comma
S9	1-255	1/10 sec	Carrier detect response time
S10	1-255	1/10 sec	Delay time between loss of carrier and hangup
S11	50-255	millisec	Duration and spacing of touch tones
S12	20-255	1/50 sec	Escape code guard time

Modem Switches

Some communication software packages require special signals that must either be present or absent between the computer and a modem for the software to function properly. For example, the PC-TALK communications software requires that the Data Terminal Ready signal be ignored by a modem or the communication parameters cannot be changed while on line with a host system. Otherwise, the carrier is lost during the parameter change and the connection with the remote computer is lost. Modems normally allow you to set these signals either through software controls or manual *switches*. The ideal design allows both manual and software changes in these signal switches.

The location of a modem's switches is an important consideration if the position of the switches require frequent changes. The switches for the Hayes Smartmodem 300 and 1200 are behind the front cover and switch changes can be difficult for a hardware novice. The switches for IBM modems, on the other hand, are on the rear of the modem unit and are easily accessible for switch position changes.

Modem Self-Tests

The built-in *self-test* features in a modem are pattern generator and error-checking circuitry. These features allow the modem to be tested as a stand-alone device or with a similarly equipped remote modem. The tests verify the modem's ability to accurately send and receive data. The three types of test modes are: the analog loop-back self-test, the digital loop-back self-test, and the remote digital loop self-test.

The *analog loop-back* self-test verifies the operation of a local modem as a stand-alone unit. Data are sent from the self-test circuit through the modem's transmitter. The transmitter output is then routed back into the modem's receiver where the data are then routed back to the self-test circuit. The self-test circuit compares transmitted patterns to received patterns and notifies the modem user if errors are detected.

The *digital loop-back* self-test verifies the operation of a remote modem. With the help of the remote modem operator (switch positions have to be changed on the remote modem), data are sent from the local modem and looped through the receiver and transmitter of the remote modem. When the data are received back at the local modem, they are compared to the original transmitted data. If errors are detected, the modem notifies the local user. The remote digital loop self-test is identical to the digital loop-back self-test except that it can be performed without remote operator assistance.

IBM modems provide two test capabilities. The TEST command provides options that allow the execution of all the types of tests described in the previous paragraphs. The DQuality command is unique to IBM modems made for Personal Computers and allows the modem user to monitor the quality of incoming data. The response to this command is either

```
DATA QUALITY GOOD or
DATA QUALITY POOR
```

This command provides an indication of how likely you are to have data transmission problems using the current telephone connection.

Modem Indicator Lights

Most stand-alone modems have *indicator lights* on the front panel that show action and status. Those indicator lights are labeled with cryptic symbols that do not mean much to the communications novice. The symbols are also not the same on all modems, which leads to further confusion when a person uses more than one modem. The following definitions will clear up some of the confusion around modem labels.

Auto-Answer—Indicates the auto-answer status of the modem. When this indicator is on, the modem will automatically answer the modem.

Carrier Detect—Indicates whether the modem has detected a carrier signal from a remote modem. This indicator has to be on for data to be transmitted.

Data Terminal Ready—Indicates whether the terminal is ready to receive and send data. This indicator must be on for the modem to maintain the connection with a remote modem.

High Speed—Indicates the modem operating speed. When the indicator is on, the modem is operating at its maximum rated speed (i.e., 2400 bps for a 2400 bps modem). When the indicator is off, the modem is operating at the next lowest speed or at another programmed rate less than its maximum rated speed.

Modem Check—Has an assigned special meaning for modem testing. The modem manual specifies the exact meaning of this indicator.

Modem Ready—Indicates the operating status of the modem. When this indicator is on, the modem is ready to receive and send data.

Off Hook—Indicates the status of the data line connected to the modem. When the modem is using the telephone line, the indicator is on. This indicator is also on when a modem is making the telephone line appear to be busy.

Receive Data—Indicates the receipt of data from a remote modem. When this indicator is on, data are coming in from the remote modem.

Send Data—Indicates the sending of data to a remote modem. When this indicator is on, the modem is sending data to the remote modem.

Test Mode—Indicates that the modem is in a test mode.

Stand-alone modems versus Board-mounted modems

Although they perform the same functions, *stand-alone* modems and modems mounted on *adapters* have advantages and disadvantages particular to their design. The type you choose will likely depend on your specific communications application and the advantages provided by one modem type.

Tables 3-10a and 3-10b show the general pros and cons of the stand-alone and *board-mounted modems*. In almost every case, an advantage for one type is a disadvantage for the other type. From this list, you can see that a board-mounted modem is a logical choice for the owner of a portable or laptop computer who plans to travel with the computer and wants to minimize the number of gadgets that have to be carried separate from the computer system unit. People who want a complete communications hardware package that does not require external cables, boxes, and power supplies might also want a board-mounted, internally installed modem.

Table 3-10a. Stand-alone modems.

Pros:

- Can be used with any computer or terminal.
- Has indicator lights that show action and status.
- Heat load is external to computer system unit.
- Can be removed from serial port so port can be used for other applications.
- Has power on/off switch for last-resort modem reset.
- May have DIP switches that can be easily set.

Cons:

- Requires space adjacent to computer.
- Has to be transported when computer is taken on trip.
- Requires a power supply connection.
- Requires an RS-232C cable.
- Requires a serial port connection.

Table 3-10b. Internal expansion-board modems.

Pros:

- Requires no space outside computer system unit.
- Requires no serial port connection.
- Requires no RS-232C cable.
- Requires no external power supply.
- DIP switch settings can be software controlled.
- Does not have to be transported separate from computer.

Cons:

- Consumes one expansion slot inside system unit.
- Cannot be used with incompatible computer.
- Provides no indicator lights to show action and status.
- Provides no hardware reset switch.
- Requires installation inside system unit.

A stand-alone modem is a good choice for people who use several different computers and terminals that require a modem for communicating with other devices. This type is easily moved from one device to another. A stand-alone modem is also a good choice for communications software developers and bulletin board operators. The indicator lights on a stand-alone modem serve as helpful diagnostic tools and busy-signal indicators. Just by watching the data send and receive, the auto-answer, and the bps rate indicator lights, a software developer can eliminate many hours of debugging time. An external modem's indicator lights also provide problem and activity indicators for auto-answer software operators. A host or bulletin board system operator can determine the system's status at a glance by observing the modem lights.

Modem Summary

With this exposure to some of the characteristics and capabilities of modems, you should be able to make a better selection of the type you need. A sample modem-evaluation matrix is shown in Table 3.11. You may want to use a similar matrix when selecting one for your own use. The Hayes V-series Smartmodem 2400 V.42 and the IBM 5853 Modem are shown on the sample matrix, so you can compare their capabilities to other available modems. For current comparisons of specific makes and models, you should subscribe to PC monthly magazines. You may also be able to get this kind of information from local IBM Personal Computer users' groups; many of them have Communications Special-Interest Groups that keep a current matrix comparing available modems.

The material in the rest of this chapter is for PC owners who plan to use the PC's RS-232C interface for a modem or direct computer-to-computer communications. We have covered all the information that pertains to internal modems.

Table 3-11. Modem evaluation matrix.

Modem Feature	Hayes V-series Smartmodem 2400 V.42	IBM 5853 2400 bps Modem
Modem Type:		
Stand-alone	o	
Expansion board		
Transmission Protocols:		
Bell 103	o	o
Bell 212A	o	o
Racal-Vadic		
V.22	o	o
V.22bis	o	o
V.32	o	
Error Controls		
MNP	o	o
LAP-B	o	
LAP-M	o	

Table 3-11. Modem evaluation matrix. (continued)

Modem Feature	Hayes V-series Smartmodem 2400 V.42	IBM 5853 2400 bps Modem
BPS Rate Capability:		
300	o	o
1200	o	o
2400	o	o
Duplex Modes:		
Half		
Full	o	o
Switch Position Control:		
Manual switch only		
Software switch only	o	
Both		o
Neither		
Built-in Test Modes:		
Self-test	o	o
Analog loop-back	o	o
Remote digital	o	o
Line Quality		o
Communication Modes:		
Asynchronous	o	o
Synchronous	o	o
Modem Operating States:		
Off-line command	o	o
On-line communication		o
Quit (dormant)		
Command Help File:		
Available on-line		o
Available off-line		
Command Compatibility:		
Vendor unique mode		o
Hayes compatible mode	o	o
Parameter Change Recognition:		
From Dormant State		
From Command State	o	o
Both		
Dial Types Available:		
Pulse (rotary)	o	o
Touch tone	o	o

Table 3-11. Modem evaluation matrix. (continued)

Modem Feature	Hayes V-series Smartmodem 2400 V.42	IBM 5853 2400 bps Modem
Detect and switch		o
Call/Answer Modes:		
Manual originate	o	o
Manual Answer	o	o
Auto-answer	o	o
Dialing Modes:		
Keyboard input	o	o
Software disk directory	o	o
Modem-stored directory	o	
Automatic Dial Design:		
Dial from menu		
Dial by host name		
Redial busy number		o
Redial x times		o
Repeat dial last number	o	o
Link alternative number		
Tone Recognition:		
First dial tone	o	o
Secondary dial tone		
Busy signal		o
Dead line		
Blind dial	o	o
Commands Available:		
Set disconnect code		
Set answer-back code		o
Set backspace code	o	o
Set attention code	o	o
Wait delay during dial	o	o
Make line busy	o	o

Communications Adapters

To communicate with modems and other serial devices, electronic circuitry must be provided to convert the parallel bit stream used within the IBM PC system unit into a serial bit stream that is compatible with these devices. As discussed in Chapter 2, there are several techniques used in this conversion process. Common adapters used for parallel-to-serial data conversion are discussed in the following paragraphs.

Asynchronous Communications Adapter

The expression *asynchronous communications adapter* is often used to describe the circuitry that permits the Personal Computer to communicate externally with serial devices, but this label is only one of many used to describe the adapter. Other names for this circuitry are *serial port*, *asynchronous communications interface*, and *Universal Asynchronous Receiver/Transmitter*, or *UART* (pronounced you-art). All these descriptions refer to a circuit board or a part of a circuit board designed to perform parallel-to-serial or serial-to-parallel conversions of binary data and other functions described in the following paragraphs.

As explained in Chapter 2, the IBM PC communicates internally with a data bus composed of 8, 16, or 32 parallel wires. By using this technique, an 8-bit character can be transferred by sending all 8 bits to a device simultaneously, resulting in rapid internal communications. When data have to be transferred over long distances, however, routing cable containing eight or 16 parallel wires becomes costly. Instead of dedicated computer cables, most computer communications arrangements use ordinary public telephone equipment. Thus, the eight parallel bits that are transmitted by the computer must be funneled into a stream of sequential serial bits that can be sent over ordinary telephone lines. The serial port performs the chore of an "electronic traffic cop." A graphic representation of the process is shown in Figure 3.5, page 60. At the receiving end, a serial port converts the serial flow of data bits back into a parallel flow so the receiving computer can process the information on its internal parallel buses.

Because of the serial nature of telephone communications and because of the potential for the introduction of communications errors from the telephone system, the serial port performs more than just parallel-to-serial and serial-to-parallel conversions of bit streams. Some of the other functions performed by this device are listed in Table 3-12. To perform these diverse functions, the RS-232C interface is supplied with a small microprocessor, a separate clock, and random access memory. The serial port is actually a self-contained microcomputer and its sophistication allows many of the functions described earlier to be performed without the need for user involvement.

Transmission Speed

One vital function of the serial port is to control the rate of data throughput. As explained in Chapter 2, data transmission is measured in *bits per second* (*bps*), which is called *bit rate* for asynchronous communications. Most IBM PC, XT, and AT serial ports support transmission bit rates from 50 to 9600 bps; PS/2 models with the Micro Channel go as high as 19,200 bps. These bit rates are selected through software control and, once selected, allow the communications software to transmit and receive data through either modem or direct-connection interfaces with other peripherals or computers.

Table 3-12. Serial port functions.

- Monitors the communications link with the modem to prepare the communications line for data transmission.
- Allows software control of communications parameters.
- Regulates data transmit and receive speeds to predetermined fixed rates from 50 to 19,200 bits per second.
- Adds start bits to character bit strings being transmitted.
- Adds error-checking parity bits to the end of transmitted characters if instructed to do so by the communications software.
- Adds stop bits to character bit strings being transmitted.
- Buffers data waiting to be transmitted or waiting to be received by the computer.
- Detects and ignores false start bits.
- Deletes start bits from received character bit strings.
- Checks for errors between characters received and their associated parity bits if parity is being used.
- Sends parity error indication to the communications software.
- Deletes stop bits from character bit strings received.

The important thing to remember regarding the selection of a bit rate is that the transmitting and receiving computers have to operate at the same rate for data to be communicated properly. Otherwise, the data being received will appear to contain many transmission errors. Some auto-answer intelligent modems can detect and switch rates to match that of the incoming call. Some unattended communications software packages can also perform this switching function. If neither the modem nor the communications software you use is capable of automatically performing a switch to match the bit rate of a remote system, you must manually switch the communications bit rate with your communications software.

Data Framing

Since asynchronous communications is, by definition, not continuous, an asynchronous port receiving this type of data must know when data transmission is starting and stopping so the receiving computer's timing device can *synchronize* with that of the transmitting device. This synchronization is done on a byte-by-byte basis using *framing bits* or signals. Contained between these framing signals are additional bits that contain the transmitted data.

As discussed earlier, *data framing* begins with a *start bit*. The serial port adds a start bit to each string of data bits (an alphanumeric character when transmitting ASCII) as it passes through the serial port to tell the receiving computer to prepare itself for the receipt of data. The serial port on the receiving end, after synchronizing with the incoming signal, must strip the start bit from the data because it serves no further purpose. It would only occupy valuable space when stored with the transmitted data.

The serial port may also add a *parity bit* to each byte of data it transmits. By adding the parity bit to each string of data bits, the serial port can make the total number of bits per character even or odd. The receiving computer's serial port can then check each set of data bits it receives to be sure the set contains either an odd or even number of 1 bits. If the receiving serial port detects an error, it can signal the user, through communications software, that a transmission error has occurred.

Following the transmission of a byte of data, the serial port must signal the receiving computer that transmission is finished. The port accomplishes this task by adding *stop bits* (equivalent to binary 1s) to each byte of data it transmits. This "test period" tells the receiving serial port that it has received a complete byte of data. The port can then translate the serial data into parallel data and create an interrupt signal that tells the receiving PC's CPU that data have arrived. The stop bit also allows accurate measurement of the start point for the next byte of data. Stop bits may be 1-, 1.5-, or 2-bit times in length. Normal use requires 2 with 110 bps and 1 with 300 bps and higher.

Speed Matching

The members of the IBM PS/2 and PC families provide *DMA control* to transfer data from memory to nonvolatile storage. The speed-matching of communications between these processors and other computers, however, is accomplished through software control. The asynchronous adapter will accept data to be sent to another computer and will receive data from another computer, but neither the PC system unit nor the PC-DOS operating system provides a built-in adapter handler or device driver to facilitate the movement of data to and from the adapter. The communications software must provide the data conduit between the asynchronous adapter and system unit memory, and must provide interrupt service and temporary buffer storage in order to achieve speed-matching between the data transfer speed of the system unit and the data transfer speed of the asynchronous adapter.

Other functions performed by the serial port will not be discussed here because they are normally transparent to the user and beyond the scope of this book. It is worth noting, however, that the functions provided by the serial port can be combined with that of parallel printer circuitry and additional memory capacity in a single adapter. Most of the vendors marketing these combination boards have duplicated the functions of single-function boards so well that users cannot detect the difference between the operation of single-function boards and of these combination boards.

Synchronous Communications Adapter

The second type of communications adapter used with the IBM family of Personal Computers is called the *synchronous adapter*. This device performs parallel-to-serial and serial-to-parallel conversions of binary data similar to the asynchronous adapter with one significant difference—the data stream between two such devices is continuous and continuously synchronized, compared to the discontinuous stream of character-by-character synchronized data between two asynchronous adapters. In addition to this difference, synchronous adapters adhere to specific protocols.

Synchronous adapters are named for the protocol compatibility they provide. The two most frequently used synchronous adapter types are *SDLC* and *BSC*. Both of these adapter types are used in IBM SNA communications, although the SDLC adapter is by far the most popular. These synchronous protocols are described in Chapter 2.

Multiprotocol Adapter

In a business environment that may require communications between the IBM PC and devices or host computers in a variety of protocols, a multiprotocol communications capability may provide advantages. To conserve the use of system unit expansion slots and to provide programming flexibility, IBM offers a *multiprotocol adapter* that provides asynchronous, Bisync, and SDLC protocols in a single expansion card. With the advent of Personal Computer modems that provide both asynchronous and synchronous capability in the same unit, this multiprotocol capability allows communications with a large variety of devices.

The RS-232C Standard

When shopping for data communications equipment, you will frequently see the phrases "standard RS-232C" and "RS-232C compatible." These statements usually mean the device or cable uses a *DB-25 connector*, but it does not guarantee that all the signals defined by the *RS-232C standard* are supported by the device. Many standard RS-232C cables have been purchased to connect modems and serial printers to home computers, but were returned when the user found that some of the modem or printer features could not be activated because of signals that were not being transmitted by the cable. Because of a lack of conformity in the implementation of the RS-232C standard, some serial printers will not work at all without special cables designed specifically for the make and model being used.

The RS-232C is a standard published in 1969 by the *Electronic Industries Association (EIA)*. The RS is an acronym for Recommended Standard and the 232 is the identification number for that particular standard. The C designates the last revision made to the RS-232 standard. The purpose of this standard is to define the electrical characteristics for the interfacing of *data terminal equipment (DTE)* and *data communications equipment (DCE)*. For the IBM PC user, these terms refer to the PC and a modem, respectively. Other devices, such as serial printers, may be configured as DCE or DTE devices, depending on the manufacturer. The differences between these configurations are discussed in the following paragraphs. Figure 3.9 is a diagram of the application of the RS-232C interfacing cable with the PC. From this figure, you can see that the RS-232C interface performs a critical role in personal-computer communications. It is the link that facilitates the transfer of data to and from another computer via the telephone system.

Other pertinent facts regarding the application of the RS-232C standard to the PC are the bit rate and cable lengths supported. The standard applies to serial data transfer rates in the range of 0 to 20,000 bps, which adequately covers the PC's 50- to 9600-bps range. The standard limits the cable length to 50 feet, which should also cover most PC communications hardware configurations. Cable longer than 50 feet can be used (and are often used on mainframe systems), but such applications should be thoroughly tested to ensure signal quality before being relied on.

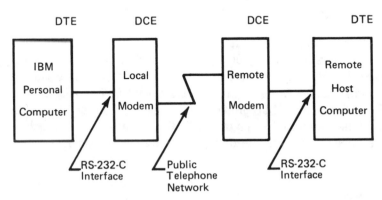

Figure 3.9 RS-232C interface application.

RS-232C Signal Characteristics

To ensure that binary data are transmitted properly and that equipment controls are properly performed, it is necessary to agree on the signals that will be used. The RS-232C standard provides voltage ranges for data and control signals to satisfy this requirement. These ranges are shown in Table 3-13 and Figure 3.10.

Table 3-13. Interchange voltage standard.

Interchange Voltage	Binary Logic State	Signal Condition	Interface Control Function
Positive	0	Space	On
Negative	1	Mark	Off

The IBM PC user is not normally concerned with the voltage ranges and signals associated with those ranges as they pertain to communications. These signals are of concern to hardware vendors and are used during the design of serial ports and modems; but when properly implemented, the operation of these signals will not require PC user interaction.

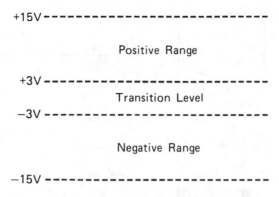

Figure 3.10 RS-232C signal voltage ranges.

RS-232C Pin Assignments

The physical implementation of the RS-232C standard is shown in Figure 3.11. This figure illustrates the *pin assignments* used in the design of the DB-25 connector normally used on each end of an asynchronous communications cable. Although these pin assignments are defined under the RS-232C standard, the actual design of the connector is controlled by the International Standards Organization document ISO 2113. Also, the female version of this connector is supposed to be used on modems and the male on serial ports, but equipment vendors do not always follow that standard.

The pin assignments shown in Figure 3.11 would lead you to believe that data are always transmitted on the wire assigned to pin 2 and that data are always received on pin 3. Both the computer and a modem or printer cannot, however, transmit and receive over the same wire, which makes the pin assignments somewhat confusing. A discussion of each pin assignment is provided next, to eliminate some of the confusion. Also, the pin labels assigned by the RS-232C standard are from the perspective of the DTE (PC, in this case), which should help clear up some of the confusion.

Transmit Data (TD, Pin 2)

The signals on this pin are transmitted from the PC to a modem or printer. The serial port maintains this circuit in the marking condition (logic condition 1, equivalent to a stop bit) when no data are being transmitted.

Receive Data (RD, Pin 3)

The signals on this pin are transmitted from a modem or printer to the PC's serial port. This circuit is also maintained in a marking condition when no data are being transmitted.

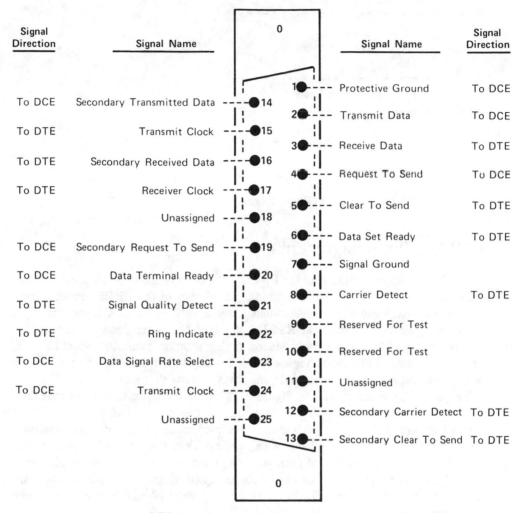

Signal Direction	Signal Name		Signal Name	Signal Direction
		0		
		1 — Protective Ground		To DCE
To DCE	Secondary Transmitted Data — 14	2 — Transmit Data		To DCE
To DTE	Transmit Clock — 15	3 — Receive Data		To DTE
To DTE	Secondary Received Data — 16	4 — Request To Send		To DCE
To DTE	Receiver Clock — 17	5 — Clear To Send		To DTE
	Unassigned — 18	6 — Data Set Ready		To DTE
To DCE	Secondary Request To Send — 19	7 — Signal Ground		
To DCE	Data Terminal Ready — 20	8 — Carrier Detect		To DTE
To DTE	Signal Quality Detect — 21	9 — Reserved For Test		
To DTE	Ring Indicate — 22	10 — Reserved For Test		
To DCE	Data Signal Rate Select — 23	11 — Unassigned		
To DCE	Transmit Clock — 24	12 — Secondary Carrier Detect		To DTE
	Unassigned — 25	13 — Secondary Clear To Send		To DTE
		0		

DTE=Data Terminal Equipment (Personal Computer)
DCE=Data Communications Equipment (Modem)

Figure 3.11 RS-232C pin assignments.

Request to Send (RTS, Pin 4)

This circuit is used to send a signal to a modem or printer requesting clearance to send data on pin 2. This signal is used with the Clear to Send circuit to control the flow of data from the PC to a modem or to a serial printer. Synchronous communications use this signal to control the flow of data between modems.

Clear to Send (CTS, Pin 5)

This circuit is used by a modem or serial printer to indicate to the PC that it is ready to receive data. When this circuit is OFF (negative voltage or logic 1 state), the receiving device is telling the PC that it is not ready to receive data. Synchronous communications use this signal to control the flow of data between modems.

Data Set Ready (DSR, Pin 6)

When this circuit is ON (logic 0), it is a signal to the PC that a modem is properly connected to the telephone line and in the data transmission mode. Auto-dial modems send this signal to the PC after successfully dialing a host computer.

Signal Ground (SG, Pin 7)

This circuit serves as a signal reference for all other circuits used in communications. It is at zero voltage relative to all other signals.

Carrier Detect (CD, Pin 8)

A modem sends the PC an ON signal on this circuit when a proper carrier signal is being received from a remote modem. This signal is used to illuminate the CD (carrier detect) LED indicator located on the front of a modem.

Data Terminal Ready (DTR, Pin 20)

The PC turns this circuit ON when it is ready to communicate with a modem. Some modems cannot signal the PC that a proper telephone connection has been made with a host system until this circuit is turned ON. If the PC turns this signal OFF during communications with a host system, this type of modem will drop the telephone connection. Modems such as the Hayes Smartmodem provide a switch that allows you to override the DTR logic. This switch, when properly positioned, causes the modem to ignore the status of the DTR circuit and maintain the communications connection even when the PC turns off the DTR signal (this is required for bit rate and parity changes while on line with a host). The function of the DTR signal, as well as the CTS, DSR, and RTS in communications with a modem, are shown on the flow chart in Figure 3.12. Figure 3.13, however, shows the typical signal combination used for most IBM PC communications.

Ring Indicate (RI, Pin 22)

This circuit is used by an auto-answer modem to indicate a telephone ring signal. The circuit is maintained ON during each ring and OFF between rings.

Not all the signals discussed in the preceding paragraphs are implemented with all personal-computer serial ports. Understanding each of the signals may help when interfacing serial devices with these system units. The following section discusses the how's and why's of cable and connector selection.

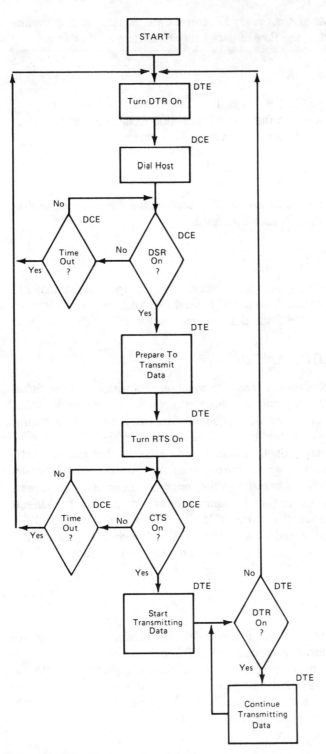

Figure 3.12 Modem signal logic.

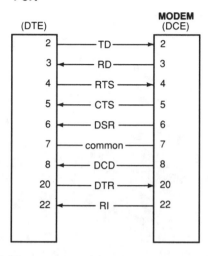

Personal Computer Asynchronous Port

Figure 3.13 Typical connection between asynchronous port and modem.

Cables and Genders

The RS-232C signals are transmitted to and from the serial port by a *communications cable*. The cable may be round or flat. The shape of the cable makes no difference in its ability to support communications, but the types of connectors provided on each end of the cable or the number of wires connected to the pins in the connectors make a difference.

When purchasing a communications cable, you should pay special attention to the cable's connectors, particularly when buying the communications adapter from one vendor and the cable from a different vendor. Almost all modems have a *DB-25 female connector*, which requires a cable with a *DB-25 male connector*. Most serial ports, on the other hand, have a DB-25 male connector which requires a cable with a DB-25 female connector. Figure 3.14 shows a diagram of the IBM PC DB-25 pin assignments.

The AT serial port is an exception to the DB-25 rule. The standard IBM serial port for the AT is a *DB-9 male connector*. Several vendors make cables that convert this serial port to a DB-25 connector that can be used with external modems. Figure 3.15 shows a diagram of the IBM PC AT DB-9 pin assignments.

As discussed earlier, there is no such thing as standard RS-232C implementation in actual hardware production. The number of pins connected in a communications cable falls into this category. The so-called *"Basic 8"* pins are 1 through 7 and 20, and many communications cables are made with only those pins soldered in place. The IBM serial port, however, requires that pin 8 also be connected. Some communications software

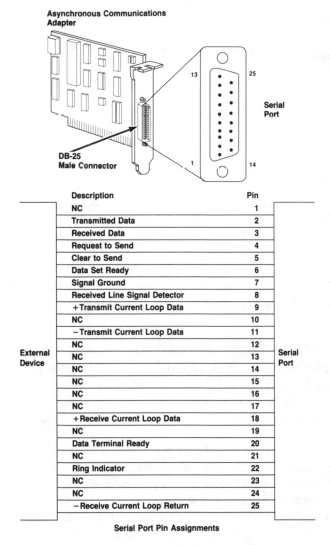

Description	Pin	
NC	1	
Transmitted Data	2	
Received Data	3	
Request to Send	4	
Clear to Send	5	
Data Set Ready	6	
Signal Ground	7	
Received Line Signal Detector	8	
+Transmit Current Loop Data	9	
NC	10	
−Transmit Current Loop Data	11	
NC	12	
NC	13	
NC	14	
NC	15	
NC	16	
NC	17	
+Receive Current Loop Data	18	
NC	19	
Data Terminal Ready	20	
NC	21	
Ring Indicator	22	
NC	23	
NC	24	
−Receive Current Loop Return	25	

Serial Port Pin Assignments

Figure 3.14 IBM PC asynchronous communications adapter.

packages also require that pin 22 (*ring indicate*) be connected for all the software functions to operate properly.

You may want to buy the parts at a local electronics parts supply store and make your own communications cable to extend the RS-232C adapter. You can buy a flat 40-wire ribbon cable, strip off all but 25 wires, then attach compression-type connectors on each end. The advantage in making your own cable is that you are assured that all 25 pins in the cable are connected, even though you will be using only nine of the pins.

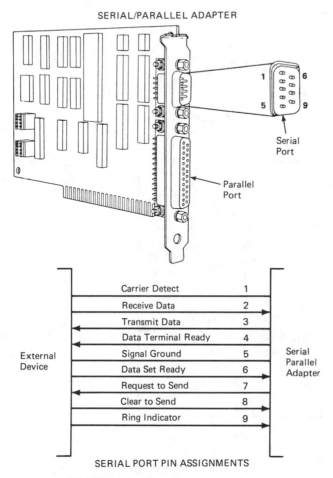

Figure 3.15 IBM PC AT serial port.

The Null Modem

If you are the proud new owner of an IBM PC, but you have several hundred programs that you developed on a TRS-80, you are probably interested in transferring some of the software over to your new PC. To do that, you may want to interface the two computers using a device called a *null modem* or *modem eliminator* instead of using two modems and the telephone system.

Actually, a null modem is not a modem at all—it is a cable or a set of connectors designed to eliminate the need for a modem. The null modem makes each computer operate as if it were communicating with a modem. In Figure 3.16, you can see that the microcomputer and the modem are sending and receiving data over compatible lines, whereas the two microcomputers are both expecting to receive and send data

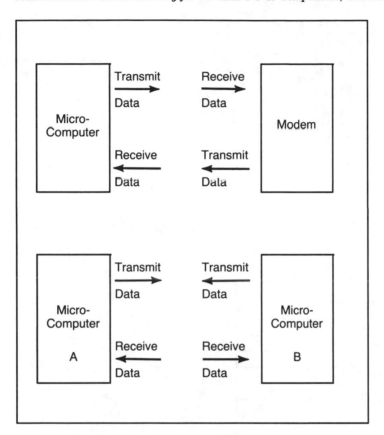

Figure 3.16 Microcomputer-modem interfaces.

on the same lines. Figure 3.17 shows the null modem solution to the incompatibility of micro-to-micro communications. By crossing the Receive Data and Transmit Data lines, microcomputer A is listening on the line microcomputer B is talking on, and vice versa.

Null modems can be purchased from a variety of computer electronics stores, but care should be taken in selecting one. There are several ways to connect the cable pins together to get two micros to talk to each other. The connections shown in Figure 3.18 should work between the Personal Computer and most other microcomputers.

By making a direct computer-to-computer connection via a null modem, data can be quickly transferred between two microcomputers. For example, data can be transferred through the a PC's serial port instead of through a modem. The serial port allows data to be transferred at rates as high as 9600 bps for older PCs and 19,200 bps for newer models compared to data transfer rates of 1200 or 2400 bps for typical modems. Direct connections not only allow rapid data transfer, they also eliminate line noise and other types of errors associated with data transfer using telephone lines.

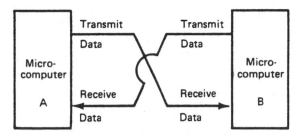

Figure 3.17 Null modem interface.

Terminal Emulation

Emulation is a technique used with the IBM PC to make it behave almost exactly like a specific type of mainframe or minicomputer terminal. The implementation of this technique often requires both hardware and software components. Some hardware and software aspects of emulation are covered here, but an exhaustive discussion is not presented.

Using the PC as a *terminal emulator* allows the user to do both host access and local processing with the same hardware. Large number-crunching programs can be processed on the bigger and faster host computer, or smaller spreadsheet or word-processing applications can be processed locally.

Hardware terminal emulators for the PC are installed in an expansion slots. These emulators can make the PC act almost exactly as a standard mainframe terminal. Most emulators of this type produce the characteristics of the IBM 3270 or 5250 families of synchronous terminals. With the proper hardware and a matching software package, the PC can be connected to an IBM 3274 or 3174 control unit and participate as a mainframe work station. The IBM 3278/79 Emulation Adapter is an example of such an emulator. The Token-Ring Network adapter can also be used with some 3278/79 terminal emulation software packages to provide 3270 connectivity through a Token-Ring attached to an IBM 3270 Information Display System.

Software terminal emulators are often used alone to make a personal computer appear as a standard ASCII terminal to a minicomputer or a mainframe. Terminals most often emulated are the IBM 3101, DEC VT 100, DEC VT 52, and ADDS Viewpoint. If a large computer is already set up to expect one of these terminal types, it is easier and less expensive simply to make the PC look like one of these terminals, rather than add software to the large computer to accommodate the Personal Computer. The difference between the terminal types are the escape codes used to create certain screen functions. If you do not use the same codes with your Personal Computer that the large computer expects, you may get screens full of garbage instead of legible text.

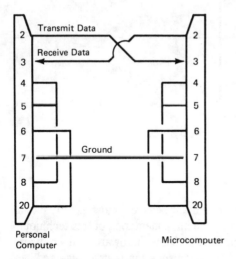

Figure 3.18 Null modem diagram.

4

Terminal Communications Software

After assembling the pieces of hardware described in Chapter 3, there is one more item that has to be added before the PC can communicate with other computer systems: A terminal communications software package must be added. Before delving into the subject of communications software, however, it is a good idea to review the relationship between IBM PC software and hardware. The following paragraphs review this relationship.

Software Layers

As shown in Figure 4.1, the *central processing unit* (*CPU*) is the piece of hardware that directs the flow of communications within the PC. Three kinds of software control this processor. The first layer of control comes from instructions stored in memory chips called *read only memory* (*ROM*). An operating system provides the second layer of instructions and control. Communications software provides the final layer of control. This software draws upon the capabilities of the ROM and the operating system to execute user-directed data communications functions. Figure 4.2 shows the logical relationship between these three layers of software and the hardware that supports data communications.

ROM BIOS Software

When the computer first starts up, it must have software built into the hardware to ensure proper start up. This same software must also support more powerful software

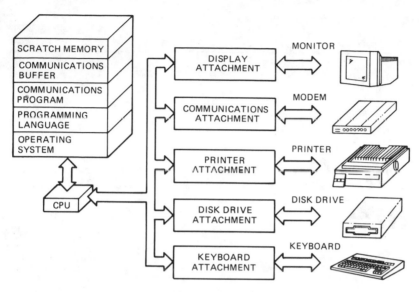

Figure 4.1 IBM PC communications overview.

that loads from disk after start up. ROM software, stored in a variety of hardware chips in the PC, performs this function. The ROM software is permanently embedded into the hardware in such a way that it cannot be erased or changed for the lifetime of the computer. Each time the computer begins operation, this software executes an identical set of start-up operations, and then stands by with an identical set of *basic input/ output system(BIOS)* functions to support system operations. The PS/2 series of microcomputers has BIOS functions not contained in the earlier PCs. This set is called the *Advanced BIOS (ABIOS)*.

Although important to proper system start-up and reliability, the initial start-up ROM does not play a role in later operation of communications software. This portion of ROM performs several tasks as shown in Table 4-1. The following paragraphs describe these tasks and the roles they play in support of data communications.

Table 4-1. Initial start-up ROM routines.

Executes initial system error and reliability tests.
Performs initial system chip and equipment set up.
Performs initial optional equipment tests.
Sets up initial interrupt-handling vectors.
Loads operating system from disk.

The initial system error and reliability tests are brief routines that test certain hardware components in the PC to be sure the system meets a minimum set of requirements. These tests are not exhaustive, but ensure that such things as disk drives and

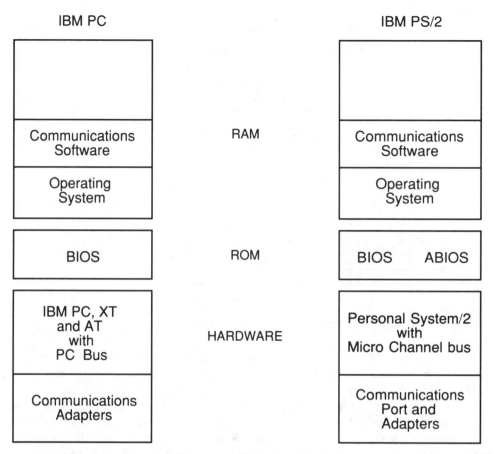

Figure 4.2 Communications software and hardware.

memory operate properly to support applications software. For example, the ROM checks each block of memory to be sure there are no bad memory chips that will abnormally affect later operations. This set of instructions does not, however, test such things as RS-232C communications ports for proper operation. You must run a more exhaustive set of maintenance tests to verify proper operation of this hardware. For the RS-232C port, these maintenance tests require a special cable to support a *loop-back* test. The test verifies that the port properly transmits and receives predefined bit patterns.

The next initialization process the ROM performs is crucial to later communications operation. Besides reading system switches and checking optional hardware installed in the computer, the ROM initializes *interrupt vectors* that tell the CPU what to do when it receives specific interrupt signals during later operations. Some of these vectors are pointers to ROM BIOS routines that handle input/output with the RS-232C port(s) or adapter(s) installed in the computer. Chapter 3 provides more information about these interrupt routines.

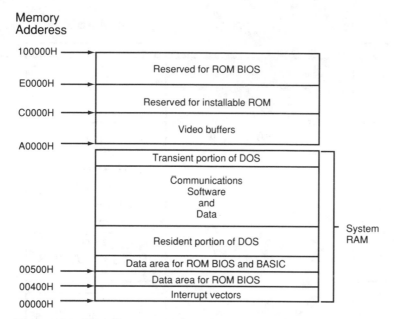

Figure 4.3 PC software required for communications.

The final step ROM takes after the computer starts up is the loading of more powerful system control software. For a PC that includes a disk drive, a ROM-based *bootstrap loader* starts the disk drive operating. It also loads a more powerful *disk operating system (DOS)* into the PC's memory. This disk operating system, normally *MS-* or *PC-DOS*, assumes control of the PC after it loads into memory. DOS has the necessary commands to control all the peripherals shown on the right side of Figure 4.1. It also controls the transfer of programs and data between disk files and RAM memory (whereby it gets the name disk operating system). DOS also controls many of the design characteristics of the software that can be loaded and run in the PC. Figure 4.3 shows a technical diagram of the various layers of software required to support communications.

Operating System

The *operating system* contains several software programs that direct the operation of all internal IBM PC components. Without the existence of the operating system, the power and flexibility we have grown to expect from microprocessor-controlled personal computers would be sorely lacking. All PC operations and applications build upon this foundation of software layers.

Language Interpreter

The next layer of software required for communications is either a *language interpreter* or a communications software package. This layer should be a high-level language interpreter such as BASIC if the communication application is written for operation in an interpretive mode. Interpretive BASIC software does not require an assembly or compilation process before it executes. Instead, a software developer writes the BASIC software with an editor and stores it as ASCII text or as a meta-language. When you run the software, an interpreter reads, interprets, and executes the software one line at a time. These interpreter applications normally have filenames that have extensions other than EXE or COM. For example, interpretive BASIC programs have a BAS filename extension.

Communication applications written in languages that require a compiler or assembler load and execute without the support of a language interpreter. These *directly executable* applications programs have filenames that end with EXE or COM, and, when loaded into PC memory, have the relationship with ROM BIOS and DOS shown in Figure 4.3. These machine-code programs operate faster than interpretive programs because they do not interpret source code one line at a time. They can also have direct links with the RS-232C communications hardware, which improves their execution speed. Software developers write these communications software packages in the C language or assembly language in order to achieve high execution speed and obtain direct access to the system unit hardware.

Communications Software

In the sequence of software loading from disk to memory, the *communications software* is the last to load. When a communications application loads, it sets aside a certain amount of random access memory for the *communications buffers* described in Chapter 2. For communications software written in BASIC, there is a section of memory used for software house cleaning, a space for reorganizing data, that will not be of concern for most communications users. Software developers monitor memory usage to be sure there is enough free space for this house cleaning. Users of these packages do not concern themselves with this level of detail unless they choose to modify the software.

Communications software performs both high-level and low-level operations. This software must interact with a user or a set of user-written procedures at one end and translate these interactions into information the communications hardware will understand at the other end. On the other hand, the communications software must monitor the communications hardware and execute operations dictated by signals generated by this hardware.

Software-hardware Compatibility

A key factor in the proper operation of communications software is compatibility between the BIOS and operating system that controls the CPU and the communications software. The communications software must be designed to operate with the specific operating system the user has chosen for the PC. Software interrupts and system calls issued by the communications software must be understood and properly executed by

BIOS and the operating system. If not, communications will fail in one way or another. For example, a communication package written for execution under the PC-DOS or MS-DOS operating system will not operate properly under Operating System/2 (OS/2) or the AIX operating system.

The introduction of the PS/2 has added to the potential software-hardware incompatibilities. The PS/2 has two more communications-related functions in its *Advanced Basic/Input Output System* (*ABIOS*) than the IBM PC, XT, and AT have in their BIOS. This makes it possible to write software that will work perfectly well with the PS/2 but fail in an older PC. A good software developer will provide a technique to ensure that the communications software matches the hardware if there are subtle differences such as this BIOS extension. For example, the developer can provide an operational profile that is modified during installation to tell the communications software whether to use special or hardware-dependent extensions.

Software Design Concepts

Communication software, like most other types of software, can be designed in several ways and still accomplish the same objectives. The software design may affect the performance of the package or it may affect only the user interface. We discuss in the following sections the four major design models vendors use for communications software.

Data Handling Techniques

Besides communicating properly with an operating system, the software must provide a mechanism for transferring data from one device to another. The operating system can control each of the PC's peripherals, but the software must decide the device destination for data. After selecting the device to receive certain data, the software must handle the process of moving the data from one device to another. The software must also tell the user when a communications error occurs and provide the user with a method to terminate operations when errors are excessive. Software designers use either polling or interrupt-driven techniques for these data-transfer and error-handling operations.

Although both *polling* and *interrupt-driven* communications software accomplish the same objectives, they differ significantly in the methods they use to accomplish these tasks. Both accept input from the keyboard and transfer data to and from the communications link. They also display user input and data received from a distant computer. The major differences between the polling and interrupt-driven techniques is the method designers use to determine the need for action and the time it takes to execute the action.

Polling Software

The polling technique can result in slow reactions to changes. This method typically forces the CPU to continually check the keyboard and the serial port buffers to see

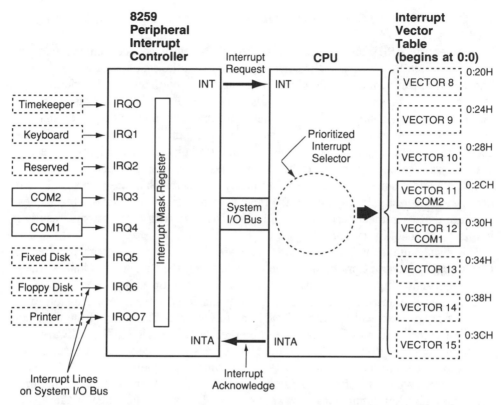

Figure 4.4 Hardware interupt logic of the IBM PC.

which of these devices has data available. A software developer can combine this continuous polling technique with one of several ways to handle data it finds in a device's buffer. A developer can require the CPU to process all data it finds in a given buffer before continuing the polling process. A developer can also write the software to handle only part of the data it finds in a buffer, then continue with its polling process.

Regardless of the polling design, it may respond too slowly to user commands or incoming data. If the user of such a package wants to terminate an operation that is in progress, the CPU might be emptying a communications buffer when the user executes the termination command. Several characters might continue to display on the monitor before the termination is completed. If data are coming into the serial port at a rapid rate and the user decides to send a file to the remote computer at the same time, incoming data may be lost while the CPU is busy sending out data.

Interrupt-driven Software

The interrupt-driven input/output control technique, on the other hand, causes a program to react quickly to changes under most circumstances. The interrupt technique allows the CPU to continue executing a designated task until it needs to perform a different task. No time is wasted in the polling of devices. When a device has data available, it sends the CPU an *interrupt request*, as shown in Figure 4.4, indicating the need for service.

Whether the CPU stops an activity to service a device depends on the *interrupt priority* given to that device by the operating system and the communications software. The software can turn off or *mask* minor interrupts to keep them from interfering with other important tasks. The software can also give interrupts different levels of priority that determine their *order of execution* when more than one interrupt requires simultaneous service. For example, a software author can program the ESC key to transfer the user from the conversation mode to the command mode instantaneously, regardless of other operations under way when the user presses the ESC key. A software designer can also make a software package react quickly to specific characters or signals that arrive at the serial port. Because of the rapid response of interrupt-driven techniques, software that uses these techniques can keep better pace with host systems, resulting in a lower probability of data loss.

The disadvantage of interrupt-driven software is the complex design required to assign proper interrupt priorities. In the polling design, the CPU always knows where data are coming from and handles interrupts one at a time, based on the *polling sequence*. With interrupt-driven design, however, an interrupt can occur at any time during a program execution. The software has to recognize the origin of the interrupt and determine what action to take, based on preselected priorities. The software also has to preserve the status of the operation in progress when the interrupt occurs, then return to that same point when the interrupt service is complete.

Software developers often use packages of interrupt-driven routines or *libraries* when they develop communications applications. By using a package of these routines, a developer can quickly design and write a communications application. The library vendor is responsible for developing, testing, and maintaining the interrupt library. The communications application vendor is responsible for developing, testing, and maintaining the application. With this division of responsibility, each vendor can concentrate his efforts on one level of software development, thereby providing end users with more powerful software. Two popular vendors of communications libraries for the PC are Greenleaf Software and Blaise Computing. These DOS-based libraries provide communications functions that are linked directly to applications.

IBM provides a library of communications functions, called *Dynamic Linking Routines*, in the OS/2 Extended Edition. The OS/2 EE Communications Manager contains an *Asynchronous Communication Device Interface* (*ACDI*) that provides interrupt-driven support for PS/2 serial ports. Vendors can write communications applications that call these standard routines to send and receive data. The application programming interfaces in ACDI are similar to the Presentation Manager APIs that provide standard screen and keyboard input/output.

The techniques vendors use to transfer data to and from serial ports are normally *transparent* to users. If the techniques work, the user is not aware of their presence. If they do not work, the user is aware there are functions in the software that are not performing as required. A feature users are always aware of, however, is the interface the vendor provides for control of the communications software.

Predominant User Interface

Software vendors design communications software as either *conversation-mode* or *command-mode* predominant. When the user starts a communications software package, the software goes directly into either the conversation mode or the command mode. The user must instruct the software to make a switch to get to the other mode. The active mode determines where the user interactions go.

The command mode provides *off-line* communications between the PC keyboard and the communications software. This mode allows the user to perform functions that do not involve the computer at the other end of the communications link. For example, the user can store a telephone number in a dialing directory or change the software's operating profile, neither of which require interaction with the remote computer. When the user finishes off-line command-mode functions, however, he or she may return to the *on-line* conversation mode to resume interactive communications with the remote computer.

Conversation Mode

Conversation-mode predominant software assumes the user will normally be in the *conversation* or *terminal mode* when communicating. This design is excellent for interactive communications with bulletin boards and information systems and is the design many vendors chose for their software. With this type of software, a user goes into the command or off-line mode only when he or she needs to change a communications parameter, select a telephone number, or execute some other nonconversation action. No data move between the PC and the remote computer while the software is in this mode. When the user completes off-line action, the software immediately returns to the conversation mode.

Command Mode

Command-mode predominant software, on the other hand, assumes the user will frequently want to be in the off-line mode when communicating. Businesses prefer this type of software when they frequently execute batch-mode file transfers. Command-mode software is also easier for a communications novice to use. The command menus prompt users for input.

With command-mode software, the user remains in the command mode until he or she requests a switch to the conversation mode. After switching to the conversation mode, the user can return to the command mode at any time during a communications session by striking the required conversation-mode escape key. This option allows the user to execute several off-line operations without returning to the conversation mode.

The user can list a file, delete a file, or change communications parameters without switching back and forth between off line and on line.

Command-mode software also helps to eliminate the confusion some users experience when switching between the off-line and on-line modes. Conversation-predominant software does not always provide a clear indication when it changes from on line to off line or vice versa. Command-mode software provides a better indication because menus appear on the screen when the user is in the off-line mode.

The IBM DOS includes a simple command-mode predominant communications program called COMM.BAS. Figure 4.5 shows the command menu for this program. Although COMM.BAS is an interpretive BASIC program, it can provide low-speed, terminal communications between the PC and a remote computer. It also provides good examples of communications software design techniques. Most commercial communications packages for the IBM PC are more complex and offer many more features than COMM.BAS, but many of these packages are just as easy to use.

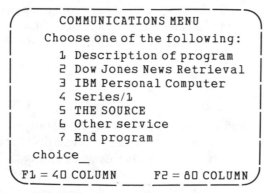

```
      COMMUNICATIONS MENU
   Choose one of the following:
      1 Description of program
      2 Dow Jones News Retrieval
      3 IBM Personal Computer
      4 Series/1
      5 THE SOURCE
      6 Other service
      7 End program
   choice_
   F1 = 40 COLUMN     F2 = 80 COLUMN
```

Figure 4.5　COMM.BAS command menu.

Off-line Command Mode

The off-line mode of communications software is either *menu* or *command driven*. Menu-driven software always provides the user with a list of options to choose from in the off-line mode. Command-driven software, on the other hand, requires the user to execute commands without a list of available options. Both types of software often provide help files to explain command functions, but the command-driven type may provide two levels of help. The first level of command-driven help may only list the available commands, whereas the second level may provide more specific details about each command.

Menu-driven Software

Menu-driven communications software is generally easier to learn and use for communication novices. The command prompts lead the novice through a sequence of easy-to-follow choices. The selection of a choice at one menu often leads to another list of alternatives. The menus provide a decision tree with two or more branches at the end of each branch.

Although easy to learn and use for the novice, menu-driven communications software packages often become inconvenient and frustrating to use as the novice becomes familiar with data communications. Going from one menu level to another can become an annoying chore. Users of packages that contain several levels of menus often develop "menu disgust."

Command-driven Software

Command-driven communications software is a good choice for the experienced communications user. The user can go from conversation mode to command mode and execute several commands in quick succession, without going through a series of time-consuming menu prompts. The user can always ask for help when commands fail to produce desired results. This type of software is sometimes intimidating for the novice and often requires more frequent use of the software documentation or on-line help. The intimidation may also cause the user to overlook features and not take full advantage of the package.

The ideal communication software package offers the best of both worlds. The novice can start using the package in a menu-driven mode, then switch to a command-driven mode after achieving proficiency with the package. This type of software may also offer a configuration feature that allows different users to default to one or the other of these modes automatically when the software begins operation.

Software Screen Displays

With the introduction of Microsoft Windows and the OS/2 Presentation Manager, yet another method of categorizing communications software has emerged—*character based* and *windows based*. A character-based design uses the original character-based DOS command screen, whereas windows-based software uses one of two panel techniques. Both provide display and user input control, but the window technique may provide a more consistent user interface.

Character-based Display

Character-based software provides its own vendor-specific screen layout, menus, and user input techniques. This type of software may also use graphics-based panels or windows for output display. The problem with these windowing techniques is that vendors of different packages often use different techniques to display information and obtain user input. Vendors who develop windows-based software from either a Microsoft Windows or a Presentation Manager toolkit, on the other hand, provide user interfaces that are consistent with all other applications developed for these environments.

Windows-based Display

Windows-based communications software, by its nature, provides a menu-driven user interface. This does not, however, dictate either a command or conversation predominant design. The software may be in either the command or conversation mode when it first begins operation, and require user input to change to the other mode. With the pull-down menus available in a windows environment, it is easy to combine these modes of operation. The software can allow the user to pull down menus while a conversation is in progress with a remote computer. Scroll bars can also allow the user to scroll back through information received earlier. A developer's imagination is the only limit with this powerful and rich operating environment.

Although the design of a software package often heavily influences its operating efficiency and ease of use, the potential software buyer may be more concerned with the features available in a package. These features determine how well a package matches the user's requirements for communications with another device or computer.

Software Intelligence

The number of features included in a communications package determine its level of *intelligence*. Software packages range from dumb to smart. Software vendors design *dumb terminal* packages to provide only the basics, whereas they design *smart terminal* software to provide many automated functions. The prices of these packages usually match their level of intelligence.

Dumb-Terminal Software

Dumb-terminal software allows the PC to *emulate* an asynchronous ASCII terminal that has no disk drives or other data-storage devices attached. This type of software is often used for data entry and display. Such a package cannot store and retrieve information to eliminate the complexities or tedium of logging onto host computers. Dumb-terminal software also provides no file transfer capability.

A good example of dumb-terminal communications software is the COMM.BAS program included in the IBM DOS software. This program allows communications with other computers through either an internal or an external modem. COMM.BAS also provides all the capabilities required for data entry with a minicomputer and mainframe computer that support asynchronous, dumb terminals. However, this software provides only a small subset of the functions contained in other communications software available for the PC.

Smart-Terminal Software

Smart-terminal software refers to packages that give the PC real communications power. Besides data entry and display, these systems allow the user to store and retrieve host telephone numbers, automatically dial telephone numbers, and transfer disk files. Smart-terminal software usually provides many built-in features that make the task of data communications easier. This type of software often includes features that allow the user to customize features and functions to give the package a personal touch.

Some smart-terminal packages are available in the *public domain* and others are commercial packages. The commercial status of a package, however, does not always reflect its level of performance or quality of documentation. Some of the best smart-terminal software is also available as *freeware*. If you continue to use these packages after an initial trial run, you are expected to make a contribution to the software vendor. Qmodem and ProComm are two examples of high-quality, communications software that have versions available as freeware. Other communications packages are only available as commercial products, and many of these packages have loyal fans who will not use another package even if it is free. Long-time owners of the Crosstalk and Relay packages, for example, often feel lost with any other communications package.

Because of the variety of options available in smart-terminal communication packages, the selection and purchase of a commercial package may be time consuming. One element that makes the selection of a package difficult is the jargon vendors use to describe software capabilities. Software publishers use terms such as *download* and *break signal* without prior definition. Software publishers also use different terms to describe the same process or capability, thus adding to the confusion. To eliminate some of this confusion and to make the selection and use of a communications package easier, the following paragraphs provide a detailed explanation of most of the terms used to describe asynchronous communications software capabilities.

Smart-terminal Software Capabilities

Smart-terminal communications software is like any other applications software. No single package is likely to satisfy all wants and needs. The best you can hope to achieve is to obtain a package that provides most essential features and some nonessential but desirable features. Table 4-2 provides an overview of the features included in many smart-terminal packages.

Table 4-2. Communication characteristics and capabilities.

Installation and Set Up:

Operating system required	Manual and auto-dial modems
Modem speed flexibility	Documentation manual
User help files	User support
Error handling	Display width selection
Parameter selection	Duplex mode selection
Command files	Batch mode
Prestored strings	Password storage security

Modem Controls:

Originate/answer mode switch	Dialing directory
Disk directory listing	Auto-redial
Clock-controlled operation	Telephone hang up

Data Redirection and Flow Control:

Data capture to printer	XON/XOFF protocol
Data capture	Data upload
Upload throttle	Upload/download local echo
Binary data transfer	Protocol file transfer

Data Manipulation:

Line feed control	Blank line expansion
Character filter	Translation table
Terminal emulation	Case conversion
Tab-to-space conversion	

Special Features:

Split screen	Elapsed time of call
Break signal	Remote takeover
External file manipulation	Return to operating system

Although many features are common to both business and personal communications software, vendors often implement these features in different ways to match the needs of a target market. The following paragraphs briefly discuss communications software features and emphasize the differences between business and personal applications.

Installation and Set-Up Features

Vendors use a variety of features in the initial installation and set-up of their packages. These features are described in the following paragraphs.

Operating System Required

You must define the operating environment before selecting a communications package because a package may operate only under the *DOS, OS/2,* or *AIX* operating system. Though some packages will operate under only one of these systems, others are available for more than one operating system. A package designed to operate under one system will not operate under another system. Files downloaded using an AIX communications package cannot be accessed later under PC-DOS because the disk formats are different.

Manual and Auto-dial Modem Support

A user may have only a *manual-dial* modem, but when selecting a software package it is a good idea to get a package that will support both manual and *auto-dial* modems. Having a communications package that supports only manual-dial modems or only auto-dial modems limits flexibility in hardware configurations. With the rapid increase in the capabilities of modems and the rapid drop in their prices, a new auto-dial modem may become a necessity long before expected. An auto-dial modem might also have to be relinquished for repairs for a period of time, resulting in the need to use a spare manual-dial modem.

Modem Speed Flexibility

A communications package should be able to support communication speeds from 300 bps to as high as 9600 bps. The user should be able to upgrade from a 1200-bps modem to a 2400-bps or 9600-bps modem without having to buy a new communications package; this can save a great deal of cost associated with changing software and retraining personnel. Just about all communications packages use different commands to perform the same function, so going to a new package means communications users have to learn new commands.

Again, because of the faster data-handling speed of assembly language and C software, most communications packages written in these languages can send and receive data at speeds up to 19,200 bps. Almost all commercial communications software is written in one or a combination of both of the languages. Some freeware communications packages, however, are written in BASIC and have some serious speed-matching limitations. Some of these packages written in interpreter BASIC are advertised as supporting data rates above 300 bps, but their slower operating speeds often limit data capture at 1200 bps and higher to files under 10 kb. Compiled BASIC programs, on the other hand, can be designed to capture data to a disk at 1200 bps without special hardware assistance—the *PC-TALK* communications software published by The Headlands Press is a good example of this type of compiled-BASIC software.

Documentation Manual

A communications package is incomplete without a good *documentation manual*. A package that contains all features just discussed is of little use without a manual that tells how to use the features. A documentation manual does not have to contain the background information on communications provided in this book, but it must fully explain every package feature.

User Help Files

User *help files* are important for communications packages that are not to be used frequently. They are also helpful for the user who is not accustomed to that particular package. Help files are not a replacement for a good documentation manual, but they provide a *quick reference* for the keys required to perform certain functions. These help files should be readily accessible (single key stroke) and written in clear, concise English.

A package should also provide 25th-line (bottom-of-screen) messages and *abbreviated menus* unless the user elects to turn them off. These menus indicate commands that are available under certain modes of operation and help novices learn to use the package more quickly. Expert users may not want to have the menus on the screen and should be allowed to toggle them off.

User Support

When all else fails, a user must be able to get support from the software publisher. Good user support means that a technical person is available, when required, to help solve application problems. No communications software package is perfect, particularly new ones coming out on the market, and most of the problems encountered cannot be solved by a software salesperson. Before purchasing a software package, check with local IBM PC users' groups and other people who own and use the package to be sure it is well supported.

Error Handling

A software package's ability to handle errors is vital. A good package should either warn the user before an error occurs so that preventive action can be taken or provide a clear, understandable error message when an error does occur. The package should also allow the user to continue with communications if a minor error occurs. Operations that can result in significant errors should also be designed to give the software user the opportunity to abort a command before the error is made. For example, a user should be told that captured data will be lost when an attempt is made to return to the operating system before the data have been saved. The user should be given the opportunity to go back and save the data before finally returning to the operating system.

Display-width Selection

Some communications packages allow the user to operate in either the 40- or 80-column display mode. This is particularly useful when a user is doing a great deal of communicating using a monitor that does not produce easily readable 80-column text. This feature is also necessary for PC use with a standard home television set; most of them will display only 40 columns of readable text. Software packages that use windows also provide the capability to change the size of the windows—even the ones that are displaying a communications session in progress.

Parameter Selection

To properly communicate with other mainframe and microcomputers (collectively called *host systems*), a communications user must be able to select the appropriate *communications parameters* required by the host system. These parameters include bps rate, number of data bits, type of parity error-checking, and number of stop bits. The software package may provide *default values* for these parameters, but it must also provide the option of modifying the default values both before and after a connection is made with a host system.

A good communications package also allows the user to modify the standard (sometimes called *global*) default values. A new set of default values replace the original set. These new default values are normally stored in a disk file for later use. Some software packages also allow the user to store specified sets of parameters for each host or service system. A user loads a *parameter command file* or selects a host system from a *displayed directory* to put the specific parameters into effect.

Several communications packages are designed to work with direct-connect auto-dial modems, and the communications parameters associated with each telephone number are stored in a file with the number. When the software is instructed to dial a number, the associated communications parameters are automatically put into effect before the number is dialed. These parameters remain in effect until modified by the user.

In each of the cases discussed above, the default or selected parameters are communicated to the PC's internal modem or serial port to set the stage for communications under a specific protocol. The software must *initialize* the serial communications hardware automatically, or it must be instructed to initialize the hardware before communications with a host is established. If any of the parameters are modified during a communications session, the software must reinitialize the communications hardware to put the new parameters into effect.

The option of listing selected parameters is another good feature. If difficulty is encountered during a communications session and the selected parameters cannot be listed, troubleshooting the problem becomes difficult. Establishing proper communications parameters to use with a new system may require some experimentation with different parameters. That trial-and-error process is difficult to perform without the ability to list the communications parameters.

Duplex-Mode Selection

A communications package should allow a user to switch between *half-duplex* and *full-duplex modes*, because business and personal communications applications often require connection to both half-duplex and full-duplex host systems. Most information services and bulletin board systems operate in the full-duplex (*host echo*) mode, but other microcomputer and mainframe systems may operate in either the full- or half-duplex mode.

To properly communicate with a variety of systems, a user must be able to switch between the full- and half-duplex modes both before and after a communications link is established. Some bulletin board and host systems may require a user to switch duplex modes after establishing a communications link. If a host system operator (SYSOP) answers a page or interrupts your communications session to deliver a message (switches from automatic operation to the conversation mode), the host software may also switch from full duplex to half duplex. When this happens, characters are no longer echoed back to the user's terminal. To see the characters typed locally, the user has to make a modem switch to half-duplex or a software switch to *local echo*. A software package that offers a single-key-stroke toggle switch between full-duplex (remote echo) and half-duplex (local echo) is useful under these circumstances.

Some software packages allow the duplex mode or host echo mode to be changed through a menu selection. This method is acceptable if switching to the menu does not disconnect the telephone connection. Modems that monitor the Data Terminal Ready signal generated by the serial port will drop the telephone connection when the user enters the menu mode to change parameters. An external Hayes Smartmodem has a switch that allows the user to override monitoring of the DTR signal, but some modems do not have this override option.

Command Files

Command or script files allow a user to store several parameters in a disk file for repeated use. These files can contain many or all the software package commands that can be entered from the keyboard. Communication parameters, such as parity and number of data bits, may be modified, and a telephone number can be automatically dialed by a command file.

Command files offer several advantages for business applications. First, they save users from repetitive typing of commands. Second, different user disks can be set up, containing passwords and system log-on information specific to certain individuals. Third, command files can contain telephone numbers and passwords, eliminating the necessity for separate lists that have to be kept to call and log on with remote systems.

Batch Mode

Batch-mode operation is similar to command-file loading and execution, but it supports several commands that are not supported by command files. A *command file* can modify communications parameters and dial a telephone number when used with an auto-dial modem, but a communications operator must take over to continue the session after the communications link is established. A *batch file* can modify communications parameters and dial a telephone number, but it can also continue the communications session after the connection is established with a remote system. Log-on messages can be sent and files transferred between the IBM PC and any other system without operator assistance. A batch file can also be written to delay execution until a specified period of time has elapsed; unattended file transfers can be performed late at night when telephone rates are lowest. This capability could be a valuable asset for a business with branch offices in different time zones.

Many software packages now contain support for script files. This capability allows a user to create software commands using an editor or capture operating sequences as they occur. In either case, the script file can be executed later to automate operations in the same manner as command or batch files. Some vendors offer complete communications applications based on these script files.

Clock-controlled Operation

Clock-controlled operation can combine the automated capabilities of command, batch, or script files with operation that is controlled by the internal IBM PC clock. The user can design these files to execute specific operations at certain times of day or night. The user can set up the software to dial a remote system at 3:00 A.M., perform all log-on functions, upload a text, data, or program file, log off the remote system, then return the IBM PC to the operating system—all without the attendance of a local or remote system operator. Clock-controlled operation can be used to take advantage of low, late-night telephone rates and to transfer files, freeing the machine for other tasks during business hours.

Clock-controlled operation is sensitive to proper communications when it is used for unattended operation. The software has to be able to perform rudimentary *artificial intelligence*. After a command string is transmitted to a host, the software must be able to check to see that the host response indicates proper receipt of the command and repeat the command if the response is not correct. This eliminates the problems encountered with noise-generated command transmission errors.

Predefined Strings

Frequent communications with systems that require log-on commands can result in repetitive typing. In such cases, *predefined strings* that can be uploaded to a system can be a useful feature for both business and personal applications. Many IBM PC communications software packages allow predefined strings to be uploaded with either a one-key-stroke or a two-key-stroke combination, which makes this feature even more convenient. When predefined strings are provided by a package, the user must be able to easily and quickly list the strings while logged on with another system; it is easy to forget which string goes with each key and a quick reminder is sometimes necessary.

Password Storage Security

For software packages that allow the user to store and retrieve character strings, security for stored passwords should be considered. The listing of stored character strings on the monitor should allow the user to omit stored password strings. This keeps onlookers from stealing passwords to time-sharing or information services.

Modem Control Features

Good smart-terminal software packages are designed to take full advantage of the features included in popular, intelligent modems. The features discussed in the following paragraphs are associated with the use of auto-dial, auto-answer, intelligent modems. Examples of these modems are the Hayes Smartmodem 2400 and the IBM 5853 Modem.

Originate/Answer Mode Switch

It is necessary to switch a modem from the *originate-mode* to the *answer-mode* when receiving a call from a remote terminal or another microcomputer. Manual-dial modems provide a switch that activates the mode change, but intelligent modems may be switched manually or through software control. Communications packages often allow the user to switch from one of these modes to the other by pressing either one or two IBM PC keys. *Menu-controlled* originate/answer mode switches can be more cumbersome to use than single-key toggle switches unless the package contains only one command menu.

Dialing Directory

When a software package allows the user to store telephone numbers that can be used with auto-dial modems to access remote systems, the package should also allow the user to list the *dialing directory* of stored telephone numbers. Numbers that are buried in command or batch files are inconvenient to locate when the number has to be dialed without use of the command or batch file. A brief summary listing of the major communications parameters that will be automatically invoked when a number is dialed from the directory is also a good feature.

Disk Directory Listing

The ability to list the *disk directories* of all disk drives is another good communications software feature. When uploading files, this function allows the user to select files for transfer. When downloading files, this function allows the user to select filenames that are not currently in use. If the package stores communications parameters in disk files, the disk directory listing provides the user with a menu of parameter files. For packages that support batch file operation, this option allows the user to view the menu of available batch files.

Auto-redial

Some local information services used by the hobbyist run on microcomputers and allow only one user at a time, whereas others have a limited number of incoming connections. The telephone numbers of these services are frequently busy. Instead of manually redialing a number from the keyboard, an auto-dial modem can be software-controlled to redial a telephone number until a connection is made. Software packages that offer this capability also provide an alarm signal that gets the user's attention when the carrier of a remote system is finally detected. It is often necessary to use an *auto-redial* to get through to a bulletin board system on weekends or holidays.

Telephone Hang-up

Some business communications involve systems that do not automatically break the telephone connection when a user logs off. To break a connection with one of these systems, the user should be able to execute a software command that "drops the line" when an auto-dial/auto-answer modem is being used. Without this option, the modem might have to be turned off to break the connection, and frequent off/on cycling of a modem could shorten its life.

Software packages that offer the *telephone hang-up* feature generally require that the modem respond properly to the serial port's DTR signal. The modem should be set up to drop the *carrier signal* and the telephone connection when the *DTR signal* is turned off by the software. If the modem is not properly configured, the telephone-hangup command will not work properly.

Data Control Features

Smart-terminal software allows the user to redirect the flow of data to different devices. It also allows the user to transfer data to and from the PC. The following paragraphs describe features associated with these capabilities.

Data Capture to Printer

A communications package should allow the user to send data to a printer at the same time the data are being displayed on a monitor. Sometimes it is necessary to *log a conversation* with another person or print a download menu contained on a bulletin board, to eliminate repeat listings of the menu during selection of a download file. A user may also want to log sessions with time-sharing systems to refer to later; this is particularly useful when transactions result in the transfer of funds. Logging conversation-mode transactions is also a good way to develop training material for later time-sharing or information service system classes.

The simultaneous communications and printing capability offered by most software packages is usable only in the conversation mode. A dot-matrix printer can keep pace with conversation-mode data transfer rates but may not be able to keep pace with file transfer rates. A general rule to follow is to print only the data being continuously transmitted at a rate less than the speed of your printer. An 80-character-per-second printer can keep pace with a 300-bps (30-character-per-second) modem, but the same printer cannot keep pace with a 2400-bps (240-character-per-second) modem. A difference in communications speed and printer speed may not be a problem for assembly-language software packages because of the way they buffer incoming data, but it will likely be a problem for BASIC software packages.

Spooler software can be used with the printer option to facilitate simultaneous printing and downloading of data when using a slow-speed printer. A user can scan the messages on a bulletin board and mark messages of interest, then go back and list those messages while simultaneously printing them. After listing these messages, the user may go on to other bulletin board functions or download a file while the print spooler continues to send the messages to a printer. A print spooler can also be used to handle print-screens without interrupting data transfer. By pressing the shift and PrtSc keys simultaneously, a user can send screen contents to the printer as communications continue.

A *single-key toggle* that allows the user to turn the print function on and off without interrupting the transfer of data is also a desirable feature. This option allows the user to selectively send text to a printer by pressing one or two keyboard keys. Software that requires the user to go into the command mode to turn the print function on is cumbersome and requires either data receipt interruption or a pause in data transfer before printing can be initiated. This frequently results in desired data scrolling off the screen.

Care should be taken when using the simultaneous print option with certain printers. Some non-IBM printers go off line when they receive XOFF characters, which could cause the PC keyboard to lock up (not respond to key strokes) until the printer is manually returned to the on-line status. Printers may also respond to format effector characters, such as form feeds, that are transmitted for monitor control and waste paper.

XON/XOFF Protocol

Most file-transfer applications that involve data-transmission rates greater than 1200 bps require *XON/XOFF communications speed-matching protocol*. This protocol allows the software designer to use less memory for a communications receive buffer because communications speed-matching will not have to be handled solely by the buffer. Most mainframe computers use the XON/XOFF protocol, so business applications that involve file transfers with mainframe computers can make good use of this capability.

Assembly-language communications software packages often provide XON/XOFF support because they can rapidly respond to these characters, but BASIC-language software packages may support the protocol only when they are receiving files. If a BASIC program is advertised as an XON/XOFF protocol package, it should be thoroughly tested before being relied on to performed XON/XOFF speed-matching.

File-transfer protocols that provide XON/XOFF support are required for communications with some host computers, particularly older IBM mainframes. The two protocols that support XON/XOFF for the IBM PC are Kermit and Zmodem. Without this support, a file transfer can exceed the buffering capability of the host computer, resulting in data loss or abnormal termination of the file transfer.

Data Capture

Data capture is the process of storing received data in memory or in a disk file. The process is also called *downloading*. Most communications applications will require this capability. Some packages allow data capture directly to a disk file, whereas others only allow data capture to random access memory for later storage in a disk file. Some packages provide both options. Most personal-communication applications require *direct-to-disk capture* capability, but many business applications require the *memory-capture* option because the captured data must be modified before they are sent to a disk file or because the file-transfer rate is too great for capturing data on a diskette.

Capture to Memory

Data capture to memory removes the need for disk-emulator software to provide communications speed-matching at 1200 bps and above. The capture buffer is a portion of unused RAM that is set aside to temporarily store received data. Most software designers provide at least 20 kb of capture buffer. To keep the receive buffer from overflowing and to allow operation with small receive buffers, some communications packages may also be set up to automatically dump the capture buffer contents to a disk file when the buffer becomes full. For the transfer of large files, a large capture buffer and automatic buffer dump are recommended.

Data capture to a memory buffer has several advantages compared to data capture directly to disk. First, it is at least three times faster than data captured directly to disk, which allows data transfer rates of 1200 bps and higher. Second, data capture to memory can usually be *toggled* on and off by pressing a single key. The toggle allows a user to capture segments of received data instead of capturing and storing all incoming data. Third, captured data can be easily and quickly erased if the user decides not to save the data to disk. Hand in hand with that advantage, however, is the disadvantage that data captured to memory can be easily lost because of power surges or errors that require the system to be reset as part of the recovery process.

Capture to Disk

Data capture to a hard disk is the best option for two reasons. First, a hard disk allows data transfer from memory to a file at high speed. Second, data stored on disk is nonvolatile and will not be lost in the event of a power failure during the file download. This option is more expensive than data capture to memory or diskette because of the cost of the disk, but the data integrity and transfer speed could easily justify the extra cost.

Data Capture Selection

In addition to the selection of where to capture data, some communications packages allow the user to select the type of data to be captured. The user can elect to capture only incoming data transmitted from a host system, capture only data entered from the local PC keyboard, or capture both incoming and outgoing data. This option is good for business applications, but most personal applications do not require it. If only local keyboard input is being captured, a file can be opened and a series of batch-mode commands entered into the file. Then the file can be closed and immediately put into operation. Frequent use of this option can improve the efficiency of data communications and reduce communications cost for a business.

Data Upload

The term *upload* is used to describe the process of transferring a local disk file to a remote host system. Both business and personal communications applications make use of this capability to transfer files containing memos, reports, data, or software to remote computer systems. File transfer protocols are normally used to ensure error-free data transfer, as discussed in Chapter 6.

Some communications software allows data to be transferred directly from memory to the communications port. This option requires the user first to transfer the file to a *memory work area*; then the file can be sent directly out via the communications link. This capability reduces the workload placed on a disk drive when frequent file transfers are performed.

Upload Throttle

When files are being uploaded to a mainframe system, it may be necessary to match the file transfer rate with the response of the mainframe. Some large host systems will not allow you to send a line of data until you are *prompted* to do so. The prompt may be a letter, a character, a number, or a combination of all three, and it is a signal indicating that the mainframe is prepared to receive more data. Data sent before the prompt is received are usually lost. Uploading a file to such a system without providing a mechanism to wait for prompts results in the *truncation* of each line; a later listing of the file would show the beginning of each line missing. To match the upload speed of the IBM PC with the system response of a mainframe, it is sometimes necessary to throttle the upload.

Communication software packages provide several types of upload throttles. The three major types are time delays, character-receipt delays, and character-prompt delays. A *time-delay throttle* allows the user to select the length of time delay between the upload of each line of data. A *character-receipt delay throttle* allows the user to specify the number of characters that must be received from the mainframe before a new line of data is uploaded. A *character-prompt delay* allows the user to specify the exact character string that must be received from the mainframe before a new line of data is sent.

Of the three types of upload throttle, the time-delay throttle is the least effective because it requires the user to specify the longest expected mainframe response; selecting a long time delay to reduce the probability of losing transmitted data could result in long and costly data transfers. The character-receipt delay is effective if the mainframe continues to properly receive data. If an error occurs and the mainframe begins to reject data, the IBM PC will continue to transmit data if the proper number of characters (error messages in this case) keep coming in over the data line. The character-prompt delay is the most effective because it ensures that data will be transmitted only when the proper signal is received from the mainframe.

Upload Local Echo

For file transfers that are performed without a file transfer protocol, such as the upload of a text file to a host text editor, a software package may include a provision for displaying the data as they are transferred. A communications novice may need this type of feature to prevent improper file transfers. If a user selects the wrong file to upload to a host or bulletin board system, the user may have no way of discovering the error. With local echo of the file during transmission, operator errors can be noted and file transmission aborted, saving the user time. The same is true for downloading text files. While viewing a file being downloaded, a user can elect to abort the download process if the file turns out to be the wrong one or contains unexpected data.

The disadvantage of local echo during a file transfer is that the screen scrolling slows down the movement of data on the receiving end. This is normally not a problem when the PC system unit operates fast enough to keep pace with the incoming data. Screen display can be a problem for slow system units (less than 6 MHz CPU clock speed) equipped with the IBM Color Graphics Adapter for data communication speeds above 1200 bps.

Binary Data Transfer

A business communications package must allow the transfer of non-ASCII files. It is often necessary to transfer *machine-code* files to protect the source code from being stolen or modified by users. Some BASIC language communications software will not send or receive machine code because some of the binary strings contained in the files appear as *end-of-file markers* causing the transmit or receive mode to terminate abnormally. Communication software can be designed to overcome this problem and is usually required for business applications.

File Transfer Protocols

The term *file transfer protocol* refers to special *error-checking* techniques used during file transfers. There are several of these techniques used in communications software, but they generally do the same thing. The *protocol signals* (sometimes called *handshaking*) used by these packages allow them to transfer text, data, and machine-code files, and to perform sophisticated error-checking to be sure files are transferred properly. The handicap in using these protocol file-transfer techniques is that the computers on both ends of the communications link must be using the compatible software; there is no standard that controls these protocols and no two are exactly alike. This means that a business must standardize its microcomputer communications software to take advantage of protocol transfers.

Besides allowing the user to transfer machine-code files, the protocol technique offers other advantages. First, some protocols allow transfer of multiple files by allowing the user to invoke "wild card" commands in much the same way as multiple files can be copied to the printer with the IBM PC. All files with a particular extension or with a specific string as part of their filename can be transferred by entering one file transfer command. Second, data are transferred in *blocks* and some packages allow the user to select the block size. Each block is checked for transmission errors and blocks containing errors are retransmitted. For transmission over noisy telephone lines, the file-transfer block size can be set small to force frequent checks for errors. For transmission over low-noise telephone lines, the file-transfer block size can be set large to speed up file transfers. Third, the error checks performed under protocol file transfer are usually of the cyclic redundancy check (CRC) type described in Chapter 2. The CRC is a mathematically computed checksum, and its value is uniquely calculated for each block of data. This type of error checking is superior to asynchronous parity error checking because it results in bad data blocks being retransmitted; the parity error-detection technique simply signals that an error has occurred.

Microcom Networking Protocol

One vendor-specific file-transfer protocol that is becoming widely used is the *Microcom Networking Protocol* (*MNP*). This technique is based on the International Standards Organization model for Open Systems Interconnection. The protocol allows one or multiple files to be transferred and provides greater than 99.9 percent error-free data transmission. The protocol is included in the several PC products that have communication options, and is often included in modems. The protocol is proprietary and can be included in a software or hardware product only through a licensing agreement with Microcom, Inc.

XMODEM Protocol

Besides vendor-specific proprietary protocols, there are several protocols that have become default standards in microcomputer communications. One of these is the *Ward Christensen XMODEM protocol*. Many public bulletin board systems use the XMODEM file-transfer option. This protocol is similar to the vendor-specific protocol file-transfer techniques in that it requires a protocol-matched system. Software that supports this protocol during file receipt allows the user to take advantage of 99.6 percent error-free file downloading from bulletin boards that support XMODEM file transfer. The XMODEM protocol performs checksum error detection for transferred blocks of data, and blocks containing errors are automatically retransmitted. More advanced versions of the XMODEM protocol called CRC XMODEM and YMODEM provide the more advanced CRC type of error detection.

Kermit Protocol

The *KERMIT protocol* is also becoming widely used in communications because of four powerful features it provides. KERMIT can handle any kind of file and can be used with just about every kind of computer. The protocol is capable of converting all data into the equivalent of printable 7-bit ASCII characters and numbers when necessary. When KERMIT is forced to communicate 8-bit binary files, it sends the extra bit by itself. This *prefixing* or *8-bit quoting* process overcomes the 7-bit limitation of some old mainframe front-end processors.

KERMIT can transfer files through control character-sensitive data communications equipment. When Kermit is asked to transmit a control character, it encodes the character in a process that produces a printable character. The receiving Kermit must translate the characters back to the original data.

KERMIT allows *wild card* file transfers. An asterisk can be used in place of several file name letters in order to sequentially and automatically transmit many files with common filenames or extensions.

Minicomputer and mainframe versions of KERMIT often include a *SERVER mode*. After the host KERMIT is placed in the SERVER mode, the local KERMIT performs all handshaking necessary to both send and receive files. A detailed presentation of file transfer protocols is contained in Chapter 6. Chapter 6 also contains a comparison of the popular IBM PC protocols.

Data Manipulation Features

Smart-terminal software allows the user to select certain options that pertain to received or transmitted data manipulation. The following paragraphs describe some of these features.

Line Feed Control

Not all communications software packages add *line feeds* after each *carriage return* received or transmitted. Business communications software should allow the user to decide whether line feeds should be sent following each carriage return or added after each received carriage return. Without this capability, transferred files may have to be edited to remove or add line feeds, and conversation-mode communications may be difficult to perform.

The need for line-feed control depends upon the operation in progress. If a line feed is being added to each transmitted line by a remote system and another one is being added by the PC's communications package, the received data will have a blank line between each line of data. If line feeds are not being added to the end of each transmitted line by the host and the PC's communications package is not adding one, the data received by the PC cannot be listed and edited until line feeds are added. If data are being received in the conversation mode and neither the IBM PC software nor the remote station software is adding line feeds at the ends of data lines, each line will overprint the previous line on the PC monitor, making it difficult for the user to read the data.

Blank Line Expansion

Some host-computer software packages change modes of operation in response to blank lines; this requires the use of communications software that eliminates undesired mode changes. The message-receive functions of many electronic mail systems change from the message input mode to the message edit mode when a blank line is received. The file-creation mode of some mainframe editors also changes from the input mode to the edit mode when a blank line is received. A line containing only a carriage return means ''end of text'' to these systems. To avoid mode changes when the user wishes to upload text containing blank lines to such a system, a communications package must convert lines containing only a carriage return into a space followed by a carriage return—a technique called *blank line expansion*.

Character Filter

Some mainframe and microcomputer communications software transmits control characters. These characters do not print on most computer terminals, but the characters are printed on an IBM PC monitor. To eliminate these annoying and sometimes confusing characters, it is necessary for software to *filter* them out of the incoming stream of data. Some PC software packages allow the user to turn the filter on or off by executing a command string. Business applications that require remote demonstrations of software running on a computer that transmits control characters would benefit from the filter option.

Translation Table

Translation tables allow the user to redefine incoming or outgoing character codes. Any of 256 ASCII character codes can be redefined so that a different character is passed back to the IBM PC than the one represented by received data, or a different character is sent out of the communications port than the one that is entered at the keyboard. ASCII code can be converted into EBCDIC code or vice versa. Certain characters can be redefined as nulls or spaces or can be left out of the translation table entirely to filter out incoming or outgoing data.

Terminal Emulation

Another form of the translation table is called *terminal emulation*. Terminal emulation in a communication hardware package allows a user to communicate with a host system that is set up to communicate only with a specific type of terminal. Terminal emulation causes the PC to act almost exactly as the type of terminal the host is programmed to expect. Terminals that are often emulated include the Digital Equipment Corporation VT 52 and VT 100 and the IBM 3101, because of their popularity in business computing.

Terminal emulation, according to the strict data communications definition, is achieved only through hardware. Emulation that is achieved only through software translation is defined as *terminal simulation*. Most software vendors use the term *emulation* to describe the terminal simulation performed by their software, and that definition will be used here.

Terminal emulation usually pertains to keyboard key assignments and screen displays. Terminal-emulation software translates certain PC key combinations to character strings that are produced by keys of the emulated terminal. Terminal-emulation software also translates received character strings to strings that cause the PC screen display to perform like the terminal being emulated. These screen control characters are called *escape codes* and are used to clear the screen, locate the cursor in a specific row and column, and control screen attributes such as reverse video and blinking characters. Additional terminal emulation features found in several commercial products are shown in Table 4-3.

Table 4-3. Popular terminal emulation features.

Supports graphics displays.
Provides user programmable keys.
Allows multiple configurations to match several hosts.
Provides command or hot key switch to/from PC-DOS.
Provides smooth scrolling of screen text.
Allows the user to select color combinations.
Provides true underlining of text.
Provides or simulates boldface characters.
Displays double-high, double-wide characters.
Provides on-line help.

With a terminal-emulator equipped PC, the user can access and use a remote host system without keyboard and screen display incompatibilities. The other two alternatives to terminal emulation are emulation on the host end of the communications link and emulation between the PC and the host. The host can be programmed to respond to PC keyboard input and to transmit screen controls the PC will understand. This emulation allows the host and the PC to work efficiently and effectively as a team. Terminal emulation may also be combined with *code and protocol translators* to achieve communications with a host computer. These translators are normally used to connect an asynchronous device to a synchronous network such as IBM BSC and SDLC networks. An example of such a device is the IBM 7171; this translator allows IBM 3101 terminal or IBM PCs with 3101 terminal emulation software to access an IBM host that is normally accessed with 3278 or 3279 synchronous terminals. These translators eliminate the compatibility problems associated with *vendor-specific protocols* that are typical of host computers and older model word processors.

Terminal emulation is sometimes combined with local area networks to simulate the operation of terminals connected to a *cluster controller* or *control unit*. When a PC is equipped with terminal-emulation software and connected to the network, the user can access a remote mainframe computer and execute programs or edit files. If the host does not support direct connection to the network, a *gateway* on the network acts as a traffic cop to direct the flow of data to and from the host. A single Token-Ring Network allows over 250 microcomputers to access an IBM host with this technique. Using the PC as a mainframe terminal can be cost effective because the cost of a Personal Computer is sometimes less than the cost of a stand-alone mainframe terminal. A PC equipped with terminal-emulation hardware and software also eliminates the need for both a Personal Computer and a host-specific terminal.

Data Compression

Some smart-terminal software packages support data compression to improve the throughput of data between two computers. Data compression is the conversion of repeated bit patterns to coded bit patterns that reduce the total number of bits transferred during a communications session. The receiving computer must perform data expansion to reconstruct the original bit patterns that were compressed by the sending computer. In order to work properly, the communications software on both ends of the communications link must use matching data compression and data expansion techniques. This technique is used in the BLAST communications software, the MNP protocol, and the Kermit file transfer protocol to reduce file transfer time by as much as 40 percent for text, data, and binary files.

Data Encryption

Some smart-terminal software packages support data encryption to provide communication security between two computers. Data encryption normally uses a cryptography key to encipher transmitted bit patterns and to decipher received bit patterns continuously during a communications session. In order to work properly, the communications software on both ends of the communications link must use matching data enciphering and data deciphering techniques. Because of the computing overhead required to encipher and decipher data, this feature is often provided with an option to turn the data encryption on and off. Data encryption with this on/off option is often used in terminal-emulation software that provide IBM SNA compatibility.

Case Conversion

Many older computer systems do not recognize lowercase letters. Some of these systems will automatically convert lowercase to uppercase, but many systems will not perform that function. To overcome this problem, an IBM PC software package must perform the conversion from lowercase letters to uppercase letters before the characters are transmitted.

Tab-to-Space Conversion

Some IBM PC text processors such as the IBM Personal Editor use tab (Control-I) characters to represent spaces in stored files. These tab characters save valuable disk space by representing up to eight spaces each. Other systems, however, do not always follow the same convention. To keep files that contain tab characters intact, it may be necessary to convert tab characters into spaces. Several IBM PC communications packages allow the user to turn this automatic conversion on and off by executing a command from the keyboard.

Special Features

Smart-terminal software packages often provide other features that do not fall into any well-defined categories. These special features are described in the following sections.

Split Screen

When communicating with another person or a group of people through a data communications link, it is less confusing to have a split-screen communications option. When the communications package splits the screen horizontally, displaying received characters in one window and transmitted characters in another window, the PC can both transmit and receive text without confusing the user. Without a split screen, simultaneously transmitted and received text cannot be distinguished. The split screen is especially useful for the on-line conferencing and CB simulation offered by CompuServe.

Elapsed Time of Call

It is convenient to have an *elapsed-time-of-call indicator* when communicating with a time-sharing information service. Information services generally charge a rate based on *connect time*, so the elapsed-time indicator can help a user save connect-time costs. This feature can also serve as a reminder of costs when calling a long-distance number to get in contact with a host computer system.

Break Signal

Many mainframe and some information services require a *break signal* to interrupt program execution. A communications package should be able to send a 200-to-600 millisecond *sustained high signal* (equivalent to a logical 0) with either a single or a dual key stroke. This signal will interrupt program execution or get the immediate attention of an information-service system. Most software packages fix the duration of the break signal, but some allow the user to specify the signal length.

It should be noted that the break signal is not the same as the IBM PC *Ctrl-Break* key combination. The Ctrl-Break is actually a Ctrl-C and will terminate the running of a BASIC communications program. The true break is a sustained voltage signal (not a control character) and will not interrupt the operation of the user's software.

Remote Takeover

Some IBM PC communications packages allow remote users to call in and *take over* the operation of a Personal Computer. To perform this function, both the remote and local PC systems normally have to be equipped with communications software from the same vendor. Businesses can use this capability to transfer files without having to provide computer operators at both ends of the communications link. A branch office can send a file to a branch office in another time zone either before or after the normal working hours of the receiving office. This capability is also used to provide help desk support for remote users; the help desk calls in an executes software on your PC while you watch or participate in the operation.

External File Manipulation

Users often need to delete old files as new ones are being created during a communications session. Users may also need to rename files that have been created by a communications software package (for example, a command file) or files that have been improperly named during file downloading. Users may further need to run an *external program* or execute a DOS program (for example, FORMAT or CHKDSK) during a communications session. These operations can be done more quickly and easily if the user can perform them without exiting the software package. The IBM PC communications packages that provide these options can save time and money when file transfers are frequently performed.

Return to Operating System

The ability of a communications package to return the user to the operating system is often overlooked when a package is being evaluated. A user should not have to reboot the system unit each time a communications session is completed. A user should be able to terminate communications and return to the operating system to perform other computer operations by entering a simple command. Many packages program a function key or the Alt key combined with another key to provide a shortcut back to the operating system. Other packages require that the user go through a series of menus before returning to the operating system. Either option is acceptable, but the single- or dual-key shortcut is faster to execute and easier to remember.

Some packages allow the user to return to the operating system without breaking the telephone connection with a host system. This feature allows the testing of a downloaded program to be sure it was properly received before terminating the connection to the host system. It also allows the user to view a downloaded file, then return to finish the communications session.

Background Operation

Several communications packages support a background mode during certain operations. They provide *background operation* of time-consuming tasks such as file transfers.

Software packages that allow file transfers in a background mode also allow the user to perform other foreground tasks while the file transfer is executing. Other packages allow the communications software to reside in RAM but remain in the background until needed. The user can press a *hot key* to bring the software operation to the *foreground*.

Some communications packages offer compatibility with *multitasking operating environments* such as DESQview, Microsoft Windows, and Operating System/2 (OS/2). These environments allow the user to switch from one active or foreground task to another. This feature provides the user more flexibility in communications and often reduces the time required to switch between communications and another task.

Background communications software ranges from simple terminal emulation to full-feature, smart-terminal software. The popular Sidekick software allows the user to pop up a menu from the background, automatically dial a remote host, then perform a terminal session with the host. The Softerm PC Software is a full featured package that can reside in the background until needed and can perform file transfers while other activities are performed. The IBM PC/HOST File Transfer and Terminal Emulation Program also provides background file transfers.

There are several limitations with background communications software that must be understood in order to prevent communications failures. First, loading more than one software package into a background "stay resident" mode may cause *interrupt conflicts* such that the operation of one package interferes with the operation of another. Second, communications software has to be *tightly coupled* to the PC hardware in order to respond quickly enough to support high data throughput rates; this tight coupling prevents communications software from being swapped to disk in a multitasking environment. Third, background operations, such as file transfers, must adhere to a strict set of rules to prevent file creation and expansion damage to other files being simultaneously created or changed by a foreground task. Good background operation software will take care of these limitations for the user and explain the limitations in the accompanying documentation. OS/2 Extended Edition provides excellent support for both foreground and background communications in a multitasking environment.

Evaluating Communications Software

The evaluation and selection of a communications package may not be an easy task. Changing needs and capabilities in a business environment and changing budgets in a personal situation contribute to the complexity. But, as is the case with other software packages, decisions have to be made based on the best information available at the time.

The initial approach to selecting a software package is to first assess communications needs. A list of all essential features should be developed. This should be followed by the development of a list of nonessential, but desirable, features. Only then should available communications software packages be considered.

To place communications packages in proper perspective, it is a good practice to produce an *evaluation matrix* similar to the one shown in Table 4-4. Information can be recorded on such a matrix by reviewing the manuals provided with software packages. Newsletters and magazines also publish software reviews containing data that can be used in completing the matrix. Local IBM PC users' groups often have a special-interest group (SIG) dedicated to communications. Information can be obtained through conversations with the members of such a group. Software vendors can also be solicited for information; many of them have toll-free telephone numbers.

Table 4-4. Smart-terminal communications software matrix.

Software Feature	COMM.BAS	Pkg #1	Pkg #2
Data capture direct to disk file	—		
Data capture to memory buffer	—		
On-line display of capture buffer	—		
On-line editing of capture buffer	—		
Filtering of received control characters	—		
Blank line expansion	—		
Optional add/delete of linefeeds	—		
Upload wait for host prompts	—		
Upload text throttle (delay between lines)	—		
Menu of prestored uploadable strings	—		
Transmission of prestored strings	—		
Transmission of a true break signal	—		
Tab to space conversion	—		
XMODEM protocol file transfer	—		
KERMIT protocol file transfer	—		
XON/XOFF support during file send/receive	E		
Non-ASCII (binary) file transfer	—		
Operation with nonautodial modem	G		
Autodialing telephone directory	—		
Autodialing modem support	—		
Auto-redial of last telephone call	—		
Auto-redial of last call until connect	—		
Modem/telephone hangup	—		
Return to operating system without hangup	—		
Elapsed time of call display	—		
On-line switch between originate/answer	—		
On-line selection of duplex with toggle	F		
On-line selection of comm parameters	F		
On-line listing of selected parameters	F		
On-line printer on/off toggle	—		
On-line viewing of disk directories	—		
On-line viewing of disk files	—		
Deletion and renaming of disk files	—		

Save/reload of customized parameters	F
Batch operation from operating system	—
Command file power/flexibility	—
Remote takeover and operation	—
Efficient use of available memory	E
Display of help files	F
Line 25 abbreviated help menu	F
Terminal emulation	—
Split screen option	—
Ease of command key use	G
Quality of user manual	—

Legend: E = Excellent, G = Good, F = Fair, and — = Not Supported

The sample evaluation in Table 4-4 compares the COMM.BAS dumb-terminal program with the capabilities found in many smart-terminal software packages. As you can see from this comparison, there are significant differences between the capabilities of a dumb and a smart terminal. To select a smart-terminal package that best fits your needs, you may want to complete a matrix of this type.

Experience using a package is a valuable part of determining your communication needs. Public-domain and inexpensive BASIC programs are excellent learning tools. A user can experiment with these programs and learn a great deal about communications through trial and error. There are many bulletin board and public host systems operating in major metropolitan areas that can be used as guinea pigs during this learning process.

To prevent telephone-bill shock while experimenting with bulletin board and host systems, many IBM PC users have subscribed to a GTE Telenet service called PC Pursuit. For a one-time initiation fee and a low flat rate, home computer users are allowed to make an unlimited number of calls to any city connected to the service. Although calls can only be made during the evenings and weekends and each session is limited to one hour, most callers experience an average savings of 75 percent compared to normal telephone rates during these same hours. The other advantage of this service is that it uses the normal Telenet *packet-switched network* equipment, which offers excellent error detection and correction for data. For file transfers with this service, most users have found that *sliding-window protocols* such as Kermit, Zmodem, and the BLAST and Relay Gold proprietary protocols provide the greatest data throughput. Chapter 6 discusses these protocols in detail.

5

Unattended Communications Software

Although considered by many as a hobbyist application, unattended communications systems have become popular in business and personal data communications applications. During the past ten years, unattended communications systems have gone from home-grown bulletin boards to powerful business support systems. This type of software provides many communications novices with their first taste of communications between one personal computer and another. After this experience, many PC users are ready to move on to more powerful applications of unattended host, bulletin board, and electronic mail systems that are run by some of the country's largest information suppliers.

The first microcomputer-based, unattended communications system available to IBM PC users was a Radio Shack TRS-80 electronic bulletin board. Wes Merchant, an IBM PC specialist working for IBM, set up the system in 1982 for the Capital PC Users Group. Although limited in its capability compared with current unattended systems, the Radio Shack bulletin board became a popular medium for information exchange in the Washington, D.C. area. After only six months of operation, it was necessary to use an auto-redial communications package to get into the bulletin board during the evenings and weekends. The telephone line was always busy with local and out-of-town callers posting public information about the IBM PC.

HOSTCOMM was the first unattended communications software released for the PC. The system, written in interpreter BASIC, allowed remote PC users to call in and transfer files or execute other BASIC programs stored on diskettes. For people who had gotten tired of scheduling electronic meetings with friends to transfer files,

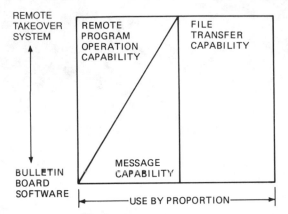

Figure 5.1 Remote takeover and bulletin board systems.

HOSTCOMM was a welcome relief. Files could be transferred to or from HOSTCOMM any time of day or night without the attendance of a system operator.

During the past nine years many software vendors have released powerful and useful unattended communications systems for the PC. The Close-Up and Carbon Copy packages are excellent examples of *remote takeover systems* (*RTS*). The Major BBS and the Total Communications System (TCOMM) are examples of *bulletin board systems* (*BBS*) that provide electronic mail, file transfers, and the execution of external programs. Transcend PC is a good example of a PC-based *electronic mail system* (*Email*). These commercial packages are usually written in the C programming language and provide high performance and rich functionality. There are a few unattended communications packages still around that are written in interpreter or compiled BASIC, but many packages that started this way have subsequently been translated to C.

There are several unattended communications systems available that provide an introduction to this type of software at low cost. The *Remote Bulletin Board System for the PC* (*RBBS-PC*) is a good example of this type of software. Originally ported from the CP/M operating system to run on the IBM PC in 1982 by Russ Lane, this software has become a favorite for weekend software hackers and hobbyists. Thomas Mack, an active member of the Capital PC User Group, coordinates most of the "official" RBBS-PC enhancements, and members of the user group make many of the enhancements. The user group distributes the source code, executable object code, and documentation for RBBS-PC for a nominal fee.

Remote Software in Perspective

Users often categorize remote communications systems as remote takeover, bulletin board, or electronic mail systems, but there are systems that provide all three capabilities in one package. Figure 5.1 illustrates the difference between remote takeover and bulletin board systems. As you can see from this figure, an RTS-equipped personal computer primarily provides remote program operation, whereas a BBS-equipped personal computer primarily provides message exchange. A remote takeover system can accept calls from remote terminals and execute commands received through the serial port in the same way that it executes local keyboard commands. A bulletin board system, on the other hand, is capable of storing messages received from a remote computer and is capable of transmitting messages to that same remote computer. Some special-purpose bulletin board systems can automatically transmit and receive messages; these systems are called electronic mail or Email systems.

Normally, both RTS and BBS software can receive and transmit files. Some electronic mail systems also allow you to transmit files as attachments to messages or mail. These systems allow users to transfer ASCII text files and binary program and data files between a local microcomputer and a remote, unattended PC. Special error-checking protocols transfer the files and correct errors caused by the telephone system.

Remote Software Capabilities

Unattended communications software is both a personal and business productivity tool. In addition to eliminating the need for an operator at one end of the communication link, these packages offer strong support for specific types of information exchange. The following paragraphs explore the practical uses of this software. Later sections of this chapter explore the capabilities associated with specific types of unattended systems.

Practical Applications

Bulletin board software serves as a tool for enhancing productivity and scheduling. How many times have you wanted to get information to members of a group quickly and had to resort to letters or post cards because of the lead time required for normal group newsletters? Have you had a need to collect written text or data from several sources on a tight schedule but had to wait for several days for the information to arrive by mail? Unattended remote communications software can solve these problems for you as well as providing other data-transfer power.

Availability Mismatches

Unattended communications software eliminates the need to have two communicating parties available simultaneously to transfer files or data. With unattended software operating on a 24-hour-a-day basis, other parties can call in and leave or retrieve messages or transfer data at any time, day or night, without disturbing the system operator. An author can work halfway through the night and still meet a 9:00 A.M. deadline halfway across the continent by transmitting the work to a remote, unattended IBM PC when he or she finishes the work. Many newsletter and magazine editors who use unattended communications software to collect articles appreciate the lack of operator attention required with these systems. They go to bed the night before an article deadline date and wake the next morning to find a disk full of valuable information.

Availability mismatches also occur between company offices located in different time zones. Remote takeover and bulletin board software provides an extra three hour communication period in the mornings and evenings for offices located on opposite U.S. coasts. Reports, data, or messages can be transferred while the recipient is still at home asleep or watching the evening news.

Order Taking

Bulletin board systems often serve as *electronic order-taking* devices. The system presents callers with bulletins on the latest merchandise available and allows them to order from a menu by selecting a number associated with an item of interest. The software also may be capable of taking charge card information and validating the identity of callers based on data stored in an on-line database. This application of bulletin board software allows a retailer to get notices of product and price changes to potential customers quickly. It also speeds up the ordering process by eliminating mailing delays.

A Tool for the Handicapped

Bulletin board software is a useful communication tool for the hearing and speech impaired. Information on upcoming social or educational group events can be posted on an electronic bulletin board to eliminate or augment the need for telephone answering machines or operators. Information left on a telephone answering machine is of no use to the deaf and people with certain hearing impairments. Bulletin board software not only provides these people with information, it allows them to interact with the system to select specific information of interest. The BBS also allows the users to exchange messages with others who have similar impairments.

Transport Elimination

Unattended communications software can eliminate the shipping or mailing of information or software. Some situations make the transport of information, both printed matter and electronically stored data, impractical and thus can make good use of remote, unattended communications software. Some hospitals eliminate the need to decontaminate notes and records made in infectious-disease wards by entering the information into a terminal located in the contaminated area. The information transfers electronically to a remote bulletin board system in a "clean" area of the hospital. This electronic transfer of information saves a hospital time and money by eliminating complex physical decontamination procedures.

True RTS "host" software gives an IBM PC owner the power of his or her computer from any location equipped with a terminal, modem, and public telephone. An unattended host software system allows a remote caller to take over the PC and operate it through a telephone link almost as if the caller is sitting at the PC's keyboard. A person can take a laptop or portable computer on a trip and use any remote telephone connection to tap into his or her PC at home if it is equipped with an RTS software package. A writer can create a news article during an airline flight to a distant location, then transmit the article back to a PC at home from his or her hotel room. The only limitation to host software application is the user's imagination.

Software Support

Many software vendors have found remote takeover systems invaluable in the support of their own software packages. A software vendor can dial into a remote computer equipped with both an RTS and the vendor's software. The RTS allows the vendor to execute the software on the PC to diagnose a problem or to help the user understand how to use the vendor's software. The user can watch the operation to learn more about the vendor's software package or participate in the execution of the vendor's software as part of a training exercise. This type of remote operation can save a vendor many hours during problem diagnosis. It can also save a user the same number of hours in learning to use a new package.

Group Electronic Mail

A PC equipped with an unattended electronic mail system can eliminate travel and enhance communications between the members of a working group. Two or more of these systems can exchange messages and mail between group members at specific times of day or on a 24-hour-a-day basis. Users can submit mail for delivery to a remote system by simply designating the name of the recipient. The electronic mail system takes care of storing the mail, then calling the remote system to deliver the mail. These PC-based systems can act on a stand-alone basis or in conjunction with a local area network. LAN-based systems are discussed in Part II of this book. Stand-alone systems are explored in greater detail later in this chapter.

Remote Takeover Software

Remote takeover software, as its name implies, allows callers to dial in and take over the operation of a remote PC. Figure 5.2 shows the logical connection between the local and remote PC after the connection is made. This type of communications requires a matching set of software on the local and remote PCs. The PC that supports remote takeover is sometimes called an *asynchronous remote takeover server* (*ARTS*). The ARTS software normally runs in a hidden, background mode on the remote PC and supports asynchronous communications with, and complete takeover, of operation from a remote PC. The PC that performs the remote takeover must execute an *asynchronous remote takeover terminal* (*ARTT*) version of the same software in a foreground mode. The ARTS and ARTT software work together to ensure synchronization of operation between the local and remote computer.

After a successful security screening, the keyboard and the screen of the local ARTT PC and the remote ARTS PC act as one. A copy of all screen output on the remote PC is trapped by the ARTS software running in the background on that computer, and sent out the communications port. The local ARTT-equipped PC receives that output and produces the same display results that appear on the ARTS-equipped computer. In a

Software Feature	RBBS-PC	Pkg #2	Pkg #3	Pkg #4
Parameter detect/switch	G			
File protection	G			
ASCII file transfer	E			
Xmodem protocol	E			
CRC-16 protocol	–			
XON/XOFF flow control	G			
File size indicator	G			
Operator chat mode	E			
Operator page hours	E			
Case conversion	E			
Help files	E			
Message storage	G			
Message retrieval	G			
Message maintenance	G			
Message scan	G			
Message protection	F			
Message word processor	E			
Local snoop toggle	E			
Log-on bulletin design	E			
File directory listing	G			
Directory maintenance	G			
Callers data log	E			
Users data base	F			
Users log maintenance	E			
SYSOP special controls	E			
System configuration	G			
Caller defaults recall	E			
Terminal emulation	–			
Expert/novice menus	G			
Remote operation	G			
Disk area restriction	F			
Unattended reliability	G			
Unattended security	F			

Legend: E = Excellent, G = Good, F = Fair, – – = Not Supported

Figure 5.2 Host and bulletin board software evaluation matrix.

similar manner, the ARTT and ARTS software work together to make keyboard input from either the local or remote computer perform the same functions at the ARTS-equipped computer.

The ARTS software can operate in a stand-alone or LAN-attached personal computer. First, it can run in the background while a work station user executes either stand-alone or LAN-based application software in the foreground on the same PC. Second, it can operate in a LAN-attached PC set up solely for remote access to the LAN. In the first mode, the ARTS allows either the local or remote user to initiate a call to link the ARTS and ARTT computers. In the second mode, a distant ARTT computer can dial into a modem connected to the LAN-attached ARTS computer and execute LAN-based software. The ARTS and ARTT software packages must work together and work with the LAN operating system to provide proper support for remote takeover of the ARTS work station/server.

Although the ARTS/ARTT combination provides only a one-on-one relationship between the ARTS server and the remote ARTT terminal, this type of software is invaluable for remote support of software applications. This software pair allows the ARTT user to execute software on the ARTS computer while allowing users at both ends of the link to observe the screen output from the software. Both the local and remote user can interact simultaneously with application software executing in the foreground mode on the ARTS-equipped PC. This software combination also allows an ARTT user to dial into the ARTS computer and run any stand-alone or LAN-based software at full ARTS-computer execution speed.

Remote Takeover Software Features

RTS software can provide great productivity enhancements for remote execution of applications or for problem diagnosis if the right package is selected. Although many of the features contained in commercial RTS packages are similar, there some subtle differences that may determine the success or failure of an implementation in a specific situation. Because of the uniqueness of some user needs, it is important to understand the characteristics and capabilities available in RTS software before purchasing a package. The following brief descriptions of the RTS features listed in Table 5-1 will help you make the right selection of this type of software.

Table 5-1. Remote Takeover Software features.

Configuration Control
System Security
Remote Dial-in
Software Execution
Error Correction
File Transfers
User-to-user Chat
Screen Capture
Remote Printer Support
System Logs

Configuration Control

The configuration control required for RTS software is simple compared to the elaborate configuration required for other types of unattended communications software. Both the ARTS and ARTT software modules require separate configuration profiles, but the total number of parameters that must be set up are a small fraction of the number typically required for a full-blown BBS that supports multiple users. The reason for the simplicity is the one-on-one design of RTS software and the limited number of total users that normally access such a system. A PC is also supplied with ARTS for a single purpose—to allow someone to run the machine from a distance. Other unattended systems have a variety of information and file transfer features that must be customized for the circumstances. The following paragraphs explore just a few of the most important configuration parameters required for ARTS/ARTT software.

Modem Type

Both ARTS and ARTT software must allow you to designate the type and model of modem you will use with the system. Some systems allow you to define your own modem features and characteristics. This feature is important because it allows the system to take advantage of the specific capabilities of your modem. For example, a modem that provides its own built-in error detection and correction protocol would not require the same level of protocol for file transfers that is required with modems that contain no error correction protocol. In order to take advantage of these modem features, the RTS software must be smart enough to recognize that certain features exist in a modem and that the modem at the other end of the link is using the same features.

Dialing Type

Some RTS packages do not provide a choice of touch-tone or rotary dialing, thereby limiting some applications of the software. System operators may want to use a rotary line because the telephone company charges less for that type of service. An RTS that supports only touch-tone eliminates that alternative.

Reboot on Hangup

A system that provides access for multiple users may require a system reboot after each call. A *cold reboot* is identical to the operation of the PC after it is first turned on. A *warm reboot* is identical to the restart you can perform at the PC keyboard by pressing the Ctrl, Alt, and Del keys simultaneously. If the RTS allows you to invoke either type of reboot after each caller hangs up, the system ensures a clean start for each new caller. This feature helps enforce the security features contained in the package or the security features provided by the LAN if the ARTS is a LAN server.

Screen Type

An RTS that allows you to specify the screen type provides optimum performance with your hardware. Older display adapters require more time to scroll the screen and require the operation of special software timing routines to prevent the display of snow during screen write operations. Without a Screen Type configuration parameter, the RTS must detect the type of display you have and adjust the software operation to match.

Screen Update Speed

RTS packages may allow you to select the speed of screen display updates. A slow update speed may provide cleaner output, but slow down remote operations when the communications link is less than 9600 bps. A fast update may provide quicker response with some decrease in synchronization between the ARTT and ARTS. A system such as Close-Up, that lets you dynamically switch between fast and slow speeds, is ideal.

Action Keys

One configuration parameter most people find impossible to live without is the definition of *action keys*. The user must be able to select the "hot Keys" that invoke ARTS/ARTT menus and functions to eliminate conflicts between the factory settings of this type of background software and those provided with other foreground software. If the same keystroke is required to bring up the ARTS main menu that is used to exit a foreground package, such as a word processor, the conflict will keep one of the modules from working properly.

File Transfer Protocol

Most RTS software packages allow you to transfer files between the ARTS and the ARTT. You should be allowed to select the file transfer protocol you wish to use each time you start a file transfer, or you should be able to designate one protocol for automatic use every time a transfer operation starts.

Printer Operation

Most RTS packages allow you to determine the method of handling printer output for all remote applications that produce printed results. You can specify that output goes to the remote printer only, the local printer only, or to both. This is an important configuration setting because it may determine the need for an operator at the ARTS end of the link. Most printers require some attention for proper operation.

Passwords

An ARTS must be given one or more passwords that control caller access. Most ARTS packages provide a built-in editor that allows you to input or modify access passwords. If an ARTT allows you to store passwords associated with specific remote ARTS computers, it must provide some kind of security to prevent unauthorized access to the passwords.

System Security

System security is crucial with an RTS because callers often have full access to the ARTS PC. When an ARTT dials into an ARTS, the ARTT must provide the proper password before the ARTS provides access. The ARTT/ARTS software normally do this security handshaking automatically after the dial-in operation is complete and the ARTT modem is communicating with the ARTT modem. If the ARTT and the ARTS cannot agree on a proper password, the ARTS must terminate the connection. Some systems provide a *call-back* whereby the ARTS drops the connection after the password exchange and calls the ARTT computer back to ensure that it is the proper ARTT terminal. For this type of operation, the ARTS must store the telephone number for each remote user and associate the number with a unique password or user name.

Remote Dial-in

Most ARTT packages provide a *dialing directory* to make the task of dialing an ARTS computer easier. Such a directory must provide a built-in editor that allows you to enter and edit ARTS telephone numbers and names. If the editor allows you to store passwords for ARTS computers, it must not display the passwords unless specifically instructed to do so. Passwords must be encrypted on the disk to prevent unauthorized access.

Software Execution

An ARTT/ARTS combination must allow you to execute any *well-behaved* software from a remote terminal. Well-behaved software uses standard DOS and BIOS routines to display information on the screen and to obtain user input. An ARTS may be able to handle some forms of nonstandard input/output, but most of them do not because of the number of different techniques vendors can use to speed up operation of their software. If the ARTS cannot capture an application's display output and redirect it out the communications port, the ARTT user will simply get a blank screen when the software executes. The ARTT user can normally execute ARTS application commands even if the ARTS cannot redirect the applications screen display.

Error Correction

The error detection and correction technique included in an RTS determines both the quality of communications and the performance of remote application execution. Most ARTS/ARTT combinations include a *continuous* error detection and correction process to ensure proper communications throughout a session—not just during file transfers. If this protocol uses the checksum technique, you are assured of 99+ percent error-free communications. If the protocol uses the CRC technique of error detection, you will have near error-free communications. If the protocol uses a *stop-and-wait* technique like the one used in the Xmodem file transfer protocol to signal proper receipt of data, the execution speed for remote software may be slow. If the protocol uses a faster, *nonstop* technique such as the one in the Zmodem file transfer protocol, the execution speed of software will not be affected by the error detection and correction. The ideal situation is to have all such error correction performed at the modem hardware level, but all modems do not include these protocols.

File Transfers

A good ARTS/ARTT combination allows you to transfer files between the local and remote computer with the same ease as transferring files from one local disk to another. If you have to go through elaborate file transfer menus or controls to start a file transfer, you avoid using the feature. Once started, the transfer protocol should provide a good visual status of progress. Some packages provide a bar chart to show you how much data you have transferred and how much is remaining.

User-to-user Chat

For RTS packages used to support other application software packages, it is vitally important to have a means of communicating between a local and remote user. The package must allow both of these users to go into a chat mode and exchange messages from the keyboard. It is also important to allow either user to move the *chat window* around on the screen to keep it from masking screen output. Some RTS packages go one step further by allowing you to go back and forth between data and voice communications over the same telephone line. For proper operation of this *voice-to-data toggle*, both the modems and telephones require special wiring configurations. Many popular modems—including the Hayes series—support this operation without additional hardware.

Screen Capture

For complete diagnoses of an application software problem, it is sometimes necessary to capture one or more screens of information to disk. You can then send these screens to the vendor for analysis. Some packages also allow you to continuously capture screen output to disk so you can later "play" the output back for further analysis.

Remote Printer Support

As discussed earlier in the configuration presentation, printer support is an important aspect of remote takeover operations. If you cannot control the direction of printer output flow, you may have limited success in operating a computer from a remote ARTT PC. If an application sends output to the printer, the ARTS computer may stop operation if the printer jams or runs out of paper. You must be able to redirect printed output to the local printer or completely disable printer output.

System Logs

Systems used for financial applications may require a log of all activities. This log must provide full *audit trail* support. It is not normally used as a failure recovery technique in the same sense that a transaction log is used with a mainframe computer. If this type of recovery is needed, the support for rollback is normally provided by software beyond the RTS. A database or application would supply this capability.

Remote Takeover Summary

As you can see from the features normally contained in RTS software, this type of software can provide powerful communications services. Companies use RTS software to perform remote tests of systems and to update software contained on these remote systems. Companies also use RTS packages as a part of a training program to educate remote users on the features and functions of application packages. Specific employees may also use RTS to perform work from home. These users dial into their ARTS-equipped PCs at work to perform application operations from home.

Although RTS software packages provide a robust set of communications features and functions, they may not meet certain communications requirements. Organizations that need systems that support groups in the transfer of information, files, and messages will find the unattended software described in the following section more appropriate than RTS. We discuss bulletin board systems next, then follow that presentation with a discussion of Email systems.

Bulletin Board System

Bulletin board systems are by far the most popular unattended communications software. These systems provide access to wide varieties of information, from serious business ventures to home-computer games. From a grass roots beginning, the BBS developed into a powerful business tool along with the IBM PC. The original BBS software came from the homes of personal computer hobbyists. This software was in the form of interpreter BASIC and was widely distributed to anyone interested without charge. More recent implementations are written in either the C language or assembler and are full commercial packages.

The wide distribution of BBS software is good for the PC owner because these packages provide a good place for you to get started with PC communications with a small investment. You need a PC, a modem, and a smart-terminal communications package to dial into one of these systems and browse to your heart's content. Most BBS packages work in the *TTY* output mode, which means you do not have to run in any specific *terminal emulation* mode for proper screen and keyboard operations. The simplest and least expensive terminal communication configuration will work with these systems.

Bulletin Board System Features

Although the operation of a BBS is transparent to most callers, the details of its operation are important to someone interested in setting up and operating one for the first time. The following brief descriptions of bulletin board system features listed in Table 5-2 will help you make the right selection of this type of software.

Table 5-2. Bulletin board system features.

CONFIGURATION CONTROL:

Remote access code	Expert mode
Ring-back control	Disk drive assignments
System file designation	Prompt sounds
Maximum time on system	Maximum number of messages
User inactivity limit	Number of system bulletins
User activity display	Communication port
Modem sound control	Operator availability
Caller options	Local display
Help files	Communication parameters

FILE TRANSFER:

File directories	Error-checking protocol
XON/XOFF protocol	File statistics

CHAT MODE:

Available hours	Operator paging

SYSTEM OPTIONS:

Case conversion	Line feeds
Nulls	Prompt sounds
Screen size	Expert mode
Terminal emulation	

MESSAGE SUBSYSTEM:

Message privacy	SYSOP comments
Message scan	Message word processor

SYSTEM LOGS:

Caller log   User data base
Data base maintenance

REMOTE TAKEOVER:

Remote Execution   File protection

RELIABILITY:

Normal operation   Abnormal operation

Configuration Control

Unattended communications software must allow the system operator to configure the system for operation under a variety of circumstances. Different hardware combinations and applications require installation flexibility. Configuration control provides this flexibility. The system configuration utility allows the operator to establish a profile of desired operating characteristics. The utility stores this profile in a default-value file. Each time the system begins execution, it reads this file and operates within the rules it finds there. The following paragraphs describe some of the configuration choices offered by bulletin board systems.

Remote Access Code

The operator should be able to specify a password or code that will allow system operator control from a remote terminal. The code may be a special password or it may be a special name that the system operator uses. If the system operator uses this code after dialing-in, the system allows the operator to execute special controls and commands. Callers that do not have this access code cannot execute these special features.

Ring-back Control

Some unattended systems allow the operator to use one telephone for both voice and data communications by providing a *ring-back* feature. The ring-back design allows a caller to call in, let the telephone ring once, then call back within a short period of time to get into the system. The system will answer the call on the first ring during the second (ring-back) call. If the call is not a ring-back, the system will not answer the call until a specified number of rings have taken place. The system ring-back configuration allows the operator to turn this feature on and off. It also may allow the operator to specify the number of rings that must take place before the system will answer for calls that are not ring-backs.

Disk Drive Assignments

The configuration utility should allow the operator to select the disk drive or drives that are available for file uploading or downloading. It should also allow the operator to choose the drive that will contain the system files. These are simple choices for a PC with only one drive, but they may be important for systems that have several drives. One drive may be reserved for system files, such as the caller log and message file, and other drives may be reserved for file upload or download only.

System File Designation

The configuration utility should allow the operator to designate files that are important to system security. These files will be recorded as *system files* and callers will not be able to download them regardless of their location on the disk. One of these files will always be the configuration file because it contains the system operator's remote access code. Message files are also system files because they sometimes contain protected messages. The operator comments file may fall into this same category because it can include private comments from callers. Some of the comments may be personal or may contain information about hidden or system files. Finally, the system caller log and user database could be included because they contain private lists of caller activities and user passwords.

Prompt Sounds

The operator should be able to turn input *prompt sounds* on and off. Some operators like reminders of required input and others do not. The operator should be able to choose the default for prompt sounds.

Maximum Time on System

The operator should be able to select the maximum length of time a caller can stay on the system during a single session. A system that only operates at 300 bps will generally require a longer maximum time limit than one that operates at 1200 or 2400 bps. An operator may also want to reduce the time limit as the system becomes more active. Time limits usually vary between 30 minutes and two hours.

Maximum Number of Messages

A bulletin board operator will want to designate the maximum number of messages the system will allow because of disk space limits. If the system does not limit the number of stored messages, the message storage disk can become full and cause the system to malfunction. This can result in a total loss of all messages with some bulletin board systems.

User Inactivity Limit

Some systems keep a log of all users and their system operation preferences in a user database. Such a system will need a function that deletes inactive users from the database. The configuration utility should allow the operator to select the length of that period of inactivity.

Communications Port

The system configuration profile must tell the unattended communications software which communications port to use. Systems that have more than one serial port installed in the PC system unit need a default port specified in the system configuration or the system may not operate properly. Some systems that allow more than one caller on the system at a time may need two or more active serial ports.

Modem Sound Control

The configuration utility should allow the operator to select the modem sound condition if the system modem uses a speaker to indicate operating conditions. Some system operators like to hear the high-pitched modem carrier sound when the modem answers a call, and others prefer to have the sound turned off.

Operator Availability

Systems that allow callers to page the system operator must allow the operator to select his or her office hours. Without control over paging hours, callers could ring the page bell at inappropriate times. The operator should be able to select the time of day for the page option to start and the time of day for it to stop. When a caller requests an *operator page*, the system should check the configuration file before initiating the page. Most systems provide the caller with a friendly message indicating the operator is not available if the page request is not within normal "business hours."

Caller Options

Some system configuration utilities allow the operator to specify special conditions for selected callers. Some callers may be allowed access to file directories that other callers do not get to see. Other callers may be allowed to run selected programs that are resident on the system. BBS systems use this facility to determine the level of system control callers should get. This type of option should allow the operator to designate several caller names or passwords that match system options.

Local Display (Snoop)

The display screen of the bulletin board-equipped system should be protected from prolonged *display burn-in*. The system should clear the screen and leave it blank within a specified period of time after start up. This temporary blanking of the screen should, however, be independent of caller activity display. Some operators, especially new ones, like to sit and watch all caller activity. Others like to turn off the display of caller activity most of the time. The system configuration should allow the operator to choose to have local *snoop* on or off. When snoop is on, the system should begin to display user activity as soon as the modem answers a call. When snoop is off, the system should clear the screen a short time after start-up and keep the screen blank under all subsequent operating conditions. Some systems provide the operator with a "snoop toggle" that will temporarily override the default snoop condition. This override allows the operator to turn on the display of caller activity and usually only lasts for the duration of the call in progress.

Besides turning the local screen display on and off, the snoop designation should also turn all system sounds on and off. The bells (Control Gs) sometimes used to signal the end of ASCII file transfers and to prompt callers for input may become annoying after several weeks of system operation. The system operator should be able to turn them off locally without affecting the sounds transmitted to remote callers.

Help Files

Help files are key elements in the introduction of novice users to a remote system. Each subsystem of an unattended software package should provide user help for all commands available in the subsystem. The help files should elaborate on the information provided in the novice-user menus. The system should also allow the operator to modify the help files to match the needs of specific users.

The help provided in the downloading subsystem of an unattended system is especially important. Interactive communications are usually easy for most communications novices to grasp, but file transfers are more difficult to master. Each system usually has a unique syntax required for file transfers and that syntax should be well documented in help files. These help files are often divided into several levels of detail, with the lowest level showing a step-by-step procedure for file downloading and uploading.

Communications Parameters

A well-designed unattended software package should allow callers to use several data communication speeds and formats. The software should *detect and switch* bit rate and parity to match that of the caller. Software that will operate at only one bit rate or parity type eliminates callers who cannot reconfigure their systems to match the software's default data format. Most unattended packages switch to match the data format used by the caller, but some must be set up by the operator for operation using a single format. Typical single-format options are seven data bits and even parity or eight data bits and no parity.

Fixed-parameter software limits the power and flexibility of the remote PC. Software that supports only a format of seven data bits eliminates the transfer of the special IBM 8-bit graphics and symbol characters. This format also eliminates the use of error-checking file transfer techniques, such as Xmodem and Ymodem. Software that supports only a format of eight data bits, on the other hand, sometimes eliminates the use of dumb-terminal access to the PC. Some dumb terminals operate only in a seven data bit mode.

There are many other features and options available in system configuration utilities, but the ones listed give you an idea of the value of the system configuration. This feature provides the operator with total control of the system environment. As hardware and system applications change, the operator can change the configuration of the system to match.

File Transfer Features

One powerful feature of unattended communication software is the capability to transfer files. The ideal bulletin board system should allow a caller to interact with the system to download a file from the system, or upload a file to the system. The system should allow the transfer of ASCII text and source code files and binary data and program files. Systems that require the conversion of binary files (files with COM and EXE extensions) into another form before they can be transferred are cumbersome to use. The following paragraphs provide additional requirements for transferring files.

Error-checking Protocol

The file-transfer capability of unattended communications software should include an *error-checking protocol* transfer option. This option should provide either a checksum or a cyclic redundancy check (CRC-16) error-checking technique that causes retransmission of data blocks found to contain transmission errors. As a minimum, the *Ward Christensen Xmodem* protocol should be provided. This protocol is available in many public-domain and commercial smart-terminal software packages. The Xmodem protocol uses a checksum error-checking technique to ensure 99.6 percent error-free file transfers. This magnitude of error detection and correction is acceptable for most hobby and business data transfers. For data transfers that require greater than 99.9 percent error correction, use of a CRC-16 technique, such as those used in the *Kermit* and *Ymodem* protocols, may be required. Chapter 6 provides more details regarding error checking and file-transfer protocols.

ON/XOFF Protocol

Unattended communications software should also provide the XON/XOFF file transfer speed-matching protocol. This protocol prevents one computer from sending more data than another computer can handle in a given amount of time. The *XON/XOFF protocol* allows the receiving computer to halt a file transfer temporarily until it can catch up with the flow of data. This protocol is required for the transfer of files without the use of a file transfer protocol such as Xmodem or Kermit. The absence of XON/XOFF support can result in communication buffer overflow and a loss of data on the receiving end.

File Directories

One major distinction between remote takeover and bulletin board systems is the *file directory*. Bulletin board systems normally have text files that serve as directories of files available on the system. A BBS directory normally contains the name and a brief description of each file available for download from the system. Each disk may be provided with one directory or disks may be divided into several directories. RTS software, on the other hand, provide a standard listing of files using DOS to generate the list.

The technique used to select files for transfer from the unattended PC to the caller's system may also differ. Some systems allow file selection by number from a menu, while other systems require that the caller specify the exact name of the file. Some callers like the menu selection design because it does not require the entry of filenames. Others like the filename entry technique because it does not require switching of file menus to access all files.

File Statistics

The file-transfer subsystem of unattended communications software should provide *file size* and *available disk space* information. When preparing to receive a file, a caller should be told the size and transfer time for the selected file. The system should allow the caller to terminate the transfer after receiving these data. The caller may not have enough free disk space to receive the file or may not be willing to pay the long-distance toll charge for a long file transfer. When preparing to transmit a file to an unattended communications system, the caller should be told the free disk space remaining on the disk that will receive the file. The system should allow the caller to terminate the transfer because of insufficient free disk space on the unattended system.

System Options

Unattended communication software should allow the remote user to select options that configure the unattended system to desired characteristics. These options should appear as choices each time a user logs on, or they should be requested once and stored as a user profile for use each time that specific user logs on. If the system stores user profiles, users can log on quicker because they do not have to key in their required options each time they call.

Most user options pertain to screen size and text display, but some pertain to sounds and level of user expertise. The following paragraphs provide more details regarding these configuration options.

Case Conversion

Some dumb terminals only operate in uppercase and require remote system support in uppercase only. A bulletin board should ask the caller whether lowercase is acceptable immediately after the caller gains access to the system. If the system limits output and input to uppercase only, the system should convert all letters to uppercase before transmitting the characters to the caller. As terminals become more intelligent with new hardware releases, the need for case conversion will be eliminated.

Line Feeds

Some users prefer that each line of text transmitted by the unattended system end with a line feed. A remote terminal that requires line feeds at the end of each line will write each new line over the top of the previous line without the line feeds. Other users have their local systems set up to add line feeds to the end of each line and do not need line feeds added by the unattended system. The unattended system should allow the user the option of turning line feed addition on or off.

Nulls

The request "Do you need nulls?" that appears on the screen when a user logs on a bulletin board may be confusing for a new user. Most systems that ask this question do not provide the user with help in answering the question. Hard-copy printing terminals need these nulls when moving to a new line of output. Personal Computers do not need nulls. When this option is turned on, the system transmits a string of nulls as a time delay at the end of each new line of text.

The nulls are *nonprinting characters* and provide a *time delay*. The time delay allows the print head of the terminal to return to the left margin before a new string of characters is transmitted. Without the time delay, the next string of characters could start printing before the print head reaches the left margin. PCs and CRT terminals do not need this option because there is no time delay needed for the terminal's cursor to return to the left margin at the end of each line.

Prompt Sounds

Unattended systems often allow the user to turn input *prompt sounds* on or off. When the operator turns on prompt sounds, the unattended system sends beeps each time it wants more data or commands from the caller. These beeps remind the caller that the system is waiting for input. Many users find the sounds irritating and turn them off.

Screen Size

A caller should be able to change both the screen width and screen height assumptions made by the system. Small screen terminals and some portable computers are difficult to use with a remote system that assumes a full 24-line by 80-column monitor when it transmits text and messages.

Expert Mode

Unattended software should be menu driven to guide novice callers through the system, but should provide an abbreviated menu or command structure for the expert user. Menus are a welcome sight for the timid communication novice, but are annoying for frequent system users, particularly at 300 bps. At 1200 bps or higher, even the expert can tolerate long menus; but at 300 bps, menus seem to go on printing forever. The *expert mode* should be user selectable—a user should be able to switch between the novice and expert mode at any time. The expert mode should also provide abbreviated versions of novice menus because expert users sometimes forget available commands or functions.

Terminal Emulation

Some BBS systems allow the caller to select certain screen and keyboard attributes to match a particular type of terminal. The system stores the *terminal emulation* selection in a user data-base—the system operator or the caller selects the emulation mode as a normal default condition. The system activates the selected terminal emulation mode each time the caller dials into the system. The BBS system may also allow a user to select another terminal type while on line. This allows the user to call into the system with several different terminal types.

Message Subsystem Capabilities

The message subsystem is a predominant part of bulletin board systems. This subsystem should allow callers and the system operator to leave messages for other callers or retrieve messages left by other callers. It should also allow callers to retrieve message summaries and mark messages for later retrieval. The following paragraphs discuss other desirable capabilities.

Message Privacy

When entering a message, the caller should be allowed to specify whether the message is a private or public message. Private messages should be readable only by the recipient and the system operator and should be encrypted when stored to ensure message security. Public messages should be readable by any caller, but the person entering the message should be able to select the level of protection required to avoid message deletion. The system should allow the message recipient, the caller who left the message, and the system operator to delete a protected message.

Comments for Operator

Most bulletin boards also allow a caller to leave private comments for the system operator. These comments should be protected from normal caller access by data encryption or file-location protection. The system should place the comments in a sequential data file so they can be edited by a text editor or word processor. System operators often use these comments in response letters or in help files for other users.

Message Scan

The message scan capability of an unattended system should allow a caller to search messages in ascending numerical order (forward search) or descending numerical order (backward search), beginning with a specific message number or date. Some systems also allow a caller to scan or read only those messages entered since the caller was last on the system. Other systems allow callers to retrieve messages based on selected subjects. The system may also provide an automatic scan of the message file to locate messages directed to the caller.

Message Word Processor

One often overlooked aspect of a message subsystem is the message word processor. Message entry that does not provide automatic word wrap or search and replace editing is cumbersome to use. The quality of messages left on a system, and the frequency of use of the message function, will often depend on the quality of the message editor. Callers spoiled by high-quality message processors on other systems may not use the message function on a less sophisticated system.

Log-on Bulletins

Log-on bulletins are the system operator's opportunity to get to you before you get into the system. Bulletins can be delivered to a caller several different ways, but the two most often used techniques are sequential file one-time delivery and menu-selectable text files. The sequential file method forces the caller to either read the entire file or abnormally terminate the file listing by sending the remote PC a special character. After displaying the sequential bulletin, sometimes called "general mail," the caller can only read the bulletin file again by terminating the session and calling back. The menu-driven bulletin technique allows a caller to skip all system bulletins or read selected bulletins. BBS systems normally allow users to reread bulletins any number of times. The menu technique is superior to the sequential file technique because bulletins can be categorized by the system operator. The caller has more flexibility in selecting and reading the bulletins.

System Logs

Unattended communications software should keep a log of all callers. Systems may also collect other user data. Some systems record the communication data format of callers and files transferred. Other systems collect data on users that provide default system operation parameters. When a caller logs on, these systems search user databases to determine whether the person has been on before. If the person has been on before, the system automatically invokes the parameter selections used during the last session. The caller may modify the selection for the current and future parameters with each call.

The user database provides the system operator with a tool to lock certain users (by name only) out of the system. Pranksters can be eliminated or forced to change their log-on names. The lockout does not keep crank callers from logging on under another name, but it does keep them from developing a following with name recognition.

Remote Takeover

Remote system takeover is often provided in BBS systems in a limited form. Remote takeover should allow callers to access the system through password control and perform as many normal local IBM PC functions as possible from a remote terminal or personnel computer. A caller should be able to execute DOS internal and external commands such as DIR, COPY, ERASE, and CHKDSK. The system should allow a caller to run any application that prints on the monitor one line at a time; software IBM refers to as "well behaved."

Remote Takeover Limitations

The greatest limitation of remote takeover is execution of *direct-video, memory-mapped* software. Most remote takeover capabilities in BBS systems will not support operation of such application software because of the time required to send full screens of information. The system must transmit complex escape codes to format the remote display. PC-DOS and all its utilities print each line of output individually on the screen using standard DOS and BIOS functions. These commands can be operated remotely. WordPerfect, dBASE IV, and Lotus 1-2-3, on the other hand, are direct-video, memory-mapped software and cannot be operated from a remote terminal without special RTS software at both ends of the communications link, as described earlier in this chapter.

True remote takeover software, such as Carbon Copy and Close-Up, allow remote operation of direct-video software. These packages intercept all screen output and repackage the images for transmission to the remote PC. The system sends only the actual screen changes over the telephone line, which speeds up the display process significantly.

File Protection

Disk file protection is critical in bulletin board systems that allow remote access and unscreened caller access. Unattended software should allow only selected callers to delete files. The software should either provide *password protection* of files or allow only the system operator to delete or rename files. Without this protection, callers can delete files intended for other callers' use or delete files that are necessary for system operation.

Some systems provide several password levels. The system operator determines the access level each caller is to have by entering the information in the user database. When a caller logs on, the system retrieves the caller's authorized access level from the database. If the system is located in an area that is physically accessible by system users, access to the system-maintenance utilities must also have password protection.

System Operator Controls

Unattended communications software should allow the *system operator* to access the system both locally and from a remote terminal. Operator access is necessary for file and system database maintenance. Files often have to be added to the system directories or messages have to be deleted. The system operator may also want to enter messages for callers or revise system bulletins. Table 5-3 lists a summary of necessary and desirable system operator functions.

Table 5-3. Bulletin board system operator controls.

Necessary Controls:

System bulletin, menu, and file revisions
Message entry and deletion
User database listing and modification
Selective user lockout
Disk file directory listing
Disk file viewing
File directory modifications
Listing of caller comments file
Deletion of caller comments file
Modification of caller time limit
Modification of system default parameters

Desirable Controls:

Caller log statistical analysis
Caller log deletion
User database statistical analysis
Disk and file directory mismatch analysis
Password-protected remote takeover

System operator access should be protected by a password. A special password or name should allow the system operator to gain access from a remote terminal. A special key combination should also allow the system operator to access the system locally. The system may need a special local-access password for applications used for financial transactions.

Besides the operator access capabilities listed in Table 5-3, an operator should have several local controls that can be activated with keyboard function keys or hot keys. The following paragraphs describe three typical local controls.

Forced Chat

A good bulletin board system allows either the caller or system operator to initiate a conversation-mode *keyboard chat*. The system operator should be able to force the system into the chat mode at any time, except during a file transfer.

SYSOP-on-next

When someone is using the system from a remote terminal, the local operator should be able to toggle the system to let him or her on next. This toggle sets a system flag and holds the system open for operator use when the current caller logs off. Without this feature, the operator has to interrupt caller use of the system to ask for local access or standby until the user logs off. With the *SYSOP-on-next* feature, the operator can toggle the flag, then come back later to use the system.

Exit to DOS

Another desirable feature for the system operator is the ability to exit the unattended communications system to the disk operating system without entering a series of system commands. The operator may wish to do file maintenance with an external editor or run another application. A function key that allows a quick exit to DOS saves the operator time in performing these operations.

System Reliability

An important characteristic of bulletin board software is *system reliability*. The system should continue operating under all anticipated conditions for long periods of time without operator attention. A system that frequently crashes or runs out of disk space can become a nuisance for the system operator. Such a system can require the attention of assistant operators if the primary system operator is away on travel or vacation. Reliability requirements under both normal and abnormal operating conditions are described in the following paragraphs.

Normal Operation

The system should not "crash" as a result of normal problems such as the disk becoming full and too many active messages being created. It should also recover from loss of the communications carrier signal regardless of the activity in progress at the time of the loss. Some systems have a tendency to "hang" if the carrier is lost while a file is being transferred. When a hang occurs, the system operator must restart the system. Other errors that occur should be either logged to a special file or the caller should be asked to leave the operator a note indicating the type of error that occurred.

Abnormal Operations

Many remote communications systems recover well from power outages and equipment malfunctions. A good unattended system should recycle properly if power is lost for a period of time. Another typical problem is a disk drive door left open; the system should recover from this operator error and inform the caller that the drive door is open.

As you can see from the remote takeover and bulletin board characteristics and capabilities just described, this type of software can provide the PC with significant unattended communications power. There is yet another type of special-purpose unattended communications software, however, that is popular with PC owners. Electronic mail software allows the PC to send and receive messages between one or more users. This software, described in the following paragraphs, does not require an active user at either end.

Electronic Mail Software

Electronic mail software and the bulletin board software just described have many things in common, but electronic mail software usually provides more powerful message delivery capabilities. Bulletin boards allow the system operator or callers to leave messages for other callers, but callers do not receive the messages unless they call the bulletin board. Commercial *store-and-forward systems*, such as The SOURCE's SOURCEMAIL and CompuServe's EMAIL, provide more sophisticated versions of this passive *computer-based mail system(CBMS)* design. The power of these CBMS systems, however, can be tapped only if message recipients actively participate in the process by periodically calling into the CBMS to retrieve messages.

A CBMS is a good choice of message system if message recipients have access to only dumb terminals. These store-and-forward facilities allow several widely dispersed users to exchange mail. The advantage of CBMS systems is that users do not have to purchase computers and electronic mail software; they just call the store-and-forward service and send or retrieve their mail as required. The trade-off is network-service subscription and connection costs for a commercially operated facility versus long distance telephone rates and a dedicated microcomputer required to operate a private electronic mail system.

PC owners have another alternative. If the PC owner is willing to leave the computer unattended and dedicated to communications, electronic mail software can be used to send and receive messages, reports, and files. A PC can be set up in a business office as an electronic intraoffice memo system to eliminate "telephone tag" and to reduce the frequency of face-to-face meetings. The increase in office productivity produced by such a system could easily justify the cost of the computers and the dedicated telephone lines needed to establish the "PC network." The exchange of messages outside the local area could still be conducted through commercial CBMS facilities or public data networks to reduce long-distance telephone costs.

The major advantage of unattended electronic mail systems is the control it provides the local operator. An electronic mail system operating on a PC can provide all the capabilities of commercial CBMS software plus additional control over the delivery and the delivery timing of information. You can tell the system when to deliver certain messages and files, and the system will automatically call other systems to deliver the specified information at the specified times.

Electronic Mail System Features

Table 5-4 lists the features included in some PC-based electronic mail packages. PC-based electronic mail systems are usually designed to work with standard PC hardware containing limited disk space and the system features are based on the assumptions that a single individual or small group will use the electronic mail system, and that each user will have system operator privileges. There are no callers in the same sense as bulletin board operation because the software and hardware do the calling without operator attendance. Some of the features of these software packages are described in the following paragraphs.

Table 5-4. Electronic mail software features.

SYSTEM CUSTOMIZATION:

System configuration

CORRESPONDENCE ADDRESSING:

Assign mailboxes	Group addressing
Hidden distribution	Address maintenance

SEND MAIL:

Send to mailbox	Send to list
Send to phone number	Blind copy
Reply requested	Express delivery
Registered mail	Delayed delivery
Outgoing mail	Automatic retry
Protocol transfer	

RECEIVE MAIL:

Mail scan	Mail search
Display mail	Print mail
Forward mail	Reply to mail
Delete log entry	Save mail file
Delete mail file	

FILE MAINTENANCE:

File editing	Choice of editor
File merge	

MISCELLANEOUS:

On-line help	Input prompting
Single-level password	Multi-level password
Calendar	Correspondence template
Database update	Gateways

System Customization

Before a system is used for the first time it will have to be configured for the specific application. System customization allows the system operator to tailor certain features to meet the specific needs of groups or organizations. This capability also allows the operator to customize the system to match the hardware available. Items that should be included in this system setup are the number of disk drives, type of printer, and type of monitor available. The customization may also include the passwords required for operator access; several levels of access may be needed for group use of the system.

Correspondence Addressing

The *correspondence addressing subsystem* of an electronic mail system allows the user to establish "mailboxes" for persons or sites that are going to frequently receive mail. These subsystems are usually menu driven and allow the user to perform several addressing functions without returning to the system master menu. Some addressing options that may be included are described in the following paragraphs.

Assign Mailbox

The *mailbox* for another electronic mail system contains the addressee's name, the telephone number of the remote computer, and the data communication parameters used by the remote system. The mailbox is sometimes given a name that can be later displayed in a summary list of all mailboxes. The mailbox must also contain the formal name of the addressee that will be included in message headers. Generally, a *message header* consists of a "TO:" line followed by "FROM:" and "SUBJECT:" lines that are provided when a message is later sent to the addressee. The telephone number included in the mailbox must contain all special PBX codes required to get through to the telephone system and the area code of the addressee if the remote system requires a long-distance call.

The communication parameters of the remote computer may include several data items. The data rate of the remote modem must be included, but the system may also require the parity, number of data bits, and the number of stop bits associated with the addressee's system.

The mailbox feature usually includes the ability to display all mailboxes or selected mailboxes. Mailbox selection may be based on criteria such as location, company group, or project title. The selection feature may also allow the user to use Boolean logic in the selection command. Some systems allow you to print the mailboxes on an attached printer. This feature may include a pagination option as well as selection criteria.

A well-designed electronic mail system should make the addressing function transparent to users after a system operator has installed the system and created the mailbox list. In other words, the sender should be concerned only with an account number or name of the recipient. The message should find its way to the proper receiving station no matter what combination of modem or local area networks is in use. Provisions must be made for the common occurrence of addressee names or a project moving from one physical mail station to another in the same building or in another city. The software and communications protocols required to make this happen are not trivial and are a major factor in the cost of a software package.

Group Addressing

Group addressing allows the user to specify multiple mailboxes that fall into a category. These groups or *lists* can be used later to send a single piece of correspondence to several addressees. Several of these distribution lists may contain some of the same mailbox addressees. When you direct mail to one of these lists, the mail is automatically sent to each addressee on the list as if you had sent the mail to each addressee individually. This feature usually includes the ability to display all addressing lists categorized by group. The system may also include a print list option.

Hidden Distribution

This is a variation of a blind copy. The *hidden distribution list* of addressees will automatically get a copy of correspondence when they are included in a mail distribution. Addressees do not see the hidden distribution list unless you specifically designate them as hidden list recipients.

Address Book Maintenance

An electronic mail system must allow the operator to periodically maintain *address book* mailboxes. The telephone numbers and operating parameters of remote systems sometimes change, and the operator must be able to modify the system mailbox data to match the changes. Mailboxes may also have to be deleted or group addressing lists modified.

Send Mail Features

A well-designed mail system provides several send-mail options. The electronic mail-send process controls the originator's intended distribution and disposition of the mail. The process also controls the type of information sent to addressees. Some system options may include the features described in the following paragraphs.

Send to Mailbox

The *send-to-mailbox* option allows the operator to send messages, files, or data to a particular mailbox. The system may also require the operator to specify which type of information is being sent so that it can tell the addressee what to expect when the transfer is made. For example, an addressee will need to know that particular files contain *binary data* instead of readable text.

Send to List

The *send-to-list* option allows the operator to send messages, files, or data to a group-addressing list. As is the case with the send-to-mailbox feature, the system may also require the specification of which type of information the operator is sending so that it can tell the addressees what to expect when the transfers are made.

Send to Phone Number

The *send-to-phone-number* option allows the operator to send messages, files, or data to a telephone number that is not contained in a mailbox. This feature is useful for sending information to a number that is going to be called only once. It would be a waste of time to set up a mailbox that will receive only one mail delivery.

Blind Copy

The *blind-copy* feature allows the operator to send a copy of the correspondence to an addressee without indicating such to other recipients. This is an extension of the hidden distribution discussed earlier; it allows specific additional blind copies to be sent to people not on the hidden distribution list.

Reply Requested

The *reply-request* feature allows the operator to request a reply from the addressee. This feature may also allow the operator to specify a time span within which the addressee has to respond.

Express Delivery

Express delivery means that an addressee will immediately be called after the piece of mail is posted. Some express-delivery options may provide an automatic hard-copy delivery if the addressee's system cannot be reached within a specified length of time. This automatic hard-copy delivery would have to be handled by a third-party service company.

Registered Mail

If mail is designated as *registered*, the system will record whether it was delivered properly. Some systems always record whether addressees get mail sent to them and do not provide this as a separate feature.

Delayed Delivery

The *delayed-delivery* feature allows you to designate the date and time you want the system to start attempting delivery of mail to a specific addressee. A system that offers this option must also be certain to obtain the correct date and time from the operator or be able to use a system clock.

Outgoing Mail

An electronic mail system must keep a record of all *outgoing mail*. The operator should be able to review the list of outgoing mail to see the status of all mail that has been sent. The list should include the addressee's name and the subject of the correspondence. If the system records whether the addressee received mail properly, this information should also be displayed.

Automatic Retries

Most PC-based electronic mail systems will retry a telephone number a specific number of times if mail sent cannot be delivered. Some systems automatically retry a telephone number at a set interval for a given number of times. Other systems allow the operator to designate the number of retries and the retry interval. The number of retries required to deliver mail should be recorded in the outgoing mail log for later review by the operator. If certain addressees could not be reached or were difficult to reach, the operator may want to change the retry parameters associated with that addressee, assuming the system allows that option.

There are many factors that may keep a system from delivering mail. The addressee's computer may not be in the mail mode or it may not be on. If the addressee's computer is on and in the mail mode, it may not be configured as expected. A bad telephone connection also may result in an aborted attempt to deliver the mail. The system also may not have enough free disk space for the mail being sent or a file-storage error may occur. There are several other reasons for improper mail delivery, which makes it important to keep a record of attempted deliveries so problem addressees can be investigated.

Error Checking

For systems that are used for important file transfers or binary file transfers, it is desirable to have file transfer error detection and correction. Error checking can also be used to verify proper mail delivery for the originating system; mail deliveries that are not properly completed can be retried later. Error checking is more important for electronic mail systems than for bulletin board systems because most PC-based electronic mail systems operate unattended on both ends of the communications link. Bulletin board systems generally have an operator in attendance on the caller end of the communications link, and the operator can abort a file transfer if the systems fail to communicate properly. Totally unattended file transfers that occur between electronic mail systems require more integrity checking. Error-checking protocols such as the *Microcom Networking Protocol* (*MNP*) are ideal for this application. They not only perform CRC-16 error detection and correction, but they perform system-integrity checks throughout a communication session.

Receive Mail Features

Receive options allow system users a degree of flexibility in dealing with received mail. The user should have an incoming mail menu that provides some of the features discussed in the following paragraphs.

Mail Scan

Mail scan allows the user to browse through pending mail and review only mail originators, subject lines, and mail origination dates and times. This feature also allows the user to select important messages that must be read first. The system may allow you to mark selected messages for immediate display or printing.

Mail Search

The *mail-search* feature allows the operator to scan or read messages by date interval; that is, all before, all after, or between designated dates. It also allows searches by key word, subject line, or originator. This feature may also allow mail to be marked for display or printing.

Display Mail

The *display mail* feature should allow the operator to view any message file still current in the system. This feature should also prevent you from displaying nontext data such as binary program files; the system should automatically mark binary data files when they are delivered.

Print Mail

System operators often want to keep printed copies of messages as reminders of action items. The system should allow the operator to print messages. It should also be set up to paginate long messages.

Forward Mail

A desirable feature is the capability to *forward mail* along with system operator comments to another mailbox not on the original addressee list. This gives the operator a shortcut in re-sending the file or message; otherwise, the file has to be saved to disk, then redirected as a new piece of mail.

Reply to Mail

The *reply-to-mail* feature allows an immediate reply to received correspondence. The reply is sent to the originator of the mail, based on the telephone number and other data contained in the mail. This feature may require that the originator be included as a system mailbox.

Delete Log Entry and Save File

This feature allows the operator to remove the entry from the incoming mail log and retains the mail in an existing or new file for later editing, merging, or review. This is an important maintenance function because it keeps the incoming mail log from getting so long that it becomes meaningless. It also allows the piece of mail to be used in other items of information.

Delete Log Entry and File

This feature allows the operator to perform maintenance on the incoming mail log and to dispose of messages and files at the same time. Deleted mail is erased from the system diskette. This feature should ask for confirmation before a file is deleted to prevent accidental deletions.

File Maintenance Features

File maintenance is a vital part of operating an electronic mail system. Good file maintenance features can make a system easy to use and can improve mail productivity. The following are some file maintenance features to look for in an unattended electronic mail system.

File Editing

One feature that is indispensable in an electronic mail system is the ability to create and edit text files without exiting the system. Some systems allow the operator to use an external editor and others provide their own built-in editor. A system that allows either option is ideal because it allows the operator to choose a familiar editor if he or she already has one or it allows the operator to use the built-in editor if he or she does not already own one.

File Merging

File merging allows the user to insert boiler-plate text or nontext material, such as Lotus 1-2-3 spreadsheets, into the outgoing mail. It also allows newly prepared text files to be merged with files received as mail.

Miscellaneous Features

Beyond the basic features of sending, receiving, filing, and addressing, there are several features that can be categorized as unnecessary but desirable, although some of these may be important for a specific application.

On-Line Help

On-line help provides descriptions of system functions and usage for novice users. Each help message must be related to the specific actions that are being contemplated by the user, based on the menu in use at the time help is requested. If the system does not use menus, the user should be able to get a list of available commands and information related to each command.

Input Prompting

Input prompting leads the operator through the procedure of setting up mailboxes, sending or receiving mail, or performing system maintenance. Some systems use menus to achieve input prompting. Others respond to requests for help with data input prompts.

System Security

For corporate and financial applications, correspondence security and access control are often necessary. Generally, a *single-level password scheme* for system operator access is sufficient; this requires that all participants in a given group have a unique password. Security of this type of password scheme can pose a problem over time and should not be considered for highly sensitive applications.

Multilevel access is another means of achieving security. It allows more flexibility and control in retrieving messages and can be combined with a scheme for classifying messages. This security design provides several passwords based on assigned security level.

Another approach to security is the use of *mail encryption*. This type of protection is more difficult to achieve and is more costly because each electronic mail station in a network must have a device to encrypt data. With the recent emphasis on the prevention of computer misuse, encryption is becoming a popular security measure.

Calendar

The *calendar* feature automatically notifies a mail originator of the recipient's upcoming schedule or absence. This feature could also allow the operator to select mail originators that are to receive calendar information.

Correspondence Templates

A *correspondence template* can provide prestored formats for certain specialized correspondence and is useful in organizations that use forms for authorizing work or ordering parts. It can also be used to improve report-preparation productivity.

Database Update

Database update is used to place selected portions of messages into a database. This could be used to keep track of warehouse stores or to log field sales information.

Gateways

Electronic mail systems may sometimes be used as *gateways* to other types of electronic communication services. They can be used to send messages to an unattended TELEX machine. Gateways can also send and receive messages from electronic mail systems made by other vendors. For example, a local system may be set up to send messages from local users to remote users through the Email capabilities of service providers such as The SOURCE. Many electronic mail systems also provide routing through MCI Mail so that hard copies of messages are delivered to users who do not have data communications. These are valuable connections for local inhouse systems that must communicate with other offices.

The international *X.400* electronic mail standard will provide the common denominator for message exchange between dissimilar electronic mail systems in the future. This Open System Interconnect protocol ensures compatibility between the source and destination information contained in electronic mail messages to ensure proper delivery of the messages regardless of the number of systems they pass through. The CCITT *X.500* recommendations define the directory services that X.400-compliant systems must use to determine the proper destination address of the intended recipient of a message. This recommendation defines a database for mail recipients that is equivalent to the telephone White and Yellow pages.

As electronic mail becomes more widespread and sophisticated, an increasing number of features will become available. Integration of unattended electronic mail systems into other applications will be an area of continued growth. Examples of these combinations are the merging of voice, data, and image into electronic form that is stored on a hard disk or optical disk for delivery to other users. Electronic mail systems are also moving into the financial world through Electronic Data Interchange (EDI). These systems allow corporations and government agencies to exchange electronic documents and make financial transactions without the need for paper or human interactions. Most of these electronic interchange systems are in their infancy. As their level of sophistication increases, users and consumers will have additional options for service transactions not available today.

Evaluating Unattended Communications Software

Because of the number of aspects a PC owner must consider when selecting an unattended communications package, the task of making a single choice could be overwhelming. To make the task easier, a structured approach should be taken similar to the approach shown for terminal communications software.

The first task in selecting a package is to assess unattended communications needs. A list of all essential features should be developed. This should be followed by the development of a list of nonessential, but desirable, features. Only then should available unattended communications software packages be considered.

Table 5-5. Remote takeover system evaluation matrix.

Software Feature	Pkg #1	Pkg #2	Pkg #3
Configuration Control			
Select Modem Type			
Touch-tone Dialing			
Rotary Dialing			
Reboot on Hang Up			
Select Screen Type			
Screen Update Speed			
Action Key Definition			
Protocol Selection			
Printer Operation			
Store Passwords			
System Security			
Password Encryption			
Dial Back			
Remote Dial-in			
Dialing Directory			
Password Protection			
Software Execution			
Well Behaved			
Other			
Error Correction			
Stop-and-wait			
Non-stop			
File Transfers			
Natural commands			
Xmodem protocol			
CRC-16 protocol			
User-to-user Chat			
Chat Window			
Movable Window			
Screen Capture			
Snapshot			
Continuous			
Playback			
Remote Printer Support			
Remote print			
Local print			
Disable print			
System Logs			

Legend: E = Excellent, G = Good, F = Fair, — = Not supported

Table 5.6 Bulletin board software evaluation matrix.

Software Feature	Pkg #1	Pkg #2	Pkg #3
System configuration			
Parameter detect/switch			
File protection			
ASCII file transfer			
Xmodem protocol			
CRC-16 protocol			
XON/XOFF flow control			
File size indicator			
Operator chat mode			
Operator page hours			
Case conversion			
Help files			
Message storage			
Message retrieval			
Message maintenance			
Message scan			
Message protection			
Message word processor			
Local snoop toggle			
Log-on bulletin design			
File directory listing			
Directory maintenance			
Callers data log			
Users database			
Users log maintenance			
SYSOP special controls			
Caller defaults recall			
Terminal emulation			
Expert/novice menus			
Remote operation			
Disk area restriction			
Unattended reliability			
Unattended security			

Legend: E = Excellent, G = Good, F = Fair, - = Not supported

Table 5-7. Electronic mail software evaluation matrix.

Software Feature	Pkg #1	Pkg #2	Pkg #3
System configuration			
Assign mailboxes			
Group addressing			
Hidden distribution			
Address maintenance			
Send to mailbox			
Send to list			
Send to phone number			
Blind copy			
Reply requested			
Express delivery			
Registered mail			
Delayed delivery			
Outgoing mail			
Automatic retry			
Protocol transfer			
Mail scan			
Mail search			
Display mail			
Print mail			
Forward mail			
Reply to mail			
Delete log entry			
Save mail file			
Delete mail file			
File editing			
Choice of editor			
File merge			
On-line help			
Input prompting			
Single-level password			
Multilevel password			
Calendar			
Correspondence template			
Data base update			
Gateways			

Legend: E = Excellent, G = Good, F = Fair, — = Not supported

To place packages in proper perspective, it is good practice to produce an *evaluation matrix* similar to the ones shown in Tables 5.5, 5.6, and 5.7. After a matrix is completed showing the strengths and weakness of packages in a given category, it becomes easier to select the appropriate package.

As you can see from Tables 5.5, 5.6 and 5.7, there are significant differences between the capabilities and features of the different types of unattended communications packages. Remote takeover software packages provide the greatest level of support for the execution of native software stored on the remote PC. Bulletin board software packages, on the other hand, provide the greatest level of support for information and data exchange among the members of a specific group of callers. Finally, electronic mail software provide the greatest level of support for the exchange of mail among the members of a specific group of users. Although all three types of software provide unattended operation and have some overlapping features, they are different in concept and implementation.

Because of the differences in packages, it is a good idea to experiment before making a significant commitment to one particular type of software. Experience using a bulletin board package is a valuable part of determining your communication needs. Public-domain and inexpensive programs such as RBBS-PC are excellent learning tools. A user can experiment with these programs and through trial and error discover the power and limitations of unattended software. The RBBS-PC source code, system files, and documentation can be obtained by downloading the files from many public bulletin board systems.

Operating Tips for Unattended Systems

If you decide to become the operator of an unattended communications system, there are several important facts to consider before you start. The following paragraphs contain information that may save you time, money, and frustration.

Required Equipment

Other than the software described in the previous sections, unattended communication systems require several pieces of hardware besides a microcomputer. The minimum requirements and some recommendations are discussed in the following paragraphs.

Telephone Line

Most applications require a dedicated voice-grade telephone line. Systems that provide the *ring-back* feature may be operated on a line that is normally used for voice communications, but the ring-back operating mode is not recommended. Most system operators find it too confusing and frustrating to use only one line—someone is always on the system when you need to make a call. A dedicated line can be used 24 hours a day without interfering with normal home or business voice communications.

It should also be noted that a "data line" is not needed for most unattended communications systems. *Voice-grade lines* are not as good for data communications as dedicated *data lines*, but for most PC applications voice-grade lines are sufficient. Voice-grade lines are much less expensive to install than data lines. You may also find that you can get *pulse (rotary) lines* at less cost than *touch-tone lines*; most auto-dial, auto-answer modems provide both options.

Modems

All unattended communication systems require auto-answer modems. Auto-dial is required only for electronic mail systems. The communications package you choose may specify a particular modem make and model to be used with the system. You should read the documentation manual carefully. Many new operators have spent several frustrating hours trying to get a system to work with the wrong modem before reading the system modem requirements.

Most system operators prefer *stand-alone modems* to internal *modem adapters*. Problem diagnosis is easier with a stand-alone modem that has *indicator lights* for auto-answer, high speed, off-hook, receive data, send data, terminal ready, and modem ready. Modem reset is also easier when the system "hangs" (all systems do this occasionally) because most stand-alone modems have external reset buttons or switches for turning the power off.

Disk Drives

Many new or prospective system operators worry about wear and tear on disk drives. This worry is normally unfounded for the IBM family of Personal Computers. Many systems have logged over 15,000 continuous hours of use without a single disk drive failure or malfunction. It does make system operation faster and smoother if you have enough memory to set up an *electronic disk drive* for frequently accessed system files. The system should not use an electronic disk for files that are updated during calls because a power failure will erase the updated information before it can be saved to disk. A hard disk is the ideal storage device for a system operator; it could be a necessity for frequently used business systems.

Power Line Protection

Many system operators use power-line *surge suppressors* to eliminate power-line spikes that occur during lightning storms. This device is useful only if it is designed for fast-response and high-voltage filtering; such a device is usually expensive. Several IBM PC systems have operated around the clock for thousands of hours without surge protection and without system damage, even in areas that have frequent storms. These systems were found "locked up" on many occasions, but no internal or external damage was found. These system operators may have just been lucky. If it makes you more comfortable to have a surge suppressor, you should get a good one.

Some unattended communications systems are equipped with an *uninterruptable power supply* (*UPS*) to protect against power failure. These devices include rechargeable batteries that are continuously charged while normal electrical power is available. When normal power is lost, the UPS converts stored energy into *alternating current* (*AC*) to keep the PC system unit operating for a short period of time. The duration of UPS operation after power loss depends upon the electrical load connected to the UPS and the power rating of the unit. A 500 KVA UPS rating provides a few minutes of operation for a typical PC system unit—enough time for the system to get through a short power outage.

Telephone Line Protection

Power-line surge suppressors normally provide adequate system protection. To prevent modem damage during lightning storms, additional protection from telephone-line power spikes may be required. To prevent this problem, it is necessary to install surge suppression devices on the telephone line between the wall jack and the modem. These devices are inexpensive and can be purchased from most electronic parts suppliers. Some power-line surge suppressors also include telephone line surge suppression— two telephone jacks allow the line from the wall and the line going to the modem to be connected to the surge suppressor.

System Maintenance

Most unattended communication systems require periodic maintenance. Files must be deleted that are no longer needed and old messages must be erased. If the system keeps caller logs, these logs may have to be archived or deleted at least once a week. If a system has a user database, the database may have to be packed periodically to remove users who have been marked for deletion or users who have not been active. This usually has to be done once a month. If the system keeps comments for the operator, these comments have to be periodically archived or deleted. Some comments may also require operator response. There may be additional duties and actions required, depending on the system design and capacity of the system hardware.

Long Unattended Periods

Some systems do not use much disk space to log users or record caller activity and can be left unattended for long periods. Others are "disk hogs" and can be operated for only a few days without system maintenance. You will be able to judge this after operating the system for a while. The maximum unattended period will usually also depend on caller and message activity. Often-used systems require more frequent maintenance than systems that do not see much activity.

If you operate an unattended system at home, you should not inform callers that your system will be out of operation while you are away from home. The reason for this caution may be obvious to some people but not to others. It may be a courtesy to tell system callers you will be away, but it may also invite thieves to your house. You could say that your system will be in the shop for maintenance for that period of time, but you could also say nothing. People who call while you are away will simply think your system "crashed" and has not been restarted.

Caller Activity

A new system operator is often frustrated because the system does not get much activity at first. This is especially true for hobbyists. Some operators get so frustrated that they shut down the system before its use becomes popular with callers. This is unfortunate because it usually takes time for a new system telephone number to get into circulation. Most systems receive only a few calls during the first two months of operation. Some new business electronic mail systems are also slow to catch on because people take time to adjust to new ways of corresponding. For system operators that get beyond this "break-in period," however, there are new experiences in store.

Demanding Callers

Public bulletin board users can sometimes be demanding. They may ask for advice or counsel or they may ask for files you have removed from the system. After answering these demands several times, most operators learn to say "no" politely. If you are a professional in a certain trade or business, you also have to be careful about providing advice or counsel on a public information system. You may be technically liable for actions taken based on your advice. This is particularly true for lawyers and medical doctors.

Prank Callers

Almost all electronic information systems receive prank calls. Some callers just want to have fun and others want to interfere with the operation of your system. Good unattended systems are designed to handle these callers, but a person seriously interested in "stopping the show" may find a way to do so. You should keep track of these callers and devise methods to lock them out of the system. Handling prank callers may require changing passwords frequently or using a system utility that allows you to exclude certain callers. You may also want to leave messages for people you suspect as pranksters so that they are aware of your observations. Knowing there is someone watching may be enough to keep some ill-intentioned callers away.

Profanity

There are some system callers who insist on using profanity. Your system may be designed to scan messages and files for certain words, but most systems do not have this feature. You will have to monitor messages and files frequently to be sure they meet your standards. Text that does not meet your standards will have to be purged.

Upload Rules

If your system allows public access and file uploading, you should post rules for the files you will accept. Some callers like to upload *copyrighted files* to public systems just to see what kind of response they will get. You may be held responsible for public access to that copyrighted material. Besides posting upload rules, you will have to monitor uploaded files to be sure none of them are commercial software packages.

You may also want to post rules on the types or quality of software you will accept. If you operate a public-access bulletin board for a special interest group, you may want to limit files to those that would be of interest to the group. You may have less control over the quality of files you get. Some system operators test all software uploaded to their systems, but this is impractical for active board operators. You may just want to post a *disclaimer* on the quality of software found on your system.

Conclusions

As you can see from the number of characteristics and considerations described in this chapter, unattended communications software is somewhat complex, but can offer some users great communications power. Unattended communications software provides the PC owner with a communications tool that can both receive and deliver messages to callers. It can also provide callers with software. Unattended communications software can also provide an excellent vehicle for experimentation with the types of smart-terminal software described in Chapter 4.

6

Error Detection and Correction Protocols

$\mathbf{M}$any users of data communications find the concepts of data integrity and communications system control confusing. Many communications articles add to this confusion by mixing discussions of data communications error detection with computer hardware error detection. This chapter clarifies these concepts by providing a complete review of asynchronous error detection and correction. This chapter also provides a review of the most popular types of error-correcting protocols used in asynchronous data communications.

Before delving into the details of error detection and correction, however, we wish to provide some background information regarding data communication lines and data networks. Communication novices sometimes misunderstand the concepts of voice networks and data networks. *Voice networks*, such as the public telephone system, transmit and receive voice-frequency sounds as discussed in Chapter 2. You can transmit and receive data through these networks at rates up to 19,200 bps with current modem hardware without special amplifying and switching equipment. *Data networks*, on the other hand, may be specially conditioned telephone lines or packet-switched systems. You can lease special *data lines* from several vendors (including AT&T) that support data rates substantially higher than 19,200 bps. You can also subscribe to a *public data network* (*PDN*) to communicate with a remote computer or service company. These *packet-switched networks* (*PSN*s) provide special error detection and correction for data and cannot be used for voice communications. This chapter provides information on all three types of communication systems.

Asynchronous Error Detection and Correction

Data communication errors can often produce catastrophic results if not quickly detected and corrected. An error in the transmission of financial data can cause accounting books not to balance or the amount of a transaction to be recorded wrong. An error in the transfer of an executable software program can cause the software to malfunction or can keep the software from operating at all. To prevent these types of problems, it is necessary to detect and correct data communication errors before the transferred data are put in use on the receiving end of the communications link.

To understand the process of detecting and correcting errors, it is first necessary to understand the cause and effects of data communication errors. Errors can be introduced into a communications link at any point along the route of the data flow. When a Personal Computer sends data out the local serial port, a bad set of communication chips in the port can generate data errors. A poorly designed or manufactured modem can add errors to data as it passes from the serial port to the telephone line. Errors can be generated by faulty telephone company equipment. Finally, errors can be generated on the receiving end of a link by either the modem or the serial port.

Data communication errors are undesirable changes in the bit patterns of data that occur after the data go from the internal PC data enroute to an external device or computer. The only acceptable changes that occur in data beyond that point are intentional changes created to alter data in a manner that can be reversed on the receiving end. For example, hardware or software may *compress* data on the sending end to speed up communications; hardware or software must *decompress* that same data on the receiving end. Hardware or software may also *encrypt* data on the sending end and *decipher* the data on the receiving end to provide secure communications. This same hardware or software must detect and eliminate data changes that occur in the communications link that are not intentional.

Typical data communications errors are created by electrical noise or faulty equipment. A bolt of lightning near a telephone line carrying data will induce electrical noise and alter the bit patterns of the data as shown in Figure 6.1. A poorly designed or manufactured modem may create electrical noise on the telephone line that alters data. A person or piece of equipment can also generate line noise. When someone inadvertently picks up another telephone on the same line you are using for communications, bursts of noise may go into the telephone system. A motor can start near a telephone line and create noise also.

Data communications systems must detect and correct the damage telephone line noise cause. A system must detect interferences of short duration that only change one bit in a byte of data. The same system must detect interferences of long duration that create bursts of errors. All error-detection techniques are not, however, equally adept at handling both types of errors, as you will see later in this chapter.

Hardware or software can execute error detection either continuously for the duration of a communications session or for specific portions of a session. Asynchronous communications may use either of these techniques, whereas synchronous communications always use the continuous error-detection method. Asynchronous communica-

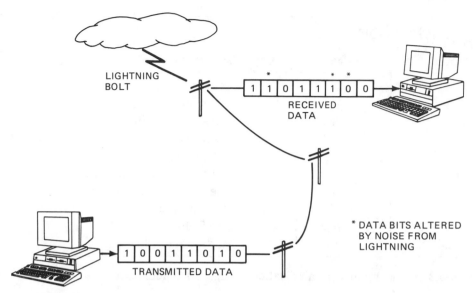

Figure 6.1 Lightning induced noise.

tions may also execute error detection at the *data byte level* by examining the bit pattern in each byte of data or at the *data packet level* by examining the bit patterns of groups of bytes. Synchronous communications normally execute error detection at the packet level only.

Asynchronous communications hardware or software can perform three forms of error detection and correction. The simplest form of error detection is the *parity check* described in Chapter 2. The asynchronous communications adapter or the internal modem adapter executes this form of error detection for each byte of data the PC receives. Communications software operating in the PC must detect these errors by reading certain hardware registers and notify the user. The next level of error detection for asynchronous communication is the *file transfer protocol*. Communications software normally execute these error-correcting file transfers. The highest level of error detection and correction is the continuous *packet assembly and disassembly* technique. Communications hardware or software may execute this procedure. The following paragraphs provide detailed discussions of these three popular error-correcting techniques.

Parity Error Detection

Parity error detection, as discussed in Chapter 2, has several limitations in the reliability of error detection and effectiveness of error correction. Vendors have used parity error detection in data communications hardware and software since the 1960s, but this technique provides little value today.

Parity error detection served a useful purpose for communications between dumb terminals and large computers. The absence of detected parity errors was an indication

I/O Decode (in Hex)		Register Selected
COM 1 Adapter	COM 2 Adapter	
3F8	2F8	TX Buffer
3F8	2F8	RX Buffer
3F8	2F8	Divisor Latch LSB
3F9	2F9	Divisor Latch MSB
3F9	2F9	Interrupt Enable Register
3FA	2FA	Interrupt Identification Registers
3FB	2FB	Line Control Register
3FC	2FC	Modem Control Register
3FD	2FD	Line Status Register
3FE	2FE	Modem Status Register

Figure 6.2 Asynchronous communications element I/O addresses.

of a good communications connection, whereas the presence of detected parity errors was an indication of a poor communications connection. The keepers of the company computer hardware could make decisions regarding the need to reconfigure communications connections based on the level of parity errors on specific communication connections. With the introduction of the IBM PC with its *8-bit character set* and high-speed communications capabilities, parity error detection became an antique. Because of its continuing presence in asynchronous hardware, however, the following paragraphs provide a brief explanation of this technique.

Input/Output Registers

Input/Output (I/O) registers in an asynchronous communications port or modem adapter activate, initialize, and monitor parity error detection. The registers that provide this capability for the *COM1* and *COM2* asynchronous ports are shown in Figure 6.2. The *Line Control* and *Line Status Registers* provide the initialization and monitoring windows into the communications hardware. The *Interrupt Enable Register* allows these registers to execute their tasks. Figure 6.3 shows the relationships between these registers for a typical PC asynchronous communications port.

As shown in Figure 6.4, the *Line Control Register* (*LCR*) selects and enables specific types of parity. LCR bit 3 turns parity error detection on and off. By setting bit 3 to a value of 1, you activate parity detection. By setting bit 3 to a value of 0, you deactivate parity detection. If you activate parity, LCR bits 4 and 5 allow you to specify the type of parity you want. If you deactivate parity, LCR bits 4 and 5 are ignored.

LCR bit 4 selects even or odd parity. When you activate parity and set bit 4 to a value of 1, the port sends an even number of 1 bits in each byte and checks for an even number of 1 bits in each byte it receives. When you activate parity and set bit 4 to a

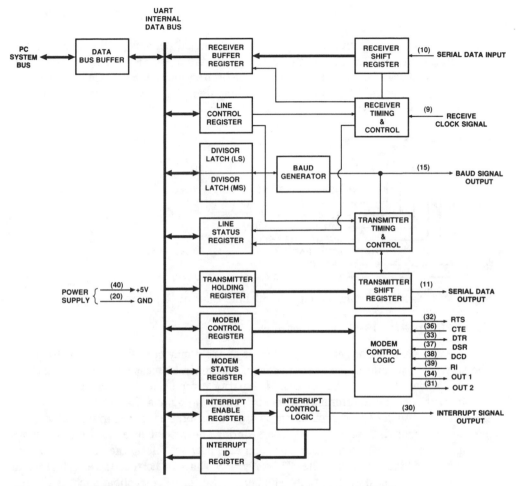

Figure 6.3 A block diagram of a typical asynchronous port UART.

value of 0, the port sends an odd number of 1 bits in each byte and checks for an odd number of 1 bits in each byte it receives.

LCR bit 5 selects mark or space parity. When you activate parity and set bit 5 to a value of 1, the port sets the parity bit to 0 for space parity for each byte it sends out. When you activate parity and set bit 5 to a value of 0, the port sets the parity bit to 1 for mark parity for each byte it sends out.

As shown in Figure 6.5, the *Line Status Register* (*LSR*) monitors the data stream for parity errors. If the LSR detects a parity error, it places a value of 1 in bit 2. The only way the IBM PC user will know about the error, however, is through communications software. If the communications software turns on the asynchronous port's interrupt logic, the detection of a parity error results in the generation of an interrupt signal for the IBM PC's CPU. The communications software must respond to this interrupt and determine its cause at the *Interrupt Identification Register* (*IIR*) shown in Figures 6.2 and 6.3.

After the software identifies the interrupt as a signal pending at the LSR, it must check all the bit positions at the LSR to determine status. If LSR bit 2 contains a value of 1 when the CPU reads it, the LSR resets the bit position to 0 to enable the detection of future parity errors. After reading the LSR and detecting a parity error, the communications software must tell the user about the error.

LINE CONTROL REGISTER (LCR)

3FB

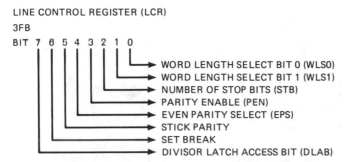

Figure 6.4 National Semiconductor 8250 Line Control Register.

Parity Limitations

The entire parity error detection process is fast, but may be of limited value to users. The software may inform the user of errors through screen messages, but may provide no mechanism to correct the errors. If a parity error occurs during an interactive session with a host, the error may be an obvious alteration of a character or symbol. An error detected under these circumstances should not present an insurmountable problem for the user. If a parity error occurs during the receipt of a file from a remote computer, however, the communications software may not inform the user. It may also store the bad data in a disk file. The only way you can correct these errors is to combine parity error detection with a higher level of error correction, such as the file transfer protocol.

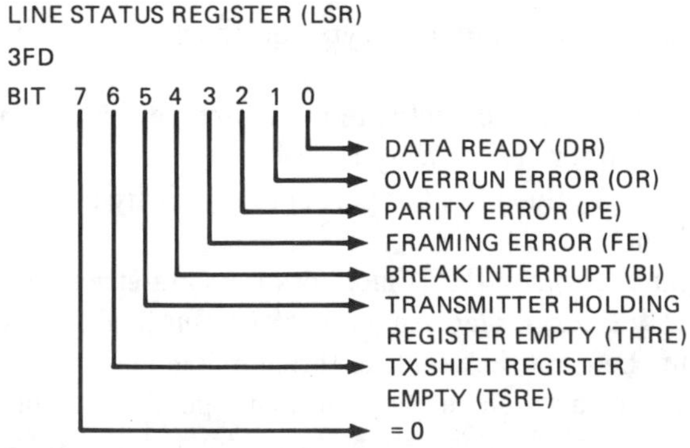

LINE STATUS REGISTER (LSR)

3FD

BIT 7 6 5 4 3 2 1 0

→ DATA READY (DR)
→ OVERRUN ERROR (OR)
→ PARITY ERROR (PE)
→ FRAMING ERROR (FE)
→ BREAK INTERRUPT (BI)
→ TRANSMITTER HOLDING REGISTER EMPTY (THRE)
→ TX SHIFT REGISTER EMPTY (TSRE)
→ = 0

Figure 6.5 National Semiconductor 8250 Line Status Register.

File Transfer Protocols

Transferring files between computers requires special communication techniques to detect and correct errors and to keep extraneous data or keystrokes from entering the files. Personal Computer users often have difficulty transferring files because of the jargon used to describe or control the process. Software vendors sometimes write file transfer procedures in generic terms that may not work with the user's communications software and hardware configuration. The following paragraphs discuss file transfer techniques and the jargon vendors use to describe this process in order to take some mystery out of this useful application of communications.

A simple but time-consuming technique of transferring files between two computers with assurance of file integrity is to transfer the entire file at least twice. You can send the file from one computer to another twice and store the file under two unique names during the process. You can then compare the transferred files with a utility such as the DOS COMP command to be sure the contents of both are the same. If the sizes of the two files are the same and a file comparison indicates the files are identical, then you can assume with a high degree of certainty that neither of the files contains data communications-induced errors.

If a file is transferred twice and the two copies are not identical, there may be no way of knowing which file contains errors. If the files contain readable text, you may be able to perform a manual review of the two files and identify errors that can be corrected. If the original file contained binary data or program object code, a visual comparison of the two files you received may not provide much insight into communications-induced errors. It could be impossible to determine which file is correct if they are different; both files could contain errors. The only way to be sure you have successfully transmitted good data using this technique is to continue retransmitting the file until two received copies contain no differences—a process that could consume much time and resources when telephone lines are of low quality.

Data Packets

To make the process of file transfer error detection and correction a manageable undertaking, vendors often provide communications software that divide a file into *packets* as it moves from one computer to another. These packets include error-detection information that enable the receiving computer to determine the presence of communications-induced errors.

Instead of transmitting a packet twice and comparing the first copy to the second, the sending computer derives information from the data it transmits and attaches the information to the packet. The file transfer protocol calculates a byte called a *checksum* or a pair of bytes called a *cyclic redundancy check* (*CRC*) and attaches this information to the end of the packet. The receiving computer executes the same calculation and compares the results to the checksum or CRC it receives with the packet. If the checksum or CRC comparison is favorable, the data transmission continues with the next packet. If the checksum or CRC comparison is not favorable, the sender must

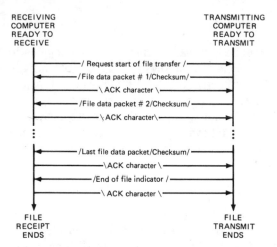

RECEIVING COMPUTER READY TO RECEIVE

TRANSMITTING COMPUTER READY TO TRANSMIT

/ Request start of file transfer /

/ File data packet # 1/Checksum/

\ ACK character \

/ File data packet # 2/Checksum/

\ ACK character\

/Last file data packet/Checksum/

\ACK character \

/End of file indicator /

\ ACK character \

FILE RECEIPT ENDS

FILE TRANSMIT ENDS

Figure 6.6 Protocol file transfer.

retransmit the bad packet of data. The file transfer protocol must repeat this process, as illustrated in Figure 6.6, until it transfers the entire file. The checksum is an easy error-detection technique to implement, but its accuracy may not be sufficient for serious communications. Most IBM PC communications software packages implement the checksum by adding the ASCII value of all the bytes in a packet, and then calculate a *modulo 255* byte from the results. The software then transmits the modulo value with the data packet as an additional byte. Figure 6.7 illustrates this process with a segment of C source code.

Because it is easy to implement in most software languages, the software on both ends of the communications link can quickly calculate the checksum in a few short steps. This translates into a low overhead for a file transfer protocol. The protocol can spend most of its time sending or receiving data and little time calculating or sending the error-detection data.

Because of its simplicity, the checksum does not provide the high degree of error detection that can be achieved through the more sophisticated CRC techniques. The sequential addition of ASCII values of data and the modulo arithmetic performed in the calculation of a checksum give it a reliability of approximately 99.6 percent. Thus, if noise on the communications link results in errors in a data packet, the checksum provides a 99.6 probability of detecting the errors.

This probability may be misleading, however, if you do not consider the actual probability of an error occurring during a communications session. When you use good-quality telephone lines where noise appears as bursts, which is the usual case with data communications through telephone lines, the probability of transmitting a file without errors with the checksum technique is greater than 99.9 percent. This level of error detection is sufficient for most hobbyist, but may not meet the stringent requirements of a business environment.

The CRC type of packet check is more reliable than the checksum and is gaining high acceptance in most asynchronous communications. The CRC technique handles

```
/*
 * makepack ()
 * make the next Xmodem packet to send with checksum error check
 *
 *Returns: TRUE if end of file encountered during read
 *         FALSE if not end of file read
 *
 */
bool makepack(foo, blockcnt)
int foo;
unsigned char blockcnt;
{
    extern unsigned char packet[134];
    extern long goodbyte;
    unsigned char sector[SECSIZE];
    int bytesget;
    int index,checksum,eoxmfile,n;

    packet[0]=SOH;                          /* here is our header */
    packet[1]=blockcnt;                     /* the block number */
    packet[2]=~blockcnt;                    /* the block number compliment */

    checksum=0;
    bytesget=read(foo,sector,128);          /* get next 128 bytes from disk*/
    goodbyte=goodbyte+(long)bytesget;       /* how many do we have total */
    if (bytesget==0) return(bytesget);      /* end of file */
    if(bytesget<128)                        /* if not enough for full packet, */
            {                               /* pad it to 128 with NULLs */
            for (index = bytesget; index<128; index++)
                    {
                    sector[index]=NULL;
                    }
            }
    for (index = 0, n = 3; index < SECSIZE; index++, n++)
            {                               /* make packet & calc checksum */
            packet [n] = sector[index];
            checksum +=packet[n];
            }

    checksum = checksum & 255;              /* get rid of excess bits */
    packet[131] = checksum;                 /* map it into packet */
    packet[132] = '\0';                     /* we need null end of string */
    return(bytesget);
}
```

Figure 6.7 Xmodem checksum calculation, C source code.

the data in a packet as a string of bits. It works on the low order bit of the first byte first and the high order bit of the last byte last. The CCITT recommends a 16-bit CRC that is the remainder after dividing the packet bit string by the polynomial $x^{16} + x^{12} + x^5 + 1$, in which the value of x is 2. A sample implementation of the CRC is shown in Figure 6.8. This technique will detect all *single-* and *double-bit errors*, all packets with an odd number of bits in error, all error bursts that are shorter than 16 bits, and 99.9 percent of error bursts that are longer than 16 bits. This level of error detection is the preferred level for serious business file transfers.

```
/* --------------------------------------------------------------------

updcrc()

updates the crc accumulator, if 'crc' is TRUE,
else updates the checksum.

'x' is the byte to be added to CRC or checksum.

CCITT polynomial used for CRC calculation.

References globals: crc;
Modifies globals: crcaccum, checksum;
---------------------------------------------      --------------------- */

void updcrc ( x )
unsigned char X;
{
        extern int crc;
        extern unsigned int crcaccum;
        extern int checksum;

        unsigned shifter, i, flag;
        if( crc )
            {
            for( shifter = 0x80 ; shifter ; shifter >> = 1 )
                {
                flag = (crcaccum & 0x8000);
                crcaccum << = 1;
                crcaccum |= ((shifter & x) ? 1 : 0);
                if( flag )
                        crcaccum ^= 0x1021;
                }
            }
        else
            checksum += (int)x;
}
```

Figure 6.8 Ymodem CRC calculation, C source code.

Asynchronous file transfer protocols have been evolving since 1977. The early ones such as the *MODEM* protocol had many limitations, but more recent vintages have become quite robust. Because of the unique features and capabilities of these protocols, we discuss some of the most popular in the following paragraphs. We also provide a comparison of these protocols later.

Xmodem Protocol

Ward Christensen developed the *Xmodem* file transfer protocol, originally called the MODEM protocol, in 1977 to facilitate error-checked file transfers between microcomputers operating under the CP/M operating system. Mr. Christensen designed and implemented the protocol during a single weekend. The MODEM protocol provided a simple and easily implemented technique to ensure near error-free transfers of text and

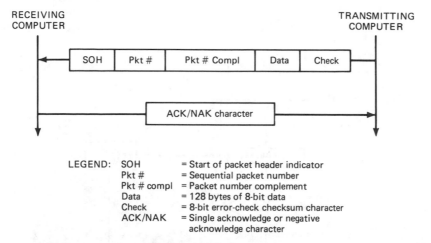

LEGEND: SOH = Start of packet header indicator
Pkt # = Sequential packet number
Pkt # compl = Packet number complement
Data = 128 bytes of 8-bit data
Check = 8-bit error-check checksum character
ACK/NAK = Single acknowledge or negative
acknowledge character

Figure 6.9 Xmodem data packet and ACK/NAK response.

binary files. The protocol did not provide a solution for all communications problems, and its weaknesses are just beginning to surface. The enhanced MODEM protocols—MODEM7, Xmodem, XmodemCRC, and Batch Xmodem—have extended the life of Ward's original design, but they share common weaknesses. Because of the widespread use of the Xmodem version of the MODEM protocol, we discuss this version in detail in the following paragraphs.

Figures that depict its operation best describe Xmodem. Figure 6.9 shows the basic elements of the protocol, including the framing and error checking performed with each

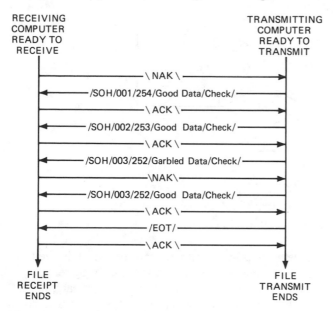

Figure 6.10 Xmodem protocol file transfer.

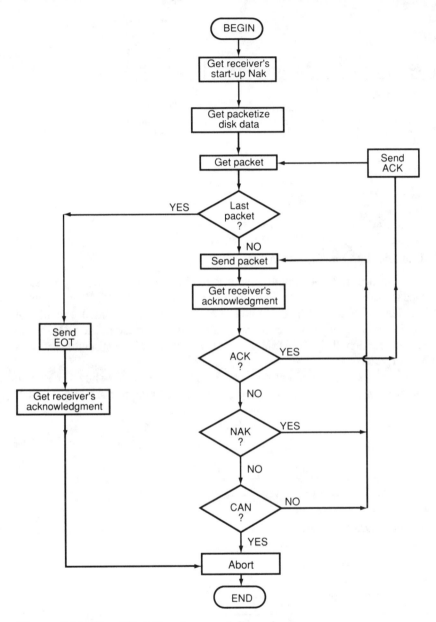

Figure 6.11 Simplified Xmodem send flow chart.

packet. Figure 6.10 shows a complete file transfer with an error occurring in the third packet. As you can see from this figure, Xmodem recovers from an error by retransmitting bad packets immediately after discovering an error. After receiving each packet, the receiver checks its contents to be sure there are no errors. If the receiver finds no errors in the packet, it tells the transmitter to send the next packet. If the receiver

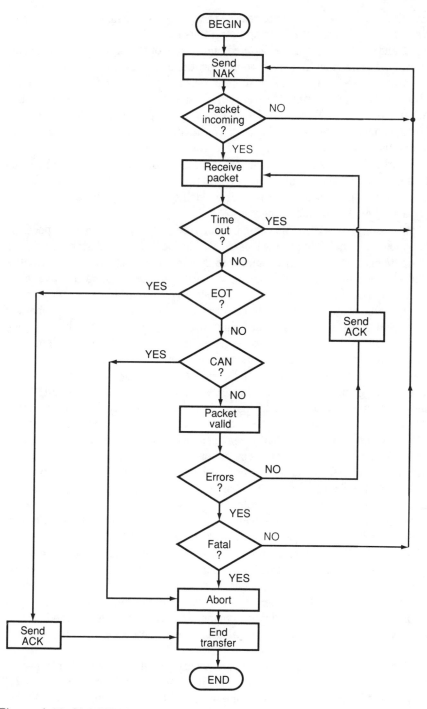

Figure 6.12 Simplified Xmodem receive flow chart.

finds an error, it tells the transmitter to resend the last packet. Xmodem can resend a single packet up to 10 times before giving up and aborting the file transfer.

Figures 6.11 and 6.12 provide more detailed indications of the signalling that occurs on the sending and receiving ends of a communications link during an Xmodem file transfer. The protocol uses the control characters described in Appendix B for protocol signalling. It uses the NAK character to start a file transfer and to indicate an error in a data packet. It uses the ACK character to indicate receipt of a good packet and to acknowledge the completion of a file transfer. The Xmodem sender uses an EOT character to signal the proper completion of a file transfer, and a CAN to abnormally terminate or abort a file transfer. Xmodem considers more than ten attempts to resend the same data packet a fatal error and aborts the file transfer. The file transfer protocol usually displays a message to indicate receipt of each of these signals, so the user is continuously aware of the transfer progress.

Xmodem, even though it is a simple design, is an excellent protocol for low-speed file transfers between Personal Computers located within local dialing distances of each other. The single-character signalling and 128-byte data packet translate into low overhead and efficient file transfers when good telephone connections are available. When telephone connections are low quality, Xmodem will often fail to properly transfer files. Xmodem also requires a full eight data bits in order to send packet numbers to the receiver, which may be a problem for some host computers. Most Personal Computers, including the IBM PC, can operate using eight data bits with no problems, but some public data networks and larger computers only operate using seven data bits.

Xmodem has been a workhorse for IBM PCs since early 1982. *Andrew Fluegelman* gave the protocol its greatest boost with IBM PCs by including it in the ubiquitous *PC-TALK* communications software. Xmodem gained further popularity from its inclusion in the *RBBS-PC* bulletin board system made available on large scale through the Capital PC User Group. Several national magazines also helped promote Xmodem as a minimum standard protocol for personal computers by publishing articles on the subject. Through these efforts and others, Xmodem has become widely used to transfer text and data files. Xmodem's past utility should not, however, blind communications users regarding the limitations of this protocol.

When Xmodem was written, the predominant hobbyist modem speed was 300 bits per second (bps) and most hobbyist communications were conducted through equipment provided by AT&T. The cost of modems has decreased remarkably since 1977, and the typical Personal Computer communication equipment now includes a modem that operates at 1200 bps or higher. As modem prices continue to fall, faster modems will reach the Personal Computer owner's budget level. One of the prices users pay for these faster modems, however, is a higher communications error rate. Xmodem was designed for low error rates and often fails at communication speeds of 2400 bps and higher.

The second change in communications that adversely affected Xmodem's performance was the arrival of low-cost alternatives to AT&T's communication services. Unfortunately, a hidden price users sometimes pay with these services is a higher communication noise level and data communications error rate than that experienced with the traditional AT&T services. The higher noise levels may only be annoying when these low-cost alternatives are used for voice communication, but they can be devastating for Xmodem file transfers.

The high communication error rates that occur at high asynchronous communication speeds and on low-quality telephone lines are difficult for Xmodem to handle. For example, line noise often causes a series of data bit errors that can pass through Xmodem undetected. Xmodem uses a simple checksum that is the sum of the ASCII values of all 128 data bytes, *modulo 255*. Simply translated, this means that multiple bit changes in a data packet caused by line noise can result in the same checksum as the original data. Thus, a packet error can occur without Xmodem detecting it and requesting a retransmission of the data.

Line noise can also alter the single character Xmodem returns from the receiving computer to acknowledge proper data transfer. Xmodem can properly send a packet, but the receiver's acknowledgment character can be altered to indicate receipt of bad data; this will result in the unnecessary retransmission of data packets. The receiver's response can also be accidentally altered by line noise to indicate abnormal termination of transfer. An ACK or NAK character can become a *Control-X* character, the Xmodem *CAN* signal to *abort* the file transfer, and terminate the transfer after much of a large file has been received—a time-consuming and frustrating experience.

There have been many enhancements added to Xmodem since 1977, but none of the changes overcome two major flaws in its design—the single character ACK/NAK response to packet transfers and the 8-data-bit communication requirement. By not providing a packet and a *packet number* for all data transmissions, enhancements such as *sliding windows* cannot be added to Xmodem. The 8 data-bit requirement precludes its use with some public data networks and large computers.

Public data networks (*PDNs*) such as Tymnet, Telenet, and Uninet sometimes create time delays during data communications that can cause problems with file transfer protocols. These communication services convert all data into packets and route the packets through ground and satellite equipment. The packet construction and routing can produce as much as a three-second delay in the receipt of an acknowledge or negative acknowledge to a file transfer protocol's data packet transmission. For a 48 kb file this could add 19 minutes to a normal six-minute file transfer when communicating at 1200 bps—a 300 percent increase in file transfer time!

Some file transfer protocols such as *BLAST* and *Kermit* get around the PDN time-delay problem by providing a *sliding window* of packets. These protocols can send data packets continuously unless a fixed maximum number of transmitted packets have not been acknowledged as properly received. This technique requires a *full-duplex* communications link because data packets are sent out simultaneous with the receipt of ACK/NAK responses from the receiving computer as shown in Figure 6.13. This technique also requires that the receiver's ACK/NAK response contain the packet number associated with the response. The sending computer must be able to determine which previously transmitted packets it has to retransmit because of errors detected by the receiving computer.

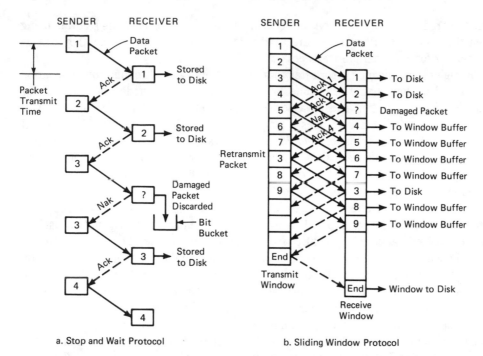

Figure 6.13 Protocol types.

Xmodem does not provide data packet numbers with its ACK/NAK responses to received data. Without this feature, Xmodem is destined to live in a *half-duplex* world where only one packet of data at a time can be transmitted; a technique sometimes referred to as *stop and wait*. The next packet can only be sent after the receiver responds to the last packet sent. Time delay caused by this half-duplex mode can be expensive and can cause protocol timeout problems that result in aborted file transfers.

Another characteristic of some PDNs that precludes the use of Xmodem is the communication parity bit. Some PDNs assume this data bit is not used and convert it into a zero or one for PDN purposes. Xmodem requires no parity and a full 8 data bits for transmission of binary data, extended ASCII characters, and its own internally generated error-checking checksum. Because of Xmodem's 8 data-bit requirement, it cannot be used with 7-bit PDNs such as Telenet.

Xmodem's 8-data-bit requirement and its 128-byte data packet size, ideal parameters for PC-to-PC communications, also preclude its use with many mainframe computers. The front-end communication processors or TTY communication ports on some large computers can only be configured for 7 data bits. Xmodem is incompatible with these machines. Other large computers, such as Honeywell, have small communication buffers and cannot accommodate the receipt of a 128-byte Xmodem packet without losing characters.

In spite of its limitations, Xmodem will remain a popular file transfer protocol throughout the 1980s. Because of its inclusion in all popular PC communications packages, Xmodem provides at least one common protocol that can be used between Personal Computers. As the need to communicate with larger computers or through PDNs becomes greater and the speed of modems continue to increase, Xmodem's popularity may wane, giving way to the other protocols discussed in the following paragraphs.

Ymodem Protocol

The *Ymodem* protocol was first introduced in 1981 as a significant enhancement to the Xmodem protocol. The protocol was developed by *Chuck Foresberg* for the *YAM* communications program originally written to run under the CP/M operating system. Chuck released this program into public domain along with the *sb* (*send batch*) and *rb* (*receive batch*) UNIX utilities that contained the same features. Aside from its robust features as a file transfer protocol, two additional attributes of Ymodem have added significantly to its acceptance in the PC community. First, it was originally written in the portable C language. Second, it was released into the public domain along with documentation showing implementation guidelines. No good PC communications software package is complete today without Ymodem.

Ymodem improves on Xmodem in two ways. First, it allows the transfer of data blocks 1024 bytes in length. This block length is almost ten times the length of Xmodem blocks, which substantially reduces the protocol overhead, allowing it to outperform Xmodem under good line quality conditions. If the line quality is not good, Ymodem automatically decreases the data block length to 128 bytes to reduce the number of bytes that have to be retransmitted each time an error is detected. Therefore, under the worst of conditions, Ymodem's block length and performance matches that of Xmodem. Second, Ymodem reduces the probability of accidental termination of a file transfer. Xmodem abnormally aborts a file transfer upon the receipt of a single Control-X bit pattern (ASCII value 024). This bit pattern can easily be created by line noise and terminate a file transfer. Ymodem requires two sequential Control-X or CAN characters before the file transfer is abnormally terminated.

Aside from reducing Xmodem's relative protocol overhead and increasing its reliability, Ymodem provides two other significant features for communications users. First, Ymodem uses the CRC error-detection technique to produce near error-free file transfers regardless of line quality. Second, Ymodem transmits file-related information to the receiving computer. The filename, file time and date stamp, and the file size are transmitted in the first block when a file transfer is started. The file size information can be used by the receiving computer to display the relative portion of the file that has been received at any point during the transfer; the file time and date information can be used to preserve the original file time and date stamp for archive purposes.

The final advantage of Ymodem compared to the Xmodem protocol is its *batch file transfer* feature. There have been several batch modes added to the MODEM and Xmodem protocol over the years, the most popular of which is in the *MODEM7* protocol, but none of these implementations have survived in the PC community. The batch capability of Ymodem has survived and offers an advantage when several files must be transferred between two computers. PC-DOS wild card and full pathname characters can be used in a filename to select a group of files for transfer to a PC-DOS, MS-DOS, CP/M, UNIX, or XENIX computer equipped with Ymodem software. The files will be automatically transferred one at a time and the original time and date stamp of each file preserved. This technique can be used as a "poor man's" file backup system when another remote computer is available with sufficient disk space to handle file storage.

Unfortunately, Ymodem suffers from some of the same limitations associated with its parent protocol, Xmodem. Ymodem requires a full 8 data bits as a communications parameter, which precludes its use with some computer systems. Ymodem also uses the stop-and-wait technique of sending a data packet, then waiting for a *positive acknowledgment* before sending the next packet. This technique is not a problem for *point-to-point communications* because Ymodem uses low protocol overhead relative to the size of its data packets. For file transfers that go through satellite links or public data networks, the time delay required to receive the acknowledge signal for each packet sent by the remote computer can add substantial time to the total file transfer period. These Ymodem limitations are overcome in the popular Kermit protocol.

Kermit Protocol

The *Kermit* file transfer protocol was designed by *Frank da Cruz* and *Bill Catchings* at Columbia University in 1981. The university had a variety of computers, including IBM mainframes, DEC minicomputers, and microcomputers made by several vendors, but university personnel could not easily move files from one type of machine to another. Improper translations of characters sometimes occurred with text files, and binary files either caused problems with the communication equipment or could not be transferred because of communication equipment limitations. Necessity became the mother of invention.

Frank da Cruz and Bill Catchings set out to design and implement a file transfer protocol that would allow any type of computer to properly receive a file sent by another type of computer. The protocol they devised became known as Kermit, a name taken from Jim Henson's famous green frog. The protocol design was based on the International Standards Organization recommendations in the Open System Interconnection model and has become available for a large variety of computers. Columbia University maintains a library of all tested and verified versions of the protocol, including many versions called "remote" Kermit that can run unattended on a host for smart-terminal access.

Kermit has been available for microcomputers since its origin and became popular with the IBM PC as the result of work done by Jan van der Eijk. A PC version of the protocol was implemented in a program called MSKERMIT in 1982. This implementation was written in assembly language and is still used in many universities and government organizations, but it does not contain the "user-friendly" interface that has been added by other vendors. Jan van der Eijk, with the assistance of William Little and his staff at The SOURCE, developed a version of the protocol in the C language in 1985 and made that version available to IBM communications software vendors on a large scale at no cost. The vendors of several popular, smart-terminal software packages have used or emulated this implementation to make it available to their users. The authors of the ProComm software used the C version developed by Mr. van der Eijk and have added significantly to Kermit's popularity because of the widespread use of the ProComm software. Jan van der Eijk's version of Kermit is also included in many unattended communications packages available for the IBM PC, including the TCOMM software coauthored by Mr. van der Eijk.

The Kermit protocol, developed by Frank da Cruz and Bill Catchings, and implemented for the IBM PC by Jan van der Eijk and others, is similar in many ways to the Xmodem protocol. The differences between Kermit and Xmodem, however, give Kermit more growth potential and allow more flexible implementations. Kermit also has capabilities that allow its use in situations that preclude the use of Xmodem.

Kermit is an excellent protocol for file transfers between dissimilar computers, for high-speed file transfers, for file transfers over long distances, and for the transfer of file groups. As you can see from Figure 6.14, Kermit has many optional features in addition to full packets with error checking for both data and ACK/NAK response data. Unfortunately, Kermit's features and flexibility add overhead to the protocol that may be undesirable under some circumstances. For direct-dial communications at speeds under 2400 bps between microcomputers made by the same vendor, Kermit's power is wasted. A protocol such as Xmodem can be ten to 40 percent more efficient under these circumstances. Kermit's power is unleashed, however, in business, government, and educational institutions where a variety of computers must communicate.

One of the capabilities that gives Kermit its power is the *feature negotiation* it performs each time a file is transferred. This "binding" process is accomplished by the exchange of *send-initiate* packets between the two communicating computers. As shown in the protocol diagram in Figure 6.15 and in the flow chart in Figure 6.16, the sending computer transmits its send-initiate packet to the receiving computer. The receiver acknowledges proper receipt of the packet and sends its own send-initiate packet along with the acknowledgment. The two computers then compare these packets and select, for the transfer of one or more files, the features that both computers can support. This send-initiate packet exchange allows any Kermit implementation to communicate with any other Kermit implementation. The transfer-by-transfer renegotiation also allows the computer operator on either end of the link to alter parameters such as packet size to optimize communication throughput based on the specific circumstances at hand.

One of the features two Kermits negotiate is the method of packet error-checking. Kermit supports three techniques: a 6-bit checksum, a 12-bit checksum, and a CRC-16. The communication overhead of each of these techniques increases with its degree of error-detection capability. The *6-bit checksum* adds one byte to each packet and is calculated the same way the Xmodem checksum is calculated. This technique is acceptable for good-quality telephone connections at speeds under 2400 bps. The *12-bit checksum* adds two bytes to each packet and is somewhat better than the single byte Xmodem checksum. This technique is better for low-quality telephone connections or high-speed communications. The *CRC-16* is based on the international CCITT recommendations and adds three bytes to each data packet. The CRC-16 technique is far superior to either the 6-bit or 12-bit checksum

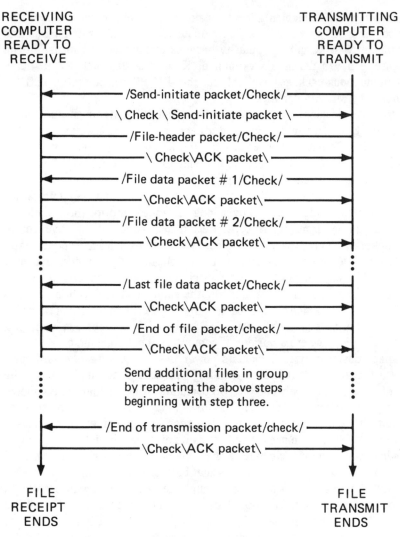

Figure 6.14 Kermit data and ACK/NAK packets.

technique and is ideal for low-quality telephone connects or high-speed communications. The CRC-16 provides almost 100 percent error detection and is good for financial data transactions. The price users pay for this level of integrity is the time required to calculate the CRC-16 and the three bytes it adds to each packet.

Aside from its error-detection power, Kermit provides three features that endear it to many users. First, Kermit can communicate through both 7-bit and 8-bit data ports, regardless of the communication hardware employed. Second, Kermit can move groups of files without interruption. Finally, Kermit is designed to facilitate the addition of new capabilities as communication needs change.

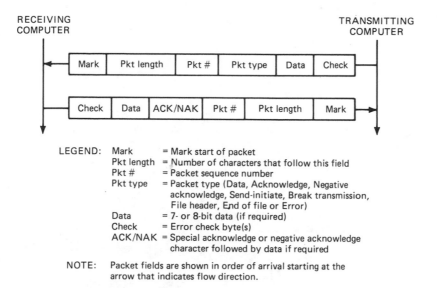

LEGEND: Mark   = Mark start of packet
Pkt length = Number of characters that follow this field
Pkt #   = Packet sequence number
Pkt type   = Packet type (Data, Acknowledge, Negative
acknowledge, Send-initiate, Break transmission,
File header, End of file or Error)
Data   = 7- or 8-bit data (if required)
Check   = Error check byte(s)
ACK/NAK = Special acknowledge or negative acknowledge
character followed by data if required

NOTE: Packet fields are shown in order of arrival starting at the
arrow that indicates flow direction.

Figure 6.15 Kermit protocol file transfer.

Kermit can transmit both text and binary files, but it converts all data into text during the transfer. During the design of Kermit, its authors discovered that some control characters (ASCII values 0-32) cannot pass through certain communication equipment without causing undesirable results. These characters were either modified by the communication equipment or caused side effects such as printer initiation. Kermit's authors also discovered that some communication equipment did not allow the eighth data bit in a byte to be used for data—the bit either had to be used for parity error detection or was converted to a one or a zero. To pass compiled programs and extended ASCII characters such as the PC-DOS 8-bit graphic characters through this equipment, the data in each byte had to be reduced from 8 bits to 7 bits.

To overcome the control character and 7-bit data limitations, Frank da Cruz and Bill Catchings added *control character conversion* and *8th-bit prefixing* to their protocol. The control character conversion is always performed by Kermit and adds to the protocol's overhead. The eighth-bit prefixing converts all 8-bit data bytes into two 7-bit bytes, but this is an optional feature and only adds to the protocol's overhead when two computers cannot communicate using a full 8 data bits.

Kermit's *file-group transfer* capability saves communication and user time. This optional *wild card* feature allows the user to transfer all files with common filename characters by executing one command. For example, the user can enter the command SEND *.EXE to archive on a remote host all files that are of the EXE type. This feature allows the same send-initiate negotiation to apply to several files, and it allows Kermit to transfer the files without additional user input. File group transfer reduces communication packet overhead and frees the computer user to perform other tasks while the files are transferring between computers.

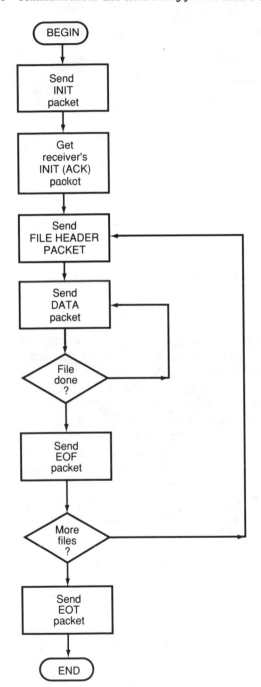

Figure 6.16 Kermit file transfer flow chart.

Kermit can agree to perform special file transfer capabilities during its send-initiate negotiation. Two special capabilities are file attribute transfers and sliding windows. The *file attribute* capability allows Kermit to send up to 94 file characteristics along with the file, including file modification time/date and file size. The receiving Kermit can use these attributes to display file transfer progress or to ensure that the file's time/date stamp is preserved. The *sliding windows* capability, developed by Jan van der Eijk in conjunction with The SOURCE, allows Kermit to take advantage of full-duplex satellite and PDN communication links to expedite file transfers. The sliding windows, along with Kermit's ability to perform repeat character *data compression*, can result in substantial throughput improvements over half-duplex protocols such as Xmodem and Ymodem.

Beyond features and capabilities discussed here, Kermit's developers have added many options that allow the protocol to perform in spite of its environment. The user is allowed to select such items as communications flow control, timeout durations, a special eighth-bit prefixing character, a packet termination character, and others. These features have been added by Columbia University as well as other educational and business institutions. With each new release, Kermit comes closer to achieving its design objective of providing one low-cost protocol that will facilitate file transfers between any two computers.

Future Protocol Directions

Xmodem, Ymodem, and Kermit, in spite of their capabilities to ensure error-free file transfers, as shown in Figure 6.17, do nothing to improve the quality of normal interactive communications with remote computers. Many communication enthusiasts have been chagrined to discover that logging into and writing messages on a remote computer when connected at 2400 bps is sometimes difficult. Greek and math symbols suddenly appear on the screen or get sent to the remote computer. These special symbols are caused by communication-line noise, and the only way to get rid of this noise with asynchronous communications is to use error-checking for all interactions between the two computers.

Continuous Error Detection and Correction

As modem speeds increase and the competition between public telephone service companies increase, the reliability of telephone systems to support data communications decreases, thereby requiring greater support for error detection and correction. The only way to ensure near error-free interactions between two computers is to provide *continuous error detection and correction* between the computers. Two contenders, Tymnet and Microcom, have emerged in asynchronous communications to provide the kind of continuous quality communications that is standard in synchronous communications. Because of the significant differences between the techniques used by these two vendors, the two techniques are discussed individually in the following paragraphs.

	Xmodem	Ymodem	Kermit
Types of File Transfer			
Single file	yes	yes	yes
Multiple files (wildcard)	no	yes	yes
Text	yes	yes	yes
Data	yes	yes	yes
Binary	yes	yes	yes
Required Data Bits	8	8	7 or 8
Error-Checking			
Checksum	yes	yes	yes
CCITT CRC-16	no	yes	yes
Error-Checking Response			
Single character	yes	yes	no
Error-checked packet	no	no	yes
Data Packet size (bytes)	128	128 or 1024	0–94
Data Compression	no	no	yes
File Attribute Transfer			
File size	no	yes	yes
Time/Date stamp	no	yes	yes
Sliding Window Support			
Single packet	yes	yes	yes
Multiple packets	no	no	1–16
Negotiated Parameters			
Packet size	no	yes	yes
Packets in window	no	no	yes
Error-check type	no	yes	yes
Data compression	no	no	yes
Xon/Xoff Flow Control	no	no	yes

Figure 6.17 Asynchronous communication protocol features.

Microcom Networking Protocol

The *Microcom Networking Protocol* (*MNP*) was originally developed by Microcom, Inc. to ensure error-free communications between the company's 1200 bps modems but has emerged as a near standard for continuous line quality assurance between modems. Although MNP may be implemented in either software or hardware, the protocol operates most efficiently when placed in a modem's *firmware*. The software or hardware implementation of this protocol also determines its supported features.

The original versions of MNP included in Microcom's modems and in the IBM Personal Communications Manager software were called the *Reliable Link Protocol* and were proprietary. A modem or software vendor could include the protocol in a product only after paying Microcom a $2,000 license fee. A few vendors paid the fee but only for the opportunity to study the protocol. The protocol did not gain popularity until asynchronous 2400 bps modems were introduced on a large scale, and Microcom released the lower three levels of MNP into public domain. The increased error rate experienced by vendors of the new 2400 bps modems drove them to investigate different forms of continuous error detection and correction. Since MNP was originally designed to be placed in modem firmware, it was a natural for modems made by other vendors. The elimination of the license fee for the lower levels also made MNP attractive.

When implemented in a modem's firmware, MNP provides an automatic throughput gain by turning an *asynchronous data stream* into the equivalent of a *synchronous data stream*. When the modems at both ends of the link support MNP, the protocol strips off the asynchronous start and stop bits associated with each data byte and forms packets of continuous data. Each packet includes the powerful CRC error-detection block check. The receiving modem disassembles the data packets and requests retransmission of damaged packets. Because of the elimination of start and stop bits, the total protocol overhead produced by MNP is less than the original start/stop bit overhead. For every 8 data bits, asynchronous communications adds one start bit and at least one stop bit; these synchronizing bits reduce total line throughput by 20 percent. The MNP protocol adds back 11 percent as synchronizing and error-checking bits for a net decrease of nine percent compared to the original asynchronous data stream. The resulting data stream is functionally like the popular SDLC and HDLC synchronous protocols described in Chapter 2.

The second advantage of MNP is its full-duplex sliding-windows capability. When communicating through a satellite link or a public data network, signal propagation delays and data routing sometimes cause significant data communications delays. MNP eliminates these delays by transmitting up to eight data packets before an acknowledgment for any of the eight is required. By continuously sending packets without waiting for acknowledgment of each before transmitting the next, MNP overcomes most of the time delays associated with slow networks or data links. Only under extremely slow data link conditions does MNP reach the limit of eight unacknowledged packets and have to stop and wait for an acknowledgment to return.

MNP offers a robust *'go back n'* method of error correction that enhances its sliding windows method of transmitting packets. When the receiver detects an error in a packet, say packet number n + 1, a message is returned to the sender indicating that an error occurred in that packet. When the error message is received, the sender goes back to packet n and starts resending data with the next packet beyond n. This 'go back n' technique sometimes require the retransmission of more packets to correct an error than the *selectively repeat* type of bad packet retransmission used in the Kermit sliding windows protocol, but the technique is easier to implement in firmware.

Beyond data packet transmission and error correction, MNP provides the necessary *handshaking* required to transmit files and preclude the storing of extraneous data with the files. The file transfer mechanism builds on the continuous error checking and error correction provided by MNP by opening a file and sending its contents from the sender and by opening a file and storing received data at the receiver. MNP also closes the file at the receiver when the entire contents of the file has been properly received and stored.

Because of the layered approach followed by Microcom in the design of MNP and its ease of implementation in firmware, many 2400-bps modem vendors now offer the MNP protocol as either a standard or as an optional feature. If MNP is included in a modem at one end of the link but not in the modem at the other end, the modems communicate using standard asynchronous techniques. If MNP is implemented in the modems at both ends of the link, the modems perform a *switch to sync* and use the MNP data stream design continuously throughout the session. This continuous error-correction approach has proven effective at 2400 bps but is of even greater importance for asynchronous data rates above 2400 bps.

X.PC Protocol

The *X.PC protocol* was developed by *Tymnet* to enhance the interface of microcomputers to its X.25 public data network. The high quality of the X.PC documentation, the portability of its original C source code, and its early release into public domain have created a niche for this robust protocol that will last well into the 1990s. Although X.PC may be implemented in either software or hardware, the protocol offers the greatest potential when implemented in software.

To provide microcomputers with greater access to the myriad of hosts attached to its X.25 public data network, Tymnet performed a study of asynchronous protocols that could be used on dial-up telephone connections to its network and provide reliable communications. After a comprehensive study of available protocols, Tymnet decided to write a new protocol based on the CCITT recommendation for PDNs. By using the X.25 design, described in detail later in Chapter 7, and trimming it down to the bare essentials required for microcomputer application, Tymnet was able to achieve complete functional compatibility with X.25.

Tymnet introduced the specifications and source code for X.PC in mid-1983 with the goal of having hardware and software vendors implement the protocol in their products. Several popular software vendors, including Microsoft and Microstuf, have since incorporated X.PC into their communications software.

X.PC offers many of the features found in the MNP protocol plus some extra networking benefits. First, X.PC converts all transmitted data into packets that contain the powerful CRC error detection technique. Second, X.PC uses a sliding window design similar to that used in MNP, including the "go back n" technique of correcting bad packets. The advantage provided by X.PC, however, is its close match with the X.25 network characteristics discussed in Chapter 7. The X.PC data packets contain *destination addresses* that allow an X.PC-equipped PC to establish and maintain up to 15 separate communications sessions with one or more host computers. With the proper windowing application software built around X.PC, a user can "hot key" between multiple, simultaneous host sessions to expedite tasks being performed by the host sessions. After a task is initiated in one session, the user can switch to another session to carry on other work until the first task is completed.

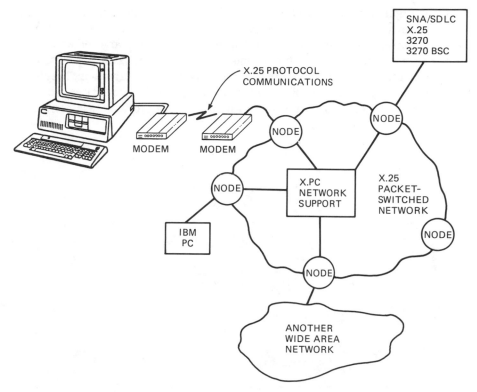

Figure 6.18 X.PC Network Support.

Tymnet offers X.25 connectivity support for X.PC through software called *X.PC Network Support*. As shown in Figure 6.18, this X.PC support allows the X.PC user to communicate with hosts that are equipped with IBM's *Binary Synchronous Control* (*BSC*), IBM's *Synchronous Data Link Control/System Network Architecture* (*SDLC/SNA*), or another X.25 network. The X.PC Network Support performs all data stream and protocol translations required to make the connections to all its host computers painless for the X.PC user. The IBM wide area network functions and capabilities that are made possible through this connectivity are explored in the next chapter.

Tymnet offers X.PC connectivity from over 500 cities. Over 10,000 asynchronous, dial-up ports ensure full and readily available access for many X.PC users. This availability and support from Tymnet should ensure a long future for X.PC.

Error Checking and File Transfer Summary

As you can see from the discussion of error checking and file transfer in this chapter, there are many options available to the PC user to ensure near error-free transfer of data. These techniques range from the simple parity error detection that we have inherited from the old teletype terminals to built-in error checking and correction at the modem hardware level. There are even options for error detection and correction combined with multiple communications sessions with remote computers. With all these asynchronous techniques available, however, there are still elements that are required in large organizations that are not provided in this technology. Large organizations, with hundreds or thousands of terminals and personal computers tied to host computers all over the world, need more than error detection and correction. They need powerful management and control of the networks that connect these devices. The next chapter provides the details of two wide area networks that provide these services.

7

Wide Area Network Architectures

Wide area networks combine the continuous error-detection and corrections techniques included in synchronous communications with robust network *problem determination* and *data routing* to form powerful *backbones* that ensure high-quality, reliable service for end users. These networks allow multiple users to access a variety of host computers simultaneously through the same physical medium, while separating each user's session such that no user is aware of another on the network. Wide area networks also operate at speeds much higher than the 9600 bps limit of normal, voice-grade telephone lines.

The most widely used *wide area networks (WAN)* are designed on the basis of well-defined layers. These layers allow certain functions to be performed to support network activity independent of the functions performed in other layers. The classic analogy used to explain network layers is human dialogue. During a conversation between two people there are three distinctive levels or layers that make communication possible: cognitive, language, and transmission.

The *cognitive level* in a dialogue requires that both parties understand the concept to be discussed. Both parties do not have to have the same degree of understanding of the concept, but at least a fundamental understanding of the concept must exist at both ends of the communications when the conversation starts. For example, when a computer user calls a software hotline to solve a software-related problem, the help desk person should be an expert in the use of the software in question. The user making the call, on the other hand, is not expected to have the software knowledge that exists at the help desk; this user must be able to understand the software well enough to explain the problem to the help desk person. The expertise at the help desk cannot solve the end user's problem without the existence of some fundamental knowledge of the computer and software on the end user's part.

The *language level* of a dialogue is concerned with the words used to convey information—not the information itself. In the help desk example, both the help desk operator and the end user may possess the fundamental understanding of the computer and software that is not working properly, but unless both parties are able to speak the same language, the problem cannot be solved. The solution to a problem spoken in German, regardless of how well explained, will mean nothing to an end user who only speaks English.

Finally, the *transmission level* of a dialogue is concerned with the physical means of conveying information between two parties. At this level, the most appropriate physical technique is selected to effectively convey the information in a timely manner. In the help desk case, it makes sense to have end users communicate with the help desk operator by telephone if the help desk is separated from the end user location by a significant distance. During the training of end users, on the other hand, the physical medium selected might be direct exposure to the speaker combined with overhead projection of figures or text.

As shown in the last three paragraphs, there are two fundamental concepts that make a conversation produce the desired results. First, each of the three layers is *independent* of the other. Each layer depends upon at least one of the other layers to be effective, but the contents of each layer is independent of the other. For a conversation to take place, a language must be spoken and the words must be conveyed between the parties, but the language chosen for the conversation does not affect the selection of the physical medium that transports the words. Second, both parties must agree in advance as to the contents of each of the three layers. This agreement on the contents of each layer, with the underlying rules for the use of these contents, are referred to as *layer protocols*. These protocols are the interactions or handshaking that takes place between layers that produce the "glue" that makes the entire process work to the satisfaction of both parties.

Network Layers

Just as conversations between two people require well-defined layers and protocols that bind the layers into an effective mechanism to convey information, computer networks must contain well-defined layers and *inter-layer protocols* to control the interactions between two computers or between work stations and a computer. The layer model frequently referenced by software vendors and used in network product design is the *Open Systems Interconnection (OSI)* model shown in Figure 7.1. This model, often called the *Reference Model*, was developed by the *International Standards Organization (ISO)*. The OSI model was developed to standardize the procedures for the exchange of information between processing systems.

The word *system* used in Open Systems Architecture is not intended to imply a large computer network, but the concept is used here to explain the inner workings of a theoretical network before specific WANs are discussed. An understanding of the

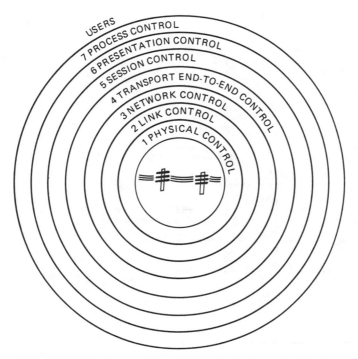

Figure 7.1 The International Standards Organization's seven layers of control for open systems.

model should provide a good background for understanding the X.25 and System Network Architecture networks described later in this chapter.

OSI Model

The ISO working groups have defined seven specific layers for the *Reference Model for Open Systems Interconnection*. These layers begin at the Application Layer, where end users interact with a system or where application software is executed and progress to the Physical Layer where logical information is converted into signals that are transported through physical media such as telephone wire.

Although the Reference Model defines the interconnection of Open Systems, the Model assumes these systems are composed of a structure of *subsystems*. As shown in Figure 7.2, each layer in each system is contained in a subsystem. Each of these subsystems contain *entities* that provide services for a subsystem of higher rank in the model. All the network-support entities in a subsystem together form a *layer* in the model. *Peer-to-peer communications* between the entities in a given layer are done in accordance with specific rules defined by OSI as protocols. Entities in one layer communicate with entities in another layer through well-defined *service-access points* using specific *interface protocols*.

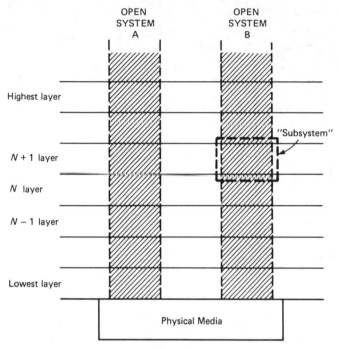

Figure 7.2 Open systems layering.

The Reference Model further defines the connections between layers and types of data that pass through these connections. The entities in a layer have *unique addresses* and communicate with entities in adjacent layers through *service-access-point connections*. Normal and expedited data and network control information are routed between entities through the service-access points. *Expedited service data* may be delivered across a connection before *normal data* that were sent earlier than the expedited data. The expedited data are never delivered later than normal data sent later than the expedited data. This interconnection of entities between layers and *priority routing* of data and control information form a complete network capable of tight control of information transfer using the layers described in the following paragraphs.

Physical Layer

The *Physical Layer* is the lowest Reference Model layer and the one that interfaces directly with the *physical media*. This layer is defined to support *point-to-point* connection of two devices or *multipoint* connection of several devices, all of which can communicate with at least one of the devices attached to a multipoint line. The Physical Layer is also defined to support both half- and full-duplex communications through either serial or parallel data paths.

The Physical Layer governs four basic areas of physical media connectivity. First, the mechanical characteristics of communication device interfaces are defined in this layer. Second, the Physical Layer governs the electrical signal design used to convey data. Third, the functional logic of electrical signals generated on certain wires in the physical media is specified in this layer. Finally, the Physical Layer defines the procedures or protocol that govern the sequence of events that must occur in order for the physical media to properly support the communications between two open systems.

CCITT Recommendation X.21 is the most important standard that has been written to control the Physical Layer. The title of this standard is "General-purpose interface between DTE and DCE for synchronous operation on Public Data Networks." This recommendation describes the interface required to operate a terminal or a microcomputer using synchronous mode of communications to transmit or receive data through a public data network such as Telenet or Tymnet.

Data Link Layer

The *Data Link Layer* provides the kinds of services for synchronous communications in an Open System Network that continuous error detection and correction protocols provide for asynchronous communications. This layer defines the protocol that detects and corrects errors that occur during data transfer through the physical media. The Data Link Layer is responsible for dividing transmitted data into *packets* or *frames* that include frame check information such as the CRC-16 discussed earlier in this chapter. This layer must also ensure that data are made *transparent* to all communications devices such that all data pass through the network unaltered by the network and without producing side effects in the network.

Error correction and frame sequencing are important features of the Data Link Layer. When errors are detected in received frames, this layer provides the request for retransmission of the bad frame. The Data Link Layer must also ensure that data are delivered to the receiver in the same sequence in which it was transmitted. This layer also provides *flow control* to keep bottlenecks from developing and frames from accumulating in the Open System.

The ISO standard *High-level Data Link Control (HDLC)* discussed in Chapter 2 is the most important standard for the Data Link Layer. This *bit-oriented protocol* is replacing the less sophisticated byte-oriented protocols such as IBM's Binary Synchronous Communications (BSC) protocol.

Network Layer

The *Network Layer* handles the routing functions for data transferred between two open systems. This layer provides the *addressing* necessary to relay data through intermediate nodes or systems that provide the connectivity between nonadjacent open systems. The Network Layer ensures that Data Link Layer frames are not lost when the frames traverse adjacent networks.

The Network Layer is the highest OSI level supported by some communication networks. As discussed later in this chapter, the PDNs that are based on CCITT Recommendation X.25 only support the first three OSI layers with the Network Layer the highest layer provided.

Transport Layer

The *Transport Layer* of the Reference Model is responsible for maintaining a specific class of service for the user and for optimizing the resources that connect the two open systems. The Transport Layer establishes transport connections between *session entities* contained in two open systems. Once a *class of service* such as batch or interactive is selected, the Transport Layer establishes this service by setting up the necessary *transport connection*. After the selected class of service is established, the Transport Layer is responsible for maintaining the service or notifying the session-entities if sufficient resources are not available to maintain the class of service.

The Transport Layer provides communications flow control beyond the frame-level control provided in the Data Link Layer. To prevent congestion in a network, this layer will *segment data* or *block data* to respectively form smaller or larger packets, thereby levelizing the flow of data between session entities.

Session Layer

The *Session Layer* of the Reference Model provides support for *session connections* between open systems. This layer manages the dialogue between systems and is dependent upon the Transport Layer in the sense that each session connection is handled by one and only one *transport connection*. Several session connections can use one transport connection sequentially, but not simultaneously. The Reference Model does, however, allow a transport session to be terminated and another initiated to overcome problems in a network—an action that might be required in order to maintain a specific class of service for a user. The Session Layer is designed to shield the higher layers from these changes in connection at lower layers.

The Session Layer manages the dialogue between two open systems to ensure that data arrive at both ends of the link in a form that is meaningful to the applications operating at these ends. These services include controlling the two-way flow of data and synchronizing the data interchange between the open systems. Beyond these services the Reference Model allows the definition of further extensions to the Session Layer, some of which have been defined and implemented in the architectures discussed later in this chapter.

Presentation Layer

The *Presentation Layer* is responsible for controlling the syntax of data originated by two open systems and the transformation of data as they pass between these systems to ensure that the exchange of data is *meaningful* to both systems. This layer negotiates the data syntax to be used at the start of a *presentation connection* between the two systems and renegotiates a change in *syntax* if one is requested or required during the connection. For example, one system may operate using the ASCII character code, whereas the other system may use EBCDIC. If the syntax of the two systems are different, the Presentation Layer must translate the data as they pass in both directions. In the example just used, the Presentation Layer would have to provide ASCII-to-

EBCDIC conversion in one direction and EBCDIC-to-ASCII conversion in the other direction.

The Presentation Layer is further responsible for *formatting data* to ensure proper output for specific devices. The mapping of screen display attributes from one system to another are handled by this layer. For example, a host application that is written for IBM 3270 terminal display must have its output reformatted if the second open system used to access this application is not an IBM 3270 terminal. The reformatting of output for an IBM PC monitor when the PC is used to emulate a specific terminal type is another example of a Presentation Layer task.

Application Layer

The *Application Layer* is the highest defined OSI level. This layer contains *application entities* that control application processes through interactions called *Application Layer Protocols*. Even though the term application is used, this layer controls operating system functions as well as application processing and end-user interaction. The interaction between PC-DOS and batch files fall into this category. In an application such as a store point-of-sale system, the interaction between the sales and the inventory portions of the software also fall into this category.

The Application Layer Protocols used in the Application Layer are normally classified in five categories or groups. The groups are:

Group 1　System management protocols
Group 2　Application management protocols
Group 3　System protocols
Group 4　Industry specific protocols
Group 5　Enterprise specific protocols

As these titles imply, the protocols range from *horizontal significance*, such as PC-DOS and its internal and external features, to *vertical significance*, such as a dBase accounting system and its combination of data and program files. The span is from national or international significance to industry significance and finally to individual store or company significance.

Reference Model Conclusion

The material presented in the above paragraphs provides the reader with an overview of the Reference Model of Open Systems Interconnection. An understanding of this model and the layer concept of communication systems aids in the understanding of specific network implementations such as CCITT X.25 or IBM System Network Architecture. Specific network architectures may not follow exactly the recommendations contained in the Reference Model, but many of the functions contained in the model may be included in these architectures.

Packet-switched Networks

The *CCITT Recommendation X.25 Level 3* is a protocol used in several popular *value added networks (VANs)* or *public data networks (PDNs)*. Tymnet and Telenet use this protocol to provide their users with near error-free communications between *data terminal equipment (DTE)*, computers or terminals, often located hundreds or thousands of miles apart. Although most people refer to these VANs and PDNs as X.25 networks, the complete end-to-end connection between a terminal and a host or between two computers may involve capabilities derived from at least three other CCITT Recommendations: X.3, X.28, and X.29.

X.25 Networks

X.25 describes the requirements for attaching a packet terminal to a packet-switched network (PSN) at three levels as shown in Figure 7.3. First, the *Physical Level* describes the interface with the physical media. Second, the *Link Level* is described as a subset of the *High Level Data Link Control (HDLC)* discussed in Chapter 2. Third, the *Packet Level* describes the protocol for data transport through a PSN.

The Physical Level of X.25 describes the connectors and wires required for connecting to and sending data bits to synchronous *data circuit-terminating equipment (DCE)* that interfaces with the PSN. This level is the same as the ISO Reference Model. Its primary functions are to perform synchronization and pass data and control signals between DTEs in the form of a user terminal or a computer and the DCE, which is normally a synchronous modem. The CCITT Recommendation that describes this digital interface is *X.21*.

The Link Level of X.25 describes the data framing technique used to carry data through the PSN. As described in Chapter 2, HDLC contains CRC-16 frame check sequences that are used for error detection. Header and trailer information is used to ensure correct routing of the data through the PSN.

The Network Level of X.25 describes the types and formats of packets used to set up X.25 connections (called *Virtual Calls*), send data over virtual circuits, control the flow of packets, and recover from failures. Since the first two levels have been discussed in detail earlier, the following paragraphs concentrate on the details of level 3.

Connections Through X.25

X.25 provides support for continuous, as well as temporary, associations between two DTEs connected to the PSN. A *Permanent Virtual Circuit (PVC)* may exist between two DTEs that require no set up. This type of circuit is typical of a leased-line connection between two DTEs that does not require a telephone call each time the DTEs need to communicate. A *Virtual Call (VC)* may also be set up between two DTEs, but this type of connection is temporary and requires a set-up procedure for each connection call and a special clearing procedure to be sure communications are properly established between the DTEs. Regardless of the type of virtual circuit, however, the X.25

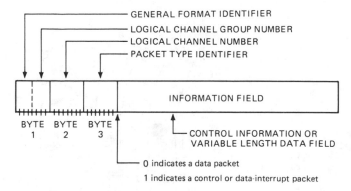

Figure 7.3 X.25 levels.

protocol must ensure that data are delivered to the recipient in the same order it was transmitted to the PSN. A typical array of X.25 virtual circuits is shown in Figure 7.4.

One of X.25's most powerful features is the ability to maintain multiple-user sessions over a single physical connection to the network. Each user session is assigned a *Logical Channel Group Number* and a *Logical Channel Number*. PVCs are assigned a *permanent Logical Channel Number*, whereas VCs are assigned Logical Channel Numbers when a call is set up. The Logical Channel Number and Logical Channel Group Number are included inside each HDLC frame delivered to the PSN as shown in Figure 7.5. The numbers allow both network equipment as well as user equipment to identify the

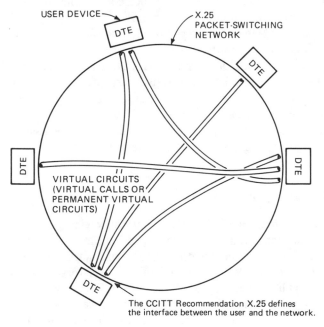

Figure 7.4 X.25 virtual circuits.

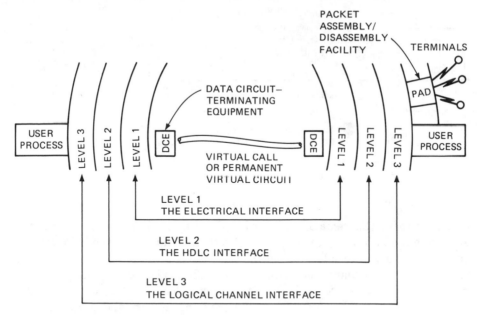

Figure 7.5 X.25 Network interface options.

source and destination of packets. Thus, more than one *Virtual Circuit* can exist over the same physical connection to the X.25 PSN because the user terminal or computer can separate sent and received HDLC frames based on the Logical Channel Number and Logical Channel Group Number contained in these frames.

An optional X.25 feature allows a PSN to be set up to provide two *classes of service*. The two classes are *high priority* and *normal priority*. A user's computer would normally select high priority for keyboard interaction with a remote host in order to achieve the best response time through the network. High-priority frames are processed before normal-priority frames. A user's computer or terminal, on the other hand, would select normal-priority processing for batch operations that can be processed overnight or without user interaction. This dual class of service and the pricing structure usually associated with it allow the user to pay a premium for better response time and keep cost down for slower operations.

X.25 Data and Information Packets

All data and information routed through an X.25 network are subdivided into discrete packets. Although X.25 recommends a maximum data field length of 128 bytes, the same as an asynchronous Xmodem data field length, options exist that allow sizes of 16, 32, 64, 256, 512, and 1024 bytes. At subscription time, a user organization selects a specific packet size that will be used with the PSN, but the PSN may have to *segment* large packets into smaller ones to match capabilities of the receiving DTE. If the receiving DTE is a dumb terminal with a 64-byte receive buffer limit, the PSN would have to segment packets larger than 64 bytes into 64-byte packets. The packet sequence numbers and a *more-data flag*, used to indicate *split packets*, allow the PSN to match the packet-size requirements of specific DTEs.

X.25 provides a robust flow control technique that is similar to the scheme used in the X.PC and MNP asynchronous protocols. Each X.25 packet contains a *sequence number* in an area of the packet called the *Packet Header. Send Sequence Numbers, P(s)* and *Receive Sequence Numbers, P(r)* are used for packet sequence verification and for packet flow control. A *sliding window* is set up between the DTEs that allow the sending of packets without immediate acknowledgment of proper receipt. The packet sequence numbers provide the identification needed to operate the window and ensure the proper sequencing of received packets. Packets received that are outside the present packet sequence number range are discarded. The receiving DTE will request retransmission of packets that are missing in the window sequence range and inhibiting the sliding of the window to a new range. This full-duplex flow control allows simultaneous, bidirectional flow of packets and prevents bottlenecks that could occur when packets are lost or damaged on a communications line.

To enhance response to special user requests, X.25 provides an *interrupt packet*. When this packet type is generated at a user's DTE, the packet is given high priority through the network. Although this packet can carry data to the remote DTE, it is normally used only for control purposes. An example of an interrupt packet would be the type of packet generated when a user wishes to abnormally terminate host processing and presses the keyboard break key. A user normally expects fast response to this action and a high-priority processing of the signal is appropriate.

An X.25 network further provides two mechanisms that support problem recovery. First, a *reset* capability allows a virtual circuit to be reinitialized without breaking the connection between the two communicating DTEs. This capability allows the network to recover from minor problems caused by host computer malfunctions or network errors. Second, X.25 provides a *restart* capability that allows the network to recover from major failures. A restart cancels all VCs from a DTE and resets all PVCs; to the DTEs connected to the network, a restart causes the association with the network to appear the same as it did when the X.25 service was first started.

Interfaces to X.25

Conventional connections of a terminal or Personal Computer equipped with asynchronous communications to an X.25 network is defined by three CCITT Recommendations. Although X.25-compatible packets can be generated directly by a dumb terminal designed to do so or by a PC equipped with an X.25 communications adapter, typical connections to a PSN are done using asynchronous communications with an X.25 *Packet Assembly/Disassembly (PAD)* facility. *CCITT Recommendation X.3, X.28, and X.29* control the communications between a PAD and a DTE.

An X.25 PAD assumes that a terminal has no data-buffering capacity. Since a PAD has to communicate with terminals that range from old teletype devices to modern microcomputers, the safest and most conservative assumption to make is that all terminal devices have the limitations of a dumb terminal. To overcome this real or assumed set of limitations, an X.25 provides *buffering* between the network and terminal devices. Outgoing keystrokes are accumulated at a PAD until enough characters have been received to fill a data packet or until the carriage return is pressed. An X.25 packet is then constructed with the appropriate header and trailer data, including the address of the recipient. When the data packet is received at the other end of the link, a receiving PAD separates the X.25 header and trailer data from the packet and sends the keyboard data to the appropriate host computer at a predetermined data rate. When a host transmits data to its PAD, the reverse of this procedure is executed by the host's PAD, resulting in the arrival of host output at the terminal at a rate that matches the terminal's capabilities.

Recommendation X.3

CCITT Recommendation X.3 describes the functions of an X.25 PAD and the parameters used to control its operation. Because of differences between terminal types and the applications executed from various terminals, a PAD allows either a host or a terminal to set or alter up to 12 parameters. X.3 defines the parameters and the PAD's response to these parameters to provide user- or host-desired PAD performance. Each terminal connected to a PAD is given a standard profile of parameters. Either the terminal or the host can modify this standard set of default parameters, as necessary. For example, a Personal Computer, when used as a dumb terminal, would want the PAD to create a packet for transmission each time the operator presses the ENTER key or a given amount of time elapses; this same PC would want the PAD to wait until a packet is filled during a file transfer operation.

Recommendation X.28

CCITT Recommendation X.28 defines the interactions between a terminal and an X.25 PAD. X.28 specifies the use of an ASCII code variant consisting of 7 data bits per character (8 bits with parity) as well as the control characters the PAD will recognize. X.28 also defines the operation of a *break signal*; a continuous binary signal (space parity bit pattern) for more than 150 milliseconds received from a terminal causes the PAD to send a *reset packet* to the host to interrupt the execution of an application. Other terminal commands are defined that cause the PAD to set up or terminate a virtual call to a host and to read or alter the PAD control parameters. X.28 essentially provides each user with a customizable connection to an X.25 network.

Recommendation X.29

CCITT Recommendation X.29 defines the interactions between a host and its associated PAD. In addition to transmitting data through a PAD for delivery to a remote terminal or PC, X.29 defines *control commands* that allow the host to alter a PADs operational characteristic. PAD parameters may be read or altered or a virtual call with a remote terminal may be cleared (terminated).

X.PC Network Support

Future connectivity between terminals and PADs may be replaced with Personal Computers and *X.PC Network Support*. The communications between a conventional terminal or PC and a PAD is based on standard asynchronous communications without error detection and correction. Although communications between two PADs through the X.25 network provides full error correction, this link between terminal devices and remote PADs has no such protection. Telephone line noise may alter data before they reach a PAD and the noise-induced errors will be transmitted as perfect errors to the receiving host.

The X.PC protocol discussed earlier and X.25 support for this protocol will result in end-to-end error detection and correction. The benefits of an X.25 PAD adapter can be achieved using a lower-cost asynchronous adapter and X.PC-compatible software connected to a remote X.PC Network Support facility using normal dial-up, voice-grade telephone lines.

X.25 Summary

A variety of X.25 connection options are shown in Figure 7.6. This figure illustrates the power and flexibility of a PSN and its support of users, regardless of their distance from application computers.

Although the X.25 PSN provides a great deal of connectivity for user devices and host computers, this type of network does not meet the needs of organizations that want strong control of the network in the form of problem determination and correction. The IBM System Network Architecture described in the following paragraphs is often chosen to meet this type of need.

System Network Architecture

System Network Architecture (SNA) is IBM's proprietary network architecture designed to ensure highly reliable and error-free connectivity between devices that support this architecture. SNA was first introduced by IBM in September 1974 with the announcement of three products that contained SNA features and functionality. At that time, SNA was little more than a statement of direction from IBM for future products, but SNA has since evolved through new product releases to become powerful "glue" in the connection of computers, terminals, and Personal Computers.

SNA is designed using a layered concept similar to that recommended by the ISO in the Reference Model for Open Systems Interconnection. IBM's architecture is based on seven layers, as shown in Figure 7.7. The major difference between the 7-layered OSI model and the 7-layered SNA design is that the OSI model is intended to *standardize protocols* at each level to allow communications between different architectures; SNA is designed to *standardize communications* between nodes of a single architecture. The goal of SNA is to ensure end-to-end compatibility between IBM products that require or support communications.

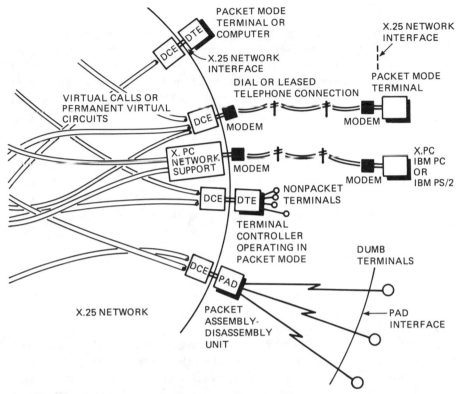

Figure 7.6 X.25 Network interface options.

Although the definition of the contents of each SNA layer may not be the same as the equivalent OSI layer, the total defined functionality is somewhat equivalent. A comparison of the layers of each of these models is shown in Figure 7.8.

SNA Features

IBM designed SNA to provide many features that enhance the efficiency, reliability, quality, and control of communications between SNA-compatible products. Some of the most significant features of this architecture are provided in the following paragraphs. The methods of SNA implementation are provided later.

Upward Compatibility

Since its first introduction in 1974, SNA ensured *upward compatibility* as new products were introduced. As new IBM products were released requiring more powerful or more robust communications capabilities, new features were added to SNA. Each new release of SNA, however, supported the functions provided in earlier releases. This upward compatibility has allowed companies to substitute one IBM product for another

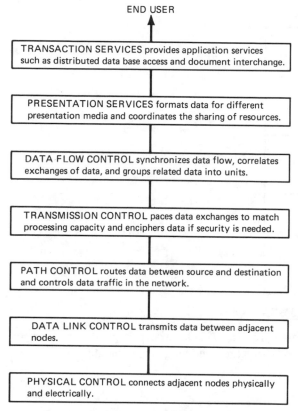

Figure 7.7 SNA layers.

and to use old products in networks that contain new products. Companies have been able to grow incrementally with technology improvements and protect their investment in older hardware and software. This upward compatibility of SNA is expected to continue.

Resource Sharing

Because of its tight coupling between remote devices, SNA allows cost reductions through *resource sharing*. By using a common communications technique for all SNA compatible devices and processors, the same communication links can connect different types of equipment. By allowing terminals or Personal Computers to access a variety of host processors, the number of unique software packages and hardware devices can be kept to a minimum.

SNA capabilities, such as *Remote Operation* and *Advanced Program-To-Program Communications*, also allow resource reductions. Remote Operation allows operators in another location to operate a minicomputer in order to reduce overall operations personnel and training requirements. Program-to-Program Communications allows more than one processor to share a common application so that the processing workload can

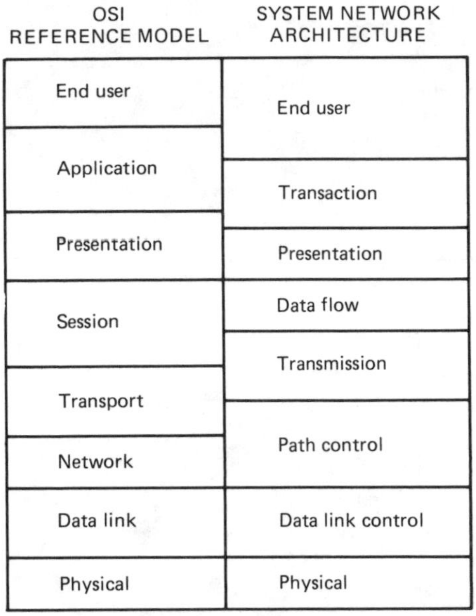

OSI REFERENCE MODEL	SYSTEM NETWORK ARCHITECTURE
End user	End user
Application	Transaction
Presentation	Presentation
Session	Data flow
	Transmission
Transport	
Network	Path control
Data link	Data link control
Physical	Physical

Figure 7.8 Comparison of OSI and SNA Layers.

be distributed to the most appropriate hardware. This latter capability allows an organization to spread processing workloads to match end-user requirements.

New Technology Growth

Because of the common architecture provided by SNA, IBM and other vendors can introduce new technology products without requiring a large investment in communications support for these products. The segregation of SNA functions into different layers allows products that implement a layer to be replaced by newer products that implement the same layer without adversely affecting the other SNA layers. For example, copper wiring may be replaced with fiber optic cabling to reduce noise interference and increase data throughput without affecting the contents of data transmitted through the media. Other new features such as digitized voice or combined text and graphics can be added at another layer without the need to change cabling or methods of error detection and correction.

Network Dependability

SNA is designed to ensure *high dependability* and *reliability*—features that are mandatory for business networks. SNA can detect lost or damaged data and ensure retransmission of the data until the problem is corrected. Built-in SNA capabilities allow devices to collect and report *error statistics* that help remote network operators make sound decisions regarding network routing or the replacement of equipment. Problem alerts may be forwarded to operators that allow them to bypass problem areas permanently or temporarily while maintenance work is performed to correct the problem.

SNA provides *network flow control* to ensure proper delivery of data and to ensure the integrity of the network. Two classes of service are supported that allow end users selection of data routing priority to ensure the proper response time for specific types of operations; *high priority* can be selected for keyboard work and *low priority* can be selected for batch remote job entry that does not require operator interaction. *Flow control pacing* is also provided to prevent data overrun of devices or nodes in the network and to prevent congestion. *Alternate data routing* and *backup hosts* can also be specified through SNA to ensure high system reliability in the event of failures of a data path or processor.

Network Interconnection

SNA products provide the hardware and software required to exchange data between similar or dissimilar networks, including X.25 packet-switched networks. Large companies often have different networks for different groups or divisions. SNA interconnection capabilities allow two SNA networks to be interconnected or allow an SNA network to be connected to a public-switched network such that users are unaware of the interconnection. Users may execute applications at hosts in two different networks without being aware of the actual location or connection between these hosts and the user terminals. These interconnections allow organizations to set up separate administrative controls for different networks without reducing the sharing of resources connected to these networks.

Network Security

SNA was designed to provide high data and application access security. *Log-on security* is provided to prevent unauthorized access to applications or data. *Data encryption* capabilities also allow users to designate data streams as high security requiring automatic encryption. Data are encrypted at one end of the link and deciphered at the other end to prevent unauthorized exposure of the data during transmission while maintaining data usability—all without the need for user attention to the process. Data encryption is particularly important in military or high-technology applications where security breaches can cost a country lives or cause a company financial hardship.

SNA Network Components

SNA is designed and implemented based on separation of function by hardware and software components. The traditional SNA hierarchy of components is shown is Figure 7.9. A more recent enhancement to SNA to support *distributed processing* is shown in Figure 7.10. In these figures, the SNA hardware components are shown as three-dimensional boxes and the SNA software components are shown as entities that reside

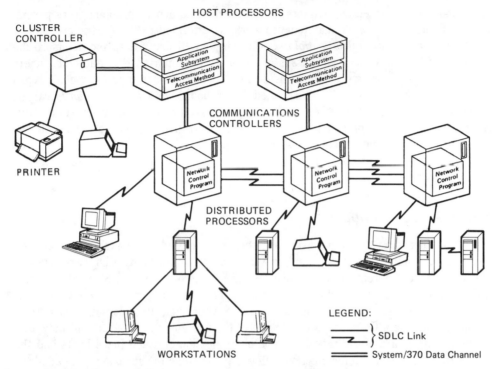

Figure 7.9 SNA hardware and software components.

inside the boxes. Each of these components is discussed in the following paragraphs, followed by a discussion of the connections between components.

Host Processors

Host processors control all or parts of an SNA network. These mini- and mainframe computers provide services such as problem solving, computation, software execution,

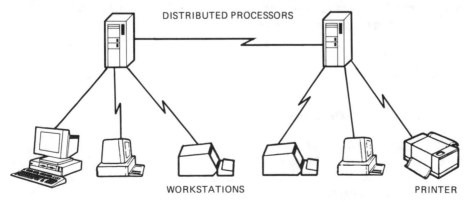

Figure 7.10 SNA distributed processing.

user access to data, disk directory services, as well as SNA network management. The traditional IBM host uses the System/370 internal architecture to provide software compatibility across a family of processors of various sizes. These sizes range from 4300 to 3090 processors and include the mid-range 9370 processor family, which are also ideal distributed processing machines. IBM host computers can be operated independently to support a variety of devices or they can be connected together to form *processor complexes*. The obvious advantage to the common System/370 architecture for these hosts is that a variety of these machines can be connected together directly or through long-distance telecommunications facilities and accessed by users as if they are parts of one large processor.

Distributed Processors

Distributed processors can provide many of the same functions provided by a host computer, but they are secondary to a host in SNA network control. Distributed-processor users may execute software directly through terminals or execute industrial and security software indirectly through the use of devices such as flow controls or badge readers. The difference between these distributed processors and an SNA host is that SNA configuration and control is performed at a higher level in the hierarchy; the distributed processor provides a path between the host and lower-level devices that are made visible to the host through SNA device descriptions and tables.

Distributed processors provide a vital link in the problem determination and control for SNA. *Error statistics* for devices can be collected at a distributed processor and passed on to a host. When properly configured at both ends of the link, a host operators can also *activate* or *deactivate*devices connected to the distributed processor, thereby reducing the operator requirements at remote computing locations. A distributed processor may also be set up to provide SNA control for attached devices that do not contain SNA compatibility.

Distributed processors usually provide high user application or connectivity features. The IBM System/3X and AS/400 families of processors provide excellent office automation and database support. The IBM Series/1 provides modularity and a variety of connectivity options including excellent support for non-SNA devices. The 9370 family of processors combine excellent System/370 computational and application features with a variety of internal connectivity options to provide formidable distributed processing.

Communications Controllers

The *communications controller* off-loads much of the lower-level SNA work from a host. The IBM 3700 family of communication controllers manage the SNA network, control communication links, and route data. These front-end processors control the flow of data between hosts in a network, between different networks, and between devices attached to a network. These SNA workhorses can also accept data at different speeds and protocols and forward that data on to a host through high-speed, channel-attached pathways. Some controller models also accept direct connection of Token-Ring Networks to provide more connectivity alternatives.

Control Units

Control units act as *concentrators* as well as controllers to manage the data flow to and from downstream devices. These control units, sometimes called *cluster controllers*, normally communicate with remote communications controllers through leased telephone lines with a modem at each end of the line. Control units may be IBM 3274 or 3174 models or IBM Personal Computers set up as a gateway that emulates a control unit. SNA gateways that connect local area networks (LANs) to remote communications controllers normally reside in IBM PC system units and emulate control units, allowing PCs connected to the LAN to emulate IBM terminals. The 3174 Subsystem Control Unit is the most versatile of the IBM control units. It can provide connectivity from a communications controller to remote PCs or direct connectivity from an IBM S/370 processor to local PCs. In both instances, the 3174 can be a Token-Ring Network gateway for LAN-attached PCs or a concentrator for several coax-connected PCs.

Workstations

SNA *workstations* provide end-user access to the resources shared through the SNA network. Workstations normally take the form of a terminal device, but may be any type of device that provides input/output for the network. The IBM 3270 and 5250 families of terminals was the standard SNA workstation before the advent of the Personal Computer. The 3278 terminal provided monochrome output, while the 3279 provided high-resolution color output; both of these devices are normally used with System/370 processors. The 5250 terminals are normally connected to System/36, System/38, and AS/400 processors. Many companies are beginning to replace these terminals with the newer 3100 family of terminals or with IBM PCs equipped with terminal emulation hardware and software.

SNA workstations include *facsimile* equipment. The IBM Scanmaster scans documents and translates text, graphics, and photographs into bit patterns that are forwarded to System/370 processors through an SNA network. These bit patterns are then sent to receiving Scanmasters, where the images are reproduced on paper for end users. SNA ensures error-free transmission of Scanmaster bit patterns just as it does for digital data transmitted by other work stations.

Modems

SNA-compatible *modems* allow the connection of IBM SNA-compatible devices to telephone lines. In addition to converting digital data signals into analog signals that are compatible with the telephone system as described in Chapter 3, SNA-compatible modems actively participate in network *problem determination*. These microprocessor-driven modems allow multidropping of several terminal devices from one line and perform *line problem determination* to assist host-based problem determination software isolate causes of failures or errors. IBM modems that perform these functions are 5865, 5866, and 5868 models.

SNA Software

Many SNA features and capabilities are implemented through software stored in SNA components or connections. Some of these SNA-related software modules are described in the following paragraphs.

SNA Access Methods

SNA access methods are software based and reside in a network host. These access methods perform SNA network control by providing an interface between host applications and the network, providing security to prevent unauthorized access to applications and providing network data flow control. The IBM *Advanced Communications Function/Virtual Telecommunications Access Method (ACF/VTAM)* is the most frequently used access method in SNA systems. ACF/VTAM monitors network performance and supports problem determination and analysis based on information provided by other SNA components in the network. VTAM also provides the support for interconnection of two or more SNA networks.

Network Management Programs

Network management programs are a family of host software packages that support *network monitoring and control*. These programs detect and report errors to network operators. They also maintain *network performance* to enable the network operator to tune the network for optimum performance. Finally, network management programs assist the network operator in the day-to-day operation of the network. Examples of older IBM network management programs are:

- Network Problem Determination Application (NPDA)
- Network Communication Control Facility (NCCF)
- Network Performance Monitor (NPM)

The latest network management software released by IBM is *NetView*. This software packages combines the best network management capabilities IBM had to offer into one integrated network management package.

Network Control Programs

Network control programs normally reside in the Communications Controller and manage the routing and flow of data between the controller and other network entities. Control programs, such as *Advanced Communications Function/Network Control Program (ACF/NCP)* control the configurations of lines to the controller and perform error recovery. An IBM communications controller equipped with ACF/NCP off-loads a great deal of the SNA workload from a host, allowing the host to perform more appropriate applications-related tasks.

Application Subsystems

Application subsystems are the end-user windows into a host computer. These subsystems make it possible to interact with application programs by locating the programs for users, loading the programs, and transmitting data to and from the user. Application subsystems retrieve data from files, update data files, and provide the graphics and text output the user views on a monitor. These subsystems also support remote batch processing—programs that do not require user interaction.

The most frequently used SNA application subsystems are *Customer Information Control System (CICS)* and *Information Management System (IMS)*. These subsystems provide terminal-oriented programming support and allow user access to databases. Other special purpose application subsystems such as *Distributed Office Support System (DISOS)* and *Airline Control Program/Transaction Processing Facility (ACP/TPF)*, provide document distribution and travel reservation services, respectively.

Application Programs

The final element in the host environment that interfaces with an SNA network are the *application programs*. These programs provide end-user services such as word processing, financial transactions, or scientific computation.

Application programs are written by end-user organizations or by outside vendors. Application programs may reside in a host, a cluster controller, or a workstation and may support a single user or multiple users simultaneously.

End Users

SNA defines the *end user* as both ends of an SNA connection. SNA end users include people who interact with network resources through workstations, as well as the application programs that provide processing services for the people using the workstations. SNA end users are both the *sources* and *destinations* of data and information that traverse the SNA network. When two processors share program execution during program-to-program interactions, the application software at each end of the link is considered an end user.

SNA Connectivity

SNA provides several means of connectivity between components that conform to the SNA specifications. Links are used to communicate between nodes, and nodes are grouped into subareas to enhance control of a large network.

SNA Network Links

SNA networks use two types of *links* to connect communicating devices, depending upon the distance separating the devices. An SNA link includes the *transmission media* used to physically connect two devices and a *data link protocol* that specifies communications controls and how data are transmitted through a link. As shown in Figure 7.9, the two most frequently used types of links are *System/370 data channels* and *Synchronous Data Link Control (SDLC)*.

Channel Attachment

System/370 data channels are high-speed connections between a host processor and another host or between a host and one of the main connectivity controllers in the 3270 Information Display System. These *channel attachments* allow data to pass between processors or between processors and controllers at significantly higher rates than can be achieved through the telephone, coax cable, or Token-Ring Network connections. Parallel data paths in a data channel allow data transfer rates in the high megabyte per second (Mbps) range compared to the high Kbps to low Mbps range available with the other connectivity methods.

Synchronous Data Link Control

SDLC provides SNA connectivity through the telephone system or through direct connections between devices and a host in special instances. In addition to data channels, an *SDLC link* can connect SNA devices to a host if the SNA access method provides support for that technique and an *integrated communications adapter (ICA)* is installed at the host. In all other cases, SDLC provides the synchronous error correction and data routing through telephone connections using modems that support this connectivity option.

As discussed in detail in Chapter 2, the SDLC link-level protocol is a subset of the HDLC protocol and provides robust error detection and correction. The CRC-16 is used as a message frame check and bad messages are retransmitted until they are correct. Like HDLC, SDLC provides *sliding window* capability for message transmission to prevent network bottlenecks and to improve communications response times. SDLC also handles data as a bit stream rather than blocks of characters, thereby allowing any type of data to pass through SNA devices without undesirable side effects—a capability called *transparent data transfer*.

SDLC frames can be assembled and disassembled in hardware or software. Because of the processing required to perform this function, SDLC is normally generated at the hardware level. For example, the SDLC and Multi-Protocol adapters available for the IBM PC perform these tasks to offload the PC's CPU to perform other tasks.

Binary Synchronous Communications

For connectivity with older SNA hardware and *packet-switched networks (PSNs)*, SNA provides support for the *Binary Synchronous Communications (BSC)* and X.25 protocols. IBM originally used BSC as the link-level protocol for SNA, but switched

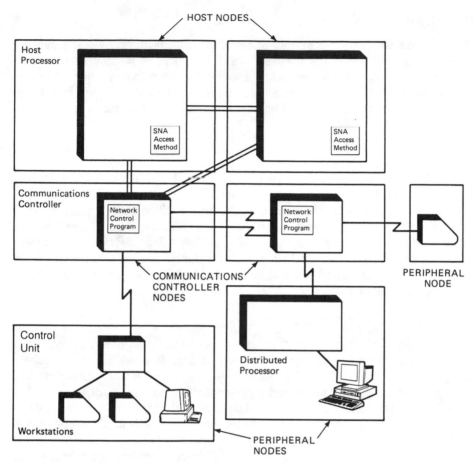

Figure 7.11 SNA Nodes.

to SDLC because of the character-oriented limitations of BSC and because of the emerging HDLC standard that IBM helped develop. X.25 interface support allows SNA networks to connect directly to PSNs and transmit data to remote SNA devices. X.25 capabilities also allow PSNs to connect two SNA networks. Both the BSC and X.25 support give SNA upward compatibility for the migration from older SNA hardware to new devices and added flexibility in the use of X.25 networks to expand the SNA span of control.

SNA Nodes

SNA is based on the concept of *node connectivity*. Hardware and software are segregated into nodes based on the SNA functions they support and the SNA layers they implement. The three groupings are host, communications controller, and peripheral, as shown in Figure 7.11. The SNA links described earlier connect these nodes.

Host Nodes

Host nodes consist of host processors that supply the SNA access method and network control. Each host and its directly attached hardware is considered a node. Host nodes normally contain ACF/VTAM and are channel-attached to other SNA components.

Controller Nodes

Communications controller nodes consist of a communications controller and a network control program. These nodes provide the connectivity between host nodes and local or remote work stations. For example, an IBM 3725 and ACF/NCP software provide the SNA "glue" between a host such as a 3090 processor and remote terminals.

Peripheral Nodes

Peripheral nodes consist of hardware and software that support end-user activity. Peripheral nodes normally fall into three categories: cluster controllers and downstream workstations; distributed processors and downstream workstations; and devices that communicate directly with communications controllers. A department, work group, or building that has its own 3174 Subsystem Control Unit or AS/400 processor is a typical implementation of a peripheral node.

Transmission Groups

SNA provides flexibility, reliability, and capacity control in the data communications across network links by supporting *transmission groups*. SNA *Path Control* combines one or more parallel links (data channels and SDLC) and makes them appear to the network as a single link. As illustrated in Figure 7.12, these transmission groups eliminate single points of failure between major SNA nodes. When all transmission group links are operating properly, the group provides a large capacity for data traffic to prevent network bottlenecks. When a link is not operating properly because a communications line or data channel has failed or is producing an unacceptable error rate, SNA can automatically route data through the remaining transmission group links. This built-in redundancy significantly reduces the probability of data loss or service disruption for end users.

Subareas

SNA defines *subareas* in order to enhance configuration control of a network. As shown in Figure 7.13, subareas consist of a host or communications controller node and its peripheral devices. These subareas facilitate the addressing of data messages to specific devices. Each subarea is assigned a unique number in the network, and within a subarea each device is assigned a unique element address. Message routing

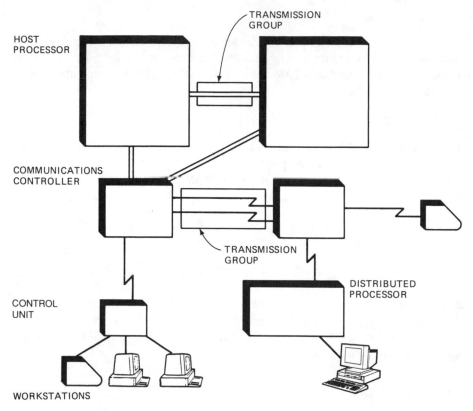

Figure 7.12 Transmission groups.

between subareas is done based on the *subarea address* only. Once a message has reached the appropriate subarea, its destination is based on the element address.

SNA Units

To enhance the functionality and control of an SNA network, different functions of the network are divided into groups called *units*. These units are ultimately managed by a host processor through a System Service Control Point.

Network Addressable Units

SNA node connectivity is made possible by two features, one of which is *Network Addressable Units (NAUs)*. In order to implement SNA in layers and to separate functions into groups, a technique of uniquely identifying network resources is required. NAUs provide this identification through *network addressees*. By routing SNA messages and control information in accordance with a path designated by these unique network unit addressees, data are transmitted to and from end users with reliability and control.

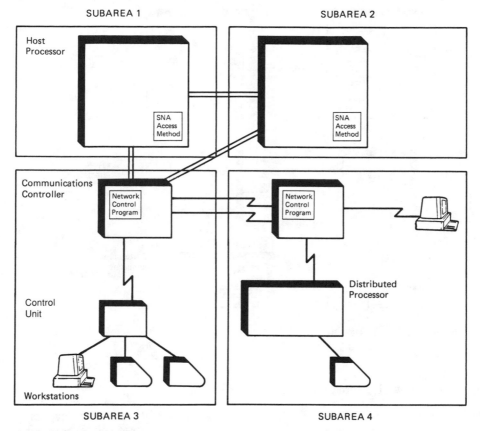

Figure 7.13 SNA subareas.

A feature called the *Path Control Network* implements the NAU addressees to ensure SNA route control and management.

NAUs are implemented in both hardware and software to provide SNA end-to-end control and SNA point-to-point data routing and pacing. NAUs reside in hosts to provide connectivity support between SNA networks and to provide the destination and source addressees of end-user applications. NAUs reside in communications controllers to provide synchronization between hosts and peripheral nodes. NAUs reside in cluster controllers to provide peripheral destination and source addressees. As shown in Figure 7.14, these NAUs are categorized as Logical Units, Physical Units, and System Services Control Points.

Logical Units

Logical Units (LUs) provide end-user access to an SNA network. These Logical Units are implemented in either hardware, software, or a combination of both to provide data exchange management between end users. The end users themselves are not visible to the SNA network; only the logical units that provide end-user services have network

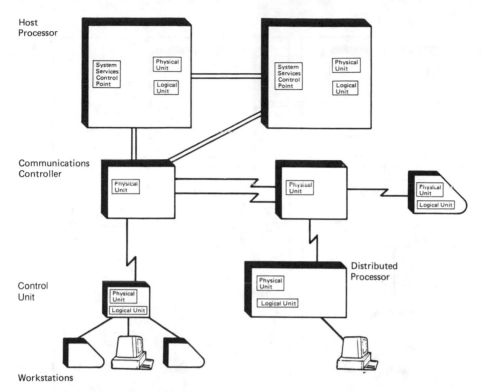

Figure 7.14 Network addressable units.

addresses and visibility to the network. This network *granularity* to the LU level provides implementation flexibility by allowing more than one user to share the resources of one LU.

LU Sessions

Logical Units communicate through relationships called *sessions* that are managed by a *Path Control Network*. Before end-users can communicate, an *LU-LU session* must be established by the SNA network. An LU representing one end user requests a session with another LU representing another LU; a *System Services Control Point (SSCP)* handles the request and activates the LU-LU session. The Path Control Network routes control data that initiates and terminates the LU-LU session and the control data that manages the routing of messages between LUs. The Path Control Network also routes end-user application data between the two communicating LUs. This same Path Control Network handles the traffic between SNA Physical Units and SCCPs.

LU Types

Logical Units are categorized into seven types based on features and capabilities. The support for these *LU types* depends upon the functions provides by a specific type of SNA node. Figure 7.15 shows the relationship between SNA LU types and node

SNA Node Type	Node Description	Architectural Description	Primary Functions of Node
5	Host Subarea Node	Subarea node Contains an SSCP Contains a PU type 5 Supports LU types 1, 2, 3, 4, 6.1, 6.2 and 7.	Control network resources Support application and transaction programs Provide network operators access to the network Support end-user services.
4	Communication Controller Subarea Node	Subarea node Contains a PU type 4	Route and control the flow of data through the network.
2.1	Peripheral Node	Peripheral node Contains a PU type 2.1 Supports LU type 6.2 in addition to LU types 1, 2, 3 and (for migration purposes only) 7 Supports direct link connections to other type 2.1 nodes.	Provide end users access to the network Provide end-user services.
2.0	Peripheral Node	Peripheral node Contains a PU type 2.0 Supports LU types 2, 3 and 7 Supports LU type 1 for non-SNA interconnect.	Provide end users access to the network Provide end-user services.

Figure 7.15 SNA node types and features.

types. Nodes that support LU types 2, 3, 4, and 7 are used in support of communications between two software entities. In all cases, however, LUs can only establish sessions with and communicate with the same type of LU in another part of the SNA network. Because of this requirement, a host subarea node normally provides multiple LU types to enable all end users to communicate.

Advanced Program-to-Program Communications

LU 6.2 is the latest IBM offering in support of end-user communications and a capability that is revolutionizing SNA communications. LU 6.2, also known as *Advanced Program-to-Program Communications (APPC)*, allows peer-to-peer communications between any two computers connected to the SNA network. When LU 6.2 is implemented in two computers and software is provided that takes advantage of this capability at both ends of the link, program-to-program communications can take place without the need for a mainframe host to control the LU-LU sessions. This capability, first announced in 1982, has been implemented by IBM and others to enhance distributed processing. For example, part of a database application can run on a host while another part of the same database application runs on an IBM PC; application function is allocated to a processor based on the location of the data to be manipulated or the CPU resources required to perform certain functions. Workload and processor capability can be more closely matched with LU 6.2 properly implemented.

Another advantage of LU 6.2 is that it is network independent. LU 6.2 was designed in such a way that it can be implemented on an SNA, X.25, or other type of network. Network independence means that LU 6.2 could eventually be used as a bridge between networks that are based on dissimilar architectures.

Complete LU 6.2 support is provided for the IBM PC in the Extended Edition of Operating System/2 (OS/2 EE). The Communication Manager included with this operating system extension provides the LU 6.2 support. This capability, along with the Presentation Manager interface included in the same package, provides software developers all the tools they need to create easy-to-use yet powerful distributed software implementation. The Database Manager portion of OS/2 EE further adds the ability to create distributed database systems.

Physical Units

Although the name *Physical Units* implies a hardware component, this SNA entity is actually a combination of hardware and software that implements several SNA functions. A *Physical Unit (PU)* represents and manages the resources of a physical entity such as a processor, controller, workstation, printer, or other end-user device. The interaction of the PUs in a host and a communications controller during the activation of a host subarea node is a good example of the services provided by a PU. During this process, the host PU provides the address of a link that can be used for communications between the host and controller and establishes the link. Once a link is established, the PUs in the host and controller negotiate to establish the optimum communications between the two devices based on the resources available at each end of the link. Before establishing or changing the communications between any two SNA nodes, the PUs of these nodes actively participate in creating and modifying links.

The PU of each node is a valuable SNA resource in maintaining high network reliability. The PU in a node can provide a *trace path* that allows the host to search for problem areas within the network. The PU can also monitor resource performance and report to the host SNA access method errors or failures associated with communication links or

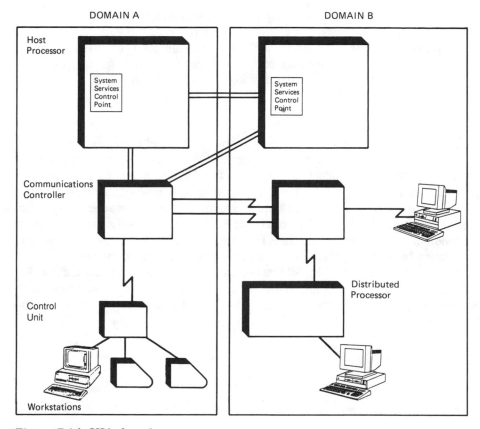

Figure 7.16 SNA domains.

components. Network operators can use the information provided by PUs to correct problems and improve network performance and reliability.

System Services Control Points

System Services Control Points (*SSCPs*) reside in host processors to activate, control, and deactivate SNA network resources. The SNA access method such as VTAM implements the SSCP to control a portion of an SNA network called a domain. As shown in Figure 7.16, two domains controlled by separate SSCPs may be connected to share resources and to provide backup capability between networks.

SSCP sessions allow the SSCP in one *domain* to communicate with the NAUs in the same domain or NAUs in another domain. An *SSCP-PU session* allows a host to control SNA nodes in the domain; network resources can be activated, monitored, or deactivated through these sessions. An SSCP-LU session allows a host to initiate and control LU-LU sessions that provide end-user access to the network. An *SSCP-SSCP session* between two domains allows LU-LU sessions to be established across domains and supports resource sharing between these domains. SSCP-SSCP sessions also allow the

SSCP in one network to act as a backup to an SSCP in another network; if one host fails, the SSCP in the other host can take over the control of all network components in both networks. This last *cross-domain SSCP capability* allows a company to set up *multiple-domain networks* that separate control and security by department or division while maintaining full resource sharing and high system reliability.

SNA Summary

SNA, although a proprietary, host-oriented network architecture for many years, has emerged as a flexible method of providing connectivity and control between communicating devices. Since its introduction in 1974, IBM and other vendors have continued to develop and implement SNA in both hardware and software products. The architecture has evolved from a rigid host-to-terminal orientation to a more versatile processor-to-processor orientation to match the evolution of communications technology, as well as workstation processing power. The IBM Personal Computer has been a major force in this evolution by providing the ideal personal workstation that can be used to access and share resources managed by SNA networks. The introduction of LU 6.2 and Advanced Program-to-Program Communications has provided the ideal SNA enhancement to support distributed processing between several IBM processors, including among those processors the IBM PC.

8

Answers to Frequently Asked Questions

Many communication novices have similar problems. To help the novice get off to a good start with electronic communications, several common questions are answered in this chapter. Since most applications of synchronous communications are in business environments that provide staff assistance to train novice users, the questions answered here are limited to asynchronous hardware and software. An index is also provided at the end of the book to help users trace key words and phrases used in the answers to these questions.

Communications Hardware

Q: I have an internal modem that does not seem to work. Every time I issue a dial command, the modem responds with a question mark instead of dialing the telephone number. How do I get the modem to dial a number?

A: The modem and the communications software may not be operating at the same data-transfer rate and data format. Try changing the software communication parameters to the modem default parameters (some modems default to 300 bps, even parity, seven data bits, and one stop bit) and dialing the number.

Q: I have installed all the hardware and software necessary to make my PC communicate using an external auto-dial modem, but the modem does not respond to my keyboard commands. How do I get the modem to talk to me?

A: You should first check to be sure that your RS-232C cable that connects the modem to the serial port has at least pins 1, 2, 3, 4, 5, 6, 7, 8, and 20 connected at both ends. If all the signal wires are connected properly, the modem "send" indicator light (labeled SD on some modems) should blink when the software is placed in the terminal or conversation mode and keyboard keys are pressed. If the modem send indicator does not blink when keys are pressed, either the cable, the serial port, or the modem is not working properly. You should substitute components that do work properly in another communication setup (borrow them from friends or coworkers), identify the component that is not working properly, and have it repaired or replaced.

Q: I just went through the last question and finally got the modem send indicator to blink, but I still cannot get the modem to auto-dial a telephone number or switch from the originate to the answer mode. What do I do now?

A: First check to be sure that you are using the proper commands described in the modem manual. If the manual specifies that uppercase letters have to be used in commands, then be sure the commands you use do not contain lowercase letters. Also be sure that all modem switches (including the ones contained inside the cover, if your modem has switches located there) are in the positions specified in your communication software package documentation manual. If your package does not specify switch settings for your particular type of modem, then use the switch settings specified in the modem manual. If none of these suggestions solves the problem, then call the software vendor to see whether there are software patches or special modem settings required to make the package work with your modem.

Q: I have a manual-dial modem that does not seem to work with my software package. After I dial the number, get the carrier signal (the high-pitch tone), and switch the modem from talk mode to communicate mode, the software package locks up. The message "check your modem" comes on my monitor and the PC no longer responds to my keyboard input. How do I get past this hurdle?

A: First check to be sure that the software is designed to work with manual-dial modems. Some packages work only with auto-dial modems. If the package is designed to operate with manual modems, try dialing the number and establishing the carrier detect signal (the modem should indicate carrier detect by illuminating an indicator light) before going into the conversation mode with the software. To do this with conversation-mode predominant software, you may have to load the software after the carrier detect is established (if the host system will allow you that much time before dropping the carrier signal).

Q: I have an intelligent modem that does not appear too intelligent. After I dial a number using a special code that makes the modem use touch-tone dialing, I cannot get it to switch back to pulse-type dialing. How do I get my modem to switch back?

A: Most intelligent modems have a special command string that can be issued from the PC keyboard that will either change the modem to another dial type or reset the modem to default settings. Before dialing a number, go into the conversation mode and issue that command string from the keyboard. When all else fails, turn the modem off and then back on again to reset it to the parameters selected by the configuration switches. If the modem is inside the system unit and cannot be turned off, turn off the system unit, then turn the system unit back on.

Q: My communications software is advertised as being Hayes Smartmodem compatible and I am using a Hayes-compatible modem. The combination works most of the time, but on occasion the modem does not respond as it should to the software. Where is the problem?

A: The problem may be with either the software or the hardware, but is most likely with the modem. Software vendors cannot buy and test their software with every modem on the market, so they limit testing to the most popular brands. If the software vendor advertises the package as Hayes compatible, then the software was probably tested with Hayes Smartmodems. Unfortunately, all Hayes-compatible modems do not provide all the same registers or operate at the same command speed as Hayes Smartmodems. These differences can cause the software/hardware combination to not work properly.

Terminal Emulation Software

Q: I cannot see the characters I input from the keyboard during conversation-mode communication with a bulletin board system operator. I can see my input displayed while interacting with the bulletin board until I page the operator and start conversing from the keyboard. The operator on the remote end of the link can read my input and I can read his, but my own input is not locally displayed. How do I turn on the local display?

A: When you are interacting with a bulletin board, you are probably in the full-duplex mode and your input is being echoed back to you from the host. When the operator comes on line, the bulletin board system probably reverts to half-duplex, which does not echo your input back to you. To see your input, you will have to switch your PC to half-duplex (sometimes called local echo).

Q: I am having difficulty reading my input when interacting with a host system. Every time I strike a key I get two characters displayed instead of one. How do I turn off the twins generator?

A: The host is probably operating in full-duplex and your PC is operating in half-duplex. The host echoes your input back to you, and your software also displays your input. Change your software setting to full-duplex (sometimes called remote echo, host echo, or echo-plex) to turn off the second character display.

Q: I am having even more difficulty than the person asking the last question. I get three of every character I type. Trying the suggestion you gave for the last question only reduced the number of characters to two. How do I get to one character for every one I type?

A: Your modem is probably set to half-duplex. Besides the character echoed back from a full-duplex host, your modem is also echoing the character back to your display. Change the modem switch setting to the full-duplex mode if it is a manual-dial modem or issue the proper command string to switch the modem to full-duplex if it is an auto-dial modem (full-duplex is normally the default for intelligent modems).

Q: I can get my modem to respond properly, but some host systems do not respond after my call to them is completed. After getting the proper carrier detect signal, there is no response to my keyboard input. How do I get the host to talk to me?

A: Check to see that you are using the proper bps rate for the system you are calling. If you are not sure of the host data-transfer rate, try changing your own software setting to different bps rates and return to the conversation mode after each change to see if the host responds properly.

Q: I connect okay with a particular host system, but the response I get is unreadable garbage. The screen just fills with graphic symbols. How do I get back to English?

A: Try changing the number of data bits and parity your software is using. If the software is normally set for eight data bits and no parity, change to seven data bits and even parity. If the software is normally set for seven data bits and even or odd parity, try changing to eight data bits and no parity. This change in parameters can be done without breaking the telephone connection with the host if your modem does not monitor the computer's Data Terminal Ready signal. If you lose the connection, change the parity and data bits and then call back.

Q: I am using seven data bits and even parity, but many characters I receive from a host have been replaced with asterisks. How do I get rid of the asterisks?

A: Some software packages replace characters that are received with incorrect parity with asterisks. The telephone connection may be too noisy, resulting in transmission errors. Log off the host system and redial the number to try to get a better telephone connection.

Q: I have call-waiting service on the telephone line that I plan to use for communications. Will that service affect my communications?

A: Call waiting cannot be used with computer communications. The communications carrier is dropped when the call-waiting signal is generated. Communications are terminated by the signal. This could be a costly problem when calling a time-sharing service that does not terminate connect charges immediately when a communication session improperly ends. If you have call-forwarding service for your telephone, you may be able to forward your calls to another number during the data communications session to avoid the problem.

Q: When I try to transmit a file to a host system or try to transmit a predefined message to a bulletin board system, the first few characters of each line are not properly transmitted. When I list the file or message after the transmission is complete, several characters are missing from the beginning of each line. How do I get the lines to upload properly each time?

A: You are overrunning the host system by sending data faster than the host can handle it. To match the data transmission speed of your PC with the speed at which the host can accept the data, you must use a transmit throttle. The PC software package has to wait a specific period of time, wait for a specific number of prompt characters to return from the host, or wait for a specific character string prompt from the host before sending each line of data. You will have to experiment with these techniques until you achieve proper data transmission.

Q: When I am listing bulletin board messages or investment information service reports on my monitor and trying to send them to my printer at the same time, my communication sessions abnormally terminate. I get what appears to be a rerun of data

I was receiving and a buffer-overflow error message. How do I get copies of this information to go to my printer without killing the whole process?

A: Many communication software packages will not allow you to simultaneously list and print information received from a host. Your printer may not operate fast enough to keep up with the receipt of data, causing data in the communication link to back up. If you can increase the size of your communication receive buffer or install a print spooler, you may be able to list and print simultaneously. You may also be able to list and print simultaneously if the software on both ends of the communications link support the XON/OFF data-flow control protocol. Otherwise, you will have to download the information to a disk file, then print that file after the communication session is completed.

Q: My communications software performs all functions except one flawlessly. I cannot exit to DOS to execute external programs. Why doesn't this feature work?

A: You may not have enough free memory to execute external programs after your communications software is loaded. This same problem could prevent the loading of overlay modules, such as file transfer protocols, that are not an integral part of the main software load module.

Q: My communications software works fine, but it causes disastrous results when I exit the program and execute other PC applications. If the telephone rings while I am executing the subsequent application, the PC locks up and I lose all my work. Why does this happen?

A: If the communications software does not turn off its communication interrupt processes when you exit to DOS, the communication interrupt handler may continue to place incoming modem response messages into an area of random access memory that was previously reserved by the communication software for a receive buffer. If that area is now used by your subsequent program, the incoming modem response will clobber your program or its data area. The usual result is a system unit lockup and a loss of all data that have not been stored to disk during the application session. If this happens to you frequently, switch to a better-written communications software package.

Unattended Communications Software

Q: I sometimes find that my bulletin board system does not respond to callers after several days of operation. It will not answer calls. What is the cause of this system failure?

A: There are many possible causes of bulletin board "lockups." It may be a bug in the software or it may be incompatibility between the modem and software. Be sure you are using the modem recommended in the software documentation manual. If you are using the correct modem, contact the software vendor for a solution. You may also want to check with other users of the same software package; they can sometimes provide more help than the software vendor.

Q: I have a problem similar to the one described in the last question. I sometimes find my monitor screen displaying an off-white color and the system will not respond to local access commands. What causes this condition?

A: A voltage surge or drop caused by a lightning storm or a power company switch change is probably the cause. If this happens frequently, you should install both a voltage surge suppressor and a low-voltage dropout relay. The surge suppressor filters out high-voltage spikes, and the dropout relay shuts down the system on low voltage. Both devices will prevent damage to the system.

Q: Someone has caused my system to malfunction on several occasions, but I have been unable to catch the person in the act. How do I catch the person and stop the assault?

A: You can sit and watch all caller activity on your monitor to identify the culprit or you can let the system do it for you. Some software packages are designed to look for system saboteur patterns, such as the use of modem attention codes in log-on names or in response to system input prompts. If your system keeps a log of all caller activity, you may be able to identify the person or persons causing the problems by reviewing this log. After identifying an individual who is causing problems, you may want to leave the person a message or lock the person out.

Q: My system does not work properly because of telephone line noise. Even with protocol file transfers, callers have difficulty downloading or uploading files. Can I have this corrected?

A: Voice-grade telephone lines are adequate for public host and bulletin board systems and for private electronic mail systems. You should contact the telephone company and request a service call. You should not mention the problems with the unattended communications system because the voice-grade lines are not guaranteed for transmitting data. The telephone company is likely to insist that you have an expensive data line installed. If a telephone company service call does not solve the problem, you may have to switch to a system that uses the CRC-16 error-checking technique for transferring files. The CRC-16 method will work under almost all conditions.

Q: I want to install a host system for public access, but I want to reserve certain files and disk areas for my own use. How do I do this?

A: There are several host systems that allow public access, but allow you to reserve areas and files for your own private use. Most of these systems use passwords to determine system-access level. The RBBS-PC package has a database of caller names and their associated access levels.

Q: I want to take advantage of an electronic mail system, but I also want to use my system for other things. How can I achieve both?

A: You have two choices. You can use a multitasking operating system and operate the mail system as a background task or you can limit the hours of your mail system operation. The first alternative is viable on most IBM Personal Computers, except those with severe memory and disk-space limitations. The second alternative is viable with any personal computer; you simply use the machine for whatever you want, then turn on the mail system when you are not performing other tasks. Most people do not use their personal computers more than a few hours a day, making the second alternative a good choice. Most electronic mail systems can automatically call yours back later if yours is not on when the first attempt to deliver mail is made.

Q: I want to use my bulletin board system to transfer files to and from word processors at work. I understand, however, that word processors embed special codes in files that do not transfer properly. How do I get around this problem?

A: Many word processors do use special 8-bit characters to mark "soft spaces" and "soft hyphens," but these files can be transferred to and from a bulletin board. If you use seven data bits as a communication parameter, all the special codes will be converted into 7-bit ASCII characters. If you use eight data bits as a communications parameter, the special codes will transfer properly, but you may get carriage returns and line feeds added in places that you did not have them before. To get around all these problems, communicate using eight data bits and use an error-checking protocol, such as XMODEM or KERMIT, to transfer the files. Most dedicated word processors will also accept Bisync communications; this synchronous protocol allows error-free transmission of 8-bit characters.

Q: I am excited about setting up my PC to act as an unattended electronic mail system, but I worry about leaving it on 24 hours a day. I have heard conflicting stories about the effects of leaving a computer on all the time. What do you think?

A: There are many host and bulletin board operators who have left their systems running 24 hours a day for years without any problems that could be attributed to continuous operation. One operator of an extremely active system used the same two diskettes for a year without any problems. Most PC systems today are designed to handle 24-hour-a-day operation without problems.

Q: I don't mind leaving my system on 24 hours a day, but I want to protect my monitor from permanent screen discoloration from continuous display of the same information. How do I do this without turning the monitor on and off all the time?

A: Many unattended systems automatically clear the screen and go into a "snoop off" mode if there is no keyboard activity for a given period of time. If your system does not provide this feature, you can get several public-domain utilities from local users' groups that will do this for you. Two of these utilities are called MONOBLANK and COLORBLANK. If none of these alternatives are available, you will just have to turn the monitor brightness down when you are not monitoring system activity.

PART II

Local Area Networks

Introduction to Part II

Thus far, this book has dealt with general-purpose communications on IBM PC, PS/2, and compatible Personal Computers—the technology and methods of exchanging information between PCs or between PCs and larger computer systems. The scope of communications discussed ranged from private networks (local bulletin boards) to public networks extending from coast-to-coast. The public communications networks we covered included the public switched telephone system (PSTN), leased (nonswitched) telephone lines, and public data networks (PDN). These networks are regulated utilities within the U.S. and have been designed for the economical transmission of voice and data over long distances.

The decreasing cost and increasing performance of microcomputers has led to a continuing integration of microtechnology into every facet of business, education, and government. This integration can only be described as explosive and has led to a commensurate growth in the application of communications between computers to a wide variety of organizational needs. Many of these applications use the regulated public networks as just described to exchange information over relatively long distances. Organizations have discovered, however, that a significant percentage of their communications occur across relatively short distances, such as within the confines of a group of offices or a building. This is particularly true for singlesite organizations.

Higher-performance microcomputers and the increasing sophistication of their software have provided a relatively low-cost and convenient foundation to automate these short-distance communications. The initial motivation for automation was the need to share expensive peripheral devices, such as laser printers, and the desire to avoid carrying floppy disks between computers in a group of cooperating users. This latter phenomenon is usually referred to as a "sneaker-net." The term *workgroup* will be used to describe any group of microcomputer users who have relatively similar work functions in an organization and who are located reasonably contiguous to each other.

The technology that has evolved to meet the needs of automating short-distance communications is a local area network (LAN). LANs are a particular form of data communications, with hardware and software optimized to support the sharing of devices and information. Shared devices are typically peripherals that are too expensive to purchase for everyone in the workgroup and include items such as laser printers, modems, plotters, and mass storage devices. Information sharing is the current focus of LAN development and the primary justification for installing a system of this sophistication and complexity.

Compared to the various forms of wide area networks, local area networks are characterized by the relatively short distances they are designed to cover, a higher speed of operation, relatively low error rates, and lack of regulation. The geographic scope of LANs is limited to thousands of feet or closely spaced building complexes. Data transfer speeds can range to 100 million bits per second (Mbps) or more, equivalent to 12.5 million characters per second (cps). Compare this rate to the more modest 64 Kbps (approximately 8,000 cps) used by the Integrated Services Data Network (ISDN) or the 2,400 bps (240 cps) common to most personal computer asynchronous communications.

In its most elementary physical form, a local area network is two or more PCs connected together by some type of wire or cable to form a data path between the computers. Once the PCs are physically connected, specially designed software controls device and information sharing and allows the cooperative use of program and data files by users connected to the network. This software also executes a variety of utility functions, including shared printing, network monitoring, and file backups.

What benefits do local area networks offer for business, government, or educational applications? First, local area networks allow the sharing of expensive resources such as laser printers and high-capacity, high-speed mass storage devices among a number of users. For the cost-conscious manager, this is a direct economic benefit. Second, local area networks allow the high-speed exchange of essential information between workgroup members in an organization. If properly managed, this sharing will promote greater efficiency and productivity and is the foundation for more sophisticated applications, such as organization-wide electronic mail. Finally, local area networks provide the catalyst to increase the range of potential applications for microcomputers.

It has been said that LANs are a solution looking for a problem. We contend this thought should be modified to state that the productive use of LANs is limited only by the imagination and resourcefulness of the user. It is most important to understand that in the final analysis, LANs are more than a communications system. They are, in fact, a productivity tool. LANs are frequently justified on the basis of sharing expensive peripherals or sharing software program and data files among a number of users. These reasons may not be sufficient to justify the cost in some situations. A LAN purchase should be studied closely in the context of the proposed LAN's contribution to the long-range interests of the organization. A LAN should be a visible contributor to increased profitability, or some other productivity metric in the case of nonprofit organizations. An even broader perspective would be to consider LANs as one of a set of tools needed to implement voice and data communications as a strategic resource in an organization. "Strategic" in this context means that communications is not just an internal service, but a direct means to increase the business base.

Part II is designed to provide you with an appreciation for the scope of software and hardware required to design and install a successful LAN. Our aim is to provide you with the basics needed to continue exploring the potential benefits of this technology as applied to the real world. Throughout Part II there will be an emphasis on the ISO 7-layer Model introduced in Chapter 8. This is done by design. Every major development in LAN systems software is inexorably linked to the ISO model and the standards derived from that model. By the end of Part II, we want you to be thoroughly comfortable with the concepts embodied in the ISO model and the role it plays in all major LAN development activity.

In Part I, we referred extensively to the PC-DOS and OS/2 operating system environments. In Part II, we will adopt the convention of using MS-DOS as the generic form, and PC-DOS as the IBM-specific form of the original IBM PC, PS/2, and compatible operating system. In the context of LANs, there is no practical difference between the two implementations of DOS. The same is not necessarily true for OS/2, and we are careful to note the distinctions between OS/2 versions as they relate to specific LAN implementation.

In Chapter 9, we start with the top of the ISO 7-Layer model and the most crucial element of LANs—the software that controls resource management and the sharing of data between users and applications working on physically separate computers. This chapter brings us to the dividing line between applications support and the methodology needed to move the data from location to location. This dividing line is between Layers 3 and 2 in the ISO model. Chapter 10 explores the two lowest layers of the ISO model—those responsible for moving data and allowing an orderly sharing of the common physical connection between computing devices. Chapter 10 is oriented to hardware elements of LANs and the physical rules of connection. Chapter 11 is an introduction to the hardware and software required to physically and logically connect multiple LANs, either contiguous or located across the continent. In Chapter 11, we show the degree of cooperation and standardization needed within the data communications industry to make useful network interconnection a reality. Finally, in Chapter 12, the more significant LAN systems available as of this writing are reviewed in detail. Each of these systems has demonstrated stability and longevity in a dynamic industry and we expect all of them to be around for the next edition of the book.

9

Local Area Networks— From the Top Down

Introduction

In many diverse organizations, a generic class of software known as *groupware* is beginning to have a profound effect on the way business is conducted. Groupware can be loosely defined as software designed to run on a multiuser system and to allow workgroup members to cooperate on closely linked activities. A prime example of groupware is a program called *Higgins*. *Higgins* is designed to allow a group to schedule its activities in a coordinated manner and to track projects in which many people contribute to goal achievement. These projects can be as diverse as building construction, magazine publishing, and software development. Another, more generic form of groupware is *Electronic Mail*. Many of these applications have been specifically designed to run in a local area network environment. Groupware applications can also be designed to run in a multiple network environment, even when the networks are 2,000 miles apart.

The ability of certain software packages to run in a network environment does not happen by accident. Like most MS-DOS or OS/2 applications, groupware relies upon the personal computer's operating system for resource support. This support includes file management, printing, and the user interface. In a LAN system, the PC operating system must be extended to support the sharing of data between applications running in different physical computers. Likewise, resource management must be extended to cover peripheral devices not connected to the application's host computer. This extension is provided in the form of a network operating system. Finally, software is required that establishes reliable and accurate communication between the user's part of an

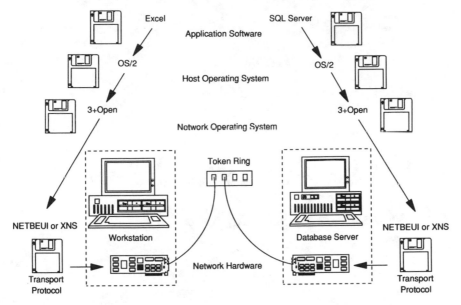

Figure 9.1 Local area network system software architecture.

application executing in one computer and that part of the application providing a service running on another computer. This communication must be established and maintained regardless of the relative locations of the two computers running the application.

The purpose of this chapter is to explore local area networks from the top down. This means that we will focus on the software that supports high-level user applications down to, but not including, the low-level means used to convey data from one location to another on the network. We give this software the generic name of *network systems software*. Network systems software includes

- The PC operating system (e.g., MS-DOS, PC-DOS, OS/2, or UNIX)
- The network operating system (e.g., Novell's NetWare, IBM's OS/2 LAN Server, 3Com's 3 + Open, or Banyan's VINES)
- The software needed to connect applications running on two or more computers on one network or across multiple networks (e.g., IBM's Network Basic Input/Output System (NETBIOS), Xerox Network Services (XNS), or Advanced Program-to-Program Communication (APPC))

Figure 9.1 shows a simplified view of these components and their relative dependency. The figure also shows how applications software running on work stations and servers relies on the underlying systems software. This chapter will not be concerned about the details of LAN physical connectivity, as represented by the Token-Ring in Figure 9.1.

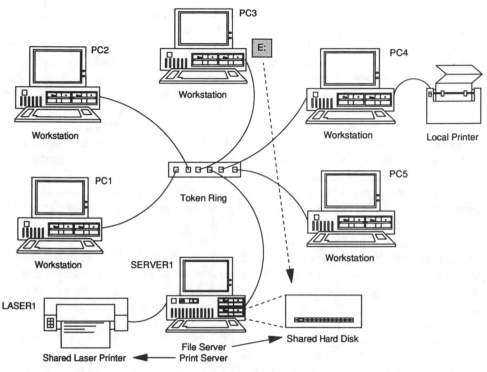

Figure 9.2 Basic local area network components.

Terminology

The local area network in Figure 9.2 will be used to illustrate some basic terminology appropriate to network systems software components. Other terminology will be defined throughout the chapter.

The term *server* refers to a software application that offers a well-defined service to network users. A server application can be run on special-purpose hardware (the dedicated file server in Figure 9.2, for example) or an ordinary PC. In the latter case, the PC often has minimum configuration requirements. The most common types of servers are *file servers*, *print servers*, and *communications servers*. *Database servers* are becoming more common with the advent of OS/2 and software such as Microsoft's SQL Server. The server depicted in Figure 9.2 is a dual-purpose file and print server. The five PCs attached to the LAN in Figure 9.2 are commonly called *work stations*, or *clients*, and are typically used for host terminal applications (discussed in Part I), graphics design, word processing, database applications, software development, project management, and a variety of other uses. Special-purpose work stations, usually higher in cost and more powerful in performance, may be attached to the LAN for computationally intensive tasks, such as simulation, computer-aided design (CAD), or artificial intelligence (AI) applications development.

On LANs, servers can be *dedicated*, or *nondedicated*. A dedicated server is set up to only provide one or more services to users on the network. A nondedicated server can simultaneously function as a work station and one or more servers. Most LANs will allow either type of operation, but vendors generally recommend that their servers be operated in the dedicated mode to maximize performance. Some proprietary servers can only function in the dedicated mode and are optimized to support one or more services for LAN users. Banyan, 3Com, and Novell all supply proprietary dedicated server hardware. IBM's LANs are designed for nondedicated operation.

The body of rules that allows the orderly, reliable transfer of data among the stations on the network in Figure 9.2 is collectively known as a *protocol*. In the context of the International Standards Organization 7-layer model discussed in Chapter 8, a protocol refers to the rules associated with a specific layer or set of layers. The protocol in any layer include *interface standards* for requesting service from the layer below and providing service to the layer above.

The original IBM NETBIOS protocol was defined in terms of Layers 5 through 1. A widely accepted protocol, such as NETBIOS, may become a *standard*. Standards are *de jure*, meaning that they are legislated by recognized national and international bodies, or *de facto*, meaning standards set by a vendor's influence in the marketplace. De facto standards often transition to de jure standards as they gain national and/or international acceptance. NETBIOS is a de facto standard. Ethernet began as a de facto standard but has been adapted to the ANSI/IEEE 802.3 Local Area Network standard in the U.S. and the ISO Draft International Standard 8802/3. The LAN in Figure 9.2 uses several protocol, the most obvious of which is the IBM Token-Ring for the Physical and Data Link layers.

The terms *virtual* and *transparent* are often used in discussions on local area networks and other data processing subjects. A process is virtual if it does not exist but appears to; a process is transparent if it exists but does not appear to. In Figure 9.2, a *virtual drive* process links the MS-DOS logical drive "E:" on the work station PC3 to a subdirectory on the file server's shared hard disk. In this case, the file server's subdirectory appears to be a local disk drive to an applications program running on PC3, but obviously does not physically exist on that work station.

The separation of physical aspects of a LAN (adapter cards and connecting cables) and the applications that run on it is a good example of transparency. The underlying physical communications protocol of a LAN (e.g., Token-Ring, Ethernet, Arcnet) is transparent to the user's application. In other words, a database software package would not operate any differently on an Ethernet, an Arcnet, or an IBM Token-Ring LAN. Closely related terms are *physical* and *logical*. A physical entity can be seen and touched; a logical entity exists as a process or an activity, but in general cannot be seen or touched. A floppy diskette is physical—software on the diskette is a logical entity.

In the context of local area networks, the term *host* can have several meanings: It refers to the microcomputer in which a work station or server application runs on the network. It may also refer to the native operating system on a work station or server. Thus, MS-DOS, PC-DOS, and OS/2 are host operating systems, and an IBM PS/2 Model

70 or an AST Premium/386C may be host to a server or a work station application. The more traditional data processing context of host refers to a mainframe or minicomputer providing centralized applications support. Our use of the term *host* in Part II may encompass any or all of these meanings.

An Overview of Network Systems Software

In terms of the ISO 7-layer reference model, user-operated applications software, such as database management systems, spreadsheets, and word processors, use the services provided by Layer 7, the Applications Layer. These applications are generally considered outside the scope of the ISO model. Network utility software and other special-purpose applications are generally considered to be either in Layer 7 or outside the scope of the ISO model, depending on the type of application. Layer 7 standards for generic applications, such as electronic mail, terminal emulation, and file transfer, are becoming more common. Host and LAN operating systems approximate functions within the scope of Layer 7 and Layer 6, the Presentation Layer. This does not imply that operating systems are recognized as standards for these layers. The boundary between these operating systems and the protocol needed to link client and server applications occurs between the Presentation Layer and Layer 5, the Session Layer.

The software defined within Layers 5 through 3 contains protocol for two primary functions:

- Support for high-level services, such as establishing sessions between client and server parts of an application or the logical naming of users and resources throughout interconnected networks.
- Support for the reliable and accurate transport of data to the desired addressee, regardless of the addressee's location.

This software exists in several well-known protocol sets, among them the original IBM NETBIOS, the IBM PC LAN Support Program developed to support Token-Ring networks, DoD's Transport Control Protocol/Internet Protocol (TCP/IP), and Xerox Network Services (XNS). These sets are sometimes referred to as *protocol stacks*. This terminology is derived from the visual appearance of the ISO model as a stack of layers, each with its own functions and characteristics.

Figure 9.3 shows the allocation of major software components to the 7-layer model. We emphasize that parts of this allocation are considered to be somewhat imprecise. In Figure 9.3, three points are particularly significant—these are shown by numbered arrows. Arrow 1 represents the manner in which applications programs request services from the host and network operating systems. Arrow 2 represents the manner in which network operating systems request logical connectivity between stations (and applications) on the network. Arrow 3 represents the manner in which the transport software providing logical connectivity requests physical conveyance of the data between network stations.

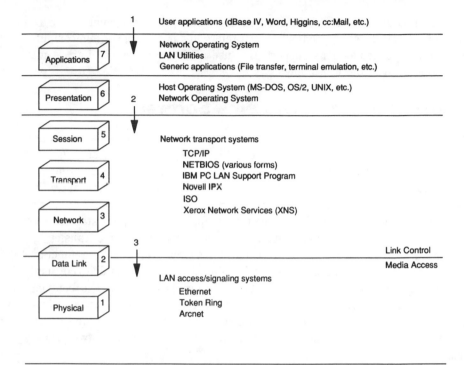

Figure 9.3 LAN system software and the ISO 7-layer model.

In the following sections, the manner in which applications software interacts with network systems software and the more significant features of network systems software components are described. The discussion emphasizes MS-DOS and OS/2 host operating systems, the major network operating systems, and alternative protocol stacks to link client and server applications across single and multiple LANs.

High-level Applications Software

There are three basic types of applications software packages that operate on local area networks. First, there are packages not designed for a multiuser environment. This software is designed to be run by one user on a single work station. Most of these software packages will run in a network environment as long as precautions are taken to prevent multiple users from opening the same data file at the same time. A typical way to use this software is to put the program files on the file server and designate them "read-only" to prevent inadvertent damage or modification. Any user on the network can then download the program file to a work station. License restrictions apply and must be enforced by network administrators. Some networks, such as LAN Manager, provide an "execute-only" privilege that prevents unauthorized copying of software maintained on a file server and publicly accessed.

The second type of software is designed for network use and has built-in provisions for multiuser protection. Capabilities of this type of software vary widely, depending on intended use. Database management software is perhaps the most elaborate because of the criticality of protecting individual records in many database-oriented applications. On the other hand, word processing software might only have minor modifications to work reliably in an LAN installation.

The third type of software is the most sophisticated and is designed to specifically support group interaction. This is the software referred to earlier as groupware. Groupware is still a relatively young, but growing, segment of the LAN software market. The program *Higgins* mentioned at the beginning of the chapter was one of the first of this type of software. Another example is the program *For Comment*, which was designed to allow a number of users to review and annotate an original document.

In each of the second and third cases above, the applications software relies upon support provided by the host and LAN operating systems. If the operating system software has built-in multiuser features and those features are actually used by the application, you would expect the software to be more effective. On the other hand, if the LAN operating system supports a sophisticated transaction tracking system and the application is not written to exploit that capability, the application loses its impact. It is the application programmer's responsibility to thoroughly understand the host and LAN operating systems and to take advantage of all appropriate multiuser features.

Applications software should be the first and foremost consideration in planning a multiuser installation. Studying a candidate application to determine its compatibility with a specific LAN operating system should be a top priority item in the overall planning process. Too often, organizations jump into LAN hardware and operating system decisions before carefully considering what work functions need to be accomplished and how their employees can best be organized to contribute to that accomplishment. Frequently, the organization is changed to accommodate the network when the better approach is to design the network to meet the needs of the organization.

Host Operating Systems

Host operating systems provide basic resource management and a user interface for a single microcomputer and its attached input/output devices. Operating systems are classified by the number of users and by the number of simultaneous tasks they are designed to support. *Single-user* systems have limited or no support for file sharing or access security, two features that are mandatory in *multiuser* systems. *Single-tasking* systems are designed to support only one program running at a time in the host computer. *Multi-tasking* systems are designed to allow execution of multiple programs nearly simultaneously.

Operating systems range from the simplest single-user, single-tasking systems such as MS-DOS to multiuser, multi-tasking systems such as UNIX and XENIX. OS/2, the proclaimed successor to MS-DOS, is a single-user, multi-tasking operating system. There are several multi-tasking add-ons to MS-DOS, the better known of which include DESQview/386 and Microsoft Windows/386. Some applications programs such as word processors and asynchronous communications packages support a limited form of multi-tasking. Typically this limited implementation supports features such as print spooling for word processors and background file transfers for communications programs. This type of multi-tasking is accomplished without direct support from the operating system.

MS-DOS

Today's generation of LANs designed for the MS-DOS environment are built on a foundation of services provided by MS-DOS Version 3.1 and its successors. This version of DOS, and its IBM variant, PC-DOS 3.1, were the first to incorporate specific functions for the sharing of devices and files. Clearly, MS-DOS 3.1 was destined to be the forerunner of newer and more powerful operating systems that would encompass the full capabilities of the 80286, 80386, and 80X86 microprocessor architectures. The successor to these MS-DOS versions, OS/2, is continuing in evolution as this book goes to press and will be a significant part of PC computing for the forseeable future. It is important to understand the basic structure of the MS-DOS series as well as its capabilities and limitations in the network environment. Many proprietary and "generic" network operating systems rely in varying degrees on the services and standardization provided by MS-DOS.

MS-DOS provides the three basic components for control and management of peripherals and the user interface: the COMMAND.COM command processor program; the MSDOS.SYS file (IBM version: IBMDOS.SYS), which is the heart of the operating system; and the IO.SYS file (IBM version: IBMBIO.SYS), which provides lower-level support for the hardware functions of certain peripherals. In addition to these software files, PCs have an installed Read Only Memory (ROM) chip set, which has firmware for the lowest-level hardware control of the more standard I/O devices. These include the keyboard, certain video displays, floppy disk drives, serial ports, and parallel ports. This firmware is called the Basic Input/Output System, or BIOS, for the IBM PC family and Advanced BIOS, or ABIOS for the IBM PS/2 family. IO.SYS, BIOS, and ABIOS are hardware-dependent elements of the operating system. The sequence of operations to load and execute a program from floppy disk illustrates the relationship between these DOS elements and is shown in Figure 9.4. It is important to keep this basic structure in mind as we investigate network operating system architectures.

The real value of MS-DOS Version 3.1 and its successors is the standard, albeit limited, support they provide for network software developers. Prior to Version 3.1, many LAN vendors had developed proprietary methods to handle the protection of files and records in a multiuser environment. This protection depends on techniques such as *file access control*, *file locking*, and *byte-range locking*. Applications developers could not rely on any one scheme to be dominant to achieve the critical mass of software development for LANs. MS-DOS provides the basic structure for LAN development through a series of network-oriented function calls. Many of these require additional network operating system software to function properly, but at least the application developer can rely upon a standard way of linking

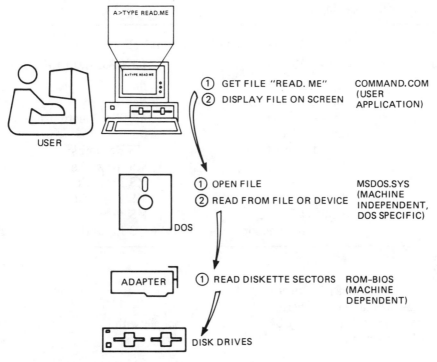

Figure 9.4 MS-DOS command execution sequence.

applications programs to a shared network environment. These function calls are summarized in Table 9-1, which also indicates whether or not additional network software is required to execute the call.

Table 9-1. MS-DOS LAN Support.

Software Interrupt 21H (MS-DOS Service)		
Function	Meaning	LAN Software Required
3DH	Open File	No
44H	Device Driver Control	No
5BH	Create New File	No (Semaphore usage[1])
5CH	Control Record Access	No
5EH(00)[2]	Get Machine Name	MS Networks[3]
5EH(02)	Set Printer Setup	MS Networks
5EH(03)	Get Printer Setup	MS Networks
5FH(02)	Get Redirection List	MS Networks
5FH(03)	Redirect Device	MS Networks
5FH(04)	Cancel Redirection	MS Networks

Notes:
[1]See the discussion under Multiuser File Management.
[2]( ) indicates subfunction number.
[3]MS Networks indicates that any LAN software compatible with
Microsoft Networks will work.

OS/2

OS/2 is the multitasking operating system that is staking its claim to the dominance of PC systems software now enjoyed by its predecessor, MS-DOS. OS/2 provides significant enhancements to the management of PC resources compared to MS-DOS, but its importance to local area networking relies on four major features:

- The Application Program Interface (API).
- Its multitasking design, which provides the vehicle for more efficient and standardized server software.
- Its support for interprocess communications among work stations and servers in a network environment.
- A new high-performance file system to eventually replace the current system (available with OS/2 Version 1.2 and later)

Application Program Interface

Whereas MS-DOS used the method of software interrupts (as shown in Table 9-1, above) to provide DOS services to applications, OS/2 uses *Applications Program Interfaces*, or *APIs*. APIs act like subprograms to a process (application) currently running in the host computer. APIs have brought an entirely new perspective to the development of sophisticated systems software and applications in a network environment.

APIs are in turn made flexible and extensible by other architectural features inherent in OS/2 design.

LAN Manager, Microsoft's LAN extension to OS/2, uses over 120 APIs for various network support services. OEM versions of LAN Manager, such as 3Com's 3 + Open, add even greater network functionality, such as Electronic Mail, internetworking, and mainframe access. A major benefit of OS/2 has been and will continue to be increased standardization of LAN functions.

Multitasking

To provide its multitasking features, OS/2 supports multiple *sessions*, *processes*, and *threads*. A session is simply a virtual computer from the user's perspective. A session supports all or a portion of the screen and attached input devices, such as the keyboard or a mouse. This level of multitasking is also supported by Concurrent DOS 386, DESQview/386, and Windows/386, among others. A process is a program in its execution mode, such as a financial program to calculate and print a loan amortization schedule. If provided with appropriate resources, such as a screen window and the keyboard, the process becomes a session. A session provides the user with a visual, manageable window into the executing process. A thread can be likened to a function or subprogram running within a process. A routine to calculate periodic interest payments in the previously mentioned loan amortization program is an example of a thread.

The key point to remember about sessions, processes, and threads in OS/2 is that they can run virtually simultaneously in a single microprocessor. That is, they may appear to be simultaneous, but in fact each is assigned a discrete time slice for execution. Hence, the utility of OS/2 in a network server environment. By their very nature, servers are multitasking network resources. They must manage simultaneous requests for hard disk access, perform print management services, and perhaps control one or more communications resources. OS/2 provides a stable, standard development platform on which to build multitasking server applications. The most common applications will be services for file management, printer management, name management, and database management.

Interprocess Communications

Interprocess Communications (*IPC*) are part of the OS/2 design to support multitasking. IPCs allow two processes or threads within the *same* computer to exchange data through a variety of mechanisms supplied by OS/2, including *Shared Memory*, *Semaphores*, *Queues*, *Signals*, *Mailslots*, and *Named Pipes*. For LAN applications, IPC allows two processes on *different* computers to communicate as if they were in the same computer. The Named Pipe and Mailslot mechanisms accomplish this task. Beginning with OS/2 Version 1.1, Named Pipes and Mailslots are implemented in the host operating system. Named Pipes and Mailslots are created by a process running on an OS/2 server node and are used by client processes running on OS/2 or MS-DOS work sta-

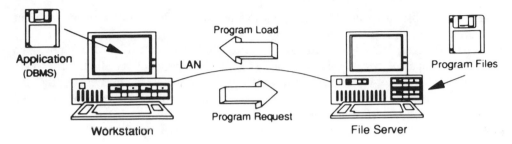

File Server Model

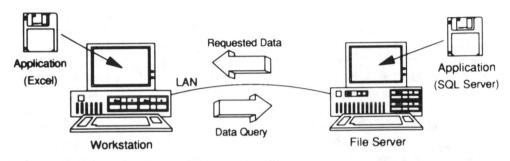

Client-Server Model

Figure 9.5 **File server and client-server models compared.**

tions. The main difference between Mailslots and Named Pipes is that Mailslots are a one-way mechanism designed for short messages, while Named Pipes are two-way virtual circuits for more complex data exchange.

As PC-based LANs continue to mature, network operating systems such as OS/2 LAN Server and LAN Manager are capable of supporting the transition from a *file service model* to a *client-server model* for distributed processing. The major difference between the two lies in the nature of the data requests passed from work stations to servers and the location of the primary application program. The two models are compared in Figure 9.5. In the file server model, these requests consist of commands to open and close data files on the file server and the movement of data files between the file server and work station. The data files in turn are used by the application program running on the individual work station.

In the client-server model of distributed processing, the total application may consist of a file server process communicating with a work station process using the Named Pipes API. The server runs the back-end (computational) application process while the client work station runs the front-end (user management) application process. The client front-end provides the user a window into, and control of, the application running on the server. A current, well-known example of this is the Ashton-Tate/Microsoft SQL Server, a database engine that executes on a server. Work stations on the network may run any compatible front-end query program from either an MS-DOS or OS/2 host operating system. The traffic between the client and the server consists of high-level data queries and the information provided by the server in response to those queries. The data passed is in the standard SQL query language format.

High Performance File System (HPFS)

OS/2 Version 1.2 introduces the *High Performance File System* (*HPFS*) as the long-awaited replacement to the MS-DOS *FAT file system*. The need for HPFS has been driven by the increasing size of hard disks, particularly in the network environment. HPFS has three distinct parts: a new means of organizing data on the hard disk, conversion of applications program file requests into hard disk device driver commands, and implementation of *installable file systems*. Table 9-2 highlights some differences between the FAT system and HPFS.

Table 9-2. FAT and HPFS Differences.

Feature	FAT File System	HPFS
Max. filename length (chars)	8 basic.3 extended	254
No. of delimiters	1	Many
Max. path length (chars)	64	260
File attributes	Bit flag	Bit flag + 64 Kbytes of ASCII or binary data
Directory structure	Unsorted linear list	Sorted B-Tree
Directory location	Root directory on Track 0	Near seek center of volume
File allocation information	FAT on Track 0	Located near each file in its Fnode
Free disk space information	FAT on Track 0	Located near free space in bitmaps
Minimum allocation unit	Cluster (4 Kbytes or more)	Sector (512 bytes)
Max. volume size	32 Mbytes (DOS)	2,199 Gbytes

The HPFS introduces some incompatibilities to existing applications software. The length of filename and existence of multiple (.) delimiters are two of the more obvious differences. Others include the use of *Extended Attributes* (*EA*) and *Access Control Lists* (*ACL*). Up to 64 Kbytes of EAs can be associated with a file, each in the highly generic form:

name = value,

where value can be an ASCIIZ string or a binary value. OS/2 APIs for querying and setting file information have been appropriately expanded to handle EAs. Support for the existing attributes of Read-only, Hidden, System, and Archive will be continued to maintain backward compatibility. ACLs will be supported by the LAN Manager version associated with OS/2 Version 1.2. As the name would suggest, ACLs will be used to store items such as access rights and passwords for users accessing that file in a network environment.

Because HPFS is a radical departure from the FAT file system, Microsoft has defined a new partition type for HPFS (Type 7). HPFS volumes can exist on the same disk as other types, including FAT, UNIX, NetWare, and others. Existing MS-DOS and OS/2 applications (written through OS/2 Version 1.1) can exploit the enhanced performance features of HPFS by using the 8.3 filename format. Since this format is a subset of an allowable HPFS filename, backward compatibility is assured.

Network Operating Systems

In PC-based LANs, network operating systems function at two levels: providing resource management for services on server machines, and providing the user and applications software a "window" to the LAN environment at each work station machine. The file server and work station components of the network operating system work together to provide an integrated system control capability to users and network managers on the LAN. The manner in which these two components interact is a major factor in LAN operating system design and network performance. You should realize that an OS/2-based file server element does not imply the necessity for an OS/2-based work station element. A typical OS/2 LAN environment could consist of one or more OS/2-based LAN servers and a mixture of OS/2-based and DOS-based work stations. Under specified conditions, this environment could also support a mixture of DOS-based and OS/2-based servers.

LAN operating systems are arguably the major determinant of overall network performance as indicated by metrics such as throughput and response times under a load of multiple users. Network server software is particularly important since server multitasking requirements can be very demanding. Work station network software, such as IBM's OS/2 Requester, has less effect on network performance but determines the major user management capability of the network. LAN utilities, which are merely specialized forms of applications software, have the least impact on network performance. Utilities provide the tools for users to more effectively manage the network and its resources. LAN utilities are most often extensions to the basic capabilities of network operating systems. These utilities may run on either file servers, work stations, or both.

Every LAN requires a control mechanism to manage shared resources, just as stand-alone microcomputers require operating systems to control their locally attached resources. Operating systems also have the responsibility to provide an orderly method for users to interact with the resources under their control. An LAN provides added value to a set of independent microcomputers by connecting them and facilitating resource and information sharing. This added value can best be managed by an operating system specifically designed for the LAN environment. Like a microcomputer operating system, a *network operating system* (*NOS*) has features that must be evaluated to determine the best match for a particular combination of applications, hardware, and budget.

Table 9-3 provides an overview of key features that prospective network purchasers and managers should look for in a network operating system:

Table 9-3. Key Network Operating System Features.

- Hardware independence—The ability of a NOS to operate in more than one vendor's network hardware environment.
- Bridging—The ability of an NOS to support the connection of two or more dissimilar hardware LANs under a common network operating system. This feature may be subsumed by the ever-increasing sophistication of third-party bridges.
- Multiple server support—The ability to support more than one server and to transparently manage communications between servers.
- Multiuser support—The ability to provide adequate and *standardized* protection for applications programs and their data files in a multiuser environment.
- Network management—The degree to which the NOS supports network utility and management functions such as system backup, security management, fault tolerance, performance monitoring, etc.
- Security and access control—The ability of a NOS to provide a high degree of network security through the control of users and resources.
- User interface—The degree of human engineering reflected in menus, screens, commands, and user control over network resources.

Figure 9.6 illustrates the relationship between applications software, host operating system, network operating system, and lower-level network communications functions. This figure is shown from the perspective of a work station on the network. The user's view of the network is through either an applications program, or menus and command lines that provide control of network functions. Many network functions are themselves special-purpose applications programs. When an application program is running in a work station, a *redirector* or *shell* program continuously screens requests for files or devices. The redirector knows what devices and drives are remote because it has been given this information by the user mapping local device names to network resources.

File requests, such as opening a word processor data file on a subdirectory on a local drive, are passed to a normal MS-DOS or OS/2 file handling routine for input and output processing. File requests to a subdirectory on a network drive located on the file server are passed to lower-level network functions. These low-level functions provide the necessary network processing, such as packetizing and proper routing. The network adapter card works just like any other adapter card in

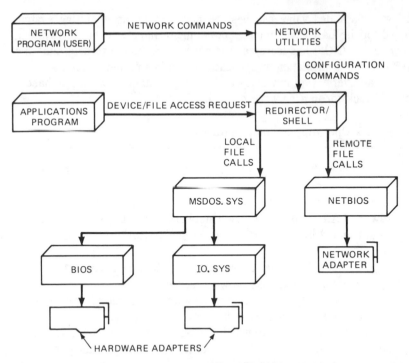

Figure 9.6 Work station system software architecture.

the work station—it provides the basic hardware and firmware support for an input/output device, in this case a local area network communications system. In this illustration, the components of the work station part of the network operating system are the network management program and its user interface, and the redirector, or shell, which is transparent to the user. The network management program and other network utilities are usually considered applications programs.

Figure 9.7 illustrates the relationships described above as they would appear on the network file server. This figure assumes that the file server is dedicated to running network services. The file server runs either a proprietary operating system such as NetWare, or a more standard multitasking host operating system such as OS/2 or UNIX. The peripherals attached to the file server, such as hard disk drives, tape backup units, and printers, are supported by the file server operating system, just as work station local I/O devices are supported by their host operating systems. Current file servers run a markedly unstandardized collection of system software. Examples are UNIX System V on Banyan's file servers, Advanced NetWare or NetWare 386 on Novell's file servers, and versions of OS/2 on 3Com's and IBM's file servers. Figure 9.8 depicts how a file server multitasking operating system is structured. This particular view shows the NetWare operating system, but the principle is similar on other multitasking systems.

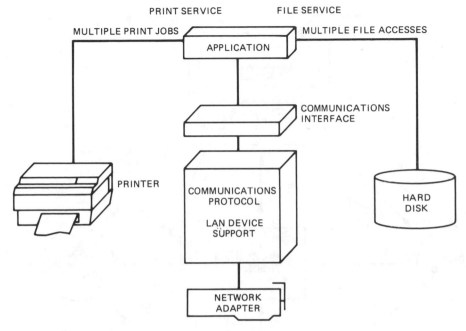

Figure 9.7 File server software architecture.

The various parts of a network operating system combine to perform a variety of tasks to support network activities. These tasks consist of shared resource support, file management, and general management functions such as system backup, fault tolerance, security management, and performance monitoring.

In general, shared resources supported by network operating systems include:

- Mass storage servers with attached media, such as hard disks, tape drives, and optical disks.
- Output servers, such as dot matrix and letter quality printers, laser printers, plotters, and large screen video displays.
- Communications servers, such as modems, bridges, routers, gateways, and facsimile.

Mass storage servers, also known as file servers, manage the attached physical storage media and offer the sharing of the logical file directory structure contained on the media. Output server processes typically use the storage facilities of the file server to queue output requests. Further discussion on communications servers will be deferred until Chapter 11, which deals with connecting multiple LANs with, and through, wide area networks.

File management is the foundation of any multiuser data processing system, and LANs are no exception. In the early days of PC LANs, multiuser file management was

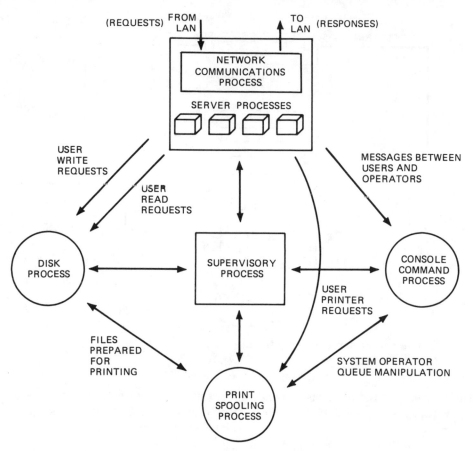

Figure 9.8 File server operating system architecture.

largely done within applications software by proprietary methods—the result was almost total lack of standardization and the paucity of network-capable software. Current and evolving host and network operating systems are rightfully assuming this reponsibility. This can be seen in the API calls within OS/2 and LAN Manager that support various multiuser file management functions.

Today's LANs provide varying selections of network management functions for users and network administrators. These functions may be built in to the network operating system or they may be stand-alone applications programs. Table 9-4 lists some LAN Manager APIs that provide Network Administrator support. A growing number of third-party network utility programs are available for the major network operating systems. The extensibility of OS/2 will contribute to continued growth of this third-party industry.

Table 9-4. LAN Manager APIs for Network Administrators.

Statistics	Access to Resources
Auditing	User Management
Group Management	Network Configuration
Remote Utilities	Network Messages
Print Queues	Print Jobs
Network Profile	Alerts
Error Logging	File Sharing Management
Remote Execution	Character Device Management

Shared Resource Support

Sharing resources was the original impetus behind the acceptance of local area networks for PCs. In this context, resources include peripherals (devices) and file directories. When printers and hard disks were more expensive than a network adapter card, buying a low-cost LAN for resource sharing made economic sense. When the prices of high-quality dot-matrix printers and hard disk drives plummeted to approximately that of a network adapter card, or even lower in some cases, resource sharing was no longer the only, or even primary justification for a LAN. There are still specialized devices that dictate sharing from an economic sense. The concept has not changed—only the complexity and sophistication of the devices themselves. Current-generation LANs support laser printers of all sizes and varieties, optical disk units, and CD-ROMs, backup tape units, modems, and, of course, the ubiquitous hard disk drives on file servers.

Regardless of the resource involved, sharing requires a concept known as *redirection*. Redirection takes place on the work station and allows logical resource names (e.g., drive designations) within the host operating system to be assigned to remote shared resources. For example, the logical printer device in MS-DOS, LPT1:, can be redirected to a network printer attached to the file server. Likewise, COM1: could be redirected to a shared modem on the network, drive F: to a subdirectory on the file server, and so on.

Inherent to the sharing process is the use of a work station-server protocol. The more common of these are Microsoft's Server Message Block (SMB) and Novell's NetWare Core Protocol (NCP). Communications between the work station's redirector or shell and the server are accomplished using this protocol. The SMB protocol has four types of server message blocks: session control, file management, print queue management, and message management. Session control establishes the dialog between the work station and server. File management blocks extend normal DOS file commands across the network. Print queue management provides control and status of print server queues. Message management SMBs control the sending and receipt of user-to-user messages on the network. Each SMB is a formatted packet with specific data meanings defined within the packet.

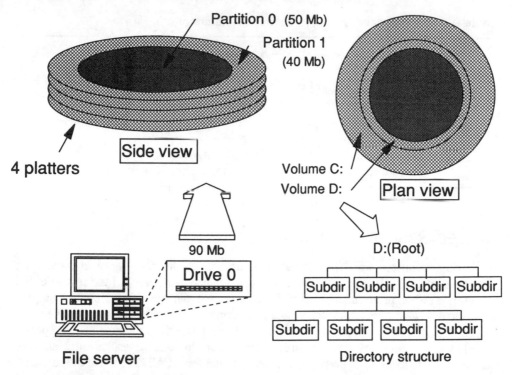

Figure 9.9 Mass storage device organization.

Mass Storage Resources

Mass storage resources and their management play a major role in effective LAN operations and in the design of network operating systems. Mass storage media are the "main battery" of the file server. An understanding of the physical and logical elements of mass storage is necessary to properly evaluate alternative LAN products. The following discussion should be viewed from the perspective of the file server.

Figure 9.9 summarizes the relationship between mass storage elements. The largest entity of mass storage on a network is the *physical drive*. Several drives may be attached to a single file server as illustrated in Figure 9-10. Most LANs allow more than one file server, thereby providing potential for gigabyte-range data storage capabilities. The LAN operating system should be checked for its ability to logically support the maximum physical storage capacity of all installed file servers. Physical drives consist of one or more rotating magnetic surfaces, or *platters*, mounted on a common spindle. Each physical drive is connected directly or through another drive to a *disk controller card* in the server.

The largest logical entity on a hard disk drive is the *partition*. A partition is mapped to a physical segment of the disk reserved for all volumes and directories under a single Disk or Network Operating System. Partitions are created by the host operating

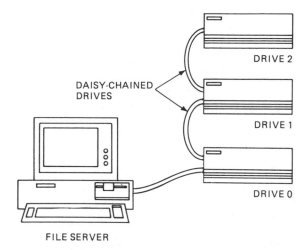

Figure 9.10 File server drive chaining.

system. For example, MS-DOS and OS/2-compatible hard disks can be divided into a maximum of four partitions. One common partitioning scheme is to put an LAN operating system, such as Novell's SFT Advanced Netware, on one partition and use a second partition for MS-DOS if the file server is nondedicated (used as a concurrent work station). Other partitions can be used for other operating systems as required by network or stand-alone applications. Typically, a dedicated file server's hard disk would be set up for a single partition for the network operating system. Partitions are physically composed of contiguous *tracks* on the disk surface. Tracks are also referred to as *cylinders* in those drives with multiple platters (the rule in current generation drives).

Once a partition is created, it is formatted by the appropriate host operating system or network operating system. The process of formatting each partition divides the partition logically into one or more *volumes*. Partitions are generally formatted to contain only one volume unless the partition size is larger than the maximum supported by the host operating system. In this case, the partition is divided into a primary partition and a secondary partition. The primary partition contains a single volume; the secondary partition can contain multiple volumes. Volumes are contiguous physical areas within a partition and are also recognized as logical entities by the operating system. A volume is sometimes referred to as a *logical drive*. In MS-DOS and OS/2, logical drives are given alphabetic device designators (Drive A:, Drive C:, Drive D:, etc.). A volume can be either fixed or removable. Examples of removable volumes are floppy diskettes, hard disk cartridges, and tape cartridges.

Tape mass storage devices also use the volume terminology, with a volume generally corresponding to an entire tape cassette, or to a single track on a cassette. However, the primary unit of physical division on a tape volume is the *block*, and the primary logical entity is the file. Blocks and files on tape volumes are physically contiguous. The tape drive is a *sequential access* device, whereas the hard disk is a *random access* device. Sequential access devices store and retrieve data in contiguous blocks during

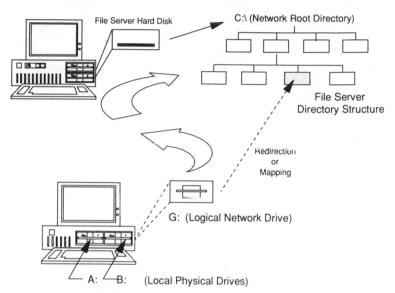

Figure 9.11 Linking directories on the file server.

I/O operations, whereas random access devices can store or retrieve data anywhere on the media surface on successive I/O operations.

Hard disk formatting is a two-part process. *Low-level formatting* of a partition creates physical tracks and sectors. These are then used by low-level device drivers for basic data storage and retrieval. *High-level formatting* establishes the root directory and file allocation tables and copies DOS system files onto the hard disk. These elements are the key to operating system file management. The operating system understands file structure and the device driver understands physical location on the disk. The device drivers support the file management requirements of the operating system.

Once volumes are created, a *directory* structure is established. Almost all LAN operating systems use some form of *hierarchical* directory structure similar to MS-DOS, which in turn is based upon long-time UNIX operating system file conventions. The hierarchical file structure consists of a *root directory* and one or more *first-level subdirectories*. Each of the these subdirectories may consist of one or more *second-level subdirectories*, and so on. This is shown in Figure 9.9. Each volume on the hard disk has a corresponding root directory. Novell's NetWare uses a proprietary directory system on its servers. This system is different from MS-DOS and is optimized for high-performance network file operations; hence, the need to create a separate partition for NetWare.

In practice, work station logical drive designators (D:, E:, F:, etc.) are linked to specific subdirectories on the file server. This concept is generically known as *redirection* and is illustrated in Figure 9.11. Any logical drive designator not assigned to a local device by the host operating system can be linked to a file server subdirectory by the network operating system. All network operating systems work in this general manner, although the command syntax details may differ.

Redirection is supported by an extension of the normal DOS pathname. For example, a subdirectory named *word5* under the subdirectory *apps* under the root directory *system* on the server named *SERVER1* would be referred to as

```
\\server1\system\apps\word5
```

in the notation used by Microsoft and IBM in their network operating systems. Similar notation is used in Novell's NetWare. Since these pathnames can get tedious to work with, *aliases*, commonly called *sharenames*, are assigned to the path to simplify reference to, and use by, work stations. The path, or sharename, then becomes a shared resource and can be linked to any number of connected work stations. For example, the pathname above could be assigned the sharename *wordpro* such that

```
wordpro=\\server1\system\apps\word5
```

Subdirectories contain files, the basic logical elements of any operating system, including those that control networks. Unlike volumes, files are not necessarily physically contiguous on a hard disk device. In the MS-DOS and OS/2 worlds, this leads to the requirement for a *File Allocation Table*, or *FAT*, to provide a road map for the operating system to locate segments of files scattered around the disk. The FAT works in conjunction with the directory for each volume to provide file identification and location services for the host operating system. In OS/2 Version 1.2, a new file structure, called the *high-performance file system* (*HPFS*), will be supported. Many of the long-standing performance limitations of the MS-DOS file system will be significantly improved by HPFS.

Because of the need to operate dissimilar work stations and a growing array of sophisticated data storage devices on networks, there is a requirement to interoperate with different file structures. These might include the MacIntosh, UNIX, DEC's VAX/VMS, HPFS, standard MS-DOS, CD-ROM, Write Once Read Many (WORM) drives, and others. This need is beginning to be met with developments such as the Installable File System (IFS) feature of HPFS and Novell's extended file system in NetWare 386.

Output Resources

Network operating systems manage output resources through the use of print servers. Print servers consist of software that places redirected print jobs into one or more queues (waiting lines), manages the queues, and routes jobs to the appropriate output device. Print servers also manage shared device configuration.

In many networks, print servers are colocated with file servers. The print server must have either (1) the required local I/O ports to attach supported printers up to a specified maximum number of serial and parallel devices, or (2) knowledge of where else on the network to send the print job. Print services must contend for the resources provided by a typical file server including processor time and mass storage access.

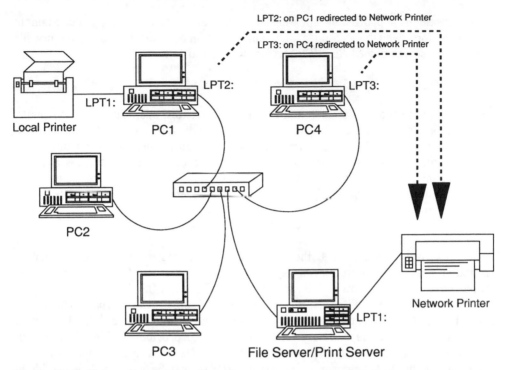

Figure 9.12 Network printer redirection.

Work station applications access a print server by *spooling* a print job from the work station to a temporary file on the file server. The print server process *despools* the print job from its temporary file to the destination printer. Think of spooling as copying a file from the work station to the server, and despooling as copying a file from the server to the printer. The application has no knowledge of where the output is actually taking place.

An important consideration for network planning is whether the network operating system supports printers attached anywhere on the network or only those attached to the file server. Obviously, the former arrangement provides the greatest flexibility. In any case, print jobs can only be sent to printers identified as shareable by the network operating system. A printer not shared to the network is a local resource for its host computer only.

Performance considerations dictate that any work station running print server software should have light-to-moderate local processing loads. The alternative is to dedicate multiple network stations as print servers, a luxury affordable only in larger organizations.

As with mass storage resources, output resources are managed by redirection from work stations. In this case, the local devices are parallel and serial communications ports, LPT1:, LPT2:, COM1:, etc. In configuring the print server, an at-

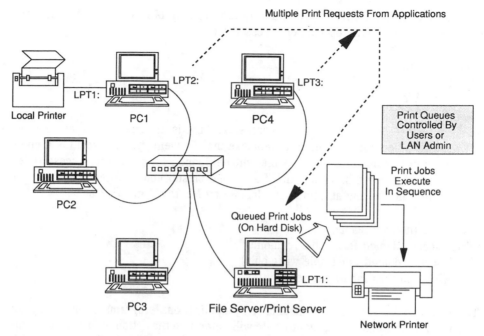

Figure 9.13 Network printer queue management.

tached printer is connected to a server physical port, say LPT1:. On one work station, the application is configured to the MS-DOS logical port LPT2:. On another work station, the application is configured to the OS/2 logical port LPT3:. The applications may be different, yet both work stations can be redirected to the physical printer on the print server's LPT1: port. Figure 9.12 illustrates printer port redirection.

The print server must accommodate multiple requests for print jobs—often arriving faster than the printer can print. The overload is handled via a queueing mechanism that generally works on a first-in, first-out (FIFO) basis. Most network operating systems provide print queue management functions that allow work station users or a network manager to designate certain jobs as high priority or to cancel jobs in the queue. The more sophisticated queue managers, such as those in 3 + Open and OS/2 LAN Server, provide time-scheduled printing, full remote queue management, and user notification when jobs are complete or an error has occurred on the output device. Figure 9.13 shows the queue management process in a typical LAN configuration.

Multiuser File Management

The unique concept of a network directory is its ability to be shared among several users. This sharing assumes that the users accessing the directory file(s) have passed network security to get there in the first place. The tools that allow sharing are *file access* and *file-sharing attributes*, *locks*, and *semaphores*. By MS-DOS and OS/2 convention, a file can be initially opened, or accessed for

Read only, or
Write only, or
Read and Write

These are termed *access attributes*. An access attribute is assigned by the application that opens the file—for example, if a database management system executes a command requiring file modification, the file will be opened for read/write access. File-sharing attributes come into play only if a second or subsequent attempt is made to open the file. File-sharing attributes are defined by MS-DOS and OS/2 as

Exclusive (non-shareable)
Write access denied (shareable read-only)
Read access denied (shareable write-only)
Deny None access (shareable read-write)

These attributes are assigned implicitly by applications programs or explicitly by users. The file's assigned sharing attribute will determine the action to be taken on the second or subsequent attempt to open the file by other users. This is illustrated by the sequences shown in Figure 9.14. A network operating system can use these features to give users control over file sharing on the network. For instance, this is done by the NET SHARE command in the LAN Manager program or by the FLAG command in Advanced Netware. Both MS-DOS and OS/2 allow the user to set the file attribute of Read-only at the operating system level via the ATTRIB command. This setting will generally override access settings made through the NOS.

If a file is opened (initially accessed) for Read/Write with a Deny None sharing attribute, there must be an additional means to control updating of the file by more than one user. The term commonly used to describe this process is *synchronization*. Synchronization of file updates can be accomplished by the use of *file locks* and *byte-range locks* or by the use of *semaphores*. File locking protects the entire file from multiple user updates—byte-range locking protects a specified range of byte offsets within a file. Locking an entire file against multiuser updates within the MS-DOS or OS/2 environments is done by assigning the sharing attributes of Exclusive or Write Access Denied.

Record locking is more complex, but absolutely essential in most multiuser applications, especially database applications. The concept of record locking is an applications-oriented term since the operating system knows nothing about records. The application context converts a record into a byte-range offset within a file. Record locking can be done through *physical locks*. Physical locks are used by MS-DOS and OS/2 and work by protecting a specified range of byte offsets within a file. The operating system ensures that another application (or process in OS/2) cannot write to, read from, or lock the protected byte range. Locks are also classified as *wait locks* or *no-wait*

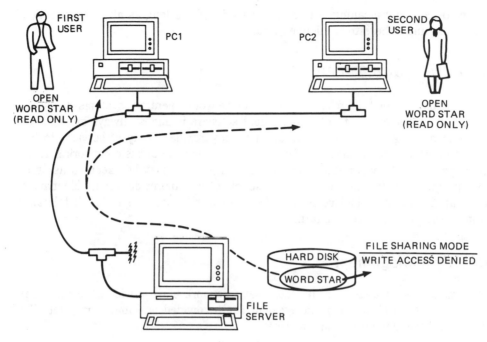

Figure 9.14 File sharing attributes in MS-DOS.

locks. Wait locks will delay and retry if the requested byte range is already locked. No-wait locks will inform the requesting application or process that the requested byte range is already locked.

Because of the intricate coordination required between processes within a multitasking environment such as OS/2, the use of byte-range locking within a file and invoking the lock interval for a minimum essential time are good network programming practices. OS/2's DosFileLocks API allows one byte range to be unlocked in the same call as another range is locked. Some systems, such as NetWare, permit multiple ranges of bytes to be locked on one call. This capability is useful in a transaction-oriented application where several records may be updated in one logical operation.

Semaphores are also not directly supported by MS-DOS, but they are provided as extended functions by various MS-DOS network operating systems. OS/2 fully supports semaphores. A semaphore is simply an addressable entity stored on disk or in memory that can be named, set, tested, changed, and cleared. Semaphores can be applied to files, a specified range of byte offsets within a file, or any sharable network device, such as a printer or modem. A semaphore is a logical control mechanism whereas a lock is an access-denial mechanism. A semaphore is more general than a lock. It can be set up to have any meaning, including access denial, as long as all using processes understand and adhere to the defined meaning.

Network Management

The final topic of this generic overview of network operating systems deals with network management. Network management software is almost always bundled with the basic network operating system and provides a wide variety of services to both users and managers. Management functions may be built in to basic network software running in both the work station and file server, or they may be executed as stand-alone programs. Networks require a basic set of utilities to provide a workable management capability. These include security (access control) management, fault tolerance, backup, and performance monitoring.

Security Management

The most basic management function that a network must provide is security management. In general, security management can be divided into four parts, not all of which are implemented in some networks:

- Network access
- User-level security
- Resource-level security
- File access

A general security architecture for PC-based LANs showing the relationship among the above four parts is depicted in Figure 9.15.

Network Access

Network access is controlled by a *network log-on process*. The log-on process works in conjunction with user-level security, typically incorporating a *user account* containing a *user name* and an associated *password*. The log-on process runs on one or more network servers and provides the initial security check since each user must log on to at least one server to share resources on a network. The server(s) maintaining the network log-on process run a validation check on the user name and associated password. Failure to pass the validation check will cause the log-on attempt to fail. In some systems, the account that is the target of one or more invalid log-on attempts will be locked from further log-on attempts until cleared by a supervisor. Network access security is only effective if the passwords assigned to users are properly protected and managed. Network access security should be mandatory for all users and uniformly administered for best results.

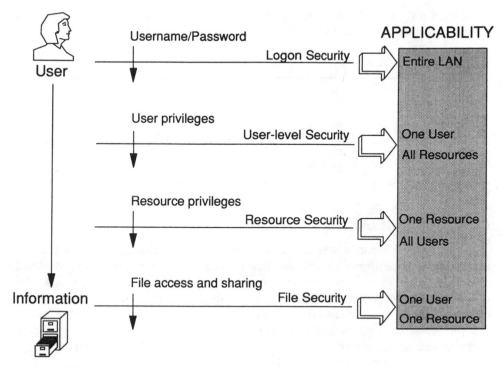

Figure 9.15 Network security concepts.

User-level Security

User-level security is designed to assign privileges to individual users according to their functions and need to access specific network resources. User-level security works by assigning basic user categories (network privilege classes) and resource-access privileges to user accounts. A *user profile* consists of a user category and a set of resource privileges assigned to a designated user. Table 9-5 compares user categories on LAN Manager and NetWare networks. Resources include file server directories, printers and external communications devices. For each registered network user, a set of privileges, permissions, or rights (terminology varies among network operating systems) *relative to that user on one or more assigned resources* is granted. Depending on the network operating system, user resource privileges may apply to some or all resources. Table 9-6 compares resource privileges granted to users by LAN Manager and NetWare operating systems.

All the network operating systems discussed in Part II implement the *User Group* concept, although specific features relative to group management may differ. A user group is a class of users who share a common function or who may have a need to access common information sources on the network. In some networks, individual users may be assigned privileges equivalent to those of an existing group, thus simplifying network administration. Group assignments (more than one group may be assigned to a single user) are usually part of the user profile.

Table 9-5. User Categories.

LAN Manager	*NetWare—286/SFT*
Admin	Supervisor
	Network operator
User	User
Guest	Guest

Resource-level Security

Resource-level security is designed to protect individual resources on the network, independent of specific user privileges. Since network resources give access to specific classes or forms of information, resource security protects information. On mass storage devices, resource security levels may apply to just a specific directory or to a directory and its child subdirectories. The latter case is generally referred to as *inherited privileges*. In some systems, such as VINES, there is no independent resource security—all access control is done through access control lists which specify authorized users for that resource.

In the case of Advanced NetWare 286/SFT, users and resources are assigned privileges (also known as rights) independently. If a user attempts to access a certain directory, the *effective access rights* are determined by comparing the user rights with the directory rights. The effective rights are simply the most restrictive between those the user carries and those held by the directory. Directory rights apply only to a specific directory level, whereas user rights apply to multiple directory levels on the user's logged-in file server. These concepts are illustrated in Figure 9.16.

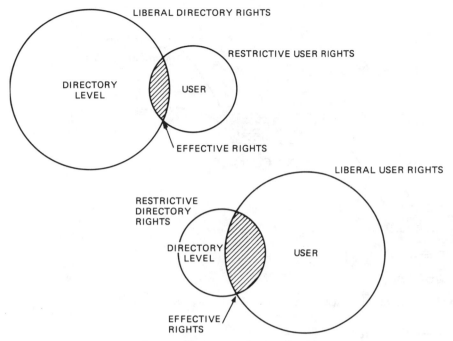

Figure 9.16 Novell NetWare effective directory rights.

Table 9-6. Resource Access Permissions.

LAN Manager[1]	*NetWare—286/SFT*[2]
Read	Read
Write	Write
Create	Creatte
Delete	Delete
Execute	Search
Change Attributes	Open
Change Permissions	Parental
Yes	Modify
No	

Notes:
[1]Applies only to designated resources.
[2]Applies to all directory resources.

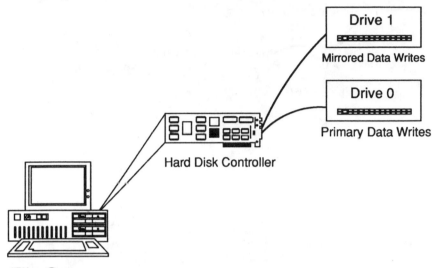

File Server

Figure 9.17 Fault tolerance with mirrored disk drives.

File Level Security

File level security generally affects whether a specific file is modifiable or shareable. File modification is controlled by the Read-only attribute. File sharing is controlled by the Shareable attribute.

Fault Tolerance

Fault tolerance is the combination of hardware and software techniques that assure a degree of network operation and file integrity under various failure conditions. The more common failures are loss of electrical power and hard disk failure. Total file server failures are possible, but more rarely encountered. The most obvious fault tolerant technique is to employ an *Uninterrupted Power Supply* (*UPS*), at least for each server, and preferably for all critical work stations. This discussion will be more concerned with fault tolerant features provided by the network operating system and its supported resources.

Novell's NetWare has been a leader in defining fault tolerant features for PC-based local area networks. Advanced NetWare with *System Fault Tolerance* (*SFT*) was originally defined for three levels of protection:

- Level I—*Surface defects* and *Disk mirroring*
- Level II—*Disk duplexing*
- Level III—*Duplexed servers* with *hot standby*

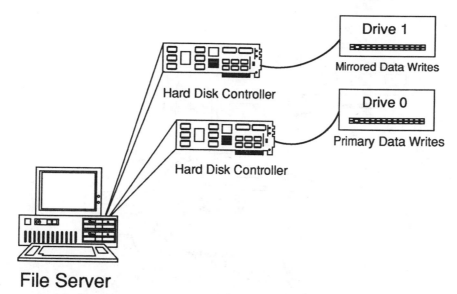

File Server

Figure 9.18 Fault tolerance with duplexed disk drives.

Disk mirroring uses a single disk controller card and two hard disk drives. Disk duplexing uses dual disk controllers and a hard disk drive on each controller. In each case, all disk operations on the primary drive are duplicated on the backup drive. Figures 9.17 and 9.18 show these concepts.

Advanced NetWare Version 2.1X with SFT supports Levels I and II. This version of SFT also includes a technique known as Transaction Tracking System, or TTS. NetWare 386 adds support for Level III. Details of Levels I, II, and III in NetWare are provided in Chapter 12.

The TTS capability of NetWare protects critical files against file server or hard disk failures. TTS works on a *transaction*, or group of related file activities. A typical transaction applies to database operations and may encompass a series of related file updates resulting from a single user activity. Transaction operations are very typical for accounting applications where a single General Ledger posting may cause updates to accounts payable, accounts receivable, and inventory files. Transactions have *boundaries*, which define where the transaction starts and where it ends. TTS works by assuring that all activity within a transaction boundary completes successfully or not at all. In other words, if a hard disk or file server failure occurs within the time period of a transaction boundary, the entire transaction is *rolled back* to its prestart state. All file updates as of the moment of failure are backed out and the entire transaction must be repeated when normal operation is restored. This process is illustrated in Figure 9.19.

TTS support can be transparent to the using application if the application uses the appropriate APIs. As an example, an application written using Btrieve Record Manager, NetWare's support for database-oriented Value Added Processes, can be program-

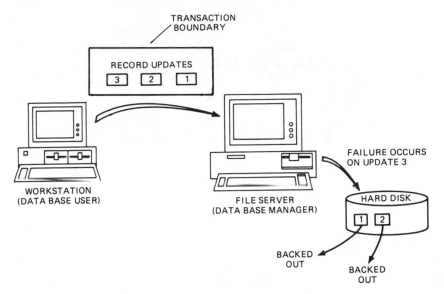

Figure 9.19 Fault tolerance with transaction rollback recovery.

med to indicate starting and stopping of logical transactions. If TTS is active, the application has access to transaction concurrency control and this access is transparent to the application user. Similar capabilities are available in the Database Manager module of IBM's OS/2 Extended Edition.

Because of the extra processing required to implement fault-tolerant features, certain performance penalties are inevitable. The proper balance between the extra reliability provided by fault-tolerant processing and maximum response time or throughput performance is a trade-off. The user organization must determine the trade-off priorities and what, if any, fault-tolerant processing will be bypassed.

Archiving and Backup

Another critical utility in multiuser environments is the ability to safely back up data files. Backup can always be accomplished by procedure and discipline, but some network systems provide additional features to make the job easier and more bullet-proof. Strictly speaking, backup systems are not fault-tolerant systems, although they may be referred to as such in vendor literature. Fault tolerance is generally considered to be a level of protection beyond techniques that can be imposed by discipline and procedure.

Several types of media are commonly used for backup: removable hard disk cartridges, tape cassettes, floppy diskettes, optical storage devices, and VCR recorders. Some systems even support the nine-track tape reels used in mainframe and minicomputer systems. In general, there is less standardization in tape and optical backup media than in hard disks; therefore, it is essential that a prospective LAN buyer determine precisely what brands and models are supported by a specific LAN

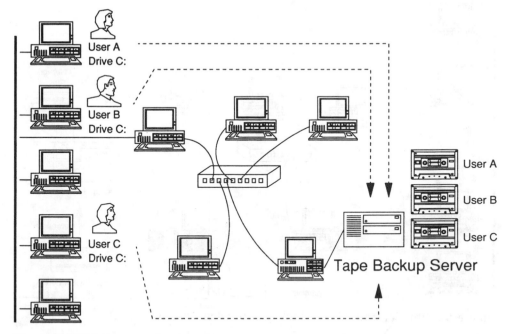

Figure 9.20(a) Decentralized tape backup with user control.

operating system. The LAN operating system must have (or be supplied from the backup media vendor) an I/O device driver specific to a given device or family of devices. In many cases, liaison with both the LAN vendor and the backup media vendor are required to ascertain compatibility or lack thereof. Another source of potential problems with backup devices is incompatibility between the network adapter card and the backup device controller card in the host computer. Interrupt channels (IRQs), DMA channels, and I/O port addresses should be carefully inventoried at all potential host computers to prevent hardware conflicts. Micro Channel Architecture (MCA) buses found in the IBM PS/2 series (except Models 25 and 30) avoid the channel conflict problem.

There are a variety of features found in backup systems. A backup drive (tape drive, for example) may be attached to the file server or to a work station. In some networks, the network must be shut down to do backups—these are referred to as *off-line backups*. In others, backups can be done concurrently with network operations, and are called *on-line backups*. Network backup can be centralized or distributed. *Centralized backup* puts one or more devices at a single location and allows only the network administrator to control backups from a single location, thus preserving a higher degree of data integrity and security. *Distributed backup* uses one or more backup device locations and allows anyone on the network to back up to this device(s). A distributed backup system is also referred to as a *backup server*, since it serves any authorized user

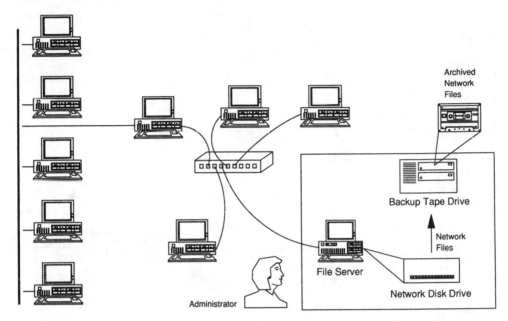

Figure 9.20(b) Centralized tape backup with administrator control.

on the network. Figures 9.20(a) and 9.20(b) illustrate the difference in the two modes of operation.

Backup systems commonly provide a scheduling feature that usually offers the option of backing up at designated clock times or at specified intervals (or both). If a particular network operating system does not support on-line backups from the file server, there are work-around options. If a tape drive is attached in a stand-alone mode to a work station, that work station can download file server directories or files and back them up locally. This system requires adherence to a more rigid discipline to compensate for lack of centralized network control over the operation. Finally, mature backup systems offer an archiving library feature. This feature typically allows the user (in a distributed system) to specify a file and the software will indicate a specific tape cartridge on which that file may be found. In a large system, time savings can be substantial.

Performance Monitoring and Audits

Performance monitoring is a management function provided by both third-party vendors and by network operating system vendors. Audit systems are more commonly found as part of the network operating system. These two related management features are important because they provide tools for the network administrator to improve network performance and user efficiency. Performance monitoring yields statistics on network throughput, server performance, hard disk performance, and network interface card operation. Audit systems provide information about who uses what resources on the network and monitors licensing restrictions for applications software.

Linking Applications Across Single and Multiple Networks

An application running in a LAN environment must ultimately communicate with compatible applications in other work stations and/or servers on the same LAN, or on other LANs or host systems that may or may not be directly connected. For this to happen successfully, the application must follow a prescribed set of rules on how it will establish a link and exchange data with the corresponding remote application. Keep in mind that "remote" in this context means any network resource not connected to the work station running the application. The remote application may be in the same room, in a different building, or across the continent.

Not every network operating system supports every transport service. However, the trend with OS/2-based network operating systems and NetWare 386 is to develop a comprehensive strategy to provide parallel support for all the major services. To view this strategy in its proper perspective, let's look at the Layer 5 and Layer 3 interfaces. Ideally, we want a particular transport service to remain transparent to the underlying hardware implementations covered in Chapter 10. In a similar fashion, we want the transport services to remain transparent to network applications. As if these requirements were not stringent enough, we also desire that multiple transport services be resident and available on demand by multiple applications.

We will discuss what transport services, or sets of prescribed protocol, are commonly available to support distributed applications and their significance in the larger context of standardization efforts. Among the more commonly used are NETBIOS, IBM's PC LAN Support Program, APPC/PC, Named Pipes, TCP/IP, XNS, and OSI. More detailed protocol aspects of APPC/PC, TCP/IP, XNS, and OSI will be discussed in Chapter 11, *Interoperability and Internetworking*.

Network Basic Input/Output System (NETBIOS)

The ability of applications to link up is directly dependent on the communications services provided to them by the network operating system. The most common example is the communications service referred to as NETBIOS, designed to allow communication between applications on a single logical LAN.

NETBIOS is the interface to a set of firmware (original broadband IBM PC Network) or software (all other current IBM LANs) that provides network transport services to applications programs, including network operating systems. NETBIOS provides roughly the analogous service between network applications and LAN hardware that IO.SYS and BIOS provide between MS-DOS applications and locally attached peripheral hardware. In terms of the ISO model, NETBIOS is the interface between Layers 7 or 6 and Layer 5. The protocol for Layers 1–5 underlying the original NETBIOS interface were developed as firmware on the IBM PC Network adapter card provided by Sytek Inc. under license to IBM. This card was part of a joint venture between Sytek and IBM to produce the original broadband IBM PC Network. The NETBIOS interface has also been adapted to the IBM Token-Ring network and to current versions of IBM's PC Network Broadband and PC Network Baseband. The Token-Ring adapter card contains only Layers 1 and 2 protocol. Depending on the specific NETBIOS emulation, some combination of Layers 3 through 5 are implemented by software in the host machine. In the IBM PC LAN Support Program, for example, only Layer 5 is implemented.

NETBIOS has been adopted as a de facto LAN-to-applications program interface standard by the LAN industry. It is important to differentiate between the NETBIOS interface and the NETBIOS protocol implementations. The application calls the NETBIOS interface and receives responses from that interface—the details of what happens within a particular NETBIOS protocol stack are unknown to the application.

One of the more confusing aspects of NETBIOS is its relationship to applications level software in non-IBM networks. There are many networks now offering "NETBIOS compatibility"—What does this mean, and how does it affect network performance? Is it really necessary? The answers to these questions are important to the network manager who is tasked with choosing the "right" network software. To answer these questions, it is important to understand what is included within the "black box" behind a NETBIOS software interrupt or API. In the original IBM PC Network, this box contains layered firmware known as the LocalNet/PC protocol. These are shown in Figure 9.21. In this implementation, all layers from the Physical Layer to the Session Layer are implemented. In the IBM Token-Ring network, the Physical and Data Link layers are different from their counterparts in the broadband IBM PC Network. Layer 5, as implemented by the IBM PC LAN Support Program, is functionally equivalent to its counterpart in the broadband network. Layers 4 and 3 do not exist in this program.

Although "NETBIOS-compatible" software may accept the standard NETBIOS calls and return the same results, the "black box" underneath NETBIOS may be significantly different. Most vendors implement an emulation of the Layer 5 protocol but use different transport and network layer protocol. These include XNS, TCP/IP, and Novell's SPX/IPX.

The most common user interface to NETBIOS consists of executing certain commands supported by the IBM PC LAN Program. This program is callable from an application or from the redirector via the software interrupt 2A. Third-party applications programs can access the services supported by NETBIOS through software interrupt 5C. This interrupt invokes a NETBIOS emulation program, as discussed above. If an applications program is written to use interrupt 2A or 5C, the emulation program will ensure a standard processing sequence. The application program provides certain required data elements, which are put into a format called a *Network Control Block*, or *NCB*. The call to interrupt 5C is then made, and the emulator handles the required LAN processing. Figure 9.22 illustrates this sequence. The advantage of this sequence is that applications programmers can use the

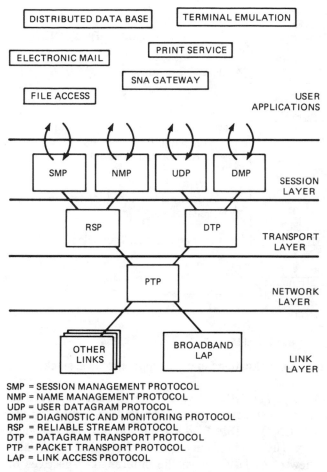

SMP = SESSION MANAGEMENT PROTOCOL
NMP = NAME MANAGEMENT PROTOCOL
UDP = USER DATAGRAM PROTOCOL
DMP = DIAGNOSTIC AND MONITORING PROTOCOL
RSP = RELIABLE STREAM PROTOCOL
DTP = DATAGRAM TRANSPORT PROTOCOL
PTP = PACKET TRANSPORT PROTOCOL
LAP = LINK ACCESS PROTOCOL

Figure 9.21 Localnet/PC protocol architecture.

standard NCB format to set up the LAN as an I/O device. This effort at standardization has a profound effect on the overall acceptance of LANs, both for software developers and for the ultimate benefactor—the user.

For applications not requiring specific session-level compatibility, a NETBIOS interface is not required. Session-level compatibility is required if the IBM PC Network-compatible *Name Management Protocol* (*NMP*) is used by a specific application software package. The naming service supported by NETBIOS recognizes human-readable names linked to a specific work station or file server on the network. This name is logically assigned to one of several possible objects active in the network node. For example, shared directories have names, attached printers have names, and names are maintained for several possible message recipients using that node. The disadvantage of this naming convention is that no central "telephone book" is maintained on the network. Each work station or file server

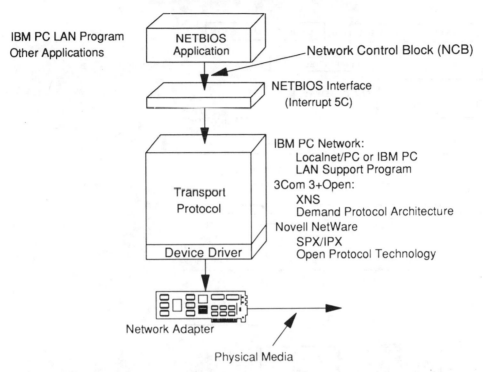

Figure 9.22 NETBIOS interface to applications and transport protocol stack.

keeps only its own name directory. The IBM network adapter card or NETBIOS emulators support up to 17 names per device, one of which is reserved for the permanent name of the device itself. The IBM PC LAN Support Program extends this name capacity to 254 names. The naming convention is shown in Figure 9.23. Figure 9.24 summarizes the view of NETBIOS from the different perspectives of IBM and non-IBM LANs.

What happens when an application desires to cooperate with its counterpart on a remote LAN? In this case, a service other than NETBIOS is more appropriate. The NETBIOS protocol was not designed for remote communications and operates somewhat inefficiently for this purpose. Lack of support for a more robust and centrally managed resource naming system is a particularly critical omission from NETBIOS.

Network Basic Extended User Interface (NETBEUI) and IBM PC LAN Support Program (PCLSP)

NETBEUI was developed by IBM for use on Token-Ring networks. It has the same basic applications interface as NETBIOS but does not use the proprietary lower-level protocol developed by Sytek under license to IBM. The Data Link Control (DLC) proto-

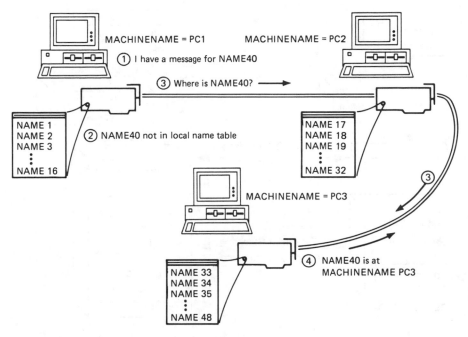

Figure 9.23 NETBIOS-compatible naming convention.

col is used with NETBEUI for compatiblity with IBM's PC LAN Program and the Token-Ring. DLC is a Layer 2 protocol compatible with the IEEE 802.2 Logical Link Control (LLC). The DLC protocol interfaces with any of the three standard IBM LAN architectures: Token-Ring, PC Network Broadband, and PC Network Baseband. These are discussed further in the next chapter. The IBM PC LAN Support Program was developed to replace NETBEUI when the PS/2 family of PCs was introduced. It functions in much the same manner as NETBEUI but is implemented as a set of device drivers rather than a memory-resident program. Figure 9.25 shows the architecture and component parts of the IBM PC LAN Support Program.

Advanced Program-to-Program Communications/PC (APPC/PC)

Whereas NETBIOS was designed as a mechanism to connect applications in the pure LAN environment, APPC/PC was developed to support IBM's vision of being able to link applications across an entire continuum of computing machinery, from mainframes to minis to PCs. Moreover, these applications would have peer-to-peer status instead of the older SNA hierarchical arrangement, in which the mainframe host controlled the entire network.

APPC/PC is the APPC interface defined for PCs connected to LANs. The protocol supporting APPC/PC parallel the NETBIOS protocol. APPC/PC's protocol is the Logical Unit Type 6.2 (LU 6.2) and consist of session, transport, and network layer ser-

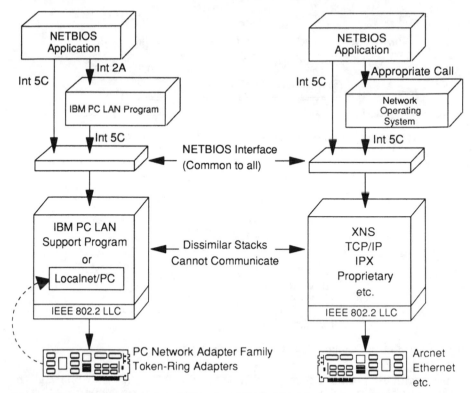

Figure 9.24 IBM and non-IBM NETBIOS implementation compared.

vices. PCs using APPC/PC are identified to an SNA network as Physical Unit Type 2.1 or 2.0 (PU 2.1 or PU 2.0). A PU 2.1 is a peer-to-peer type station, whereas a PU 2.0 is a terminal controller type station. Peer-to-peer stations are capable of transferring data with each other; a PU 2.0 station expects to be connected to a host front-end processor, or, in IBM's terminology, a Communications Controller running a version of the Network Control Program (NCP). Connected PU 2.1 stations can use either LAN physical connections or an SDLC link.

Named Pipes and Mailslots

The Named Pipes protocol was mentioned earlier as a major interprocess communications (IPC) feature of OS/2 Version 1.1 and later. For applications connectivity on a contiguous network, Named Pipes is much more efficient than NETBIOS and in all likelihood will become a dominant *intra-LAN* client-server standard by the early 1990s. Because it is a part of the OS/2 operating system and indirectly supported by MS-DOS (by virtue of recognizing Named Pipe file names), Named Pipes will have a catalytic effect on the standardization of groupware and other client-server applications development. Technically, Named Pipes is not a transport protocol, but instead is an applica-

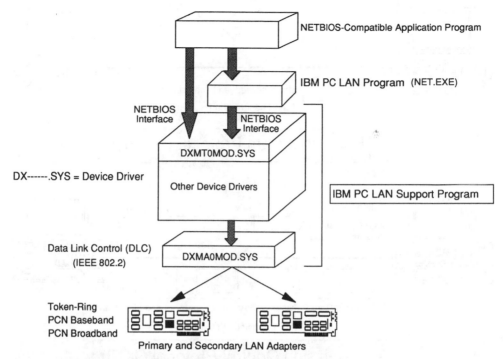

Figure 9.25 IBM PC LAN support program architecture.

tions-level interface to OS/2. However, it achieves a similar functional purpose—the connection of cooperating applications software on physically separated computers. Mailslots are set up in the same manner as Named Pipes. The chief difference is that mailslots are designed for one-way, short messaging rather than two-way sessions.

TCP/IP

TCP/IP, or Transmission Control Protocol/Internet Protocol, originated within the Department of Defense (DoD) and DoD's long-standing *Arpanet* wide-area network. Arpanet has been subsumed as one component of the Defense Data Network (DDN) but has always been one of the most sophisticated wide-area networks in the world. The ability of Arpanet/DDN to interconnect a large variety of dissimilar host computers worldwide is made possible in part by the TCP/IP protocol. Only in the late 1980s has TCP/IP transitioned from relative obscurity in the commercial world to become a major force in standardizing the interconnection of commercial networks, both LANs and WANs.

Today, TCP/IP has become the protocol of choice to connect such diverse systems as UNIX, MS-DOS, OS/2, and various mainframe and minicomputer operating systems and their dissimilar file structures. Proprietary operating systems such as Advanced Netware, NetWare 386, VINES, and 3 + Open now support the TCP/IP protocol with a variety of implementation schemes. A standard is being developed to combine the

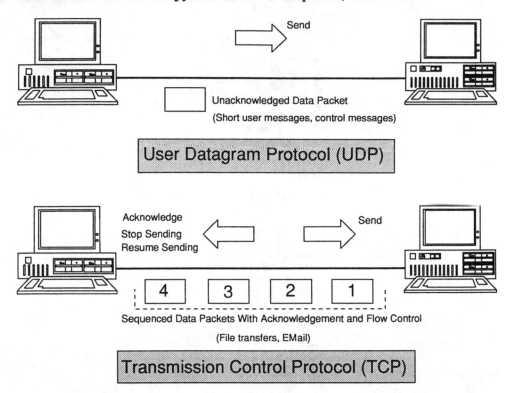

Figure 9.26 Datagram and transmission control protocol compared for TCP/IP.

NETBIOS interface with TCP/IP protocol. This standard is defined in two documents: Request For Comments (RFC) 1001 and RFC 1002. What this means is that users of otherwise incompatible operating systems can now accomplish basic file transfers across a wide variety of networks, regardless of the details of physical connection. As with other sets of transport services, however, not all TCP/IP implementations are alike; therefore, the end-user must shoulder the burden of compatibility and interoperability.

TCP/IP includes three generic application protocol: *File Transfer Protocol* (*FTP*), *Simple Mail Transfer Protocol* (*SMTP*), and *TELNET*, a terminal emulation program. Underlying these applications are two lower layers of protocol, the Transport Control Protocol (TCP) and the Internet Protocol (IP). TCP is a *reliable, connection-oriented* protocol. Reliable means that the transport-level protocol guarantees that data packets will arrive in sequence and error-free, with no missing data. Connection-oriented means that the protocol establishes a session between two remote stations or processes and maintains that session during the entire interval required to transfer data packets. TCP/IP also supports a User Datagram Protocol (UDP) designed for rapid, one-way delivery of relatively short messages. This concept is termed a *connectionless* service. UDP is not reliable, depending instead on the reliability inherent in lower-level protocol such as the IEEE 802.X series. Figure 9.26 illustrates the conceptual differences between TCP and UDP services.

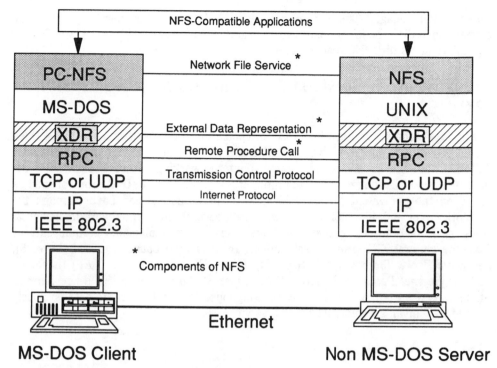

Figure 9.27 Network File System (NFS) architecture.

TCP/IP can run on any combination of Layers 1 and 2 as long as the appropriate drivers (interface software between Layers 2 and 3) are available. Although TCP/IP is most commonly found on Ethernets, it has been run on Token-Ring and Arcnet. Because of TCP/IP's importance to internetworking, from whence it was derived, discussion on protocol details is presented in Chapter 11.

One product developed to work on top of TCP/IP is worthy of discussion in its own right. The product is the Network File System (NFS) from Sun Microcomputers. NFS is a generic capability supported by TCP/IP, but not a TCP/IP protocol per se. The NFS protocol hierarchy is shown in Figure 9.27. NFS is compatible with file systems on over 100 computers, from mainframes to PCs. NFS consists of two additional protocol: Remote Procedure Call (RPC) at the Session Layer and Extended Data Representation (XDR) at the Presentation Layer.

RPC is a machine-and operating system-independent protocol designed to execute commands on a remote node of the network. NFS commands are file-oriented and pass parameters such as directory, filename, and file attributes. NFS commands are set up like subprograms or procedures in a software program, hence the name Remote Procedure Call. XDR is a way of normalizing data representation among a large number of otherwise incompatible operating systems. The normalization process involves byte-ordering (which byte in a data word is the high-order, or most significant, byte), word length (how many bytes in different types of data), and how numbers are represented (floating point usage). The NFS protocol work with all popular operating system file formats, including the MacIntosh Hierarchical File System, DEC's VAX/VMS, MS-DOS, and all versions of UNIX, among others.

Xerox Network Services (XNS), Including Novell's SPX/IPX

XNS has been the transport protocol of choice for 3Com in their 3+ and 3+Open series of network operating systems. XNS has an Ethernet heritage and, along with TCP/IP, was one of the earlier practical internetworking protocol. NetWare's Sequenced Packet Exchange (SPX) and Internet Packet Exchange (IPX) protocol stack is based on the equivalent layers of XNS. XNS spans the Session Layer through the Network Layer and, like TCP/IP, can work with several physical network implementations, such as Ethernet, Arcnet, and Token-Ring. 3Com implements certain features from the general XNS protocol set—among them are the *Courier Protocol* (Layer 5), *Sequenced Packet Protocol* (*SPP*) (Layer 4), *Packet Exchange Protocol* (*PEP*) (Layer 4), and the *Internet Datagram Protocol* (*IDP*) (Layer 3). To implement its Name Service, 3Com uses a variation of the Xerox Clearinghouse Protocol. This protocol is closely related to Banyan's StreetTalk naming service.

OSI

The ultimate dream of networking professionals is to have a single consistent set of protocols that can be used worldwide as a basis for interoperable communications between dissimilar computer systems and networks. This dream may never come to pass in reality, but if it does, it will be through the efforts of the International Standards Organization (ISO) and its model for Open Systems Interconnection (OSI). OSI is the basis for the 7-layer protocol model discussed throughout this book, and for continuing efforts to find long-range solutions to the problems of standardization. The problem thus far with the implementation of OSI protocol is the multiplicity of options developed at each layer—this inevitably leads to diverse implementation schemes and a commensurate breakdown of standardization.

The ISO protocol stack that will be supported by major LAN software vendors is the *ISO TP4*, or *Transport Class 4*. This is a connection-oriented protocol, which, as discussed earlier, means that a virtual circuit is established between the two entities communicating with this protocol. ISO TP4 is the highest grade of service available among the ISO transport protocol and assumes that the underlying network is unreliable. In other words, TP4 does its own error checking.

Multiple Protocol Selection

Microsoft, IBM, and Novell have developed different versions of a multiprotocol management scheme. Microsoft's is called Network Driver Interface (NDI) and Novell's is called Open Protocol Technology (OPT). The goal of a multiple protocol interface is to address arrows 2 and 3 in Figure 9.3, i.e., the interface between the network operating system and the transport protocol stack, and between the transport stack and the underlying physical network implementation. Ideally, we would want the operating system to have access to a selection of popular protocol stacks; likewise, the protocol stacks should be independent of our choice of Ethernet, Arcnet, or Token-Ring physical networks. Multiple protocol selection design is migrating towards a capability to load a number of supported protocol sets dynamically as needed—the alternative is to load all sets all the time.

Summary

In this chapter, LANs have been discussed from the systems software perspective. The relationship between host MS-DOS and OS/2 operating systems, network operating systems, and the software required to link applications was highlighted. These concepts and relationships are crucial to an understanding of not only how networks operate, but to making informed decisions on the specific network software architecture needed to meet an organization's business needs. In support of an application, the network operating system will eventually call on the services provided by the underlying network hardware implementation. The details of the physical aspect of moving information on the LAN and its significance will be covered next.

10

Local Area Networks—the Communications Perspective

Introduction

The purpose of this chapter is to focus on the basic terminology and concepts associated with the underlying communications technology of LANs. This technology provides the means to move data between stations on the network and to manage access to the data path common to these stations. The significance of certain LAN industry "standards," such as Ethernet, Arcnet, and IBM Token-Ring, are more related to communications considerations than to data processing and will be discussed in that context. We also will show how the shared applications and LAN systems software discussed in the previous chapter rely on the physical connectivity provided by a LAN. By the end of this chapter, the reader will have an appreciation for the physical characteristics of LANs, all of which have some significance in selecting the most appropriate LAN system for a particular location or operating environment. An objective of this chapter is to make often-used terms such as *Star*, *Ring*, *Bus*, *Broadband*, and *Baseband* meaningful to the potential network buyer and manager.

In the remainder of the chapter, we will discuss the physical components of a local area network: the network adapter card, wiring types and layouts, how data are represented on a LAN, and the basics of Physical and Data Link Layer protocol for the most common LANs. We will also cover the impact of physical factors on LAN selection and performance.

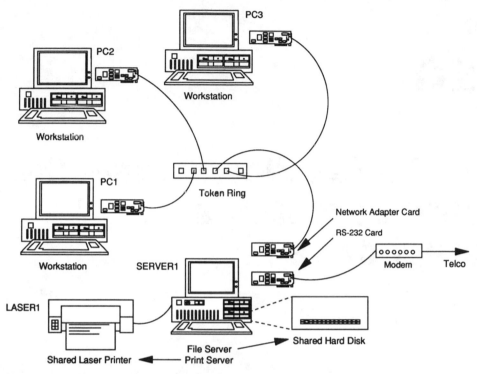

Figure 10.1 Basic LAN hardware components.

Network Adapter Cards—Getting the Data In and Out

For purposes of illustrating basic concepts, the simplified LAN depicted in Figure 10.1 will be briefly described. Hardware components consist of four PCs, with a printer and an internal hard disk attached to the PC called "SERVER1." In each PC, an adapter card is required in one of the expansion slots—this card is commonly referred to as a *network adapter card* (*NAC*) or *network interface card* (*NIC*). The adapter card has the same purpose in this network as the RS-232-C asynchronous communications card does in a modem/telephone network. That purpose is to provide the required functions for data to move from the PC to the network and from the network to the PC. This card is primarily designed for the communications function of a LAN. Each station on the LAN containing a network adapter card is referred to as a *network node*.

The network adapter card plays a major role in determining local area network performance. It is also the physical and logical link between the microcomputer hosting the NAC and the network to which it is attached. On one side, the adapter card must exchange data with the host computer's microprocessor and internal

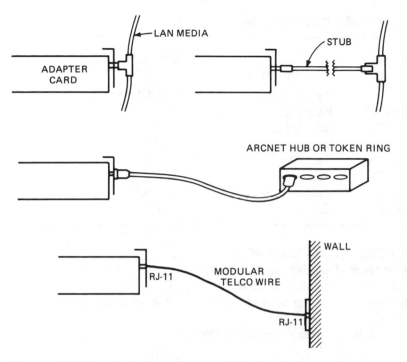

Figure 10.2 Physical connections to LANs (typical).

RAM through the computer's *internal bus*; on the other side, it must transmit and receive data at the speed and in the format required by the network physical data path, or *media*. Various means of connecting NACs to the media are shown in Figure 10.2.

One of the major factors that characterizes a LAN is the speed at which data move on the network. Table 10-1 contrasts the speeds of 10, 4, and 2.5 Mbps LANs (such as Ethernet, IBM Token-Ring, and Arcnet) with speeds of other forms of data movement to and from, or within, an IBM-compatible PC. The table points out that network data rates can vary widely from internal computer data rates. The table also shows the large disparity between asynchronous link and LAN data rates.

Local area network data transfers are done in a serial mode—bit by bit. A mismatch in data rates between the network and its host processor requires *buffering*, or temporary data storage, to prevent the loss of data as it goes into the host computer. It is the job of the network adapter card to manage data rate mismatches. Such mismatches usually occur because the network adapter card processes data packets slower than the network carries them and slower than the host computer is capable of moving data to and from the card. In other words, the network adapter card becomes a bottleneck between the network media and its host computer.

Table 10-1. Data Transfer Rate Comparison.

Transfer Type	Operation	Maximum Speed (Mbps)
Serial	Network data rate	10.0/4.0/2.5[1]
Parallel	RAM read/write	48.0[2,3]
Parallel	DMA transfer	48.0[2,3]
Parallel	Processor-initiated I/O	48.0[2,3]
Parallel	Hard disk I/O	6.5–8.0[2,4]
Parallel	Floppy disk I/O	0.25
Serial	Multiuser terminal I/O	0.0192[5]
Serial	Modem at 2,400 bps	0.0024[5]

[1]Ethernet/IBM Token-Ring (4 Mbps)/Arcnet data rate.
[2]Theoretical maximum dependent on host hardware. Figures shown are for 16-bit IBM PC/AT compatible at 12 MHz.
[3]The network sees much slower node speeds due to processing delays on the adapter card.
[4]Hard disk time does not include average read/write head access time.
[5]RS-232-C.

The adapter card may contain significant amounts of *firmware*, or software in one or more Read-Only-Memory (ROM) chips. This software is primarily designed to implement communications protocol. Firmware may include protocol up to and including any layer of the ISO model. Most commonly, the cards have firmware for Layers 1 and 2 of the ISO model.

Adapter cards are designed to communicate with the host computer through *Direct Memory Access* (*DMA*) channels, *Interrupt Request* (*IRQ*) channels, and/or Input/Output *ports*. Figure 10.3 illustrates the basic functions of a network adapter card, including basic data conversions (e.g., parallel to serial), packet assembly and disassembly, network access control, data buffering, and network signaling.

Of significance to LAN administrators is the potential for conflict between LAN adapter cards and other expansion cards in the computer that uses the same channel or port. In some designs, the adapter card uses a portion of the PC's extended RAM (addressable memory between 640 Kb and 1 Mb), which may conflict with devices such as VGA video adapters. Channel conflicts will prevent both the LAN and the interfering card's device from working properly, or at all. A well-designed adapter card will allow changing of the various interface channels through dip switches or jumper blocks.

Micro Channel Architecture (MCA)-compatible boards found in PS/2 Model 50s and above bypass this problem with intelligent channel management. A System Configuration program (SC.EXE) with its associated Adapter Descriptor File (ADF) automatically senses available interrupts, channels, and ports and provide a software-managed capa-

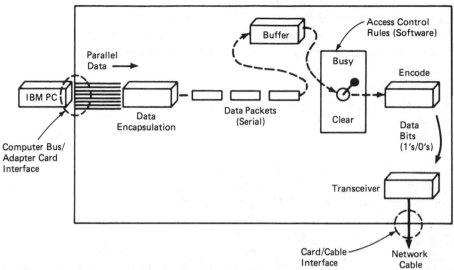

Figure 10.3 Network adapter card functions.

bility to reconfigure the adapter card. In either of the PC or PS/2 cases, a well-planned network installation should include a thorough inventory of all I/O channels in use on each work station and server.

Local Area Network Classification

From pure communications and physical perspectives, the type of network selected by an organization has a significant bearing on several factors of importance to network management. These include:

- Hardware and installation cost
- Ease of installation
- Ease of expansion
- Fault isolation
- Fault tolerance
- Performance

Thus, the prospective user should carefully weigh the inherent strengths and weaknesses of a particular network's physical configuration and its relationship to the first two layers of the ISO model. In evaluating these characteristics, some thought should be given to the vendor's strategic direction as new product lines evolve. Although the most significant LAN strategies are oriented towards the higher ISO layer functions and potential network applications, some significant directions can be seen in hardware evolution. IBM's direction in continuing to support the broadband PC Network while emphasizing the IBM Token-Ring wiring plans is a specific example of what to observe in LAN hardware trends. The increasing penetration of twisted-pair Ethernet and Token-Ring systems is another current hardware trend. In many LAN installations, hardware costs associated with the first two ISO layers can become a significant economic consideration.

Four ways of classifying networks as data communications systems are by

- Type of data path
- The means used to represent data on the media
- Physical network layout
- Media sharing

The commonly used terms for these concepts are *media*, *signaling*, *topology*, and *access protocol*, respectively. Layer 1 protol incorporates the first three of these classifications, while Layer 2 protocol addresses media sharing.

Media

Media is the general term used to describe the data path that forms the physical channel between local area network devices, or nodes. Media can be twisted-pair wire, such as that used for telephone installations, coaxial cable of various sizes and electrical characteristics, fiber optics, and free space, supporting either light waves or radio waves. Wire or fiber optics media are referred to as *bounded media*. Free space is sometimes referred to as *unbounded media*. Media differ in their ability to support high data rates and long distances. The reasons for this are based in physics and electrical engineering and include the concepts of *noise absorption*, *radiation*, *attenuation*, and *bandwidth*.

Noise absorption is the susceptability of the media to external electrical noise that could cause distortion of the data signal and, thus, data errors. Radiation is the leakage of signal from the media caused by undesirable electrical characteristics of the media. Radiation and the physical characteristics of the media contribute to attenuation, or the reduction in signal strength as the signal travels down the wire or through free space. Attenuation limits the usable distance that data can travel on the media. Bandwidth is similar to the concept of frequency response in a stereo amplifier—the greater the frequency response, the higher the bandwidth. According to a fundamental principal of information theory, higher bandwidth communications channels will support higher data rates. In this context, the media are considered to represent one or more communications channels.

Twisted-pair Wire

Twisted-pair wire has traditionally been the most limited form of data path, both in speed and in distance. In many cases, twisted-pair media required an unpleasant choice between acceptable data rates at short distances, or lower data rates at acceptable distances. It has always been the cheapest form of wiring to install, primarily because of the low cost of the media itself. Twisted-pair cable typically costs $0.05 to $0.10 per lineal foot for unshielded wire and about $0.25 per foot for shielded wire. Shielded wire would be typically used in an electrically noisy environment.

Twisted-pair cable has the added advantage of ubiquity, since it is the most common communications wiring installed in offices today. Twisted-pair wiring can take on entirely different personalities depending on the type of signaling employed. The gamut runs from RS-232-C, which is nominally limited to 19,200 bps at 50 feet, to AT&T's Starlan system, which will support data rates of 1 Mbps for distances of over 800 feet.

Continuing developments in LAN technology have made twisted-pair wiring more commonly used for LAN media. Advanced circuitry now allows the optional use of twisted-pair wiring on traditional coaxial networks, such as Ethernet and Arcnet. Token-Ring network systems use a robust form of twisted-pair wiring that includes multiple twisted pairs and individual-pair, metallic-foil shielding, all encased in a metallic braid and outer sheathing similar to coaxial cabling. Some Token-Ring cabling includes extra twisted pairs for simultaneous data and voice conveyance. This type of cable is an excellent choice for building-wide wiring systems, particularly if the communications capability is planned prior to building construction. Table 10-2 summarizes the types of cabling used in IBM Token-Ring LANS. Listed costs are approximate, with a downward trend as more Token-Ring systems are installed.

Although telephone wiring is ubiquitous in most offices, its use in LANs requires careful planning and survey. Most telephone outlets have two pairs of wires—one pair is used as the telephone "tip" and "ring" (voice) channel, and the other pair is available for other uses. As a minimum, the unused pair must be checked for continuity throughout the area in which the LAN will be installed. Planning for new office spaces should include a detailed assessment of this potential wiring source. In many cases, these spare pairs may not meet LAN electrical specifications and should be thoroughly performance tested before a commitment is made to use them throughout the organization. At the very least, the use of standard twisted pair usually results in restrictions in the size of the LAN and the number of stations that can be connected to the media.

Table 10-2. IBM Token-Ring Cabling Types.

Cable Type	Composition	Use	Cost/ 1000 Ft
1	2 twisted pairs, 22 AWG Individual foil shields braided outer shield	High-grade data	$0.40
2	Same as Type 1 except 4 additional unshielded twisted pairs	Voice/data	$0.55
3	4 unshielded twisted pairs, 22 or 24 AWG Must meet IBM specs for attenuation/ impedance	Low-grade data	$0.25
5	2 Fiber optic cables	Dual Fiber rings	$3.00
6	2 twisted pairs, 26 AWG single inner foil shield braided outer shield	Patch panels	$0.30
8	4 flat parallel wires 26 AWG individual copper shields and outer braid	Undercarpet	$6.00
9	Same as Type 1 except 26 AWG wire vice 22 AWG	Medium-grade data	$0.75

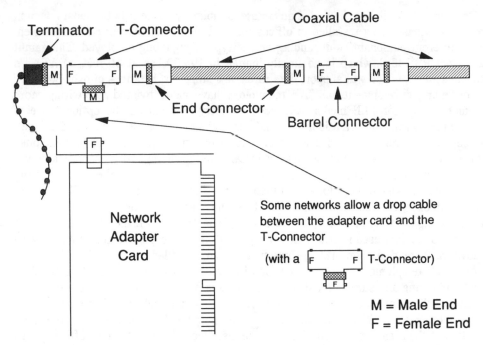

Figure 10.4 Coaxial media components.

Coaxial Cable

The next most common form of media is coaxial cable. This cable has been used for years in the communications and data processing industries. Amateur radio, cable TV, CB radio, cellular radio telephones, and various mainframe data terminals all use some form of coaxial cable. Many of today's LAN systems use coaxial cable. The more common of these are depicted in Table 10-3. The impedance values are shown because of the importance of properly mixing components of dissimilar impedances on the same network segment. These components include the cable proper and various pieces of hardware used to construct coaxial networks such as T-connectors, barrel-connectors, and segment terminators. These components are illustrated in Figure 10.4.

The cost of coaxial cable, even the higher-grade, low-loss, and double-shielded varieties, has decreased drastically in recent years due to its greatly increased use in computer installations. Coaxial cable will support data rates of up to several tens of Mbps at distances up to several thousand feet. Certain types of signaling will allow high data rates over distances of several miles.

Coaxial cable is more difficult to connect to network devices, generally requiring more planning than twisted-pair systems. Many coaxial systems require the connector on the main cable to be attached directly to the adapter on the PC—this reduces flexibility in locating work stations and servers. A better arrangement is the use of a drop cable as shown in Figure 10.4. This allows the use of wall jacks and a neater

Table 10-3. Common Coaxial Cable Types.

Network Type	Cable Type	Impedance (Ohms)	Cost/Ft($)[1]
Ethernet (Standard)	Type N	50	0.95
Ethernet Transceiver [2]	Multiwire	50	0.85
Ethernet (Thin)	RG-58	50	0.25
Arcnet	RG-62	93	0.20
Broadband (Drop)	RG-59	75	0.15
Broadband (Trunk/Feeder)	RG-11	75	0.25

[1]Costs are order of magnitude only per 1,000 Ft
[2]Required with N-type Ethernet installations

installation. Network administrators should determine the permissability of drop cables within the LAN topology rules before committing to final wiring and location plans.

Additional flexibility for planning coaxial networks is provided by hardware that allows mixing of different coaxial cable types. For example, 3Com provides a multiport repeater that allows connection of Type N Ethernet through an Attachment Unit Interface (AUI) cable port and multiple RG-58 Thin Ethernet ports. Other hardware, such as 3Com's CableTamer balun, allows the mixing of two dissimilar impedance cables, in this case RG-59 (75 Ohm) and RG-58 (50 Ohm), or RG-62 (93 Ohm) and RG-58 (50 Ohm). Figure 10.5 illustrates the configuration possibilities with this type of hardware.

Fiber Optics

The newest form of bounded media is fiber optics, which has superior data handling and security characteristics. Fiber optic cables cannot be easily tapped and will support data rates of several hundred Mbps. Connection costs for fiber optic networks are currently high, but are expected to decrease significantly in the next few years. Several vendors are capable of supplying fiber optic versions of Ethernet and Token-Ring networks. Fiber optic cable costs range from $1.20 to $1.70 per lineal foot plus approximately $100–125 per cable for termination hardware and labor. Ethernet-compatible fiber optic transceivers range from $500–750 per PC connection.

Free Space (Unbounded)

The ether was one of the first media used for experimental local area networking with the Aloha Net packet radio system. This network was used in Hawaii to connect remote terminals to a central processing facility. Amateur radio operators have been increasingly using packet radio systems in recent years and the technology appears to have promise for specialized LAN applications. Packet radio systems can extend

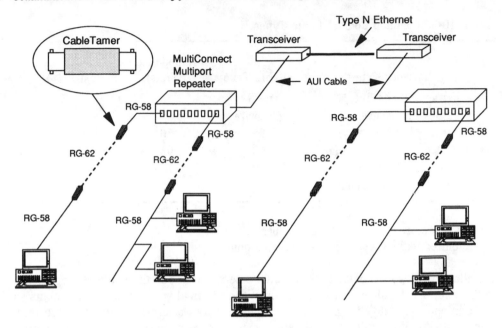

Figure 10.5 Dissimilar media mixing on LANs.

networking to ranges beyond cable-based radio frequency systems through the use of repeater stations and line-of-sight transmission. Radio-based local area networks are subject to Federal Communications Commission regulatory action since they depend on RF broadcast transport systems. Data rates supported are dependent on the frequency band used for the network—the higher the frequency band, the higher the maximum possible data rate. A potentially viable technology is the use of ultra-high frequency (UHF) radio modems operating at very low power levels for office workgroup LANs. Imagine the benefit of bypassing the detailed planning and costs involved in extensive wiring plans!

Topology

Topology is a fancy word for a simple concept—the way networks are physically connected together. Current literature most commonly classifies topologies as the *star*, *ring*, and *bus*. In terms of currently available products, a more practical classification would include *distributed star*, bus, and *branching tree*. A distributed star network has hubs that can be interconnected and that support a varying number of network stations. Bus networks consist of a single, terminated cable to which network stations connect. Branching tree networks are associated with a particular type of LAN closely related to cable TV distribution systems. Distributed star, bus, and branching tree topologies have variations as shown in Figures 10.6(a)–(c). For example, while many distributed star networks appear physically similar, the function of the star's hub (and its price) can be radically different.

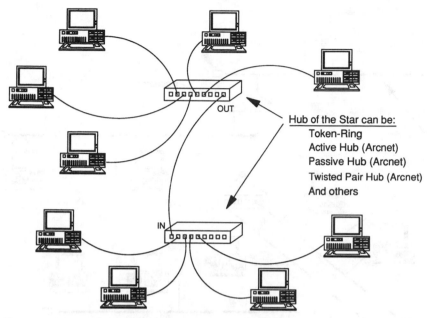

Figure 10.6(a) Distributed star topology options.

In coaxial Arcnet networks, the hubs are either *passive repeaters* or *active repeaters*. Active repeaters are responsible for amplification and retiming of data packets enroute to connected stations. Passive repeaters just reroute the data with no additional signal processing. The practical difference between the two types of repeaters is in the number of ports and the allowable distances each can support. IBM Token-Ring hubs contain electrical ring circuits, and are referred to as *Media Access Units*, or *MAUs*. In twisted-pair Ethernets and Arcnets, the hubs are *wiring concentrators* and perform both concentration and signal processing functions. The latter include amplification and retiming of the signal similar to the Arcnet repeater function. Active repeaters, MAUs, and wiring concentrators can be connected together to extend coverage of their respective LANs.

Why is topology significant? To the LAN end-user, it is not. To the LAN manager or to an organization's microcomputer-support department, topology influences certain factors important to network selection and management. These include

- The complexity and, therefore, cost of network cable installation. Cable installation can often be a major cost factor for an entire network system.
- Redundant, or fail-safe design.
- Fault isolation.
- The strategy for physically expanding and reconfiguring the network.

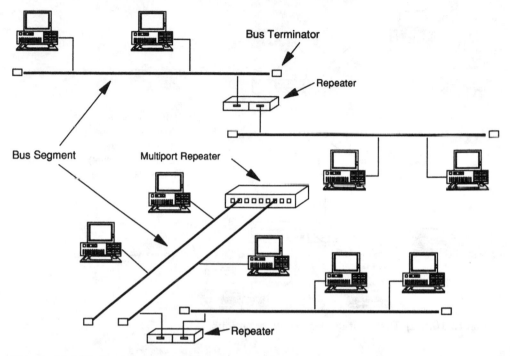

Figure 10.6(b) Bus topology options.

Star-wired networks, such as IBM's Token-Ring, Proteon's ProNET and Arcnet, are particularly well-suited for multifloor installations. Hubs on star-wired networks are frequently placed in *wiring closets*, with cable running from the wiring closet to wall outlets in selected office spaces. These networks are installed in a manner similar to standard office telephone systems. A well-designed wiring closet can simplify network reconfiguration. This is usually accomplished through the use of *patch panels*. For example, servers and other special-purpose devices such as gateways and bridges can be easily moved to different network segments. A basic example of such a system is shown in Figure 10.7. Wiring closet design also aids considerably in fault-isolation and maintenance.

An example of inherent redundancy in a PC LAN topology is the IBM Token-Ring. Media access units provide redundancy through the use of a backup wire path, as shown in Figure 10.8. The figure shows ring reconfiguration resulting from a media failure. The MAU also has built-in hardware features to isolate failed station loops from the active ring.

Star-wired networks are the superior choice for fault detection and isolation. The latter function is considerably aided if the star hub has LED indicators for connected segments. These indicators signify an electrical fault on that segment. Bus networks

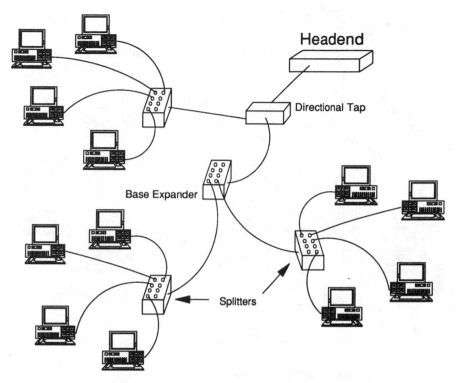

Figure 10.6(c) Branching tree topology.

are more difficult to diagnose since there is no means to isolate faulty cable segments. *Time-Domain Reflectometers* (*TDR*) can be used on a bus network to locate cable faults by measuring the elapsed time from transmission of a probe to receipt of the reflected signal.

Distributed star networks are expanded by connecting additional hubs, as was shown in Figure 10.6(a). Although bus networks are not as well suited for multifloor installations, they are well suited to linear expansion. This expansion can be accomplished both by cutting into a stretch of cable or by moving the terminator, as shown in Figure 10.9. Bus networks can also be reconfigured into a *tree* topology by the use of repeaters, as was shown in Figure 10.6(b).

Each of the three primary LAN protocol types have topology rules that must be followed to maintain specified performance. These rules are a consequence of the electrical signaling used by the LAN and the relationship between the signaling used and the LAN's access protocol. Signaling and access are discussed later in this chapter. Topology rules generally describe the following elements:

- Maximum segment length (terminator-to-terminator on bus networks or hub-to-station distance on star-wired networks).
- Maximum number of stations allowable per segment.

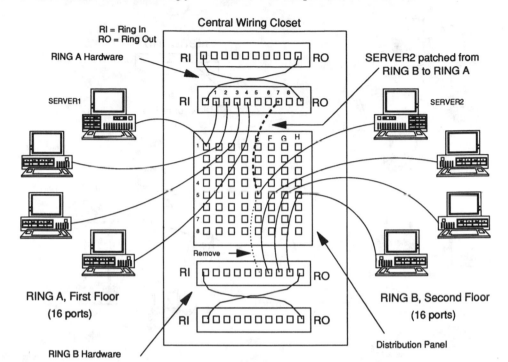

Figure 10.7 Wiring closet cable plan (typical).

- Maximum number of segments.
- Maximum total electrical length of a single LAN.
- Maximum number of repeaters allowed.
- Type of connections allowed, including placement of terminators and loops.

These rules are summarized in Figures 10.10 through 10.13 for Ethernet, Arcnet, Token-Ring, and the broadband IBM PC Network.

Signaling

Signaling is the method by which a network represents data as a serial stream of 1s and 0s on the media during its movement between the output of the source network adapter card and the input of the destination network card. It also refers to the manner in which digital 1s and 0s familiar to a computer are transmitted on the network data path. Signaling is generally the responsibility of the network adapter card. In some networks, such as certain forms of Ethernet, signaling is accomplished in a separate transceiver that is attached directly to the network media and connected to a network node by a transceiver cable, or *Attachment Unit Interface (AUI)*. Figure 10.10 shows this arrangement. This is a significantly more costly configuration than the more popular direct connection using thin Ethernet

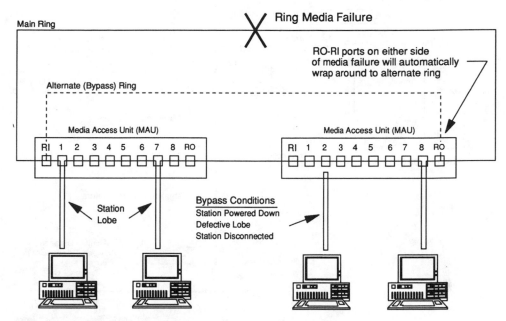

Figure 10.8 Media failure recovery on Token-Ring LAN.

cable, as is shown in Figure 10.4. In most current networks, transceivers are built in to the network adapter card. The two basic catagories of LAN signaling are *baseband* and *broadband*.

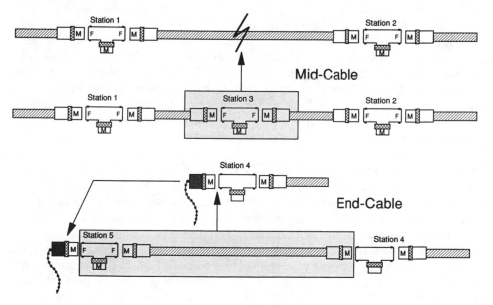

Figure 10.9 Coaxial LAN expansion techniques.

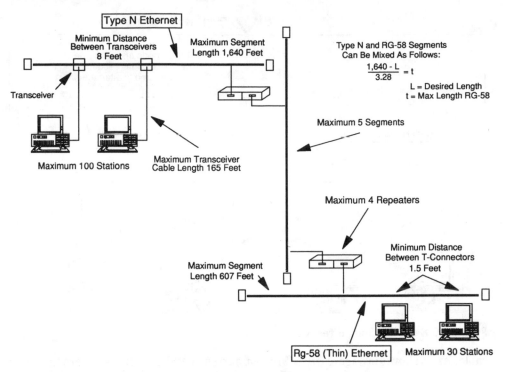

Figure 10.10 Ethernet LAN design considerations.

Before discussing baseband and broadband networks, the terms *bandwidth* and *Frequency Division Multiplexing* (*FDM*) require definition. Bandwidth can be loosely defined as the amount of information that a communications system will support. The best-known example is the AM broadcast band, which extends from 540 Kilohertz (KHz) to 1610 KHz. The bandwidth of the AM band is 1070 KHz (1610 − 540 = 1070). This band supports 107 10 KHz-wide channels in North America since the *Federal Communications Commission* (*FCC*) has defined an AM channel as 10 Khz wide. If the bandwidth were increased, the number of AM broadcasting channels supported would increase. Each AM broadcast channel carries a certain type of information—in this case, voice and music entertainment.

Another well-known example is cable TV (*CATV*). CATV has a bandwidth of 300 Megahertz (MHz) to support the transmission and distribution of 50, 6 MHz-wide TV channels throughout a specified subscriber community. For television broadcasting, the FCC has defined a TV channel as 6 MHz wide. The information in a single TV channel consists of video frames, color coding, and audio (voice and music).

There is a specific relationship between the measures of bandwidth and data rate. Remember that LAN data rate is a measure of how much serial data can be transmitted in a unit of time. In general, the higher the bandwidth, the greater the data rate that can be supported. The exact nature of this relationship is beyond the scope of this book, but suffice it to say that an information channel with a 6 MHz-wide bandwidth

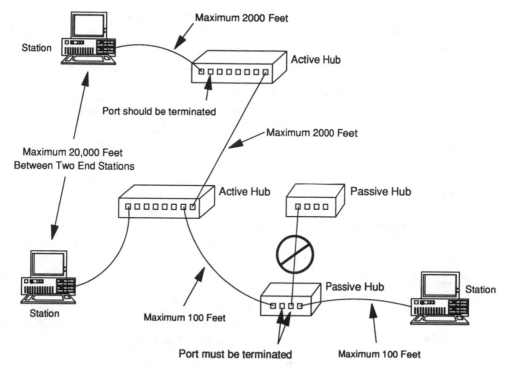

Figure 10.11 Arcnet LAN design considerations.

could support a 5 Mbps data rate LAN, or better with proper electronics design. You can see other examples of this phenomena with modems that support data rates up to 19,200 bps on a 4 KHz standard telephone bandwidth. This efficiency is achieved through advanced signaling and data compression techniques.

One might ask how it is that in some communications systems, information is funneled into discrete channels across the available bandwidth such as the AM and TV examples described above. The process of creating these channels divides the available bandwidth into well-defined frequency segments. This process is known as *Frequency Division Multiplexing*, or *FDM*. The FDM process creates a series of channels, each with its lower and upper limit frequency. Putting this another way, broadcasters and the FCC have multiplexed 107 AM radio channels into a single 1070 KHz-wide band by dividing that band into 107 equal parts, or 10 KHz-wide channels. We will return to this concept in the description of broadband networks.

In the *baseband* system shown in Figure 10.14(a), a digital data stream is sent to the network media. This data stream is transmitted at a rate that consumes the entire bandwidth available on the media. A serial stream of bits are packed into formatted data packets by the network adapter card and converted to a form suitable for trans-

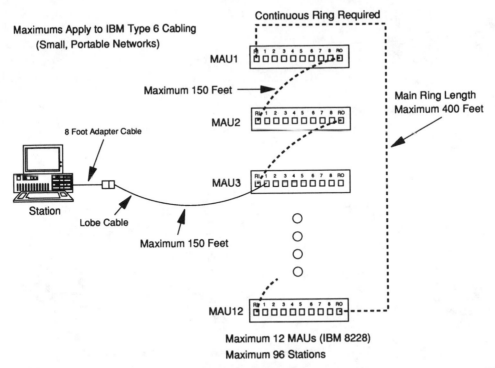

Figure 10.12 Token-Ring LAN design considerations.

mission on the data path. The serial data packets are sent and received at a specific design data rate—typically 1–100 Mbps. In a baseband network system, no signal conversion device is required between the network node and the data path. In other words, data are sent in their basic digital form, hence the term baseband. With simpler electronics, baseband LANs are generally cheaper and simpler than broadband systems to acquire and install.

A broadband LAN can make efficient use of high-capacity cable TV (CATV) distribution media. As previously discussed, this type of cable will support a relatively high bandwidth of 300 MHz. By using state-of-the-art electronic components, bandwidth can be increased to 500 MHz and beyond. This high capacity can be fully exploited in broadband local area networks. Through the FDM process, broadband LANs partition the available bandwidth into individual channels, each of which is designed for a specific service or function.

Using the TV broadcast analogy, each TV channel is fixed in bandwidth and designed for a specific function—the transmission of standard TV video and audio signals. In a broadband LAN, the channel widths remain fixed at 6 MHz, but the use of a channel will vary according to the desired data rates and connectivity

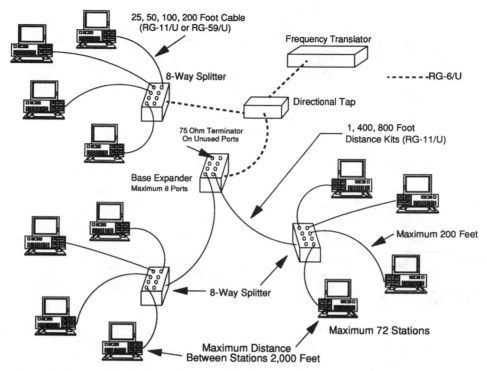

Figure 10.13 IBM PC Network (broadband) design considerations.

requirements for various services. Some examples of channel usage for broadband network services include:

- 48 dedicated point-to-point circuits, designed to allow any two stations to exchange data at rate of up to 9,600 bps. Each circuit would be functionally equivalent to a leased line typically used between a terminal controller and a host computer communications controller.
- 128, switched point-to-point circuits, designed to connect any two stations at data rates of up to 9,600 bps. This service would be functionally equivalent to a small Private Branch Exchange (PBX) used for data communications.
- A 10 Mbps Ethernet (2 channels required)
- A closed-circuit video system

In a broadband LAN, data are represented as analog signals similar to the transmission methodology employed on wide-area networks. This requires modems to convert the computer's digital signals into analog signals in the radio frequency range for transmission as shown in Figure 10.14(b). The modem must have a data rate capability equal to the desired data rate on the broadband channel. A high-speed data channel (such as a 10 Mbps LAN) requires a commensurately high-speed modem.

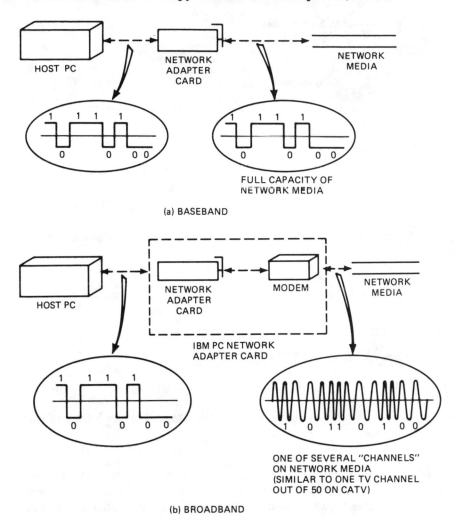

(a) BASEBAND

(b) BROADBAND

Figure 10.14(a) Baseband LAN signaling, (b) broadband LAN signaling.

Broadband modems can be *fixed-frequency* or *frequency-agile*. Fixed frequency modems are designed for a specific channel on a broadband LAN and cannot be tuned to other channels. Standard telephone modems used in wide-area networks are fixed frequency units—in this case, the frequency is an audio frequency compatible with the telephone network rather than a radio frequency. Frequency-agile modems can be tuned to different channels on the broadband network as shown in Figure 10.15.

Broadband networks are classified as either dual cable or single cable. Single-cable systems are the most practical for ordinary use since they use less components, leading to increased reliability and cheaper installation. The broadband IBM PC Network is

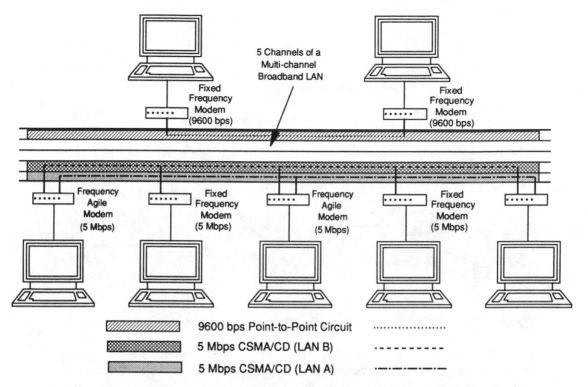

▨▨▨ 9600 bps Point-to-Point Circuit	··················
▨▨▨ 5 Mbps CSMA/CD (LAN B)	- - - - - - - - -
▨▨▨ 5 Mbps CSMA/CD (LAN A)	—·—·—·—

Figure 10.15 Broadband LAN multi-channel design.

cable network, the total available bandwidth is divided into three bands of frequencies used for *forward transmission*, *reverse transmission*, and a *guard band* in between. Forward transmission is from the headend to LAN stations. Reverse transmission is from LAN stations to the headend. The bandwidth allocated to reverse transmission determines how many 6 MHz channels can be established on the LAN.

The headend of the IBM PC Network is called a frequency translator. The frequency translator is located on the network such that it can translate a frequency in the reverse direction to a frequency in the forward direction. Figure 10.16 illustrates this scheme in the context of the IBM PC Network. There are three standards used to determine bandwidths of the forward and reverse transmission paths: *sub-split*, *mid-split*, and *high-split*. These standards support 4, 17, and 30 6-MHz channels, respectively, in the reverse band. The IBM PC Network is a mid-split system, using a reverse frequency channel of 47.75 MHz to 53.75 MHz and a forward channel of 216 MHz to 222 MHz. Dual-cable systems allocate one cable for forward transmission and one cable for reverse transmission; thus, the entire bandwidth is available for channel assignment.

As more diverse services are added to a broadband LAN, additional special hardware is required. Frequency translators become more elaborate. Special modems must be

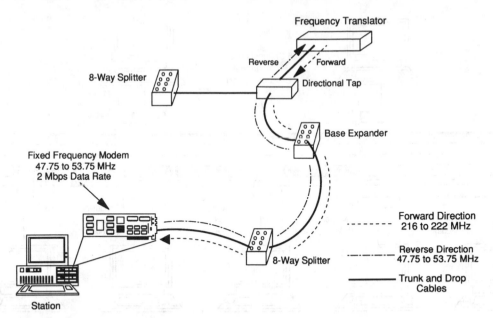

Figure 10.16 IBM PC Network (broadband) signaling architecture.

provided for video and digital voice services. A variety of RF modems may be required, depending on the specific services required. Data-switching devices are required for PBX-type services.

The added capacity and service flexibility provided by broadband LANs comes at a price. The trade-off for this highly capable type of local area network is a substantial increase in cost and complexity. The requirement for relatively expensive variable frequency and high-speed modems is a major cost factor, as is the increased complexity of the network adapter cards. Installation of broadband LANs is difficult because of the criticality of component placement and the radio frequency characteristics of the broadband media. For these reasons, it is not likely that broadband technology will find the widespread acceptance enjoyed by baseband personal computer LANs. However, increased standardization, falling prices, and more capable electronic components will ensure that broadband LANs can continue an important role in certain applications.

The broadband IBM PC Network is a well-known example of how a standard, low-cost kit approach can influence market acceptance of an otherwise expensive technology. This network is reasonable in cost and can be installed relatively easily as long as the buyer stays with the precut cable option kits. If a variance from the precut cable kits is required, the entire network must be retuned and rebalanced, increasing the installation complexity. Figures 10.13 and 10.16 showed the component parts of a broadband IBM PC Network. Unlike some other broadband networks, the IBM PC Network was designed as a small-to-medium size workgroup LAN rather than as a wide-area, multiservice backbone network.

There are at least five excellent books available that discuss the IBM PC Network in detail:

- *Networking with the IBM Token-Ring*, Carl Townsend, Tab Books, 1987
- *PC LAN Primer*, The Waite Group, Howard W. Sams & Co., 1987
- *Operating the IBM PC Networks*, Paul Berry, Sybex, 1986
- *Networking with the IBM PC Network & Cluster*, Mike Hurwicz, Tab Books, 1985
- *IBM's Local Area Networks*, David Schwaderer, Van Nostrand Reinhold, 1989

Examples of baseband systems are the various versions of Ethernet, IBM's Token-Ring network, AT&T's Starlan, and the many Arcnet systems available. Examples of broadband systems are IBM's PC Network, Zenith Data System's Z-Net, and Sytek's Localnet. The motivation for understanding the fundamental differences between baseband and broadband LANs lies more in economics than in technology. The broadband network is clearly more expensive and more complex than its baseband counterpart, but in some applications this extra cost and complexity are justified by the organization's need for multiple services on one physical cable. Because it is inherently a radio frequency (RF) system, broadband provides much greater geographic coverage than baseband. Because of this, broadband networks are very popular in educational and research institutions where widely separated facilities must be connected.

In many practical LAN installations, broadband and baseband networks have been effectively combined to exploit the advantages of each. A common use of this technique is to use a broadband LAN to connect several baseband LANs. In this case, the broadband system is referred to as a *backbone network*. This application of broadband LANs is illustrated in Figure 10.17.

Protocol

A protocol has been previously defined as the set of rules by which data communications are conducted. In the previous chapter, we applied this definition to local area network protocol that were designed to connect distributed applications software. In the context of the ISO 7-Layer model, these protocol were in Layers 3, 4, and 5. The significance of a layered communications model is ultimately economic—without a strategy to standardize protocol within well-defined layers, achieving communications compatibility would be very difficult and costly. The layered design of the ISO model allows the step-by-step achievement of standardization.

For example, Physical and Data Link layer protocol can be developed independently of the higher layers. This is precisely what the IEEE has been doing with its 802-series local area network standards. For the purposes of this chapter, the focus of protocol discussion will be on the two layers of the ISO model that correspond to the IEEE 802 standards. These form the foundation for all other LAN standardization efforts and are the most advanced in implementation. Although the ISO 7-Layer model specifies a single Data Link Layer, the IEEE 802 LAN standards provide for two sublayers: the Media Access Control (MAC) sublayer and the Logical Link Control (LLC) sublayer. This partitioning allows the same interface to the Network Layer regardless of the underlying media access technology.

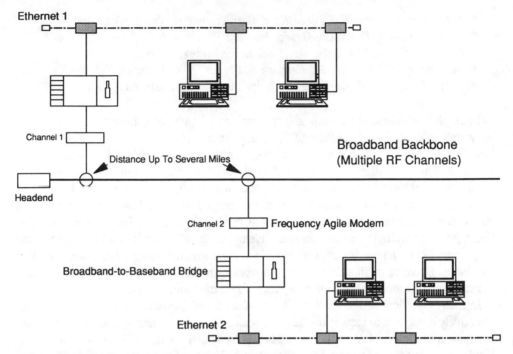

Figure 10.17 Broadband LAN used as a multi-LAN backbone.

Figure 10.18 shows the architecture of currently defined LAN physical and data link protocol in the context of the IEEE 802 standards. Ethernet has transitioned from a de facto protocol, supported by DEC, Intel, and Xerox, to the full-fledged ANSI/IEEE Standard 802.3, entitled "Carrier Sense Multiple Access with Collision Detection" (CSMA/CD). This standard is also a draft international standard (DIS), ISO 8802/3. IBM's Token-Ring has prompted the development of ANSI/IEEE Standard 802.5, entitled "Token Passing Ring." Arcnet has not yet developed into a recognized ANSI/IEEE standard, but it has achieved widespread acceptance as a de facto standard. Efforts are underway to make Arcnet a formal standard.

By definition, activity within the lowest two layers of the ISO model, as reflected in Ethernet, Arcnet, and IBM's Token-Ring, is independent of activity within the layers above. However, a Layer 3 protocol must make requests to, and receive responses from, Layer 2 protocol in order for a LAN to work properly. This request for service and subsequent response(s) are known as an *interface definition*. In theory, Layer 2 provides a standard set of services for Layers 3 and above. An example of this concept would be the Network Layer requesting the Data Link Layer to transmit a data packet to a specific destination on the LAN. The Network Layer is not concerned with how the data get to a specific destination node—that is the job of the Data Link Layer. This concept is illustrated in Figure 10.19. The idea of an interface definition applies between any two layers in the ISO model. Moreover, it applies in both directions, up and down

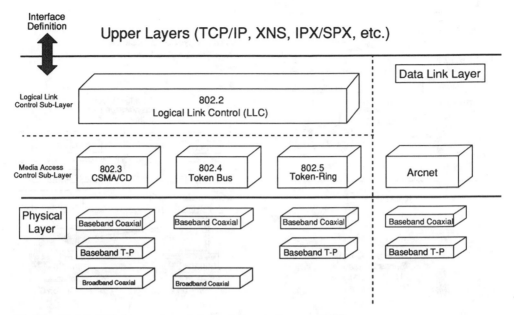

Figure 10.18 ISO layers 1 and 2 implementation on LANs.

through the model layers. A request from Layer 3 to Layer 2 will cause an eventual response back from Layer 2 to Layer 3, and so on.

If you refer back to Figure 9.3 in Chapter 9, Arrow 3 depicts the logical transport and physical network boundary in an overall LAN architecture. This particular interface is significant because it represents the ability of dissimilar physical networks to interface to a variety of transport protocol. Thus, a TCP/IP transport system can overlay an Ethernet or a Token-Ring providing the proper driver software is available.

As an example of the importance of standard protocol, consider the case of a business that purchased a low-cost Ethernet LAN from Vendor A. This LAN is advertised as "IEEE 802.3 compatible," which means that the protocol for layers 1 and 2 follow the ANSI/IEEE specification. If, in the future, this business desired to equip newly acquired work stations with more robust IEEE 802.3 adapter cards supplied by Vendor B, network compatibility would be maintained in the upgraded LAN. In this case, the network side of the adapter card maintains IEEE 802.3 standards while the host computer side can be upgraded to enhance performance.

As a different example, consider the same business with the LAN adapters from Vendors A and B, which now decides to expand its operation into another city. The physical characteristics of the LAN in the new city are not required to conform to the Ethernet-compatible standard. If this business uses a different LAN standard (such as Arcnet) in the new city, at least some of the higher layers must be equivalent if linking applications between the LANs in the two cities is a requirement. This application linkage might take the form of electronic mail or a file transfer. The general rule is:

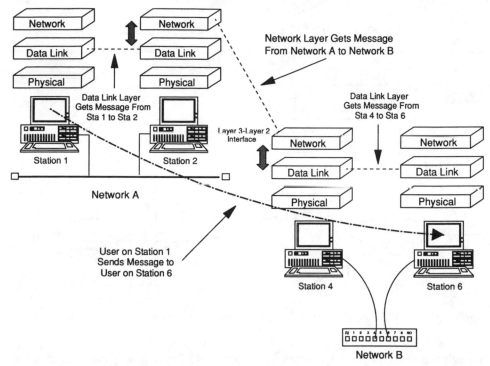

Figure 10.19 Comparative roles of data link and network layers in ISO model.

Networks not physically joined do not have to be equivalent at Layers 1 and 2, but unless higher layers are protocol-equivalent, meaningful communications between individual users on the separated LANs is not possible.

Physical Layer

The two most stable protocol layers for LANs are predictably at the lowest levels of the 7-layer model. Physical protocol deal with how signals are transmitted to the data path, the electrical representation of data, network cable pin definitions (such as found in the RS-232-C standard), and design data rates. The Physical Layer also provides certain services for the Data Link Layer. In the Ethernet protocol for example, the Physical Layer indicates the presence or absence of a data signal on the network media. The Physical Layer also detects collisions and signal errors. Physical layer compatibility allows the network adapter card from one manufacturer to communicate with cards from other manufacturers on the same network.

Data Packets

The network shown earlier in Figure 10.1 must distribute processing and data storage tasks among a number of users who may require near-simultaneous access to the

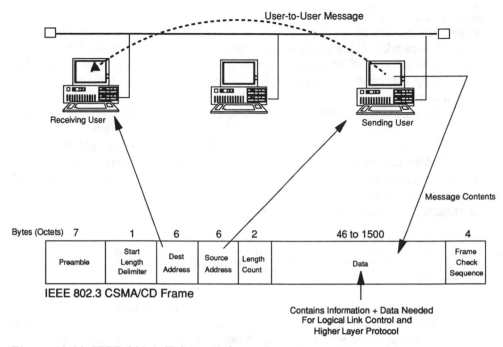

Figure 10.20 IEEE 802.3 (Ethernet) frame format.

server PC. Basic network control requires placing a structure on the data flow in a well-defined manner. Basic control implies the following elements:

- An orderly means of allowing each device to access the network (link establishment).
- Delivery of the data to the correct recipient (addressing).
- Assurance that transmission errors have been minimized (error detection and correction).

A prerequisite to basic network control is the placement of serial data streams into formatted packets, or *frames*, by the Data Link protocol. These frames are then transmitted according to Physical Layer protocol. An example of a formatted data frame and its relationship to the physical network for the commonly found Ethernet is shown in Figure 10.20.

Data frames are characterized by a well-defined format consisting of a number of fields, as indicated by the example in Figure 10.20. As a minimum, LAN data frames contain header, or control field(s), a source address field, a destination address field, the information field, and a means to detect and correct errors (frame check field). The information field of a frame has many uses. Any control data required for the processing of ISO layers above the Data Link Layer is embedded in the information field. An example of such data is source and destination network numbers used by the Network Layer. These numbers are required to route frames between widely separated networks. Other parts of the information field may be used to support processing requirements for the Transport and Session Layers. The application being supported by the network protocol takes the balance of the information field for usable information.

LAN data are packaged differently from data transmitted by asynchronous modems that were described earlier in the book. Asynchronous data are transmitted one character at a time, with certain characters in the ASCII set being used to control the data link. LAN data travels as relatively large blocks, packaged as described above. Asynchronous overhead is built into each character—parity, start, and stop bits represent 30 percent of each ASCII character transmitted. Thus, the efficiency of asynchronous data transmission is 70 percent when parity is used.

$$\text{Efficiency} = \frac{\text{Information}}{\text{Information} + \text{Overhead}} = \frac{7 \text{ bits}}{10 \text{ bits}}$$

LAN framing overhead is determined by the frame definition and varies with the type of protocol employed. Efficiency is dependent on the size of the information field. Some comparative efficiencies are shown in Table 10-4. For LANs, these efficiencies are the maximum attainable and assume no higher-layer protocol. The addition of protocol for Network, Transport, and Session layers will further reduce efficiencies since these protocol use additional *octets* (8-bit groups) from the information field of a frame.

Table 10-4. Data Transmission Efficiencies.

Data Transfer Protocol	Efficiency
Asynchronous w/o parity	80%
Asynchronous w/ parity	70%
Ethernet[1]	64–98%
Token-Ring[2]	0–99.95%
Arcnet[3]	9.1–70.5%

[1] Efficiency is dependent on frame size (ranges from 72 to 1526 octets)

[2] Maximum frame size dependent on Token Holding Time (maximum time station can transmit data before relinquishing the token). From a practical sense, a token transmission has an efficiency of 0 percent.

[3] Efficiency depends on frame size (ranges from 8 to 260 11-bit units. The 11-bit unit introduces an additional 27% loss of efficiency.

Media Access Control (MAC) Sublayer

Media Access Control Sublayer protocol combine with Physical Layer protocol to determine how a local network station gains access to the data path. As an analogy, think about how on-ramp traffic lights meter cars onto a busy freeway. Media access protocol also determines the format of the data packets transmitted over the network.

Media access rules for networks fall into two basic categories: *contention* and *noncontention*.

Contention protocol is designed to handle the case of two or more stations unpredictably accessing the network simultaneously—that is, they are contending for access to the network. If more than one station has data on the network at the same time, a *data collision* is said to have occurred. The rules for this case must take into account the presence of signals already on the network (*carrier sense*), and the detection and prevention of collisions (*collision detection* and *collision avoidance*). Thus, contention rules are often categorized as Carrier Sense Multiple Access, with Collision Detection (and/or Collision Avoidance), *CSMA/CD(/CA)* for short. Some LANs using this type of contention access are Ethernet, IBM's PC Network, StarLan, and Gateway Communications' G-Net. You will notice that these networks span different media types and signaling methods.

Ethernet is the most common of the contention-based networks and uses the CSMA/CD protocol. Briefly, this protocol operates as follows:

- The Physical Layer senses the network for presence of a *carrier*, indicating that data are present on the network.
- If data are already present on the network, the Physical Layer signals the Data Link Layer not to pass data for transmission.
- If no data are detected, the Physical Layer will signal the Data Link Layer to begin passing data for transmission.
- If the Physical Layer detects a collision on the network by recognition of an increase in signal level beyond a certain threshold, it transmits a collision signal to the rest of the network.
- The remainder of the network stations revert to a receive mode when they hear the collision signal.
- The transmitting station waits a randomly determined interval before rescheduling the transmission. This random back-off time makes the Ethernet protocol statistical in nature, which means that performance under loaded traffic conditions cannot be predicted with certainty.

Collision detection and subsequent actions are shown in Figure 10.21.

Noncontention protocol are characterized by a predictable order of accessing the network. Polling schemes fall into this category, as do token-passing networks. A historical example of a polling network scheme was Novell's original S-Net system. The file server software at the hub of this star-wired network sequentially polled each attached work station looking for data transfer requests.

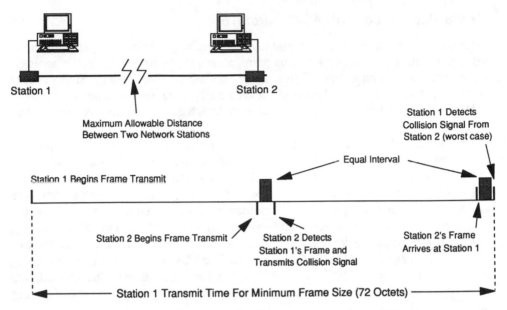

Figure 10.21 Ethernet collision detection for minimum frame size.

Token-passing networks are dominant in noncontention protocol systems and include Arcnet, Proteon's ProNET, IBM's Token-Ring, and the *Fiber Data Distributed Interface* (*FDDI*). In the IEEE LAN standards scheme, token-passing networks can have a Bus architecture (IEEE 802.4), or a Ring architecture (IEEE 802.5). The Arcnet standard is similar to (but does not specifically follow) the 802.4 definition. The Token-Ring, or IEEE 802.5 standard, is used by IBM, 3Com's Token-Link, and by Proteon in the ProNET-4 series. Proteon also has proprietary 10 Mbps and 80 Mbps token-passing ring networks. FDDI is a standard of the American National Standards Institute (ANSI) X3T9 Committee.

Because token passing is inherently predictable, tokens can be monitored to determine network performance. Token-Ring uses a *Net Management* (*NMT*) protocol, which is a part of IEEE 802.5. FDDI uses *Station Management* (*SMT*) protocol. NMT and SMT perform network management functions by exchanging certain management frames between stations on the networks.

Token-passing networks have a common characteristic of controlling access to the media by passing a special data frame, or *token*, around the network in a predetermined order. Beyond this, IBM's Token-Ring and Arcnet networks differ in protocol implementation. In the Token-Ring and FDDI, this order is sequential around the logical ring. Network stations with data to send "capture" the token and append their data by adding more frames to the token. The data packets are then "dropped off" at the destination node. FDDI's protocol is somewhat more complex and robust than the

Token-Ring. Both protocols provide a priority scheme to allow stations with critical data to have an increased share of the available network bandwidth. Priority implementation on Token-Ring and FDDI is significantly different. Higher layers of software in the sending station will determine that certain data are critical and ensure that the priority scheme is invoked at the media access sublayer.

In Arcnet, the order of token movement is determined by the network address rather than physical placement. The token is passed from lower to higher sequential network addresses. Network stations with data to send transmit a Free Buffer Inquiry frame to the destination station. The destination station responds with an ACK or a NAK frame. Receipt of an ACK frame causes the sending station to begin transmitting data to its destination.

Logical Link Control (LLC) Sublayer

The LLC sublayer is the direct interface between the Network Layer and the Data Link Layer of a local area network. Regardless of the underlying media access sublayer implementation (IEEE 802.3, 802.4, 802.5), the Network Layer sees a common set of services. LLC establishes a hierarchical set of addresses known as *Link Service Access Points* (*LSAPs*). The sending LSAP is called the *Source Service Access Point* (*SSAP*) and the receiving LSAP is called the *Destination Service Access Point* (*DSAP*). Multiple LSAPs are possible within one network station. The purpose of an LSAP is to allow the establishment of multiple data link connections in support of higher layers in a single network station. The complete address for a single connection on a specific station includes the MAC address concatenated with the LLC LSAP address. This concept is illustrated in Figure 10.22.

Protocol Summary

One might ask about the need to know anything about network protocol. The major significance lies more in standardization and economics than in technology differences. Ultimately, standardization translates to economy of scale and reduction in capital investment costs to acquire communications capability. All three of the lower-level protocols discussed in this chapter have benefited from standardization efforts.

Ethernet adapter cards have been reduced in size by half their original dimensions for the IBM PC. Reduced chip counts have been made possible by the development of specialized chips, such as the Intel 82586 Ethernet Controller. These chips have, in turn, been cost-effective to produce because the Ethernet protocol has achieved a high degree of stability. Texas Instruments has produced the Token-Ring chip that is used on network adapter cards from several LAN vendors, including 3Com and Proteon. Likewise, the Arcnet controller chip is manufactured in large enough quantities to make Arcnet adapter cards commodity items in the LAN marketplace.

Engineers have computed and debated the relative merits of token passing versus contention access schemes in various LAN configurations. It is generally held that Token-Ring networks perform better in high-traffic-load situations than Ethernet

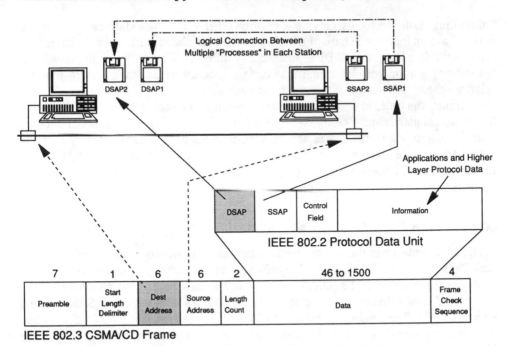

Figure 10.22 Operation of the IEEE 802.2 Logical Link Control protocol.

LANs. Conversely, Ethernet protocol supports lighter traffic loads more efficiently than Token-Ring. To the average user, however, performance differences in LANs will be less dependent on lower-level protocol than on file server and hard disk performance and network software design. A specific set of lower-level standards, such as Arcnet or Ethernet, will only guarantee the most basic compatibility within the ISO communications model.

As a concrete example of this, let's look at Ethernet in the context of its Layer 1 and 2 protocol. Two dissimilar networks, LAN A and LAN B, implement Ethernet standard protocol, but LAN A uses the *Xerox Network Service (XNS)* Layer 3 protocol and LAN B uses DoD's *Internetwork Protocol (TCP/IP)* for Layer 3. Because both LANs use Ethernet, they can be connected through a repeater or a bridge. However, applications software on LAN A work stations that uses Layer 3 protocol for communications (like electronic mail) cannot share this application with work stations on LAN B. Figure 10.23 shows this relationship.

Practical Considerations in LAN Communications

The term *throughput* is a measure that describes the total amount of data that can be handled per unit of time in a practical network configuration. Such a configuration would include the media, network adapter cards, the host computer's RAM, the mass storage device on which shared data is typically stored, and the packet structure used

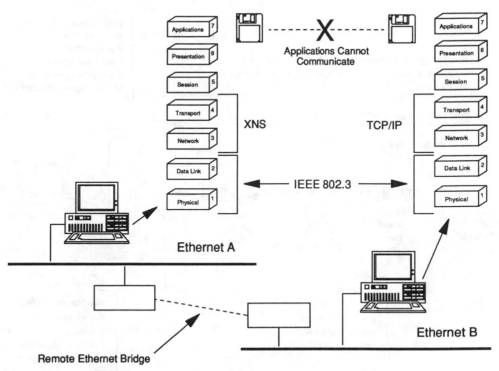

Figure 10.23 Transport stack incompatibility with common IEEE 802 implementation.

by the network. In contrast to this is the network data rate, which is a measure of how much data can be handled per unit of time between two adapter cards on a network. Throughput is a function of packet structure, network adapter card design, media access methodology, hard disk performance, and host processor speed. Data rate is a function of the Physical Layer implementation on the network adapter card and the electrical characteristics of the media.

Throughput can be thought of as data rate minus the sum of packet overhead and the processing bottlenecks inherent in a local area network. If throughput is measured at the application level (the only practical point at which to do so), packet overhead is the ratio between information bytes actually used by the application and the total number of bytes in a packet. Processing bottlenecks include network adapter cards, internal data movement within work stations and servers, and mechanical access to shared hard disk tracks (or cylinders) for data reads and writes. Throughput depends not only on data rate and design bottlenecks, but also on the manner in which the network is being used. Clearly, file transfers will put a higher processing load on the overall network than occasional record updates in a database management system. Typically, word processing has an even lighter traffic load.

Processing bottlenecks are also dependent upon the role of the network station. Servers are more prone to bottlenecks since they are, by definition, designed to handle

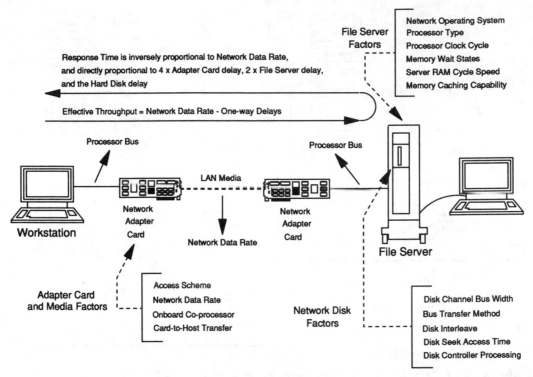

Figure 10.24 Throughput and response time derivation.

multiple network service requests. As a general rule, servers should have the fastest hard disks, the biggest disk cache memories, the fastest processors, and the most robust network adapter cards. As servers become more powerful in their ability to handle multitasking, work stations must commensurately increase their capability to avoid becoming the weakest link in the chain. There is an inherent hierarchy in the throughput chain: work station, server, and network communications capacity.

Data rate is a useful measure because it provides an upper limit on network communications capacity. Unfortunately, vendor literature tends to emphasize data rate rather than throughput, because data rate is easier to measure and because it is a constant number. In the higher performance networks, such as Ethernet or the new IBM 16 Mbps Token-Ring, current network station processing limitations mask the total capacity of the network media access and physical protocol. These limitations affect both work stations and servers. As network station hardware improves with the introduction of 32-bit network adapter cards, faster hard disks, and faster internal processing, network media access and physical protocol could become the throughput bottleneck. The introduction of fiber optic networks with data rates of

100 Mbps and above will continue to focus the performance spotlight on network station considerations.

Response time is the interval from the time a request is entered at a work station until the associated response is received back at that work station. Response time is a two-way travel measure. Response time differs from throughput in that a user can directly observe and measure response time. A slow response time on a network will cause users to lose confidence in the benefits of distributed processing. Figure 10.24 illustrates how network components affect both throughput and response time.

Summary

The network characteristics discussed in this chapter specifically describe the communications performance of LANs. This chapter extended the discussion in Chapter 9 on LANs as multiuser distributed processing systems down to the Data Link and Physical layers. We hope by this sequence to have provided you with a solid understanding of the importance of the ISO 7-layer model in understanding LAN technology, applications, and trends. A basic knowledge and awareness of communications principles as they apply to LANs is primarily useful in assisting potential managers to understand some inherent limitations in an LAN architecture. This knowledge will also provide additional insight into the economics of competing products. Other major LAN performance and selection factors are tied to noncommunications characteristics, such as the design of microcomputers used as server nodes, network adapter cards, hard disk performance, and network operating systems. These types of real-world system considerations virtually always decrease LAN throughput well below the maximum limit supported by particular communications technologies. As a practical example of this observation, consider the 10 Mbps Ethernet. The current generation of PC LAN products reduce effective throughput to a fraction of the nominal 10 Mbps data rate. Many of these products, such as hard disks and microcomputer operating systems, are not directly related to Ethernet technology.

11

Internetworking and Interoperability

Introduction

The ability to connect local networks to each other and to wide-area networks is receiving major impetus in many medium- and large-sized organizations. A major factor contributing to this impetus is an increased awareness of the value of access to, and the exchange of, information. Local area networks add value to an organization's use of desktop computers through resource and information sharing. Internetworking goes one step farther by providing physical access to public and private information and electronic mail resources available beyond the bounds of a single LAN. Interoperability between dissimilar networks, separated by distance, equipment manufacturer, and protocol, makes an internetwork seem transparent to its diverse users. Internetworking connectivity with an accompanying interoperability strategy can add even more value to an investment in LAN distributed processing.

Multisite organizations have a compelling need to move information for private electronic mail and document transfer. In the early years of PC LAN availability, individual users could access wide-area networks in a stand-alone mode by connecting a modem and a telephone line to their work station. Today's products allow the shared usage of concentrated and specialized modem resources from any location on the LAN. Hardware and software are becoming increasingly available that provide individual work stations a window through the LAN to a wide variety of commercial and private network systems. These systems span the entire fabric of today's business, government, and educational endeavor. Moreover, individual

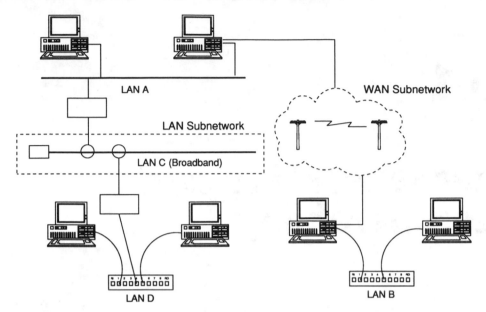

Figure 11.1. General internetworking architecture.

users can now typically dial in to an LAN with a laptop or remote PC and be a full participant on the network.

Interoperability may be defined as the ability of users on one network to transparently exchange information with those on another, regardless of differences in hardware, software, or protocol. Simply put, this means that no matter how complex or geographically, dispersed a network we build, all users can effectively share information. Typically such a complex network consists of some combination of LANs and WANs and is referred to as an *internetwork*. Individual LANs or WANs forming the elements of an internetwork are known as *subnetworks*. These relationships are illustrated in Figure 11.1.

In the best of all worlds, we would build an internetwork from products from a single vendor. This single vendor would provide all the hardware, software, and protocol needed to assure connectivity and transparency between users scattered throughout an organization. In today's communications marketplace, such a utopia rarely exists. Given today's multivendor communications environment, an interoperability strategy is required to ensure successful implementation of an internetwork system.

The purpose of this chapter is to explore the significance of internetworking as a tool, and interoperability as a strategy. We will explore the technology and interoperability factors that make internetworking productive, as well as many of the connectivity options available to current LAN users. Some examples of how internetworking is implemented by current LAN products and what services can be linked to LANs will be provided. You will discover that a well-defined interoperability strategy allows internetworking to provide an increased return on significant investments in PC and LAN technology.

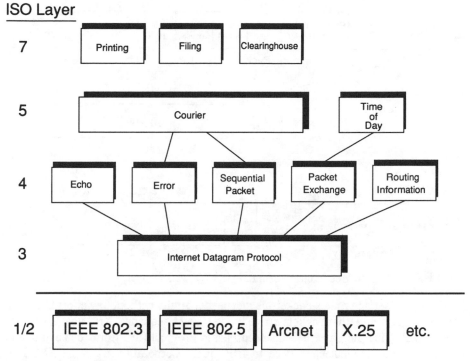

Figure 11.2. XNS protocol and the ISO model.

Internetworking, Interoperability, and the ISO Model

Before looking at some specific technology and tools in current use for internetworking, we will revisit some concepts covered in Chapter 9. In that chapter, we briefly discussed transport protocols and their connection to LAN systems software, specifically their interface to network operating systems. Three of these protocols currently play a major role in internetworking: Xerox Network Services (XNS), TCP/IP, and APPC/PC. OSI transport and network protocol will play an increasingly important role in the 1990s. These protocols are significant for internetworking systems because the manner in which they are implemented determines the degree of interoperability achievable in the internetwork. Before discussing interoperability considerations, we will revisit these protocols in greater detail.

XEROX Network Service (XNS)

XEROX Network Service (XNS) provides several classes of service for LANs that span a rough equivalence to OSI layers 3–7 (excluding layer 6). These service protocols are shown in Figure 11.2. In this section, we will discuss the class of service equivalent to ISO Layer 3. In XNS terminology, this is referred to as the Internet Datagram Protocol

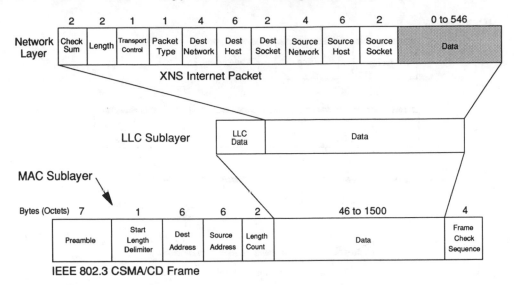

Figure 11.3. XNS internet packet format.

(IDP). Datagram service routes packets as independent units without any effort to assure delivery or to guarantee that packets arrive in the correct sequence. XNS uses datagram service for IDP since the Layer 4 Sequenced Packet Protocol (SPP) provides end-to-end error recovery and sequencing service to IDP. 3Com Corporation uses the XNS IDP protocol for its 3 + Route and 3 + Open Internet services. This protocol is also supported by 3Com in their series of gateway products. Novell uses a variation of IDP in their IPX protocol. Briefly, this protocol functions as follows:

- User interaction with applications software determines the destination of the message or file.
- The applications program passes the data and a request for routing service through the protocol stack to XNS IDP software.
- XNS uses a portion of the packet data field to insert routing information to get the data to the destination. This portion is in the header of the internet packet, as shown in Figure 11.3.
- XNS software in intermediate routing nodes determines the path to be taken by the packet as it goes to its destination (on the same network, or on a geographically dispersed network).
- The destination work station separates the routing information from the data and puts the data in an appropriate location in memory or on a mass storage device.
- The destination XNS software notifies the destination application that data have been received.

This is a highly generalized description of the XNS internetworking process. The details would be dependent on the nature of the application program. The generic process is illustrated in Figure 11.4.

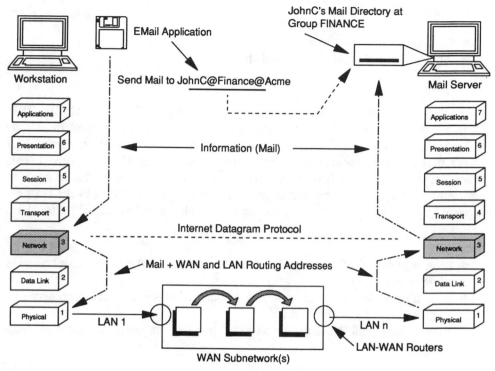

Figure 11.4. Basic XNS processing example.

IDP supports another Layer 3 protocol, the Routing Information Protocol (RIP). This protocol is used by XNS routers to maintain routing tables in an internetwork. RIP packets have the same header as IDP packets, but also implement additional fields in the data segment of an IDP packet. Figure 11.5 shows a conceptual view of the RIP process. In 3Com networks, RIP drivers are used in both work stations and servers. In both types of nodes, the RIP drivers transmit requests for routing information from a directly connected router (a specially configured network station). The router will respond with information about a route or routes available to send data to a remote network.

Transport Control Protocol/Internet Protocol (TCP/IP)

Figure 11.6 illustrates the various protocols available within the TCP/IP standards. You can see that TCP/IP Layers 3 and 4 can overlay several popular lower-level network implementations such as Ethernet, Token-Ring, and Public Data Networks. In turn, these two layers support a variety of services provided by TCP/IP systems. Our focus in this chapter is on the protocols available in Layer 3, which include

- Internet Protocol (IP)
- Address Resolution Protocol (ARP)
- Reverse ARP
- Internet Control Message Protocol (ICMP)

The Internet Protocol is functionally similar to the XNS IDP protocol. Like IDP, IP is a datagram protocol that relies on an upper-layer (TCP) protocol to provide end-to-end, reliable delivery of data. Inspection of the IP header in Figure 11.7 shows that the IP protocol is somewhat more robust than its XNS counterpart. This is not surprising since IP is used in sophisticated world-wide networks. In general, inspection of any protocol header, such as the IP header, will indicate the features provided by that protocol. Some of the features implemented by the IP protocol are

- Type of service field to provide handling instructions for the packet as it traverses other subnetworks.
- Data fragmentation, to allow for maximum packet sizes in different networks (e.g., ARPANET, Ethernet, X.25).
- Time-To-Live field to ensure the packet is purged from the internet if it becomes "lost."

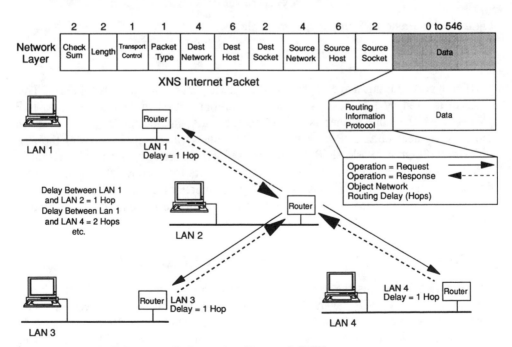

Figure 11.5. XNS Routing Information Protocol (RIP).

ISO Layer

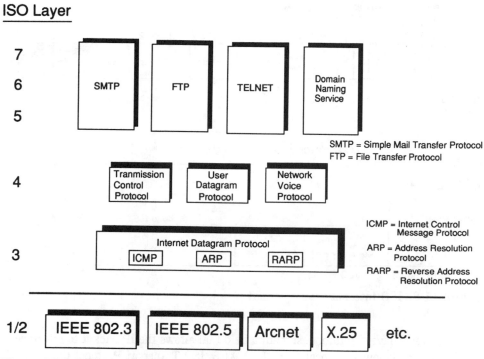

Figure 11.6. TCP/IP protocol and the ISO model.

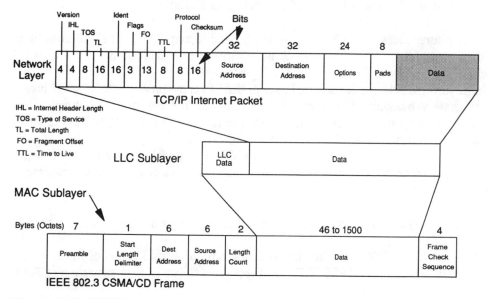

Figure 11.7. TCP/IP internet packet format.

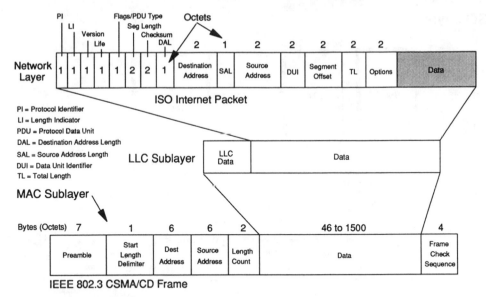

Figure 11.8. ISO internet packet format.

- An upper-layer protocol designation field that allows the IP packet to interface to different Layer 4 protocol (e.g., TCP, XNS, ISO Transport Protocol Class 4).
- An Options field that allows certain extensions to the protocol that are not normally used but may be needed for special applications.

The Address Resolution Protocol (ARP) is used to map the 32-bit IP address to an Ethernet 48-bit address. The ARP is necessary because there is no pre-established relationship between IP and Ethernet addresses.

The Reverse Address Resolution Protocol (RARP) is essentially a "who am I" broadcast that is transmitted by a new station entering the network. The broadcast is responded to by an RARP server that maps the requester's Ethernet address to an IP address appropriate to the internetwork configuration.

The Internet Control Message Protocol (ICMP) is a special-purpose set of messages that are used between internetwork nodes to resolve problems in packet processing. These messages include

- ECHO REQUEST—determine whether a destination will respond; determine path timing.
- SOURCE QUENCH—reduce transmission rate for a fixed period of time.
- ROUTING CHANGE REQUEST—redirect packets (e.g., due to expiration of Time-To-Live parameter).
- TIME STAMP REQUEST/REPLY—estimate average delay on the network (affects transmission rate on the network).

ISO Layer 3 Protocol

As with the previously discussed protocol, ISO Layer 3 provides network-level services that include

- Addressing
- Routing
- Packet fragmentation
- Packet life (datagram service)
- Class of service provided

These services are accommodated by the packet format shown in Figure 11.8. Note the similarity to the packet format and services provided by the TCP/IP Layer 3 protocol. The distinguishing characteristic of the ISO Layer 3 service is that it is defined in an abstract manner to provide the greatest possible flexibility in implementation. Unfortunately, flexible protocol are an anethema to interoperability and achieving such a condition on an ISO internetwork will be a major technical challenge.

Advanced Program-to-Program Communications (APPC)

APPC, or more appropriately the PC version, APPC/PC, works somewhat differently than the protocol described above. This is because APPC/PC's role is not general internetworking. APPC/PC is a specific architecture designed to allow peer-to-peer communications in the IBM SNA environment. APPC/PC has a session layer interface different from NETBIOS and implements a set of protocol known as Logical Unit 6.2 or LU 6.2. PCs running APPC/PC services are identified to the SNA hierarchy as either a Physical Unit 2.0 or 2.1 (PU 2.0 or PU 2.1). A Physical Unit is a classification of a type of SNA network node—each PU has certain defined capabilities, including what other PUs it can communicate with. For example, a PU 2.1 can only communicate with another PU 2.1 (peer-to-peer), whereas a PU 2.0 can communicate with a PU 4 (front-end processor, or communications controller).

LU 6.2 protocol cover the functions normally associated with Session, Transport, and Network Layers. LU 6.2 is implemented through conversation verbs and control verbs. Conversation verbs regulate the flow of data between two applications programs—control verbs are used to establish and manage the APPC/PC link. A particularly important control verb is ATTACH_LU. This verb defines which LUs will be communicating and where they are located by network and node addresses. Another important verb is ATTACH_PU, which defines how the invoking PC will be connected to other SNA nodes. Some legal connections are shown in Figure 11.9.

As mentioned above, APPC/PC has a different session-level interface to a network operating system or applications program than does NETBIOS. NETBIOS has been designed for local area network connectivity and provides a standard processing interface for that purpose. APPC/PC was designed and optimized for connectivity between PCs and designated host systems in IBM's product line. APPC/PC is the architecture

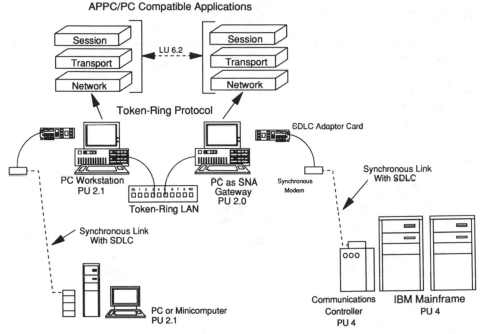

Figure 11.9. APPC/PC connectivity examples.

upon which a user can build an integrated network of IBM PCs, minicomputers, and mainframes, and thus has a fundamentally different purpose than NETBIOS.

Transport Protocol Interoperability

The key to internetwork effectiveness is whether any combination of the above protocol can coexist on the internetwork, or whether two different implementations of the same protocol can interoperate. In the pure LAN context, evolving network operating systems handle the first problem by implementing parallel protocol stacks. 3Com calls this Demand Protocol Architecture (DPA)—Novell calls it Open Protocol Technology (OPT). Parallel protocol stacks are only part of the solution since they do not, in themselves, guarantee equivalent implementation across different vendors' product lines.

You should keep in mind that the more complex a protocol is, as indicated by the number of different fields in the header, the more difficult it is to attain interoperability between systems. The syntax (format) and semantics (meaning) of each field must be implemented exactly alike or problems will occur in internetwork protocol execution. In most cases, interoperability can only be assured by compliance testing using all possible combinations of software and in the connectivity loop. One of the key tools for an effort such as this is the protocol analyzer, such as *The Sniffer* from Network General. The Sniffer can be configured to run on IBM's Token-Ring, Ethernet, Arcnet,

Starlan, and the IBM PC Network (Broadband). Protocol suites supported include all the major stacks including

- NetWare Core Protocol/XNS
- Server Message Block (SMB)/XNS
- SMB/NETBIOS/TCP/IP
- SMB/ISO
- SNA/SMB/NETBIOS

Possession of a tool such as The Sniffer is the first step in compliance testing. The next step is to determine a specific test configuration, followed by development of a comprehensive test plan. The test plan should indicate what actions will stimulate the test network and the expected responses from the appropriate protocol stacks. Data collection and analysis is handled by the protocol analyzer. Typical problems that might be discovered include errors in field coding (syntax errors), incorrect query/reply sequences (timing errors), and interpretation of field data (semantic errors). The consequences of lack of interoperability range from noncommunication to reductions in network performance.

Name Services

Although not strictly required for internetworking, Name Services contribute to the utility of widely distributed networks by providing transparent addressing and location services. As a user, wouldn't you much rather send a message to

John Jones@Marketing Group@Acme HQ

than have to look up John Jones' user name on his LAN and the phone number to dial in to that LAN? A naming service can automatically link a standard name convention such as the above to a variety of resources, among them telephone numbers, directories on file servers, mailing lists, and shared printers. Subsequent access to these resources is accomplished simply by specifying the name. Network software, supported by a Name Service, handles the details of finding the destination and delivering the data. To be most effective, name services should have two main properties:

- Persistence
- Centralized control

In a persistent name service, assigned names remain in effect until removed or changed (e.g., Banyan's VINES and 3Com's 3+Open). Nonpersistent name services remove the network name when the host work station is powered down (e.g., IBM PC LAN Program and StarLAN).

In any given network, a form of centralized control over names is desirable. Some implementations allow only one name "catalog" per logical network, regardless of the

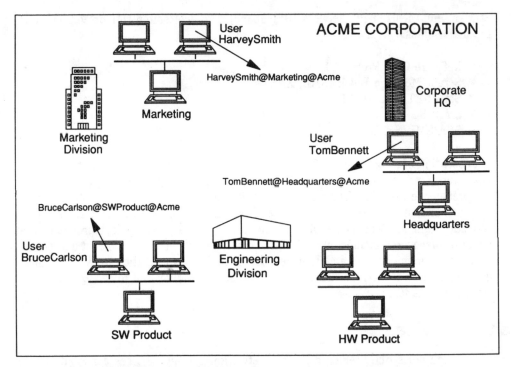

Figure 11.10. Hierarchical network naming concept.

number of servers installed; other systems assign one catalog per file server. Catalogs serve the same function as the telephone book in a city. In a distributed network, the set of network catalogs is analagous to a stack of telephone books from different cities. In a centralized system, communications between servers containing catalogs is crucial to keeping location data accurate for system-wide resources.

An example of a generic naming service that meets the two requirements above is the Xerox Clearinghouse. Variations of this protocol are used by 3Com and Banyan in their network operating systems. The XEROX Clearinghouse uses a hierarchical naming system. Its generic form is

```
Item (or name)@Group@Domain
```

In practice, the item or name is a single user, file server, printer, directory, or list of names associated with a particular physical network. The Group is typically a workgroup or department, and is equivalent to a specific logical network. The Name Service is responsible for linking the Group name to a logical network number. The Domain represents the entire organization and may be used to link the organization into a larger multiorganizational network such as a commercial electronic mail service. For example, this is currently done by 3Com with a gateway between their LAN EMail software and MCI Mail. With the appropriate mailbox information, any correspondent outside 3Com can use MCI Mail to deliver an electronic mail message directly to the recipient's workstation. The hierarchical naming system is illustrated in Figure 11.10.

NETBIOS-based networks use the Name Management Protocol (NMP), originally provided as part of the Localnet/PC protocol under license from Sytek. NMP is neither persistent nor centralized. Names are assigned to network resources only while those resources are powered up and active on the network. Because control is not centralized, NMP is not well-suited for internetworking. NMP requires that each node on the network maintain its own list of names—if a node cannot find a name in its list, a broadcast is made to the network to locate the unknown name. Broadcasts such as these would be highly inefficient in a wide-area network environment. The NETBIOS naming convention was illustrated in Figure 9-23.

Internetworking Devices

Wide-area Networks (WANs)

Wide-area Networks were extensively discussed in Chapter 7, specifically the X.25 packet-switched network protocol and IBM's proprietary System Network Architecture (SNA). In this chapter, our main concern is the connection of LANs to certain types of WANs for host connectivity, the interconnection of remote LANs using WANs as subnetworks, and access to LANs from remote work stations via WANs. Other WANs commonly used to connect LANs are T-1 links and various services offered by the telephone industry.

Proprietary networks are designed and marketed by a single computer vendor. Two of the most prominent include *System Network Architecture* (IBM's *SNA*) and *Digital Network Architecture* (DEC's *DNA*). From the perspective of a LAN user, connection to such networks is via gateways—SNA and DNA interconnects that allow LAN work stations to participate as members of the appropriate proprietary network. These types of gateways can. be connected to host communications controllers either directly or via dedicated lines using synchronous line protocol. A number of products are available for PCs that allow MS-DOS and OS/2 applications to logically connect to mainframe or minicomputer applications using SNA and DNA as routing and transport systems. Software is also available that will allow selected mainframe and mini hosts to function as servers for connected LANs.

Packet-switching is an efficient method of transmitting large volumes of data between widely separated processing sites. X.25 is an international standard of the CCITT for the interconnection of Data Terminal Equipment (DTE) devices to a packet-switching network. Local area networks can connect to packet-switched networks (abbreviated as either *PSN*, or *PDN—Public Data Network*) via a device known as an *X.25 gateway*. In this case, the X.25 gateway, or server, emulates a Packet Assembler-Dissambler (PAD), which is the Data Communications Equipment (DCE) device on a PDN. LANs can also connect to PDNs via a standard telephone subscriber line and modem. The telephone number dialed is the number of a local PDN node (PAD), which is, in turn, directly connected to the data network. This is how you connect to the CompuServe

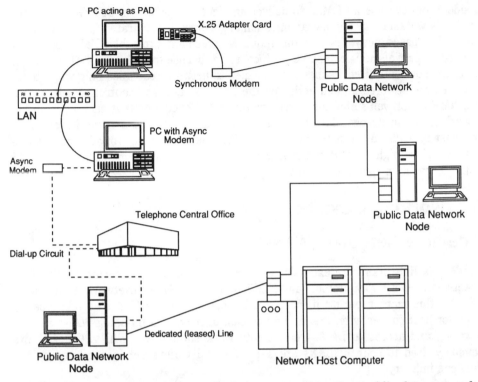

Figure 11.11. Direct and dial-up telephone connections to a public data network (PDN).

network, for example. In this situation, the PDN connection is indirectly completed through an asynchronous gateway on the LAN. Figure 11.11 compares these two methods of connecting to packet-switching networks.

WAN Line Control Devices

Working with internetworks that include wide-area networks requires knowledge of certain communications components that are used to concentrate data for economical transmission and to connect to host computer systems. The most common of these items include *cluster controllers, front-end processors, statistical multiplexers, T-1 multiplexers,* and *concentrators.* These devices are physically located between the appropriate LAN node or host computer and the wide-area transport system, usually a telephone or data network. Their basic functions are illustrated in Figures 11-12 through 11-15.

Gateways

A gateway is one of several types of communications servers. The function of a gateway is to allow two or more dissimilar networks to communicate as a single logical

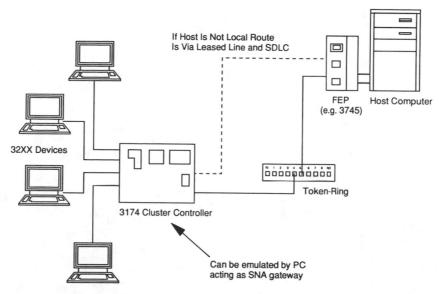

Figure 11.12. Functional concept of a cluster controller.

entity. In the context of the LAN system software discussed in Chapter 9, dissimilar means that the transport protocol are different, *and* that the underlying physical networks are different. Host and LAN operating systems may also be dissimilar. Among the more common types of gateways are those that connect LANs to proprietary mainframe architectures such as IBM's SNA and DEC's DECnet. Other common forms of gateways connect LANs to a variety of wide-area network protocol, such as asynchronous and synchronous on the public telephone network, T-1 multiplexed data on private networks, X.25 on public data networks, ISDN, international Telex, and facsimile.

Asynchronous Gateways

Asynchronous gateways are designed to convert data on a LAN to a form suitable for transmission and reception via asynchronous devices such as Bell 212A modems. Asynchronous gateways include modem servers, which allow any authorized LAN user access to one or more modems attached to the server. In this case, the function of the server is to communicate with client work stations to determine the client's desired destination service. For example, a network user may wish to connect to Dow Jones News Retrieval, while another user may wish to connect to a remote LAN for electronic mail. The server must determine the appropriate telephone number to dial (for public switched telephone networks) and the asynchronous communications parameters needed to connect to the desired service. The numbers and parameters are prestored in the server as part of the installation and configuration process.

A variety of processes are available to implement asynchronous gateways. In the most general form, a software interface at the work station allows either a third-party

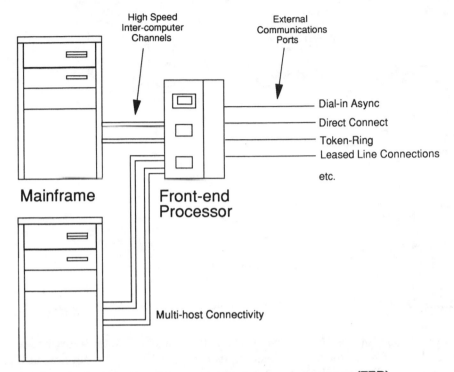

Figure 11.13. Functional concept of a front-end processor (FEP).

communications software package or some other applications program to request access to one or more dial-up modems attached to the server. This interface may take the form of a software interrupt such as IBM's INT 14 or Novell's INT 06B, or a procedure call such as IBM's Asynchronous Communications Server Interface (ACSI).

Asynchronous gateways are implemented with a variety of hardware and software design features. Many of these are illustrated below with descriptions of the following asynchronous services:

- Novell's NetWare Asynchronous Communications Server (NACS) and related products
- Banyan's Virtual Networking System (VINES) Asynchronous Service
- 3Com's 3 + Route and 3 + Open Internet for 3 + and 3 + Open network systems, respectively.
- IBM's LAN Asynchronous Connection Server (LANACS)

NetWare Asynchronous Servers

Novell's asynchronous support services include both dial-out and remote PC dial-in capabilities. Dial-out services are provided by the NetWare Asynchronous Communica-

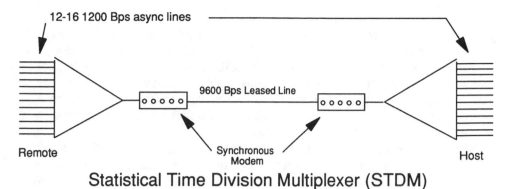

Statistical Time Division Multiplexer (STDM)

T-1 Multiplexer

Figure 11.14. Functional concept of STDM and T-1 multiplexers.

tions Server (NACS) working in conjunction with work station-hosted terminal emulation software. Work station terminal software is logically connected to the NACS through the NetWare Asynchronous Services Interface (NASI). Dial-in services can be provided in one of two ways:

- Connecting to the LAN through the NACS using the software package NetWare AnyWare.
- Connecting to the LAN through an 80386-based server called the NetWare Access Server.

All asynchronous support services use Wide-area Network Interface Modules (WNIMs) at either the NACS or the NetWare Access Server. WNIMs are multiline asynchronous adapter cards, capable of supporting up to four modems each. As many as four WNIMs may be located in an asynchronous communications server or access server. A single network can have more than one NACS or NetWare Access Server. Software implementation requires several parts:

- A WNIM control program on the server.
- NetWare Asynchronous Services Interface (NASI) for dial-out connections. This interface at the work station allows terminal emulation software packages to connect with asynchronous ports on the NACS server. NASI supports ASCOM IV and other popular asynchronous terminal-emulation software.
- ASCOM IV asynchronous communications software for dial-out connections. This package runs on up to four work stations simultaneously (per licensed copy) through the NACS asynchronous ports.
- NetWare AnyWare software for dial-in connections. This software allows a remote PC to dial in to the LAN and operate as a remote work station. Up to four work stations on the LAN can serve as hosts (per licensed copy of AnyWare). NetWare AnyWare is designed for relatively light use and requires the NACS server for remote access to the LAN.
- NetWare Access Server for dial-in connections. The NetWare Access Server functions in the same manner as NetWare AnyWare except that it is designed for heavy-duty use. The NetWare Access Server requires 80386 PC hardware and supports up to 15 individual dial-in sessions.

Figure 11.16 illustrates some typical network configurations with the above capabilities. The NACS/NASI hardware/software combination provides the following dial-out asynchronous terminal support functions through the use of ASCOM IV (upgraded

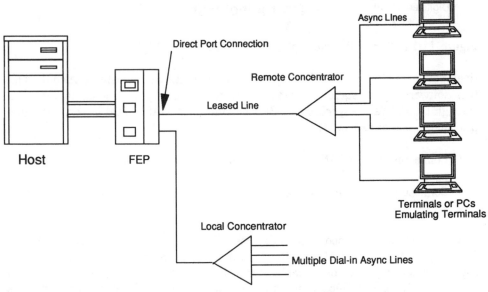

Note: Modems Not Shown

Figure 11.15. Functional concept of local and remote area administrators.

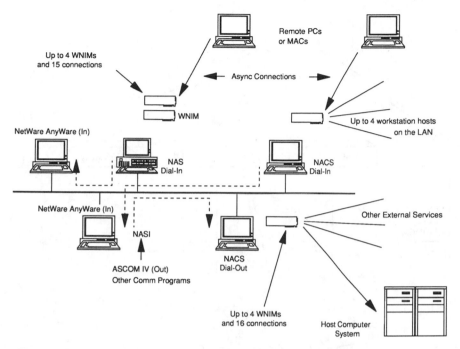

Figure 11.16. Novell NetWare asynchronous server architecture.

versions of this software or other work station terminal-emulation packages may provide additional or modified features):

- Up to 16 shared asynchronous communications lines (hardware feature through use of WNIMs).
- Communications speeds up to 19,200 bits/sec per line (WNIM hardware feature).
- Multiple file transfer protocol, including ASCOM IV, XMODEM, Kermit, BLOCK, and BLOCK V.
- Support for several common asynchronous terminal emulations.
- User-defined modem support to accommodate non-Hayes protocol.
- ASCII-to-EBCDIC conversions.
- Administrator-controlled security for limited access by LAN users.
- Script files allowing fully automated terminal operations.
- Dial directory for automatic dialing.

Banyan VINES Asynchronous Support

The VINES asynchronous communications service allows network users to connect to wide-area networks, host computer systems (mainframes or minicomputer installations) or on-line database and electronic mail services. Banyan file servers can be set up with either or both direct-line connections or any of a variety of modem communications systems. Like other Banyan services, asynchronous service uses the StreetTalk

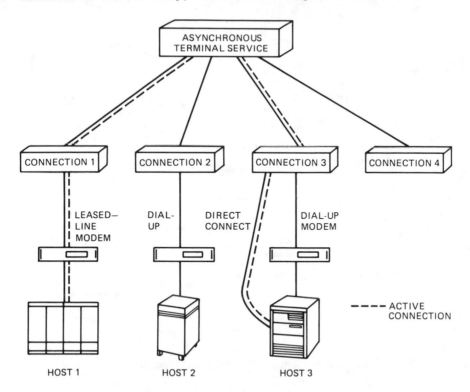

Figure 11.17. Banyan VINES asynchronous terminal service.

naming convention. The term *connection name* refers to a specific host computer or on-line service, regardless of how many or what type of communications paths exist between the Banyan server and the host system. This concept is illustrated in Figure 11.17. A server has the following capacities related to asynchronous service:

- One asynchronous service.
- Up to 30 connection names for the service.
- Unlimited dial-out lines per connection name.
- Number of direct lines per connection name equal to the number of direct line connections to the server.
- Maximum number of asynchronous hardware connections to the server depends on the specific server model used and ranges up to a maximum of 30 on the Corporate Network Server (CNS).

For each connection name, certain parameters must be specified, such as line speed, number of data bits, parity, number of stop bits, and terminal-emulation type. This process is the same as that required to use any common PC communications software. Users log on to the network with asynchronous connection names provided in their user profiles. The user profiles also contain directory search paths

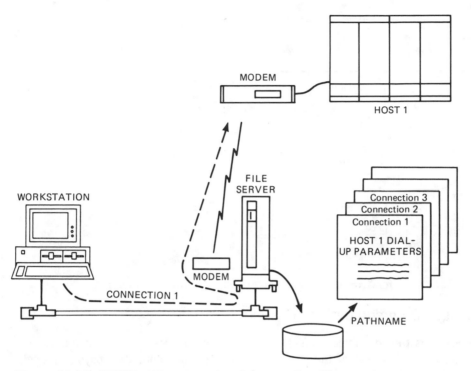

MODEM

HOST 1

FILE
SERVER

WORKSTATION

Connection 3
Connection 2
Connection 1
HOST 1 DIAL-
UP PARAMETERS

MODEM

CONNECTION 1

PATHNAME

Figure 11.18. VINES wide area network connection files.

to locate the corresponding connection files (files that contain communications parameters for a connection name). This process is shown for a typical installation in Figure 11.18.

VINES provides both dial-out terminal emulation and remote PC dial-in for asynchronous communications support. All asynchronous services use the Intelligent Communications Adapter (ICA), a six-port adapter card. From one to five of these cards can be located in the Banyan dedicated servers and generic VINES servers, providing up to 30 asynchronous ports per server attached to the LAN. ICAs support a variety of line protocols, including asynchronous, SDLC, HDLC, and X.25. Asynchronous connections are supported up to 19,200 bps.

The terminal-emulation services are integrated with the VINES StreetTalk naming service to allow emulation to be customized for individuals and groups. The terminal service is essentially a special-purpose asynchronous communications program, not unlike Crosstalk Mark 4 or ASCOM IV. It provides standard features such as the following:

- Common DEC, IBM, and TTY terminal emulation
- Autodial directory support
- ASCII file transfer
- Kermit protocol for binary file transfer
- Multiple server dial-out access for any user

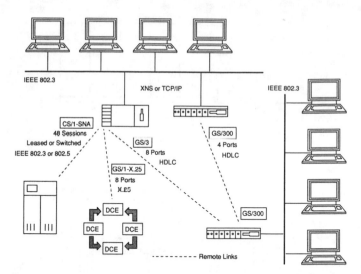

Figure 11.19. 3Com XNS and TCP/IP compatible gateway products.

3 + Route Communications Service

3 + Route is the communications service offered by the 3 + network operating system. Its purpose is to extend the sharing of resources and information beyond a single 3 + network. Internetworking is accomplished with either dial-up or dedicated phone lines. 3 + Route allows other 3 + services, such as 3 + Share, 3 + Mail, and 3 + Name service, to be transparently used across multiple networks.

3 + Route hardware consists of either a 3Server or a nondedicated PC server connected to appropriate wide-area network line devices. Remote individual PCs may also use the services of 3 + Route when they run specialized 3 + Remote software. 3 + Route's XNS internetworking protocol is compatible with several models of gateways sold by 3Com, such as the GS/3 and GS/4 Communications Servers. 3Com's gateway configurations are shown in Figure 11.19. 3Com gateways connect directly to the Ethernet and do not depend on PC-based nondedicated or dedicated servers.

3 + Route supports the following terminal-emulation capabilities:

- Microcom MNP file transfer protocol
- Time-out hang-up function with selectable time
- Program control over calling times
- Automatic telephone number look-up, auto-dial, and auto-answer
- Automatic selection of prioritized alternate numbers

3 + Open Internet

3 + Open Internet, or Internet Communications Manager (ICM), is designed to provide internetworking for XNS-based LANs through the use of asynchronous communi-

cations lines. 3 + Open Internet is backward compatible with 3 + Route and 3 + Remote, 3Com's asynchronous services for the 3 + network operating system. As with all LAN services, 3 + Open Internet is a resource manager. 3 + Open Internet's resources are communications ports and external networks. Each supported communications port is a standard COM: port and has an associated modem. Modem parameters are configurable to allow support beyond the standard Hayes, Microcom, and Telebit modems supported by 3 + Route. Network resources are associated with external LANs. Each network has an associated Network ID and a password to enhance internetwork security. 3 + Open Internet also uses standard LAN Manager network management services, such as audit trails, error logs and alerts. 3 + Open Internet can be managed from any OS/2 work station on the network by a person with proper access privileges.

3 + Open Internet consists of two parts: the service module and the user-interface module. These modules may be on separate computers or on the same computer. Communications between the user and service modules are accomplished via OS/2 Named Pipes. The service module manages communications port drivers and network routing details. The service module also uses the LAN Manager alert facility to generate messages based on predesignated events. These events may be error thresholds or certain audit conditions. The alert facility works in conjunction with the messenger facility on each work station to receive and log the alert message. If the work station has invoked the net pop-up facility, the alert will display on the user's screen at the time of receipt.

Communications ports can be in one of four states: Enabled, Disabled, Connected, or Disconnected. Networks can be either Enabled or Disabled. These status commands are used to allow dynamic management of internetwork communications. Dynamic management means that the 3 + Internet server does not have to be taken off line to accomplish network management tasks. Ports can be disabled without affecting network status—this might be done to remove a modem from the port and replace it with another, for example. A port would be connected to override a pre-established network profile. Conversely, a port could be disconnected at any time to recover from a phone line with excessive errors. Disabling a network resource would be done, for example, to prevent dial-out or dial-in during a system maintenance period.

Configuration of ports and networks is relatively straightforward. Ports have parameters usually associated with asynchronous communications, such as modem type, line speed, inactivity timeout, and whether incoming or outgoing calls are allowed, or both. Modems other than those that are standard and supported can be defined by line speed, data bit pattern, parity, whether the modem is error-correcting or capable of automatic baud-rate adjustment. Commands for modem initialization, hang-up, busy, no-answer, and connection reliability can also be specified.

Routes are logical connections between remote networks and thus are a part of 3 + Internet's network resources. The concept of routes and route configuration is carried over from 3 + Route. Route configuration parameters include phone number, comm port, network ID, dial timeout, and connection schedule. A route can be assigned

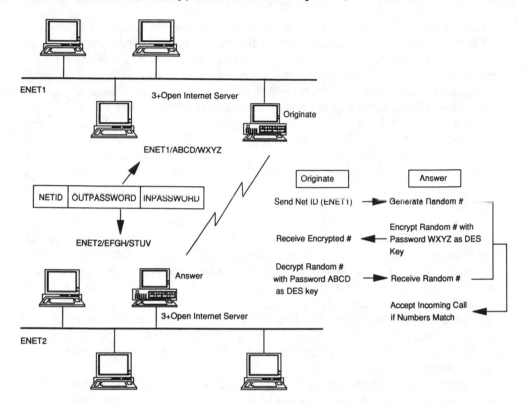

Figure 11.20. 3Com 3 + Open Internet server-to-server security protocol.

multiple comm ports. This might be done to pool modem resources to a high-usage route. Conversely, a single comm port can be assigned to multiple routes. Economical usage of a high-cost, high-speed modem would be a reason to put many routes on one port.

Network configuration includes network ID and passwords. Separate passwords can be specified for dial-in and dial-out routes. Network configuration can be bypassed to maintain interoperability with 3 + Route since 3 + Route does not support the concept of network passwords. A restricted network list may be established. Any network not on this list will be disallowed from either outgoing or incoming connections. Password verification uses an encryption scheme and an exchange protocol between the two Internet servers attempting to establish a route. Figure 11.20 shows the protocol sequence.

As an LAN Manager service, 3 + Open Internet is controlled by standard service commands. These are START, STOP, PAUSE, and CONTINUE. During a PAUSE period, existing connections are maintained but no new connections are allowed. Network dynamic management is also not allowed during a PAUSE interval. If the STOP command is issued, all connections are broken and the 3 + Internet service is terminated.

IBM LAN Asynchronous Services

IBM provides asynchronous server support through its LAN Asynchronous Connection Server (LANACS) Program. LANACS is compatible with DOS-based servers and the Real-time Interface Co-Processor (RTIC) Multiport (IBM PC/AT hardware bus) and Multiport/2 (IBM PS/2 hardware bus) adapters. LANACS provides both dial-out and dial-in asynchronous communications through a dedicated server. The server can be connected to Token-Ring, PC Network Baseband or PC Network Broadband LAN topologies. Depending on the server host hardware used and the number of RTIC adapters installed, LANACS will support from four to 32 asynchronous ports per server.

An RTIC Multiport or Multiport/2 adapter uses the Intel 80186 processor and up to 512 KBytes of RAM for on-board communications protocol support. An RTIC Mulitport can have three possible configurations:

- Four RS-232C ports
- Eight RS-232C ports
- Four RS-232C and four RS-422A ports

The RS-422A ports will support asynchronous devices (terminals, printers, etc.) over longer distances and at higher data rates than possible with RS-232C protocol.

SNA and RJE Gateways

Gateways to SNA and RJE hosts are among the most common types of gateways in LAN installations. This is the result of the large number of IBM mainframe computers found in all types of businesses and organizations. Such gateways can be direct-wired to a local mainframe or connected via synchronous modems and a leased landline, or other suitable transport system, to a remote mainframe. As with the asynchronous gateways, SNA and RJE gateways are most often implemented as servers, allowing multiple LAN users to access the local or remote mainframe facilities.

Such gateways are composed of two basic parts: the software terminal emulators that allow connected PCs to act like IBM remote terminals of various types, and the data link protocol that provide basic compatibility with IBM front-end processors. Protocols supported typically include SDLC and Bisynchronous. These are discussed in more detail in Chapters 2 and 7. Supported terminals include 3274/76 cluster controllers (typically emulated by the gateway), 3278 remote terminals, 3279 remote graphics terminals, 3286/3287 printers, and various 3770 RJE equipment. The protocols are implemented on communications adapter cards, which connect directly to the appropriate line devices (modems). Emulation software runs on the gateway and may run on work stations.

Gateway Communications' G/SNA and G/BSC

Gateway Communications provides typical SNA and RJE support through its G/SNA line of hardware and software. Non-SNA support is also provided through the G/BSC

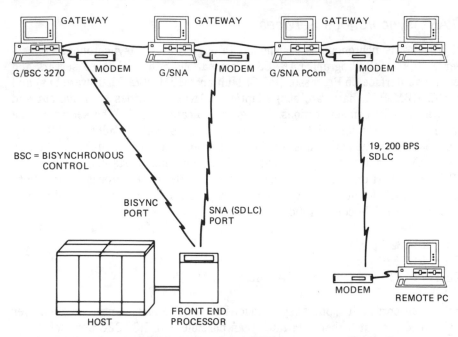

Figure 11.21. Gateway communications' SNA gateway configurations.

3270, which emulates a 3274/3278 combination on a Bisynchronous link. Another unusual subset of this product line is the G/SNA PCcom, which provides a high-speed SDLC link between remotely connected PCs. This link will support up to 19,200 bps and has superior file transfer capabilities compared to asynchronous links. Adapter cards for these products can be either IBM SDLC/Bisync cards or Gateway's enhanced WNIM-186 communications card. The latter offers speeds up to 800 Kbps and two ports, which can be configured as RS-232, RS-422, or V.35. Figure 11.21 depicts a multiple-option layout for the Gateway SNA systems.

VINES 3270/SNA and 3270/BSC Service

VINES and the Banyan file server support IBM 3274/3276 cluster controller and 3278/3279 display/3287 printer Logical Unit (LU) emulation. In the SNA system, a Logical Unit can be the session on a terminal or a printer. A cluster controller is designed to provide linkage between the SNA network and a number of individual terminals and/or printers. In the Banyan system, the server acts as the cluster controller and work stations with their attached printers emulate 3270/SNA terminals and printers. Communications capabilties with this service are:

- Up to two 3270/SNA terminal services allowed.
- Up to 32 Logical Units allowed per terminal service.
- Each terminal service requires a dedicated communications line (switched or leased as appropriate).

- Up to 30 communications lines (CNS servers) assignable on each server.

SNA terminal support incorporates reconfigurable 3270 keyboard emulation and various status displays covering on-line, connection, keyboard, printer, mode, Logical Unit, and message information. These status displays are designed to provide the user with complete information regarding the current mainframe session.

Novell's SNA Gateway

Novell also offers SNA support with its SNA Gateway. This gateway offers support for up to 32 concurrent logical sessions with mainframe equipment. IBM mainframe environments supported include the following:

- IBM 370, 303X, 208X, 43XX mainframe hosts
- IBM 3705, 3720, 3725 front-end processors
- IBM VTAM and TCAM access methods
- IBM CICS, CMS, DSPRINT, ISPF, JES, TSO/SPF applications

The Gateway functions as a 3274 Cluster Controller and work stations function as 3278 or 3279 display Logical Units. Network printers can be assigned as 3287 printer LUs. The Novell SNA Gateway does not require a dedicated server, nor does it require special software in those work stations that run SNA sessions as emulating 3278/3279 terminals. The Gateway supports dial-up and leased lines and will work with point-to-point and multidrop circuits. More than one Gateway can exist on a LAN. Three versions are provided that support either 8, 16, or 32 logical SNA sessions.

Software features include Session Hold, Hot Key, and Disk Logging capabilities. Session Hold allows the host session to remain active while the work station executes a DOS command. Hot Key is a rapid method of shifting between a host session and DOS applications. Disk Logging allows a screen of host data to be downloaded to a disk file. A typical SNA Gateway set-up is illustrated in Figure 11-22.

X.25 and Other Gateways

Gateways outside the domain of proprietary and asynchronous networks are most commonly found in X.25 packet-switched network, PSTN, or private T-1 network and international Telex applications. X.25 is an international standard sponsored by the CCITT and functions much the same for public and private data networks (PDN) as RS-232-C does for the public-switched telephone network. In other words, X.25 is a standard to connect Data Terminal Equipment (DTE) with Data Communications Equipment (DCE). In this case, the DCE is connected directly to a packet-switched network, just as a Bell 212A modem (DCE) is connected directly to the PSTN. Some X.25 gateway products allow the server to be configured as either DTE or DCE, depending on the specific application. Some examples of X.25 gateway usage are shown in Figure 11.23. X.25 gateways are available from Gateway Communications, 3Com, Novell, Banyan, and others for IBM PC and compatible LANs.

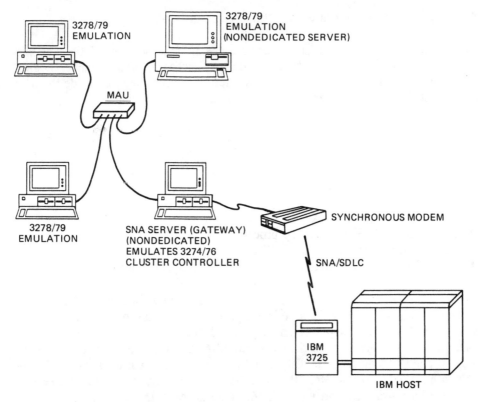

Figure 11.22. NetWare SNA gateway configuration.

T-1 gateways are designed to connect LANs directly to high-capacity public or private T-1 links. A T-1 link is a standard digital transport methodology, capable of handling up to 24 voice channels, each channel being rated at 64 Kbps. The total data rate of a T-1 link is 1.544 Mbps. T-1 links can be transported by inexpensive microwave systems, Very Small Aperture Terminal (VSAT) satellite systems, fiber optics, copper cable, or infrared light-wave links.

Telex gateways are designed to connect LANs to the international Telex network. Such gateways are capable of connecting to the older but more ubiquitous Telex I or Telex II (also known as TWX) systems, or to the newer but less common Teletex system. Telex gateways may or may not include actual Telex machines. Telex software can be integrated with a LAN's electronic mail system so that a user can send or receive Telex's as if they were any other type of EMail. A good Telex gateway will have an international directory included as well as the capability to support store and forward operations. The latter is important because many international Telex sessions are not interactive due to time zone differences. Torus Systems is one well-known supplier of Telex gateways, specifically for their line of Tapestry LAN software.

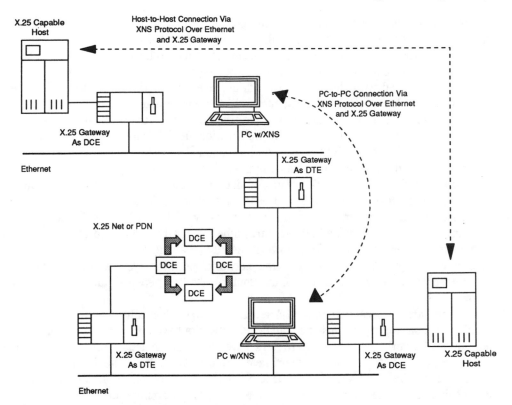

Figure 11.23. 3Com X.25 gateways in DCE and DTE modes.

Facsimile, or FAX as it is commonly called, is widely available for PCs in the form of adapter cards. Facsimile cards require nothing more than an ordinary telephone connection. Some FAX cards allow multiple work station access, in effect becoming a FAX gateway for LAN users.

Routers

Before discussing router characteristics, network addressing will be reviewed. Any work station or server on a single LAN or multiple bridged LANs will have a unique *node address*. Node addresses are assigned to a physical network adapter card serial number, thus assuring universal uniqueness. Node addresses are also known as MAC-layer addresses because they are only recognizable by the MAC Sub-Layer of the IEEE 802 standards. Packet routing on a single LAN requires only a source node address and a destination node address. Inspection of an Ethernet or Token-Ring packet will reveal a six-byte field each for source and destination address. If the packet is addressed to a user on a LAN not physically connected or bridged to the source LAN, a *network address* is needed. Network addresses are interpreted at the Network Layer of the source LAN to route an outgoing packet to a destination LAN with its own network address. One or more subnetworks may be traversed during the routing process. Addresses associated with these subnetworks are used for routing purposes. Once this packet gets to the destination LAN, the node address is mapped, or associated to a specific user on that LAN. The Data Link Layer knows nothing about the network address since it does not process the information field in either the MAC or LLC sublayers. The Network Layer knows nothing about the node address since only the information field of a MAC-layer frame is passed to Layer 3.

Routers work at the Network Layer and act as internetwork post offices. A router node forwards packets specifically addressed to that router node, and destined for one or more external networks. It is the responsibility of higher-layer software at the sending station to determine that data are to be externally routed and to ensure that the router address is correct. This, in turn, requires that the router's external communications configuration be known to the network operating system. Routers can be connected to more than two networks. Routers use the network address described above.

Routers are devices that route LAN traffic between logically separate networks. Logically separate means that the connected networks have different Layer 3 network numbers. Networks connected by routers have the same transport protocol since, in most cases, the network and transport layer protocol are linked. This is the case with XNS, TCP/IP, OSI, and Novell's SPX/IPX. Routers will support multipath routing since they can be connected to more than two networks. Router architecture and operation is illustrated in Figure 11.24.

Although routers are traditionally protocol dependent, advances in router technology have resulted in multi-protocol routers and Brouters, or bridging routers. A Brouter routes specific protocol-dependent traffic and bridges all other traffic.

Bridges

Bridges are designed to connect two physically separate LANs with possibly different higher-layer protocol stacks. Bridges work at the Media Access Sublayer and use only the destination and source addresses contained in the Layer 2 packet format. A bridge inspects (filters) all packets to determine if the destination address is on the same physical LAN as the source address. Two outcomes are possible: The packet is destined for a node on the same LAN as the source node, or it is destined for a node on the connected LAN. In the first case, the packet is ignored, since the destination node would recognize its own traffic. In the second case, the packet is forwarded to the connected LAN. Figure 11.25 illustrates basic bridge operation.

Local bridges directly connect two networks. Remote bridges connect two networks via one of several types of wide-area subnetwork as described below. Figure 11.26 shows the difference in configuration between the two types of bridges. Figure 11.26 also depicts one way of connecting more than two LANs with a multiple bridge installa-

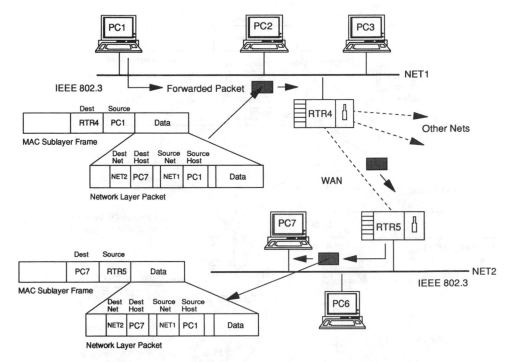

Figure 11.24. Basic router operation using Ethernet-to-Ethernet example.

tion. A more complex example, showing both local and remote bridges, is illustrated in Figure 11.27.

Common means of connecting LANs via remote bridges use the public switched telephone network, public or private data networks, and private T-1 links. PSTN bridges use asynchronous hardware and bridge software for dial-up connections to a similarly equipped remote LAN. X.25 remote bridges use either point-to-point or multipoint configurations with data rates up to 64 Kbps. In the former case, two LAN remote bridges are linked by a direct connection (leased line) or a dial-up line using the X.25 protocol. Multipoint bridges connect to a Public Data Network and can connect to multiple LANs using the PDN. Some bridges support the X.75 PDN interconnect protocol, which allows connected LAN users to access overseas packet-switched networks. T-1 bridges typically use the facilities of a private voice/data network to connect two LANs. T-1 bridges require connection to a T-1 multiplexer similar to T-1 gateways.

Proper design of bridge employment in a LAN can provide varying combinations of the following benefits:

- Logical extension of a single network
- Increased throughput
- Traffic filtering

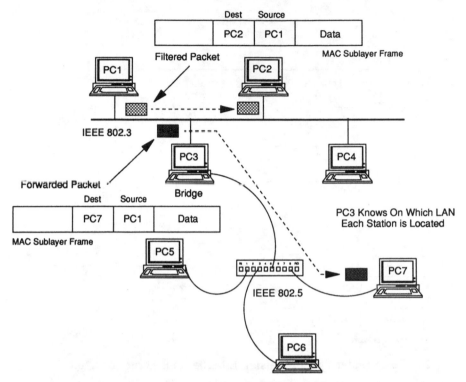

Figure 11.25. Basic bridge operation using Ethernet-to-Token Ring example.

- Protocol independence
- Higher performance than routers and gateways

Bridges commonly work in a learning mode, meaning that they automatically determine which network nodes are on each connected segment. These lists of network nodes are called routing tables, although the term is somewhat of a misnomer. For purposes of discussion, we will call the network containing the source node the first network and the forwarded network the second network. Pure bridges know nothing about routing—they only pass the packet to the second network if the destination address is not on the first network's list of addresses.

Novell's Advanced NetWare provides a unique example of bridging capabilities. NetWare supports two type of bridges: an internal bridge, designed to run in file servers, and an external bridge, designed to run in work stations. Internal bridges support up to four dissimilar network adapter cards per file server and are supported by the basic network operating system. External bridges can be either dedicated or nondedicated, and are supported by stand-alone software compatible with the network operating system. External bridges also handle up to four dissimilar LAN adapter cards.

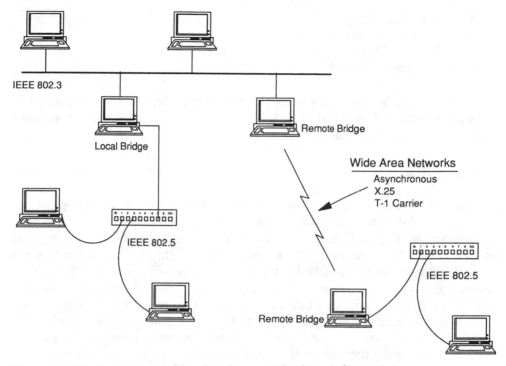

Figure 11.26. Comparison of local and remote bridge configurations.

Why pay extra for external bridge software when the internal bridge is included in the basic LAN software price? The answer is, you pay for increased flexibility. For example, the external bridge could be used:

- To provide a more flexible wiring scheme than the server might be capable of.
- To provide a repeater function to extend the effective length of a LAN.
- To add more networks beyond the four supported by the file server.

In order to properly configure a Novell bridge, certain basic rules must be followed. Each server to be bridged must have a unique name. Each network to be bridged must have a unique number. Finally, each bridge software installation must be provided with the unique network numbers of all LANs to be bridged.

Another example of a bridge operation is provided by the Banyan network server. This server provides switching between up to four LANs and multiple external service gateways. From a hardware standpoint, the Banyan approach differs from Novell in that the bridge node is always a file server and provides one or more gateways to external services. The Banyan network server may be generically described as a network data switch.

IBM uses bridges extensively in its approach to internetworking Token-Rings. IBM bridges can connect any combination of the following:

- 4 Mbps Token-Ring
- 16 Mbps Token-Ring
- PC Network Baseband
- PC Network Broadband

Token-Ring bridges are either local or remote. Remote bridges are linked with subnetwork data rates from 9.6 Kbps to 1.344 Mbps. Up to 15 bridges can be paralleled between rings, allowing redundant path routing.

Repeaters

Repeaters are not usually associated with internetworking per se, but since they are often confused with gateways, routers, and bridges, we will review their definition here. A repeater works at the Physical Layer and is designed to extend the physical length of a LAN. Repeaters are commonly used in distributed bus networks such as Ethernet and in Token-Ring networks. Specifically, repeaters allow two segments of an Ethernet or Token-Ring LAN to be connected as one logical LAN. Ethernet repeaters were illustrated in Figure 10-10. Figure 11.28 shows a Token-Ring repeater configuration using IBM 8218 Copper Repeaters. You will notice that two repeaters are required, one for the main ring and one for the alternate ring. These repeaters are designed for one-way data flow, hence the requirement for pairing. Because of physical connectivity rules, the number of repeaters allowed on a logical LAN is limited.

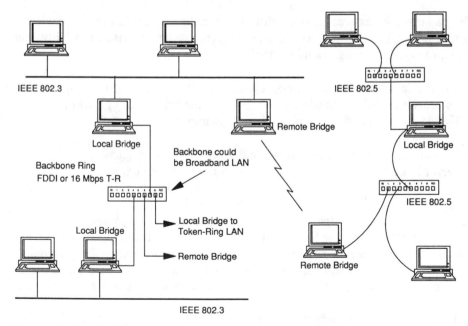

Figure 11.27. Multiple local and remote bridge configuration.

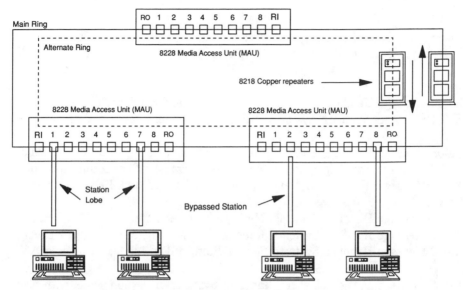

Figure 11.28. IBM Token-Ring 8218 copper repeater usage.

Internetworking Applications

Electronic Mail

Overview

In Part I, the basic features of electronic mail (EMail) software were reviewed and EMail applications were compared to Electronic Bulletin Board Systems and Remote Access software. In this chapter, electronic mail will be surveyed in relation to its use as an application for communications networks. EMail is finding a new level of maturity in American business society—this increased acceptance has been helped along by more powerful hardware, availability of software specifically designed to facilitate the use of EMail, and an increase in the linkage between dissimilar EMail systems. This last factor has been evidenced in both wide-area or public EMail systems and in the LAN industry.

Specific examples are the gateway between MCI Mail and the international Telex service, and the gateway between MCI Mail and 3Com's 3 + Mail and 3 + OpenMail. Gateways are the key to achieving *critical mass* in electronic mail systems. Critical mass in this context is having enough subscribers to an EMail service to encourage large numbers of additional individuals and organizations to sign up for service. With its various gateways, both to international services and to local area networks, MCI Mail has probably achieved this plateau. The ultimate goal would be for the dissimilar EMail services to conform to a common standard so that users would have additional leverage to reach potential correspondents.

X.400

The common standard that may bring this ultimate goal into reality is the CCITT X.400 series protocol on electronic mail systems. This series is composed of eight parts:

- X.400-Message Handling Systems: System Model and Service Elements
- X.401-Message Handling Systems: Basic Service Elements and Optional User Facilities
- X.408-Message Handling Systems: Encoded Information Type Conversion Rules
- X.409-Message Handling Systems: Presentation Transfer Syntax and Notation
- X.410-Message Handling Systems: Remote Operations and Reliable Transfer Server
- X.411-Message Handling Systems: Message Transfer Layer
- X.420-Message Handling Systems: Interpersonal Messaging User Agent Layer
- X.430-Message Handling Systems: Access Protocol For Teletex Terminals

In the above terminology, Message Handling Systems are synonomous with electronic mail systems. The X.400 series of protocols belong to Layer 7 of the ISO model, although the X.400 protocol is itself layered for ease of development and implementation. The X.400 series is quite comprehensive, and defines basic entities such as User Agents and Message Transfer Agents, several types of services, ranging from essential to optional, and connection standards to other services such as Telex, Teletex, and Group 3 facsimile. Each element in the X.400 standards can be likened to some counterpart in the standard postal service. User Agents are correspondents, Message Transfer Agents perform post office type service, addressing schemes have a purpose and design similar to Zip Codes, certain aspects of the standard are analagous to envelopes, and there is even an analogy for mail bags. Services run the gamut from required to desired. Some examples are shown in Table 11.1. Some of these have been available in other EMail systems and were described in Part I.

Table 11.1. Correspondent and Post Office Services in X.400.

Type of Service Agent	Basic	Essential	Additional
Correspondent	Message ID Type of Body	Originator ID Subject Primary Recipient Grade of Delivery	Blind Copy Encryption Status Importance Indication Expiry Date
Post Office	Message ID Date/Time of Submission Date/Time of Delivery	Deferred Delivery Delivery Notification Probe (trace)	Hold For Delivery Return of Contents Encoded Data Conversion

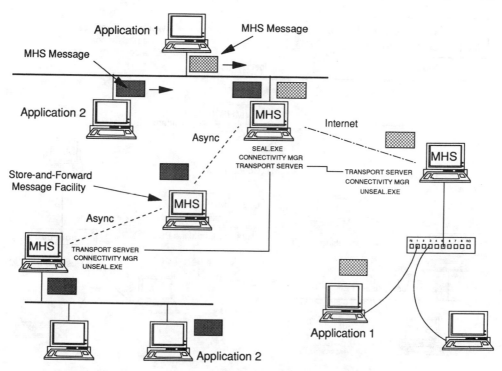

Figure 11.29. Message Handling System (MHS) software operation.

In the above table, the terms *correspondent* and *post office* have been loosely interpreted from their much more rigorous definitions within the X.400 standards. A *basic service* is inherent in the mail service; an *essential service* is required, but only invoked at the user's request; and an *additional service* is optional. It should be obvious that widespread acceptance of this series of standards will have a far-reaching effect on the future of world-wide electronic communications.

Message Handling System (MHS)

In the context of this discussion, MHS refers to the Action Technologies and Novell implementation of a store-and-forward electronic mail system. Within the LAN industry, MHS has become a de facto standard for linking applications with internetwork transport systems. From Novell's perspective, MHS is a general distributed computing architecture that can be used in a variety of applications including electronic mail. NetWare MHS handles the communications processing required for this architecture, including file transfer protocol, modem control, routing tables, transport protocol, and error checking. In other words, MHS handles all the issues associated with getting the information from the sending workstation to the destination workstation, error-free, regardless of the LAN and WAN topologies between the sender and recipient.

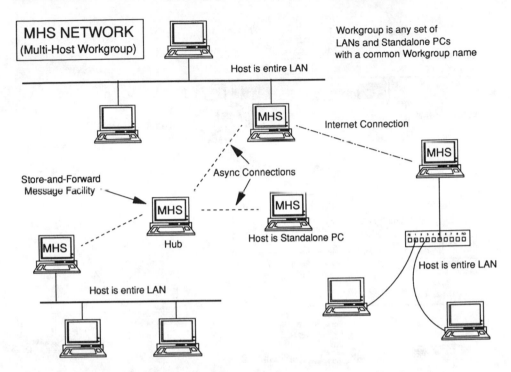

Figure 11.30. MHS network components.

MHS is invoked through a relatively simple application program interface called a *Message Control Block* (*MCB*). The Message Control Block is an 18-line ASCII file. An optional text message (cover letter) and application file(s) (the enclosure) represent the mail to be transferred by the MHS process. Any application that can create the 18-line ASCII file can interface to the MCB and the MHS transport system. The ASCII file, the text message, and the attached applications file(s) are packaged by a utility program SEAL.EXE and transmitted to the destination node. At the destination node, a utility program UNSEAL.EXE unpackages the files and transfers the text message and application file(s) to the appropriate directory(s). Figure 11.29 illustrates this process.

On the sending end, MHS is responsible for queuing the outbound messages and checking the appropriate connectivity path for availability. This might involve an asynchronous modem circuit, a remote bridge or a local bridge. The 18-line ASCII file functions as an envelope and contains information such as sender identification, destination address, subject line, and identification of the attached file(s). SEAL.EXE adds additional identifying information prior to actually transmitting the message.

Installing MHS on a LAN has internetworking implications. Before looking at these in detail, a few definitions are in order. An *MHS message* contains a header, an optional text file and an optional attachment. An *MHS application* is any end-user program that submits data to, or receives data from the MHS transport system. *MHS users* are people who run the applications that use MHS or processes that use MHS to exchange information. Each MHS installation has at least one administrative user who maintains a *routing directory* of addresses and connectivity paths within the *MHS network*. The *MHS Directory Manager* is a process that establishes and maintains the routing directory. An *MHS host* is a single workstation or LAN that runs MHS software. An *MHS hub* is a host that stores and forwards MHS messages for other hosts. An *MHS workgroup* is all users encompassed by a unique workgroup name in the MHS address form:

```
Username @ Workgroupname
```

A *multihost workgroup* is a workgroup that includes two or more hosts. Recall that an entire LAN may be considered a host. Examples of a multihost workgroup would be two directly connected LANs, LANs connected by a wide area network or a combination of multiple LANs and standalone remote workstations. A multihost workgroup would typically be an entire company or a major operating component of a company. One host in a workgroup is designated as a *workgroup-wide router* and maintains a routing directory for every user in the workgroup. A workgroup can contain internets, or multiple LANs connected by a local or remote bridge or by a router. One host in an internet is designated the *internet routing host*. Single LAN or standalone hosts must be routing hosts if connections to other hosts are required. An *MHS network* consists of one or more workgroups and comprises hosts that exchange messages among themselves.

The *MHS Connectivity Manager* is a process that runs in a routing host or a hub to transfer messages to the appropriate destination. The Connectivity Manager uses *Asynchronous Connection Transport servers*, *Internet Message servers*, and *Gateway servers* to provide the actual transport of messages within an MHS network. Asynchronous and Internet servers handle telephone and bridge connections respectively. Gateway servers provide the link between MHS networks and external electronic mail services or other computing environments. The Connectivity Manager and the servers handle the MHS network functions usually associated with Layers 3 and above in the ISO Model. Appropriate lower level LAN or wide area data link and physical protocol are used to establish links among hosts, or between hosts and external services. Figure 11.30 depicts the architecture of an MHS network and shows the relationship between an MHS network, workgroups, internets, hubs and hosts.

MHS maps well into the X.400 standard. The Connectivity Manager conforms to the functions required in the X.400 Message Transfer Agent (MTA). X.400 addressing is accommodated within the extended form of an MHS address. This strategy will allow the relatively easy establishment of gateways between MHS and X.400 electronic mail systems. The extended MHS address uses the form

```
Username.Applicationname @ Workgroupname.Enterprisename

(comment field) <X.400 address extension>

{other non-MHS address extension}
```

The real significance of a capability such as MHS is twofold: the universal interface it offers to a wide variety of applications software, and its interface to the external electronic mail world. The latter is accomplished through gateways that allow the use of commercial EMail services for transport and connection to a much larger body of correspondents. Table 11.2 lists EMail gateways supported as of this writing. The potential applications for MHS include electronic data interchange (EDI), remote job entry, daily reports from mobile sales and engineering staffs, project management from remote job sites, mobile data terminals in law enforcement, and structured telecommuting systems. The combination of MHS and internetworking technology provide the foundation upon which distributed applications can be built for business, education and government.

Table 11.2. EMail gateways supported by MHS.

cc:Mail	Infoplex (Compuserve)
DEC VMSMail	Higgins
MCI Mail	Voice mail
Banyan	IBM PROFS
IBM DISOSS	IBM SNADS
IBM CICS	Facsimile

Implementation

In deciding to implement EMail services, organizations have three basic choices on how to proceed—public EMail services, usually accessed through specialized providers or as a feature of an on-line database service, a private service, or a combination of the two. Private services are typically combinations of local area networks, stand-alone PCs, and wide-area transport services. The wide-area services may be privately owned or common carrier facilities. Private EMail services may incorporate a hierarchical structure of wide-area and local-area networks. The choice of which approach to take in the implementation of EMail is based both on economics and the affiliation of anticipated correspondents. If a large portion of correspondents are outside the organization, public EMail or a combination of private and public services are appropriate. Conversely, if most correspondence is within the organization, a private system makes more sense.

The economics of EMail implementation are based on the anticipated traffic volume between correspondents. Public Email services have widely varying rate structures, which must be carefully compared to the traffic needs of the potential customer. Charges may be based on any combination of the size of message transmitted, transmission time used for messaging, or standard on-line charges. Special service options generally cost extra. A good example of a special service option is telephonic notification of the arrival of a message in the recipient's mailbox. Most database services that have Email, such as CompuServe, only charge standard on-line fees. Specialized EMail providers, such as MCI Mail, charge by time and size of message. Some EMail services, which cater to larger businesses, have minimum monthly charges, which offer substantial savings if traffic levels are high enough. Private EMail costs are dependent on the transport system used to connect sites. Costs can range from standard long-distance telephone rates to monthly charges for leased lines or packet-switched network fees. Cost factors are based on combinations of link distance and time of transmission for dial-up telephone systems, link distance, and monthly fee for leased lines (with or without signal conditioning) or the amount of data transmitted for packet-switched networks.

Summary

In this chapter we have reviewed the concepts, hardware, and software that combine to extend the scope of the local area network beyond its immediate boundaries. Traditionally, almost 80 percent of communications in an organization are considered to occur in the immediate vicinity of a typical workgroup—the availablility of an increasing array of on-line databases and the growing sophistication of Electronic Mail may realign this traditional view of office automation communications. Clearly, an organization desiring to take the strategic view of the role of data communications in its daily activities must consider both wide-area and local-area networks and their integration. For this reason, internetworking is becoming an important element of the design and use of data communications facilities. Because of the diversity of vendors and standards in the data communications marketplace, interoperability has become a central issue in the design of internetworks. The configuration possibilities and options available to the network manager require a sound understanding of the underlying principles and their effect on the marketplace.

12

Network Implementation

Introduction

In the previous three chapters, we discussed fundamental concepts of LANs—system software, hardware, and internetworking. To put these concepts into focus in the context of today's state-of-the-art, this chapter will cover the most significant LAN system software products available for PCs. Specifically, network operating systems are the focus of the chapter because they represent the most significant area of development and have the largest influence on network performance and standardization.

Each of the chosen products represents a pattern of success and implementation excellence in the LAN world. Each of them has a strategy for pre-eminence as the LAN marketplace continues to mature. The threads common to each are the ability to support both robust internetworking plans and a variety of physical transport (hardware) systems. Each has an OS/2-capable product and a strategy to connect dissimilar computer architectures, including MS-DOS, OS/2, UNIX, and MacIntosh. Of greater significance is that each of these systems was featured in the Second Edition of this book, and is still, some two years later, a major force in the LAN industry.

The difficulty in dealing with a dynamic topic such as specific LAN implementations in a book is recognized. The reader should look more for underlying patterns of design and functionality than for specific details. The intent of this chapter is to provide representative implementations of the concepts discussed in earlier chapters. Internetworking capabilities in these systems were described in Chapter 11 because of their specialized nature. The products discussed in the following pages are Banyan's Virtual Networking System (VINES), Novell's Advanced NetWare with System Fault Tolerance (SFT) and NetWare 386, 3Com's 3 + Open networking systems, and IBM's OS/2 LAN Server and OS/2 Extended Edition.

Some of these are mature systems, some are still evolving, but each is capable of fulfilling a wide variety of demanding LAN requirements. Each of these can be compared against specific performance requirements using general criteria summarized at the end of the chapter. We emphasize that each comparison should be ranked in the context of the specific needs of your organization, rather than against some absolute measure. In other words, the only right answer to the question "what is the best network operating system available?" is the one that most closely fits your organizational objectives.

Past performance and history of these systems do provide a clue to the emphasis of each. LAN Manager and OS/2 LAN Server are based on earlier generation products with a strong leaning towards standardization and compatibility with MS-DOS. Thus, we can presume that these products will emphasize OS/2 most heavily in the future. VINES has particularly excelled in large networks with an emphasis on LAN-WAN internetworking features. Given the increased attention being placed on such systems, VINES will likely retain its strength as an internetworking product. NetWare has been a performance leader by most accepted benchmarks and continues its reputation for independence to maintain this performance leadership. These trends will continue for the new product generation, although the four systems described here will begin to exhibit increased similarity in function and performance with each major upgrade. This is the inevitable and desirable fallout from increased standardization efforts and a trend toward open architectures.

Virtual Networking System (VINES)

Overview

VINES, as the name suggests, is a hardware-independent network operating system based on the UNIX operating system. VINES is primarily designed to run on dedicated Banyan file servers, either the *Corporate Network Server* (*CNS*), the *Banyan Network Server* (*BNS*,) or the *Desktop Server* (*DTS*). Versions are available that will run on 80286 and 80386 PCs and on other third-party file servers. The discussion in this book will be oriented to the dedicated Banyan file-server implementation. The Banyan file server supports a variety of LAN hardware types and both asynchronous and synchronous wide-area networks. Multiple file servers are supported by several methods of interconnectivity. VINES software allows the establishment of large networks, combining LANs and wide-area interconnections, with the ability for users to share information without knowledge of the network routing details.

Banyan's dedicated server architecture is illustrated in Figure 12.1. The *front end* of the VINES Server provides the link to attached PC resources—whether they are located on LANs or act as independent asynchronous terminals. The *back end* of the server provides interconnect services to a variety of network types external to the local PC environment. The Services segment of the VINES Server contains the appropriate software to allow information sharing, EMail, and internetwork connectivity. These software applications run under the VINES UNIX operating system.

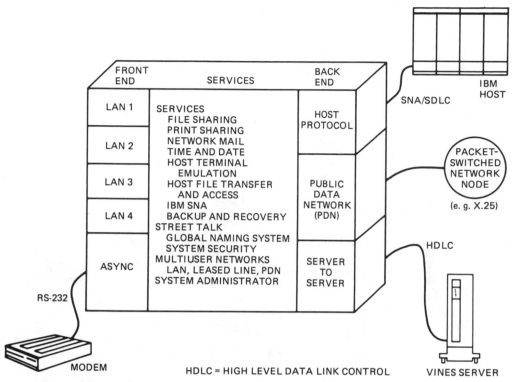

Figure 12.1. Banyan VINES file server architecture.

Major Features

Banyan's VINES software has a number of features that present its users and administrator(s) with a well-designed total network system. These are:

- *StreetTalk*—A database located throughout the network that identifies and automatically locates various classes of resources.
- File Service—Server software and work station shell that permit a work station's host operating system (MS-DOS or OS/2) to send remote file requests to a server running a multitasking network operating system (UNIX)
- Support for file and record locking conventions of Novell, 3Com, and MS-DOS 3.1.
- *VANGuard* security service.
- Print Service—Support for a default configuration of up to four parallel and three serial printers connected to a Banyan server (CNS model).
- Backup and system recovery.
- Electronic mail—A distributed mail system that is supported throughout all logically connected networks.

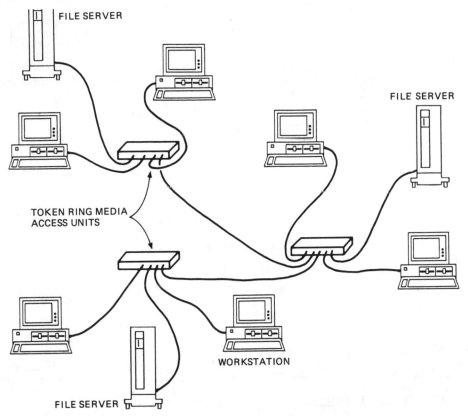

Figure 12.2. Multiple VINES file servers on a single LAN.

- VINES Network Management—A network management software application providing a variety of statistics on network operations.
- Third-party developer support (Applications Programming Interfaces—APIs).
- Asynchronous Communications—Terminal emulation, modem server capability, file transfer protocol, and multiserver connectivity. Chapter 11 covers this capability.
- IBM 3270 Communications—Complete support for IBM mainframe communications, including emulation of standard terminals and printers. Chapter 11 handles this capability.

StreetTalk

StreetTalk is the system for naming resources on a VINES network and a fundamental design feature of VINES. "Resources" in VINES parlance can be file volumes, print queues, users, lists, nicknames, connections to other computers, or any other device attached to the network. StreetTalk has three levels of definition: item, group, and organization. A typical StreetTalk name has the format

```
Doug@Marketing@SanDiego,
```

where Doug is the item (a user in this case), Marketing is the group, and SanDiego is the organization. Although items are limited to certain allowable entities, groups and organizations are limited only by imagination and common sense. One of the important features of StreetTalk is that assignment of a StreetTalk name is mandatory before a shared resource can be used by anyone on the network. All StreetTalk names are stored in a central database called the *StreetTalk catalog*. This catalog is maintained on each VINES server connected to a logical network. StreetTalk names can be used in "lists," which are in turn given StreetTalk names. A typical item in this category is a distribution list for electronic mail. The StreetTalk catalog can be reviewed by anyone on the network, but only system administrators can add, delete, or change names in the catalog.

Multiserver StreetTalk installations are possible with VINES. From the user's perspective, the number of servers on the network is transparent. Multiserver installations

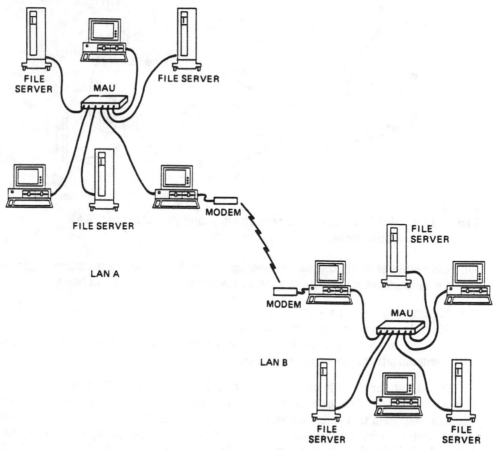

Figure 12.3. Multiple VINES file servers on interconnected LANs.

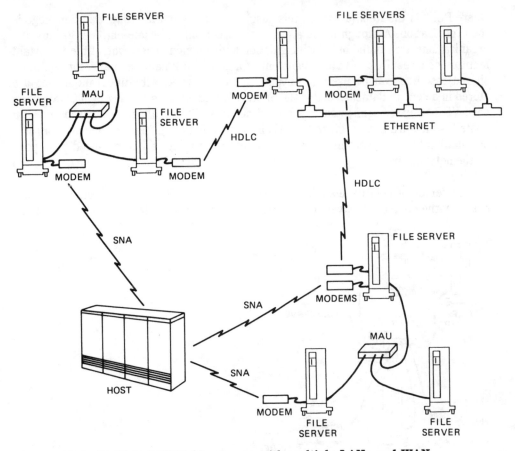

Figure 12.4. Multiple VINES file servers with multiple LANs and WAN connections.

will become increasingly common as average network sizes in organizations begin to climb. A multiserver situation can arise in several ways, among them being

- Multiple servers on a single LAN.
- Multiple servers on interconnected LANs.
- Multiple servers on dispersed LANs connected by some form of long-distance communications (wide-area network).

These situations are illustrated by Figures 12-2 through 12-4. On a multiserver network, the StreetTalk catalog is distributed among the servers according to the resources assigned to a particular server. For example, in Figure 12.5, two servers are shown, each with its own catalog of names. The total network catalog is the combination of the individual server catalogs. The important feature here is that any network user sees the combined catalog, not just the catalog of the server to which he or she is logged on.

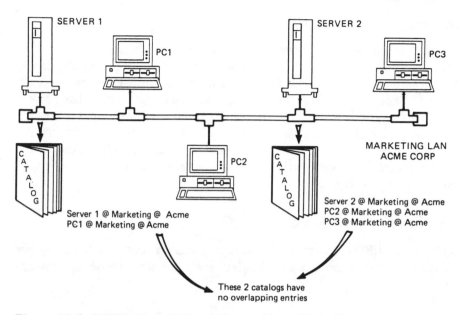

Figure 12.5. VINES StreetTalk catalogs with multiple file servers.

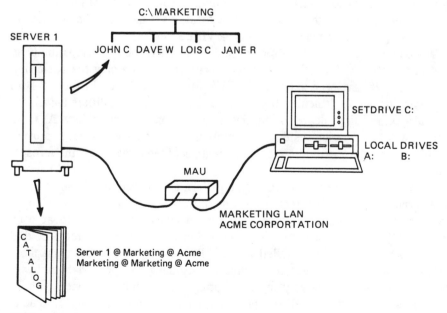

Figure 12.6. VINES file service concept.

File Service

File service consists of both hardware and software. In the former category, a volume on the fixed disk attached to a file server provides the tangible part of file service. The software portion consists of those programs required to effectively manage (create, maintain, and protect) the physical storage area. A volume on the network fixed disk is a complete hierarchical directory structure. All the usual DOS directory management commands apply. The three basic steps involved in setting up a file service are: (1) adding it to the network (making it part of the StreetTalk catalog), (2) starting it, and (3) assigning a drive designation to the network volume. VINES file service is graphically depicted in Figure 12.6.

Support For File and Record Locking

A major part of VINES support for multiuser applications resides in the *semaphore service*. Semaphore service provides the following capabilities for multiuser applications software:

- Allows concurrent operation among several PCs on a network.
- Allows file sharing on the server.
- Provides application synchronization using semaphore advisory locking features.

Banyan's semaphore services are compatible with those used by 3Com in the 3 + series, Novell in the Advanced NetWare system, and IBM in its NETBIOS service. For the user (and administrator), this means that applications designed to be compatible with those LAN operating systems will run on a VINES network.

This is a good opportunity to review the concept of multiuser locking compatibility as introduced in Chapter 9. MS-DOS 3.1 and its successors provide only the basic file-sharing services that have been extended by IBM, Novell, and 3Com. In the MS-DOS world, each vendor has implemented the extensions in a somewhat different fashion, giving the LAN community a degree of multiuser applications incompatibility. As OS/2 evolves into a mature operating system, the situation will become somewhat improved, but full applications interoperability remains more a goal than a reality for the foreseeable future.

Using a semaphore service follows the same pattern established for file service: (1) adding the service (entry in the StreetTalk catalog), (2) starting the service (making it available to authorized users), (3) modifying certain elements of software at each user's PC, and (4) connecting users to the service. Software modification requires that a memory-resident program be installed at each PC wishing to use the semaphore service. Connection to the service is accomplished by running the appropriate software at a work station PC or, preferably, by associating the semaphore service with an individual user's *network profile*. Network profiles become linked to users at the time of their logging in to the network.

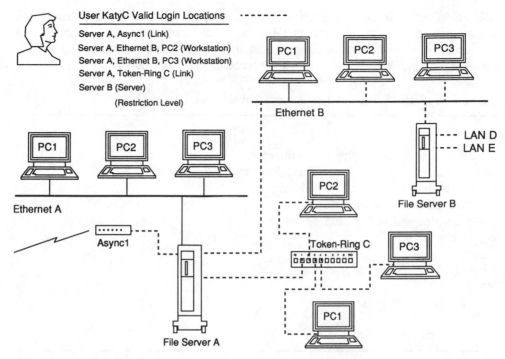

Figure 12.7. VINES logon security by location restriction level.

VANGuard Security Service

VANGuard is Banyan's name for its network security service, which includes user log-in authentication, log-in restrictions, password control, directory access controls, and internetwork security.

Part of the security mechanism for access control is the association of user passwords with StreetTalk catalog entries. The VANGuard log-in authentication process requires a person logging in to the network to use the correct password associated with that person's user name (recall that a user name is a StreetTalk item). The log-in process itself can be restricted by location, time of day, and expiration date of the user name. Location restrictions are specified by server, by link (individual LAN or serial port), or by specific work station, as shown in Figure 12.7. Passwords can be controlled by restricting users from changing their own passwords, setting a password minimum length, forcing password changes on each log in, or assigning a password expiration date.

As in most network operating systems currently on the market, VINES access control to network volumes is concerned with *who* has access to files and *what* an individual can do with the file once access is granted. Each subdirectory in the network file volume has an independently assigned Access Rights List (ARL). ARLs designate who can access that particular subdirectory. Each ARL entry can designate one of four levels of access, listed in Table 12.1 in descending order of priority:

Table 12.1. VINES Subdirectory Access Levels.

Control
1—Set access rights on the parent directory.
2—Set access rights on the child subdirectory.
3—Create/delete files and subdirectories.
4—Modify files and subdirectories.
5—Read files and subdirectories.
6—Delete the directory.
Modify
Items 2–5 under Control level
Read
Item 5 under Control level
Null
No access rights

The log-in process links users to their assigned resources and access rights. This concept is shown in Figure 12.8. Since ARLs are themselves StreetTalk catalog items, they can be addressed by linkage to groups and organizations as follows:

```
ARL@group@organization
```

Print Services

VINES print service consists of several parts:

- A printer attached to a server or a PC.
- Configuration information for the network printer.
- Standard network software on work stations to redirect print jobs to the network printer.
- A print job queue on the print server hard disk.
- Management functions.

Print service on VINES is a standard redirected operation in which print jobs originated at a work station are redirected to a specified network printer. Network printers can be attached to servers or to any work station that runs the print service software. The network print server supports spooling of the print job to its hard disk

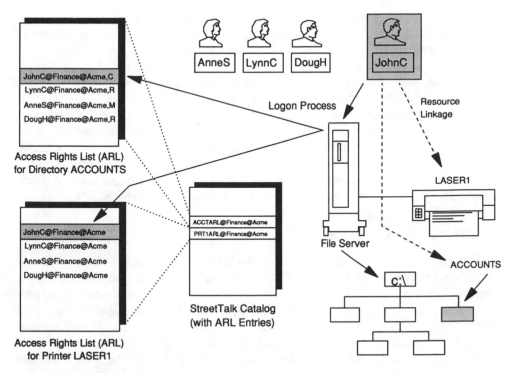

Figure 12.8. VINES logon process and user resource linkage.

and the associated queue management functions. Logical ports LPT1:, LPT2:, and LPT3: are supported at the user's work station. Each port has attributes for:

- Service name (StreetTalk).
- Redirection switch.
- Delay time in seconds prior to commencement of spooling.
- Form type.
- Banner page switch.

Multiple ports can be redirected to the same printer, each with a different form type, such as stationary, draft, or multipart.

Backup and System Recovery

Banyan provides certain automatic fault-tolerant features in the VINES/file server system. For example, the file server has a battery backup option that will cause a "graceful" shutdown process to start if normal power is lost or interrupted. Servers will reboot automatically after power restoral, whether or not battery backup is installed. The server is also designed to continually check for the proper operation of all service functions and installed LAN adapter cards. Certain other failures will cause server automatic reboots, including memory parity errors or system "hangs" (a loss of network communications). Backup and recovery procedures on the individual work stations are similar to those available in a single-user environment. Any reboot of a work station will, of course, require a restart of network log-in procedures.

Backup and system recovery operations on a Banyan file server rely upon the existence of a full system backup on cartridge tape. As with any computer system that processes critical data, file backups are a must to prevent disaster. Tape operations are controlled from the server console and would typically be done by the network administrator. Tape backups are performed on file volumes on the server. Backups may be full system, file-by-file, or individual service. Individual user local backups are that user's responsiblity and would be accomplished using normal DOS functions.

Electronic Mail Service

Electronic mail has become more than just a luxury item for LAN systems—it is now considered virtually mandatory in order for LAN software to be competitive. Going a step farther, electronic mail must address the internetworking environment to be considered acceptable for most medium- to large-scale businesses. Mail service on a VINES network is an optional feature and is designed to operate on network servers. When any server is started up, mail service is automatically initiated on that server. A user's profile specifies the mail service (i.e., server) to which he or she is attached. The mail service capability also supports multiserver installations, in part to provide alternate mail services for network users. This capability provides one element of redundancy in the VINES network system and is a direct benefit of StreetTalk design.

Internetwork, multiple-server connectivity in the mail service, is handled through serial connections or by direct, high-speed server-to-server links. VINES monitors all unsent mail and automatically attempts to deliver the appropriate correspondence when a particular serial connection is established. High-speed links are invoked when a server is explicitly named in the message address.

Optional gateways to external mail systems are available and include links to MCI Mail and CompuServe's electronic mail services. These gateways are effective in tying together VINES correspondents with users on the more popular commercial EMail services. Users outside the VINES internetwork can access specific VINES users by reference to the StreetTalk name after logging on to the appropriate commercial service. Other mail service gateways can be developed using the third-party development toolkits described below.

Mailing address lists may be maintained within the StreetTalk system or separately. Addressing features include carbon copy (CC) and blind carbon copy (BCC). A text editor is included with the EMail system and standard applications files of any type can be enclosed as a letter attachment. Message folders can be maintained by mail subject content. Mail management features allow the moving of mailboxes between existing servers and other mail services. Although third-party EMail systems with expanded functions can be used on VINES, such use bypasses the StreetTalk naming convention and much of the internetworking advantage of StreetTalk.

Network Management Option

The VINES Network Management Option is one of the more complete analytical tools provided with a PC LAN product. This option presents a real-time picture of server performance and how network hardware and software are configured. The information displayed is basically raw statistical data and, as such, must be carefully interpreted. Specifically, Network Management provides no guidance on actions to take as a result of network activity analysis. Some of the actions that could be taken as a result of Network Management data analysis are:

- Replacing a network adapter card that has excessive error rates.
- Relocating high-usage services to more lightly loaded servers.
- Adding more RAM to a server.
- Changing the physical configuration of a LAN.
- Increasing the performance of shared mass-storage devices.
- Adding additional servers to a LAN.

In order to take appropriate corrective actions as a result of Network Management analysis, the network administrator must have a solid understanding of the strengths and weaknesses of existing systems. The System Administrator manual does a thorough job of explaining the meaning and interpretation of each statistic on the various display screens. Network Management provides a number of displays, each designed to focus upon some aspect of network performance. Among these are:

- VINES Network Summary—Displays a list of all servers with loading statistics. A server may be highlighted for more data in other screens.
- I/O Statistics—Displays an overview of LAN hardware statistics (by LAN type, including internetwork links) for the selected server.
- LAN Interface Statistics—Displays more detailed data on a selected LAN hardware type within a server. The following network types are included:
  —Ethernet
  —Arcnet
  —IBM PC Network
  —IBM Token Ring
  —ProNet
  —Starlan
  —Northern Telecom LANStar
  —VistaLAN
- WAN interface statistics:
  —HDLC
  —Asynchronous
  —X.25
- Disk Usage—Displays data concerning the disk(s) on the selected server.
- Service Statistics—Displays loading information for each service located on the selected server.

- Network topology—Displays information concerning all active network devices connected to the selected server.
- File service—Displays information concerning cache performance, record locking, and open files.
- Communications statistics—Displays data on communications buffers, transport protocol connections, and sockets (local applications using network services).

Statistics are either raw counts or averaged data. The latter form uses a method known as Exponential Decaying Averages, which simply means that the most recent data have the highest weighting.

Network Management can be run from either the server console or from any PC on the network. A server without Network Management installed will appear on the Network Summary screen, but will not have statistics displayed. Network Management can retrieve statistics from anywhere on the network, including remote servers in an internetwork. Network Management is itself a service (although not defined as such on the server), and displays statistics about itself on the Service Statistics screen.

Third-party Development Support

Banyan provides a set of calls and commands designed to access the basic services of UNIX System V as well as specific VINES features such as StreetTalk, *Matchmaker*, electronic mail gateways, and communications services. Matchmaker is Banyan's remote procedure call (RPC) protocol that supports the development of linkages between client and service processes. Matchmaker has a broad functional resemblance to OS/2's Named Pipes. Communications services supported include X.25 and TCP/UDP (the TCP/IP User Datagram Protocol). The objective of these calls and commands is to allow developers to build integrated applications using the distributed processing facilities of VINES. Another objective is to allow the development of additional services that can be added to basic VINES capabilities.

Banyan Corporate Network Server (CNS)

The Corporate Network Server is a dedicated engine, with a 32-bit, 80386, 20 MHz processor operating under the UNIX operating system. UNIX is both a multitasking and a multiuser operating system; thus, it is quite suitable to manage a network environment. The file server has the following general features:

- Four to 24 megabytes RAM plus an optional 32 Kb cache.
- Up to 2.5 gigabytes of hard disk storage, 1.2 Gb internal, 1.3 Gb external.
- 150 megabyte tape cartridge drive.
- Internal battery backup.
- Support for up to four internal LAN adapter cards.

- Up to 30 serial communications ports with a maximum line speed of 19,200 bits/second. These ports can be used with synchronous or asynchronous protocol and with direct, leased, or public switched telephone lines.
- Multiple-server connections, using any combination of LANs, asynchronous, or synchronous serial lines. The synchronous serial line must use the High-level Data Link Control (HDLC) method of establishing a communications link.
- Connections for a control console and up to seven printers (three parallel, four serial)

Advanced Netware with System Fault Tolerance (SFT)

Overview

Advanced NetWare and SFT NetWare are Novell's component software products designed for the 80286-based server hardware environment. The major characteristic of NetWare from its inception has been its ability to support a large variety of LAN hardware implementations with a common software front end. System Fault Tolerance (SFT) is an evolving product development, bringing the same elements of fault tolerance that have been common in the minicomputer industry to the world of LANs. The significance of this cannot be overstated, since many vertical applications depend, in large measure, upon a reliable, fault-tolerant environment. Some examples are military, public safety, banking, and medical applications. Through a system of bridges and gateways, NetWare is capable of supporting large internetworking schemes.

Major Features

Advanced NetWare/SFT is the latest generation product from Novell that continues a tradition of unique design and support for demanding network applications. Advanced NetWare/SFT has the following major features:

- File Service—File server multitasking software (proprietary) and a user shell for MS-DOS that functions as a redirector for network resource file requests.
- File and Record Locking—Upwardly compatible with MS-DOS 3.1 with significant extensions for transaction (read-modify-write cycle) support.
- Print Service—Transparent network printing from within applications running on the network including full print queue management.
- System Fault Tolerance (SFT)—A multilevel system, featuring redundant directory management, mirrored and duplexed disk drives, an Uninterrupted Power Supply monitoring function, and a Transaction Tracking System (TTS).
- Security and Access Control—Independent user, group, and directory access controls, with eight types of access rights assignable to each.
- Virtual File Server Console allowing remote file server management.
- Value-Added Processes (VAP) and Value-Added Disk Drivers (VADD).
- Network accounting functions.

- Internal and External Bridges—Advanced NetWare support for internetworking with a unique feature of being able to configure a bridge to improve server throughput. Chapter 11 covers this feature.
- Asynchronous Communications—Terminal emulation, modem server capability (with dedicated PC), file transfers with protocol and support for up to 12 external circuits per modem server. Chapter 11 covers this feature.
- IBM SNA Communications—3270 support (3274 Controller, 3287 Printer, and 3278/79 terminals) for up to 32 sessions on a nondedicated gateway server. Chapter 11 covers this feature.
- Message Handling Service (MHS) for store-and-forward communications. MHS was discussed in Chapter 11.

File service

NetWare's file service is a significant extension of the support provided by MS-DOS. The file service portion of NetWare resides on the file server and uses a directory structure that parallels that of MS-DOS. However, the file server directory is managed by NetWare commands rather than by MS-DOS commands. Correspondence between DOS and NetWare commands is shown in Table 12.2. A NetWare shell resides on each work station on the network—this shell communicates with the NetWare operating system on the file server. Both the file server operating system and the application-level protocol (NetWare Core Protocol—NCP) between the work stations and file server are proprietary.

Table 12.2. NetWare/MS DOS Command Correspondence.

NetWare Command	MS-DOS Command
MAP	ASSIGN
	PATH
	SUBST
CHKVOL	CHKDSK
VOLINFO	CHKDSK
COMPSURF	FORMAT
NCOPY	COPY
NDIR	DIR
NPRINT	PRINT
CAPTURE	PRINT
PCONSOLE	PRINT
LISTDIR	TREE
SYSTIME	TIME/DATE
LARCHIVE	BACKUP
NARCHIVE	BACKUP
LRESTORE	RESTORE
NRESTORE	RESTORE

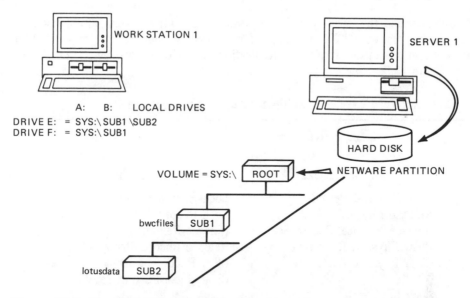

WORK STATION 1

SERVER 1

A: B: LOCAL DRIVES
DRIVE E: = SYS:\SUB1\SUB2
DRIVE F: = SYS:\SUB1

HARD DISK

VOLUME = SYS:\ ROOT ◄ NETWARE PARTITION

bwcfiles SUB1

lotusdata SUB2

Figure 12.9. Novell NetWare network drive concept.

In NetWare, the concept of "network drives" is used. A network drive is one or more of the drive letters "A:" through "Z:" mapped to a directory or path on the file server. Thus, on work station 1 in Figure 12.9, drive "E:" is mapped (logically linked) to path

```
sys:bwcfiles/lotusdata
```

on the file server. NetWare supports user attachments to a maximum of eight servers at a time. In this case, mapping must preface the server path with a server name, as in the following example

```
Server1/sys:wordpro/word
```

The user is not required to know the physical location of the servers. This task is managed transparently by the NetWare operating system.

Multiuser File Sharing Service

NetWare uses an extensive array of file-sharing calls in its file server operating system. These go beyond the basic support provided by MS-DOS. MS-DOS uses a scheme of "physical" locks, which means that an actual sector or group of sectors on the shared disk is protected. NetWare supports this scheme and also the older "logical" locking scheme, which relied upon cooperation from the application program(s). NetWare also supports a transaction locking system, which protects records during a continuous cycle of read-modify-write. This is particularly valuable for database updates and provides the hooks for the Transaction Tracking System (TTS) used by System Fault Tolerance (SFT) versions of the NOS. Semaphores are supported to provide general process or device synchronization. Extended locking function calls are listed in Table 12.3.

Table 12.3. NetWare Extended Multi-user Applications Support.

Interrupt 21h

Physical Locks	Logical Locks
Lock Physical Record	Lock Record String
Release Physical Record	Lock Record String Set
Release Physical Record Set	Release Record String
Clear Physical Record	Release Record String Set
Clear Physical Record Set	Clear Record String
	Clear Record String Set
Lock File Set	
Release File	**Semaphores**
Release File Set	
Clear File	Open a Semaphore
Clear File Set	Examine a Semaphore
	Wait Semaphore
Transactions	Signal a Semaphore
	Close a Semaphore
Begin Transaction	
Begin Transaction Update	
End Transaction Update	
Transaction Backout Available	
End Transaction	

NetWare Print Service

NetWare print service runs on the file server and controls the operation of up to five printers, three parallel and two serial. These printers must be attached to the file server. This version of NetWare does not support network printers distributed on LAN work stations. However, network printing is supported across all file servers logically attached to the network. In other words, any print job can be sent to any network printer attached to a file server, even if the user is not logged in or attached to that file server.

There are several commands that affect execution of NetWare's print service. The CAPTURE command redirects subsequent printer output to a designated print queue. ENDCAP terminates redirection. The NPRINT command sends printer output directly to a designated printer on a designated file server. Print queues are established,

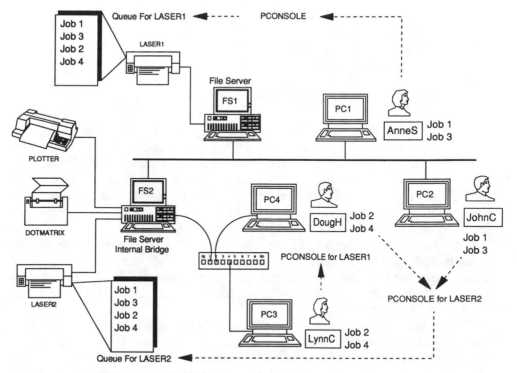

Figure 12.10. Advanced NetWare print service operation.

named, and managed by ten file server console commands. These commands allow the creation and destruction of queues and the assignment or detachment of named queues to specific printers on specific file servers. Queued jobs, all queues, and queues assigned to a given printer can be listed. Individual print jobs can be removed from queues or given higher priority within a queue. The console commands include three forms-control commands and one printer status command.

PCONSOLE allows the control of print queues from any work station on the network. PRINTDEF defines printer characteristics and form types. PRINTCON allows users to define custom job characteristics, such as number of copies, form type to be used, use of print banners, and file contents (ASCII or BYTE STREAM). The architecture of Advanced NetWare print service is summarized in Figure 12.10.

System Fault Tolerance (SFT)

Advanced NetWare/SFT provides a diverse range of fault-tolerant processing for applications critical enough to justify the higher costs. Fault-tolerant processing includes the protection of data against

- Hard disk surface defects
- Directory and file allocation table (FAT) corruption
- Hard disk mechanical failures
- Hard disk controller failures
- Power surges and failures
- System failures during database operations

The most basic NetWare SFT feature is surface defect protection. Surface defects on a hard disk platter cause certain data blocks to become unreliable. SFT employs a read-after-write verification and a real-time data redirection process called Hot-fix. This process continuously checks data written to disk against the data image still in memory buffers—any errors cause the operating system to mark bad areas on the disk and move the data to a good area. Up to 11 data bits may be detected and corrected per sector.

Redundant directory entries and file allocation tables (FATs) are maintained on separate disk cylinders (tracks). These redundant directories and FATs are verified during the power-up sequence and corrective action is taken if the data are bad. This action includes switching to the redundant directory or FAT, marking bad sectors, and moving the data to a safe area.

SFT provides additional protection against failure of a single hard disk or a hard disk transfer channel (controller card failure). Protection against a single hard disk failure is provided by a redundant disk drive on the same disk channel. This feature is called *disk mirroring*. Disk mirroring causes data to be simultaneously written to both disk drives. Should a failure occur in one of the drives, the operator is notified and the operating disk drive assumes the I/O load. Protection against a disk controller or disk channel failure is achieved by *disk duplexing*, or writing data through two separate disk channels (controller cards) simultaneously. Another benefit of disk duplexing is faster I/O performance, since file read operations can be conducted in parallel through two controller cards. NetWare is specifically designed to support this capability. Mirrored disk and duplexed disk configurations were shown in Figures 9.17 and 9.18.

UPS monitoring is supported through NetWare file servers and disk subsystems. A UPS provides constant power and battery charging when the commercial power source is operating normally. If the commercial power source fails, the UPS takes over for a predetermined interval depending on the battery size. UPS monitoring enables the server to detect activation of the UPS power source and send a warning message to all active work stations on the network. Prior to shutting itself down, the monitored server will write all data in its memory to disk and close all files.

The Transaction Tracking System (TTS) is a feature that operates transparently to an application. The application is usually based on a database management system. A database read-modify-write cycle is considered a transaction. The transaction update to disk is considered either completed, or not started. Any transaction not completed when the client work station, LAN media, or server fails will be backed out of the database at the first available opportunity. In other words, the database will be returned, or rolled back to its state just prior to the system failure. This protection is

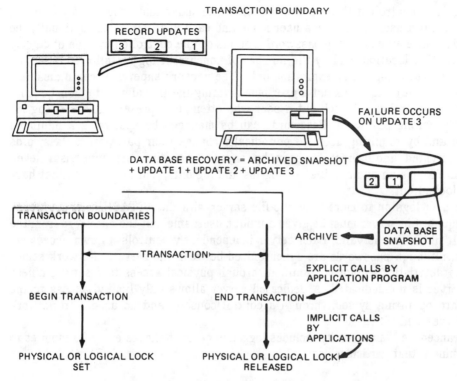

Figure 12.11. The pre-imaging process in Novell's Btrieve VAP (transaction roll-forward recovery).

called *automatic rollback recovery*. TTS must be active on the file server and database files must be flagged as transactional for TTS to operate. Transaction flagging is the responsibility of the application.

If the NetWare Btrieve record manager is used to create a Value-Added Process for a server-based database management application, a procedure called *rollforward recovery*, or *preimaging*, is available to protect database files that are not flagged as transactional. Figure 12.11 depicts the pre-imaging process. Images of database files are stored under separate filenames at the time of the first file modifications to build an audit trail of transactions. In case of system failure, archived database images and the audit trail are used to reconstruct all valid files. Preimaging is complementary to, but not a part of, TTS.

Access Control and Security

Advanced NetWare provides a high degree of network security through the use of log-in and password protection, user or *trustee* privilege levels, directory privilege levels, and file/directory attributes. Basic LAN and NetWare security concepts were covered in Chapter 9.

Log in is controlled through the use of a user name and associated password. Each network user must have a user name and each user name can, optionally, be forced to have an associated password. Log ins can be controlled by time of day, by work station location, and by the number of concurrent log ins allowed. User accounts can be assigned an expiration date. The network supervisor can o disable a user's account or can lock out a user by activating the Intruder Detection/Lockout option. This option will lock out a user who attempts a preset number of log ins with the wrong password. Passwords can be managed by specifying a minimum length and by requiring users to periodically change their passwords. Passwords are encrypted and cannot be seen by anyone, including the supervisor level. NetWare keeps an audit trail of all log ins and log outs, and of accounts that have been locked out.

If a user logs on to more than one file server with the ATTACH command, each subsequent file server must be given a unique username, but the password from the default file server is valid. Each server independently controls its own access security, although passwords are synchronized between file servers. Network security characteristics cannot be modified through physical access to a server, unless the server is nondedicated. A dedicated server allows only limited access to the NetWare operating system through a control console, and no access to network directories and files.

Advanced NetWare security includes logged-in account checks every 30 minutes to determine if that particular user:

- Can be logged in during that time period.
- Whether the user's account has expired or been disabled by the supervisor.
- Whether the user's account has reached its credit limit.

Each logged-on network user carries assigned "rights" to access various directory levels. These rights are called "trustee rights" in Novell terminology and determine *what* a user may do once access is granted. User rights may also be assigned to "groups," which are typically organizational collections of users. There are eight defined rights:

- R—Read from open files.
- W—Write to open files.
- O—Open existing files.
- C—Create and simultaneously open new files.
- D—Delete existing files.
- P—Parental rights. Control over the directory and its subdirectories.
- S—Search the directory.
- M—Modify file attributes as defined in Table 12.4.

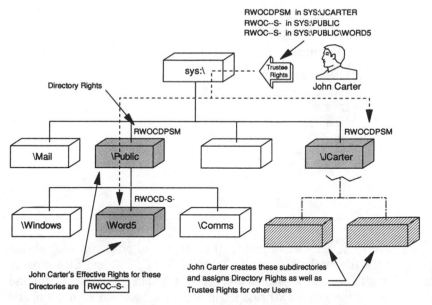

Figure 12.12. Advanced NetWare user and directory rights concept.

These rights may be granted explicitly to a user or the user may inherit them through "security equivalences." Security equivalences pass one user's or group's rights to another user or group, thus simplifying the assignment of rights. Each directory and subdirectory level is assigned a Maximum Rights Mask. The *Maximum Rights Mask* has a default value of no restrictions, or

$$[RWOCDPSM]$$

If restrictions are applied (for example, deletion of the right of any user to write in that directory) the mask becomes

$$[R\_OCDPSM]$$

The Maximum Rights Mask is designed to provide a maximum allowable level of security for a directory level and applies to all users. Thus, if directory mask does not allow a Write access as in the example above, then no user or group may modify files in that directory, regardless of what user or group rights they have assigned. User or group rights automatically extend down to all subdirectory levels unless overridden at a lower level; a directory Maximum Rights Mask applies only to that directory level. The Maximum Rights Mask is combined with trustee rights to form *effective rights* at that directory level. Effective rights are simply the most restrictive of the two levels. The overall trustee and directory level security implementation is shown in Figure 12.12.

Table 12.4. NetWare File Attributes.

Attribute	Abbreviation
Executable Only	EO
Hidden	H
Indexed	I
Modified	M
Read Only	RO
Read/Write	RW
Shareable	SHA
System	SY
Transactional	T

File-attribute security is designed to protect the integrity of programs and data on the file server. Of the file attributes listed in Table 12-4, RO, RW, and SHA directly affect security. File-attribute security takes precedence over effective rights within the file's directory. Thus, a file with an RO restriction cannot be modified even if a user's effective rights would otherwise allow that privilege. An RO file cannot be modified, renamed, or deleted. An nonshareable file (a file without the SHA attribute) cannot be accessed by more than one user at a time. The EO attribute is useful to prevent unauthorized copying of applications programs from the filer server.

Directories also have attributes. These include Normal, Hidden, System, and Private. Normal directories have no attributes set. Hidden directories cannot be seen by any users, but a user may change to that directory. System directories will not appear in directory searches. Private directories can be seen by users, but their contents are hidden. If a user has effective Search rights, Private directory contents will be visible.

NetWare Application Programming Interfaces

The Value-Added Process (VAP) application programming interfaces make certain NetWare features independently available to third-party application developers. VAPs are Novell's term for third-party services to enhance Advanced NetWare. The Btrieve record management system is an example of a VAP and is provided with current versions of NetWare. Btrieve is used for physical record management and can be combined with other VAP data management tools, such as NetWare SQL, NetWare XQL, and Xtrieve as shown in Figure 12.13. The combination of these tools with the added fault-tolerant features of TTS and preimaging can be used to create sophisticated server-based SQL and conventional database applications. VAPs can be developed as LAN services or can be used alone or with conventional program code in C, BASIC, Pascal, or COBOL to build higher-level applications.

Value-Added Disk Drivers are developed by third-party disk drive manufacturers to make their mass storage devices compatible with NetWare formatting requirements. NetWare offers their own disk subsystems but encourages maximum participation in

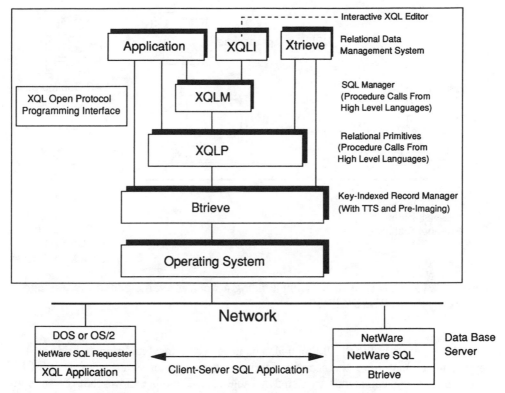

Figure 12.13. NetWare SQL value-added process architecture.

the VADD program to provide NetWare users with the broadest base possible of hard disk capability. As the breadth and depth of available mass storage devices continues to increase, the ability to link third-party hardware into the NetWare operating system becomes more significant.

The increased management functions available in current versions of Advanced NetWare provide an opportunity to make these functional programming interfaces available to third-party developers. These functions include network accounting, queue management, network diagnostics, the virtual file-server console, and network security. An example of a possible third-party application using network diagnostics would be an expert system that retrieved network statistics. The expert system would use the statistics and certain configuration rules to provide recommendations on network hardware changes. Figure 12.14 shows a conceptual view of such a system.

Virtual File Server Console

The Virtual File Server Console, or FCONSOLE, is an Advanced NetWare utility designed to allow remote execution of file-server console commands from any worksta-

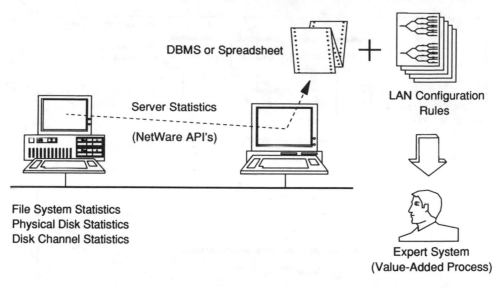

Figure 12.14. Expert system example using a NetWare value-added process and NetWare APIs.

tion on the network. FCONSOLE can also be used across local and remote bridges. The remote user must have the security equivalence of a supervisor to use FCONSOLE commands. These commands are listed in Table 12.5. The table shows that the supervisor can execute a wide variety of system monitoring and control functions through the console commands.

Table 12.5. FCONSOLE Remote File Server Monitor and Control.

Control the file server	Station's console privileges
Shut down the file server	Restrict management features
File server's current status	File system statistics
File locking activity	Disk mapping table
Broadcast console messages	Physical disk statistics
LAN driver information	Disk channel statistics
Purge salvageable files	Connection's open files
Software version	List file connections

Network Accounting

Advanced Netware supports resource accounting by allowing network supervisors to monitor network usage and bill user accounts. The supervisor can set up a credit limit for each user, monitor the account balance for each user, and create an audit trail for system use. Chargeable elements to each user account include

- Connection time to server
- Blocks read from disk
- Blocks written to disk
- Requests received from work stations
- Amount of disk storage used

Automatic billing of user accounts is not included in this feature, but can be developed as a Value-Added Process using APIs from NetWare's accounting functions.

NetWare 386

Overview

NetWare 386 is the newest of the Novell network operating systems and represents the latest in Novell's state-of-the-art. NetWare 386 is designed specifically to run in an 80386 server environment and adds significant features beyond Advanced NetWare SFT. NetWare 386 shares one characteristic of Advanced NetWare SFT—it is specifically designed as a server-based operating system. Basic user and management functions remain the same as earlier versions of the operating system, providing a degree of continuity across the product line.

NetWare 386 has been designed to take advantage of the 80386 and 80486 32-bit architecture and to provide an open platform on which extended services can be easily added. NetWare 386 also builds on the concept of Open Protocol Technology (OPT) to extend NetWare's traditional independence from network media into the logical transport software world. OPT will also provide independence from specific client-server protocol. The latter feature allows the use of different work station architectures on the same network. These might include IBM's OS/2 Extended Edition, 3Com's OS/2 LAN Manager, MS-DOS-based work stations, UNIX work stations, and the MacIntosh.

Major Features

NetWare 386 extends the services provided by Advanced NetWare SFT but retains the "look and feel" of its predecessor. The features discussed here will be implemented through a series of releases providing an incremental increase in software functions. The major functions implemented or planned for NetWare 386 include:

- Expanded security features
- Redesigned server architecture emphasizing modular design
- Open Protocol Technology (OPT)
- Expanded file service
- Expanded print service

Expanded Security Features

NetWare 386 implements several security enhancements compared to Advanced NetWare. Among these are the Secure Console Option, extended directory and file protection from unauthorized users, creation of a new user category, and increased encryption.

The Secure Console Option limits access to the server to the system supervisor, in order to prevent misuse of the server's open architecture.

The differences in capabilities and terminology for extended directory and file security support are summarized in Table 12.6.

Table 12.6. Access Control Features.
Advanced NetWare 286 Versus NetWare 386

Right	Meaning	Version
Read	User can read open files in this directory and in subdirs.	286
Read	User can open and read files in this directory and subdirs.	386
Write	User can write to open files in this directory and subdirs.	286
Write	User can open and write to files in directory and subdirs.	386
Open	User can open files in this directory and subdirs.	286
Create	User can create files and subdir's in this directory and all subdirs.	Both
Delete	User can delete files and directories in this directory and all subdirs.	286
Erase	User can delete this directory, the subdir, and files in this directory and all child subdirectories and files.	386
Search	User can search the directory.	286
Directory Scan	User can see this directory name when scanning the parent directory.	386
File Scan	User can see the file names of the files in this directory when scanning the directory.	386
Modify	User can change the name and attributes of this directory and child subdirs.	Both
Parental	User can create, rename, and erase subdirs of this directory and set trustee and directory rights in this directory and its subdirs.	286
Access Control	User can modify the trustee list and Inherited Rights Mask of this directory and all child subdir and files.	386
Supervisor	User has all rights to this directory and all child subdir and files. User can grant supervisor rights for this directory and all child subdir and files.	386

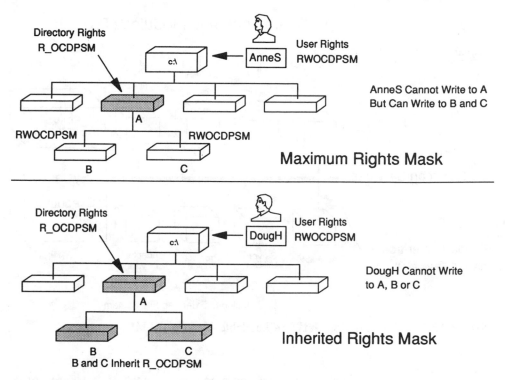

Maximum Rights Mask

Inherited Rights Mask

Figure 12.15. Comparison of advanced NetWare and NetWare 386 directory rights implementation.

In addition to expanded rights definitions, NetWare 386 extends the rights listed above (except for Directory Scan and Create) to individual files as well as to the directory structure. The concept of an Inherited Rights Mask is also new. The IRM specifies rights for directory and file trustees that are inherited from the parent directory. The Inherited Rights Mask differs from the Maximum Rights Mask in that it applies to all subdirectories of the directory in which it is established. Figure 12.15 shows the difference.

In previous versions of NetWare, two categories of users were supported: users and a supervisor. In NetWare 386, a new category has been added: Workgroup Manager. A Workgroup Manager has supervisor privileges, but the domain is limited to a designated set of users or user groups.

Redesigned Server Architecture Emphasizing Modular Design

The NetWare 386 server software design is a major departure from earlier NetWare versions. This network operating system is designed to provide multitasking and re-

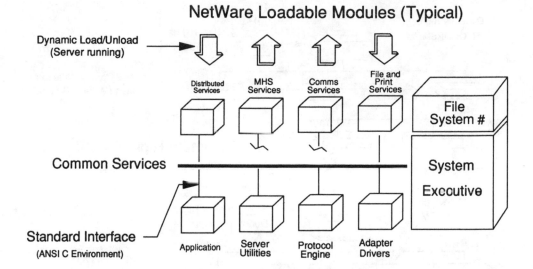

Figure 12.16. NetWare 386 NetWare Loadable Module (NLM) concept.

source management capabilities similar to OS/2, but it is not directly related to OS/2. NetWare 386 introduces the concept of NetWare Loadable Modules (NLMs). NLMs are used for disk drivers, network adapter drivers, protocol stack drivers, server utilities, and server-based applications. NLMs can be dynamically loaded and linked to the basic operating system. This concept is similar to the Dynamic Link Libraries of OS/2. NLMs are written to a standard interface specification and can access other operating system services (which are also NLMs) via the same specification. Figure 12.16 illustrates this concept. This specification commonality is referred to as a *software bus*. In practice, this means that a third-party server-based application could access the Message-handling System (MHS) service or file service to provide greater functionality.

Along with NLMs, NetWare 386 design includes dynamic resource reconfiguration, which means improved memory management. This function is provided by the System executive. The following list gives a general idea of the controllable resources, each of which requires its own memory allocation:

- Directory cache buffers
- FAT tables
- File locks
- File service processes
- Loadable modules (NLMs)
- Routing tables
- TTS transactions

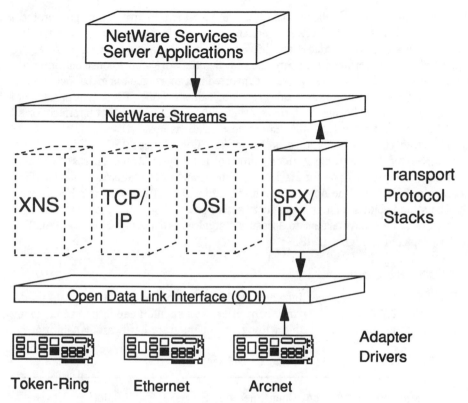

Figure 12.17. NetWare 386 Open Protocol Technology (OPT).

The bottom line of this capability is to simplify installation by not requiring the network manager to preallocate memory for these functions.

Open Protocol Technology (OPT)

Open Protocol Technology (OPT) could be the most significant improvement in NetWare 386. Any network operating system design feature that enhances interoperability would be so judged in today's multivendor networking environment. OPT encompasses media independence, transport protocol independence, and client-server protocol independence. Media independence has long been a part of the NetWare design philosophy. This has been reflected in support for a large number of network adapter cards and for bridging between dissimilar network topologies and media. Media independence continues to play an important role in the overall OPT architecture.

Novell's native transport protocol are the Sequenced Packet Exchange (SPX) and Internetwork Packet Exchange (IPX). These, in turn, are adaptions from the Xerox Network System (XNS) protocol. In NetWare 386, SPX/IPX have been decoupled from the basic operating system in favor of defining four interface layers: two to invoke transport protocol stacks from applications and NetWare services, and two to support multiple hardware adapters. The upper layer interfaces are NetWare Streams—the lower layer interfaces are the Open Data Link Interface (ODI). Streams provides NetWare with a consistent interface to all supported transport stacks and each supported transport stack is given a consistent interface to NetWare. ODI provides hardware adapter drivers with a consistent interface to supported transport stacks, and each transport stack is given a consistent interface for all supported adapters. Figure 12.17 illustrates these relationships.

Novell's native client-server protocol is the NetWare Core Protocol (NCP). NCP is equivalent to the Server Message Block (SMB) protocol used by IBM and Microsoft. Similar protocol are employed by Apple for MacIntosh systems and by Sun Microsystems for UNIX environments. These are the AppleTalk Filing Protocol (AFP) and Network File System (NFS). The stated objective for multiple client-server protocol support is to allow a heterogeneous work station environment to access the services provided by NetWare 386. This concept is depicted in Figure 12.18.

Expanded File Service

NetWare 386 provides a major increase in file system capacity relative to its predecessors. Table 12.7 lists the *theoretical* capacities. You should keep in mind that many of these capacities are not realizable without commensurate hardware capability.

Table 12.7. NetWare 386 File Service Capacities.

Maximum Concurrent Open Files Per Server	100,000
Maximum Concurrent TTS Transactions	25,000
Maximum Directory Entries Per Volume	2,097,152
Maximum Volumes Per Server	32
Maximum Drives (physical) Per Volume	32
Maximum Drives (physical) Per Server	1,024
Maximum File Size	4 Gbytes
Maximum Adressable RAM	4 Gbytes
Maximum Disk Storage Supported	32 Tbytes
Maximum Volume Size	32 Tbytes

These capacities, *when appropriately mated with available hardware*, will give PC-based LANs the I/O capabilities usually associated with minicomputers and mainframes. One of the more significant operational changes in the NetWare 386 File System is the ability of a volume or a single file to span more than one physical disk drive. The practical impact of this capacity is that I/O operations on one or more files can occur on multiple physical drives simultaneously, with an attendant increase in throughput.

The increase in file system capacities outlined in Table 12.7 supports a greater number of users on a single server, specifically 250 per server versus the earlier 100 users. Again, this increased operational limit must be tempered with factors external to the NetWare File

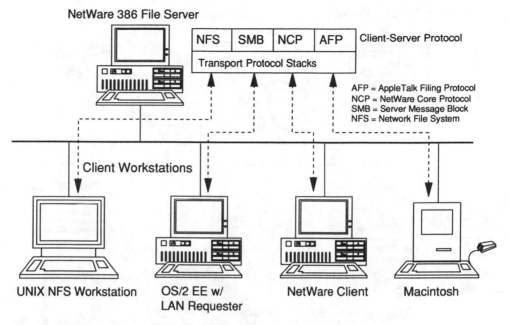

Figure 12.18. NetWare 386 support for multiple file service protocol.

System. For example, a particular application may not satisfactorily run with 250 users if not specifically written to do so. In most practical systems, the need to support 250 users would lead to a multiserver architecture to achieve workable performance levels.

Expanded file service also includes support for multiple name spaces. Support for multiple name spaces allows the use of file conventions other than those used by MS-DOS and OS/2. File conventions include items such as file name length, extension format, legal characters, case sensitivity, and other attributes. NetWare's implementation of this feature will initially incorporate MS-DOS and Macintosh file types. Extensions to UNIX are planned. Under this scheme, a single file can have more than one filename, each corresponding to a legal filename of, and accessible by, a different work station operating system. Multiple name space support goes hand-in-hand with support for multiple client-server protocol as discussed earlier.

Expanded Print Service

NetWare 386 increases the number of network-supported printers to a maximum of 16. Furthermore, the 16 printers are not restricted to physical attachment to file serv-

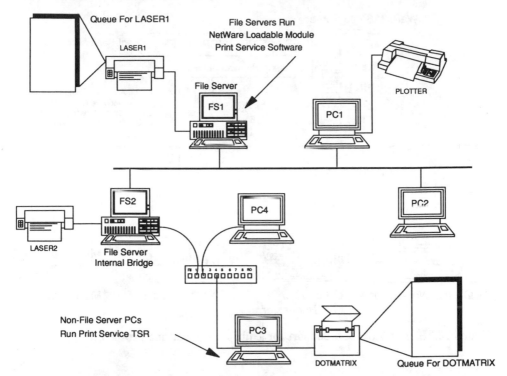

Figure 12.19. NetWare 386 print service concept.

ers, as illustrated by Figure 12.19. Print service is provided by a NetWare Loadable Module. Printers attached to the file server are managed by the print service NLM. Printers attached to work stations are managed by terminate-and-stay-resident software on the appropriate work station.

NetWare 386 supports Print Service Modes. These modes allow network managers to configure print service queues in one of four ways: queue only, forms only, queue-before-form, and form-before-queue. Print jobs will be prioritized and completed based on the number and priority of queues and associated print forms. Figure 12.20 shows an example of a multiple queue configuration.

Print service support also includes alert notification, restricted access, and the NetWare PCONSOLE utility. Alert notification will notify users of events such as completed jobs, paper out, cartridges need replacing, or other printer errors. Restricted access makes printer queues a resource similar to directories and files with the commensurate control over user access. The PCONSOLE utility allows network managers to perform certain printer management jobs for any network printer, regardless of location. The PCONSOLE utility will run on the designated print server.

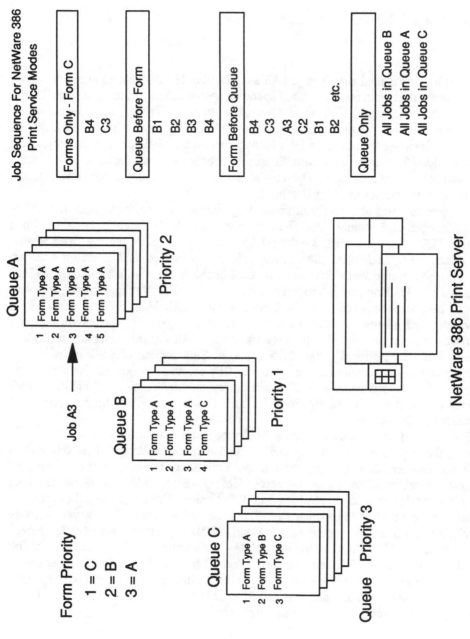

Job Sequence For NetWare 386 Print Service Modes

Forms Only - Form C
B4
C3

Queue Before Form
B1
B2
B3
B4

Form Before Queue
B4
C3
A3
C2
B1
B2   etc.

Queue Only
All Jobs in Queue B
All Jobs in Queue A
All Jobs in Queue C

Queue A

1	Form Type A
2	Form Type A
3	Form Type B
4	Form Type A
5	Form Type A

Priority 2

Job A3 →

Queue B

1	Form Type A
2	Form Type A
3	Form Type A
4	Form Type C

Priority 1

Queue C

1	Form Type A
2	Form Type B
3	Form Type C

Queue   Priority 3

Form Priority

1 = C
2 = B
3 = A

NetWare 386 Print Server

Figure 12.20. Print queue management in NetWare 386.

3 + Open and LAN Manager

Overview

3Com has broadened their line of LAN support from MS-DOS based network operating systems to encompass OS/2 based operating systems. The former product is known as 3 + and the latter as 3 + Open. 3 + uses the Microsoft Networks Redirector with a proprietary server software architecture for multitasking and value-added LAN services. 3 + Open uses Microsoft's LAN Manager as its foundation and adds proprietary LAN services. There are significant differences between the two systems, both in function and performance. Since 3 + Open is the emerging standard for 3Com networks, it is the system we will focus on in this book.

3 + Open consists of a family of proprietary, value-added products built around the LAN Manager core architecture. These products include 3 + Open Internet, 3 + Open Internet/X.25, 3 + Open Mail, 3 + Open LAN Vision, 3 + Open Name, 3 + Open Reach/X.400 and 3 + Open Maxess. LAN Manager is an OS/2-based application on a server, but does not require work stations to be OS/2-based. Work stations running MS-DOS versions of LAN Manager interoperate with the OS/2 LAN Manager server, but with limited function compared to an OS/2 work station. LAN Manager provides a set of services based on the advanced capabilities of OS/2—over 125 Application Program Interfaces (APIs) are included for network support. An enhanced version of OS/2 is installed on servers for 3 + Open LAN Manager. This version of OS/2 includes disk caching, maximum partition space up to four GBytes, and a maximum file size of two GBytes. This special version of OS/2 will be replaced by Version 1.2 of OS/2 which defines an enhanced file and directory structure. Capabilities of this file structure were discussed in Chapter 9.

3 + Open and LAN Manager share a number of features with the earlier 3 + system. Among these are resource sharing and redirection based on Microsoft Networks (MS-Net) and resource sharenaming conventions. Both share the same basic server-work station file protocol, known as the Server Message Block (SMB), although the LAN Manager version is a superset of the MS-DOS version. The differences, however, are more significant than the similarities. The major difference is the server software architecture. The server portion of 3 + Open/LAN Manager runs under OS/2, whereas 3 + runs under MS-DOS with 3Com's multitasking software, CIOSYS. Because of OS/2's inherent features, discussed earlier in Part II, the 3 + Open/LAN Manager server has a much more robust set of LAN support services than 3 + . These include expanded LAN management and auditing, expanded security features, improved user interface and support for multiple transport protocol sets.

3 + Open LAN Manager

3 + Open LAN Manager is a family of core services provided to network users. These services include resource sharing and network management. Resources include directories, files, printers, serial devices, IPC$ (remote execution of programs on a server),

and ADMIN$ (remote network administration on a server). Network management services include network security, Alerter, Messenger, Netpopup, Netlogon, 3 + Open Start, and 3 + Open Backup.

General Resource Sharing Concepts

Shared resources (server directories, printers, communications devices, remote execution, administration) are controlled by the NET SHARE command. Resources are assigned sharenames during the network administration process. A sharename is mapped to a resource as follows:

- Shared File/Directory—server directory pathname
  sharename = c: \ netapps \ dosapps \ word5
- Shared Printer—print devicename *attached to server*
  sharename = LPT1: (or LPT2: LPT3:)
- Shared Comm Device—serial devicename or pool of devicenames *attached to server*
  sharename = COM1
  sharename = COM1,COM2

Remote execution and administration are shared with the special sharenames IPC$ and ADMIN$ respectively. Network administrators use IPC$ and ADMIN$ to remotely control network security and management from any workstation on the LAN.

Network Security Management

3 + Open uses two types of security systems: network security and resource security. Network security is controlled by a log-on process and user accounts. The log-on process checks each user during log-on for a valid username-password set before allowing the user to gain access to the network. Once on the network, users are logged on to one or more servers containing shared resources. Each server invokes resource security by one of two methods: user-level or share-level. Each server on the network uses only one of these systems. The two security systems are compared in Figure 12.21. The security type for each server is determined during network configuration. User accounts consist of a username, password (optional, but highly desirable), group membership, and privilege level. Privilege levels are User, Guest, and Admin. Because of its scope of network control, the Admin privilege should be limited to the absolute minimum number of people, perhaps a primary and one alternate.

Table 12.8. 3 + Open Resource Permission Levels.

Resource Type	Permission	
Disk	C	Create
	D	Delete
	R	Read
	W	Write
	X	Execute
	A	Change Attributes
	P	Change Permissions[1]
	Y	Yes (=RWCDA)
	N	No
Spooled Print Queue	Y	Yes (=C)
	N	No
Comm Device Queue	Y	Yes (=RWC)
	N	No
IPC (Remote Execution)	Y	Yes (=RWC)
	N	No

[1] P = Administrators Only for share-level security

Log-on security only applies to OS/2-based work stations. MS-DOS work stations running LAN Manager do not support the user account concept. Log-on security can be either centralized or distributed. Under centralized log-on security, one server is designated as a central validator of all user log-on attempts. In a distributed log-on system, a log-on request is sent to multiple designated servers—at least one server containing that user's account will validate the log-on request and admit the user to the network.

User-level and share-level resource security use the same means of controlling what a user can do when the resource is accessed. Control is exercised by means of resource permissions, as shown in Table 12.8. The difference between the two types of resource security is in how the security is assigned. User-level permissions are assigned through access lists associated with each shared resource. This process is similar in concept to the Access Rights Lists of VINES. The access lists contain the names of authorized users. Access lists are permanent until changed. Share-level permissions are assigned at the time the resource is shared and persist only as long as the resource is shared. Share-level permissions for a particular resource apply to all users of that resource who have the correct resource password. Passwords are optional for each shared resource in a share-level system and are not used in user-level systems.

Shared Printing

Shared printing is managed by the use of printer queues. Queues are named with sharenames and assigned to printer ports on the server as described earlier. A single queue can be assigned to a single printer or to a pool of printers. Multiple queues can be assigned to a single printer. Queues have attributes such as authorized users, maximum number of users allowed, priority levels, authorized usage times, print job preprocessing, and separator pages. On share-level servers, queues can be given passwords. Multiple printers attached to the file server provide a choice of the type and quality of printed output. A manager could assign different queue profiles to single-printer servers to set up variations in service for separate entities in a company. One or more queues could be linked to different printers on a multi-printer server to provide a variation in output quality or to even the workload on printers.

Entire print queues and their individual job requests can be directly controlled through the NET PRINT command. Jobs can be held, restarted, deleted, or changed in priority. All existing jobs in a queue can be deleted while keeping the queue itself active. The NET DEVICE command controls the restarting and deletion of jobs on a particular printer.

Support is provided for Postscript printer queues. Postscript printers have resident software that interprets Postscript print definition files transmitted from compatible applications such as Microsoft Word or Lotus Freelance Plus. In 3 + Open, Postscript printer queues are separately defined and managed. The directory path(s) of Postscript dictionaries and downloadable fonts must be specified during the installation of print

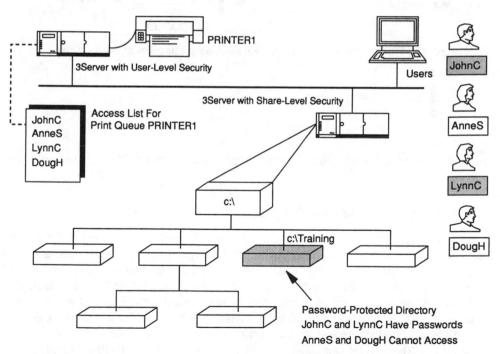

Figure 12.21. Comparison of 3Com 3 + Open share-level and user-level file server security.

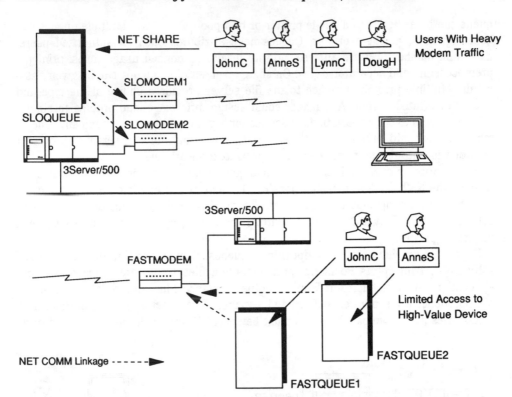

Figure 12.22. Examples of communications queue management in 3 + Open.

service. Once setup is complete, Postscript queues are managed like any other print queue.

Shared Communications Devices

3 + Open LAN Manager allows the sharing of non-spooled devices through the use of *communications device queues*. Non-spooled devices typically include some serial printers, plotters, image scanners and modems. As with printer queues, multiple queues can be established for a single device. Single or multiple queues can be linked to multiple devices. Figure 12.22 shows some configuration examples. For communications queues, the NET DEVICE command provides status only, either for a specific device or for all communications devices on the network. Queue linking to devices is controlled through the NET COMM command. The NET SHARE command controls communications queues in the same manner as printer queues.

Remote Execution of Shared Programs

Server-based applications can be shared on 3+Open LAN Manager networks. The NET RUN command invokes the remote execution service on the file server. The manner in which this service is shared depends on the type of security used on the file server: user-level security allows specification of R and X privileges for each user while share-level security has no effect on remote execution. Special server paths, called the `runpaths`, must be set up in the LAN Manager initialization file `LANMAN.INI` to contain remotely executable programs. A limit can be set on the number of simultaneously running shared programs. This limit will have a significant effect on server performance and must be set with care. In fact the entire concept of shared programs must be analyzed carefully in the context of a particular network's performance objectives since file server throughput may be significantly degraded by remote execution.

Remote Network Administration

Using the IPC$ and ADMIN$ shared resources, a network administrator can log on to one or more servers from any workstation and conduct certain admin tasks. These tasks include the establishment and maintenance of automatic alerts, server statistics, server error logs, server audit trails and user sessions with servers.

Alerter, Messenger, and Netpopup Services

The Alerter, Messenger, and Netpopup services work together to provide server-to-workstation and workstation-to-workstation messaging. The Alerter service establishes the events and conditions under which alerts will be sent from a server to the appropriate workstation. Alerts can be generated by audit, error or shared resource status events. The Messenger service supports the sending of messages between workstations. Messaging is compatible with the IBM PC LAN Program including the use of Alias names and the forwarding of messages to alternative workstations. Messages or files up to 64 Kbytes may be sent. The Netpopup service provides popup windows on user workstations for the display of alerts and messages.

3Server/500 Dedicated Network Server

The 3Server/500 is 3Com's dedicated, high-performance network file server. The file server is designed around an 80386, 20-MHz, zero-wait state microprocessor with a unique quad bus architecture. The multiple bus architecture provides an AT-compatible bus, a Small Computer Systems Interface (SCSI) I/O bus, a 32-bit processor bus and an Ethernet bus. 3Server/500 memory is triple-ported, meaning that it can be accessed from three different sources: the LAN co-processor, the main microprocessor and the I/O bus. The 3Server/500 can host either the OS/2-based 3+Open or the MS-DOS 3+ network operating systems.

Primary features of the 3Server/500 file server include the following:

- 70 ns, 32-bit RAM on one or two memory expansion boards in increments of 2, 4, 10 or 16 Mbyte
- Two internal disk or tape drive bays
- Up to 6 Gbyte of 16 ms hard disk access, 1:1 interleave hard disk capacity using 150, 320 or 630 Mbyte drives and up to 5 disk expansion units
- Support for 250 Mbyte or 2.3 Gbyte tape drives
- Ethernet and LocalTalk support built-in on motherboard
- Optional IBM 4 or 16 Mbps Token-Ring adapter
- No keyboard or CRT for increased physical access security
- Enhanced version of OS/2 for improved server performance
- Built-in disk caching
- Optional configuration of two controllers to control two disk drives for disk mirroring
- An optional external power supply with UPS backup and automatic power-loss notification to network users
- 3 + Open and 3 + network operating systems provided on tape cartridges to simplify installation
- 3 + Open Start and 3 + Open Backup software included with 3 + Open option; equivalent software provided with 3 + option

Figure 12.23 shows a potential network architecture using standard and optional capabilities of the 3Server/500. As the figure indicates, a wide variety of LAN architectures and linkages to external environments are possible.

3 + Open Start and 3 + Open Backup

3 + Open Start is software included with 3Server/500 that supports the use of 3Station diskless workstations and similar stations from third party vendors. 3 + Open Backup is the software that supports the 250 Mbyte or 2 Gbyte tape drive options on the 3Server/500. 250 Mbyte tape drives use 1/4" tape cartridge media—2.3 Gbyte drives use 8 mm cartridges. 3 + Open Backup will allow backup of any server on the network from a central source. The backup process can be remotely initiated from either a 3 + or 3 + Open workstation. 3 + Open Backup will restore the entire disk, or designated partitions, directories or files.

3 + and 3 + Open Interoperability

The likelihood of running both 3 + and 3 + Open network operating systems on the same network is relatively high, particularly in those installations planning for expansion or a phased upgrade from a 3 + to a 3 + Open environment. Some basic points must be considered when planning a mixed network:

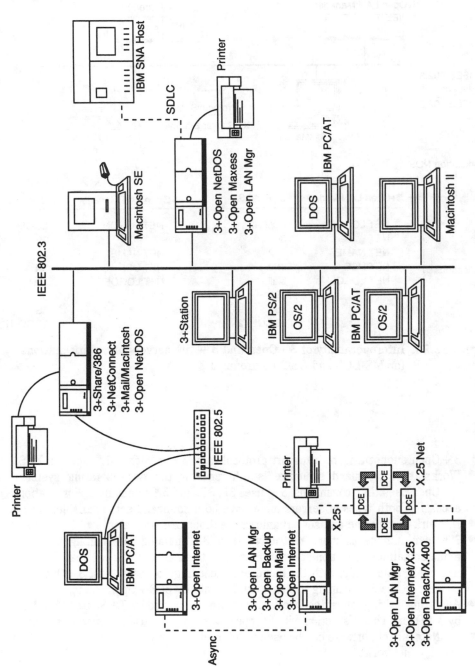

Figure 12.23. Multiple file server architecture for 3 + Open and 3 + network operating systems.

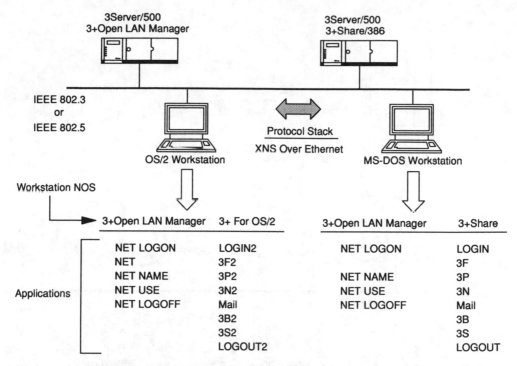

Figure 12.24. Interoperability of 3 + Open and 3 + file servers and work stations for MS-DOS and OS/2 environments.

- 3 + Open supports more transport protocol than 3 +, which only supports XNS
- Workstation command structure is different for the two operating systems. 3 + Open uses NET commands, 3 + uses 3F, 3P, and 3N commands. Workstations accessing both types of servers must have both command sets available.
- Network sharename and servername conventions are equivalent
- 3 + Open naming is more restrictive than 3 + naming. 3 + naming uses the name:domain:organization convention with up to 40 characters, whereas 3 + Open naming is name only, with the name not exceeding 15 characters. 3 + Open will convert to the 3 + naming system with availability of 3 + Open Name.
- As of this writing, Macintosh workstations are supported by 3 + Share386 but not by 3 + Open. This restriction will disappear with later 3 + Open software releases.
- 3 + Netconnect software can be used to internetwork any combination of 3 + Open and 3 + networks

- 3 + Open Backup can backup all 3 + Open and 3 + network servers. 3 + Backup can only back up 3 + servers.
- 3 + Open supports both user-level and share-level security mechanisms. 3 + only supports share-level security. Both security systems can co-exist on a mixed network, but user training considerations may dictate use of the lowest common denominator, or share-level security.

Figure 12.24 depicts the software architecture of mixed 3 + and 3 + Open workstations running on a LAN with 3 + and 3 + Open servers.

OS/2 LAN Server and OS/2 Extended Edition

Overview

OS/2 LAN Server is the server component of IBM's OS/2 LAN architecture. Its work station counterpart is the OS/2 LAN Requester and the OS/2 Communications Manager. Both server and workstation components are based on OS/2 Extended Edition (OS/2 EE) Version 1.1. As of this writing, OS/2 was transitioning to Version 1.2. OS/2 LAN Server and OS/2 EE are designed to support a specific set of network hardware: IBM Token-Ring, IBM PC Network Baseband, and IBM PC Network Broadband. OS/2 LAN Server can interoperate with both OS/2 Extended Edition and PC LAN Program Version 1.31 work stations on the same network. OS/2 LAN Server is a superset of PC LAN Program Version 1.31, which has many of the same capabilities.

Host machines for LAN Server and OS/2 Extended Edition must be 80286 or 80386/486 based; PC LAN Program Version 1.31 work stations can be any IBM PC or PS/2 version or compatible. OS/2 Extended Edition has Communications Manager and LAN Requester modules that directly support a variety of external communications and OS/2 LAN devices. The Communications Manager includes support for NETBIOS and Logical Link Control (IEEE 802.2) protocol. The NETBIOS interface is provided for LAN support and is compatible with IBM PC LAN Support Program. This NETBIOS is not compatible with the original IBM PC Network adapter (broadband). Recall that this adapter has its own NETBIOS support on the card. With Version 1.2 of OS/2 EE, Communications Manager will include protocol support for

- APPC LU6.2
- 3270 Server-Requester Programming Interface (SRPI)
- Asynchronous Communications Device Interface (ACDI)
- Asynchronous Emulation (IBM 3101, DEC VT100)
- 5250 Workstation Feature for System 36
- X.25
- SNA gateway service

The OS/2 LAN Server includes services for the sharing of files, printers, and serial devices and for the definition and management of access to resources on the server. A particular network environment may support multiple servers as a single logical entity. This entity is referred to as a *domain*. The domain includes the servers and services provided by the servers. One server in the domain is known as the *Domain Controller*. The Domain Controller, as the name would suggest, is responsible for management of all shared resources within the server domain. In context of the supported workstations, a multi-server domain is referred to as a *single system image*.

Major Features

OS/2 Extended Edition (Version 1.1 and later) and OS/2 LAN Server provide a number of features that are equivalent to those in 3 + Open and LAN Manager, as well as some unique features. Similarity to 3 + Open is to be expected since OS/2 LAN Server and 3 + Open are both based on LAN Manager core services.

- Support for a variety of services including Work station, Server, Messenger, Popup, Alerter, Netrun, PCDOSRIPL, and PCLP130. These services are similar to those in 3 + Open except PCDOSRIPL and PCLP130, which are unique to OS/2 LAN Server. PCDOSRIPL supports the independent program load (IPL) capability of attached PC-DOS work stations. PCLP130 supports interoperability of PC-DOS work stations running PC LAN Program Version 1.31.
- Ability to configure and manage the LAN from any location on the LAN. This feature is similar to 3 + Open's ADMIN$ shared resource.
- Access control system compatible with SAA architecture. This feature is similar to 3 + Open's User-level security. Specific implementation is unique to OS/2 EE and OS/2 LAN Server.
- Multiple server management. The concepts of server domains and domain controllers are unique to OS/2 LAN Server.
- Ability to execute remote commands on a server at prescheduled times. This feature is similar to 3 + Open.
- Support for printer and communications device queues including prioritization, start/stop times and multiple physical print destinations. These features are similar to 3 + Open.
- User-to-user messaging facility. This feature is similar to 3 + Open.

PC LAN Program Version 1.31 and OS/2 EE Interoperability with OS/2 LAN Server

PC LAN Program Version 1.31 users can interoperate with any server in the OS/2 LAN Server domain. A prerequisite for this interoperability is the starting of the PCLP130 compatibility service in the appropriate OS/2 LAN Server. The OS/2 LAN Server will support remote program load of the IBM PC LAN Program Version 1.31 to

PC DOS workstations. Some limitations are imposed upon the PC LAN Program workstations. The AT command for scheduling of activities and the NET RUN command for remote execution can only be run from OS/2 workstations. The Execute privilege and distributed network management are also restricted to OS/2 workstations.

System Comparisons

Having described VINES, Advanced NetWare (and SFT), NetWare 386, 3 + Open, and OS/2 LAN Server in some detail, a generic methodology for evaluating these and similar products will be provided to aid in the LAN system selection process. A typical use for questions such as these is during the formulation of a Request For Proposals (RFP) for a LAN installation or for the evaluation of vendor proposals in response to an RFP.

We emphasize that no attempt will be made here to pass qualitative judgement on the systems reviewed above, since product lines in the LAN industry undergo frequent revisions. What may be a major drawback or performance limitation today could disappear tomorrow with a major system redesign. Many real-world performance limitations may not be due to software flaws but instead can be linked to a lack of adequate hardware to support a particular feature or system capacity.

File Server Performance Enhancements

What performance enhancements from the following list are included as standard items on the file server? Which are optional items? The list includes, but is not limited to, cache memory, 16-bit or 32-bit memory transfer paths, use of 16- or 32-bit network adapter cards, disk coprocessor support, multiple disk I/O channels, high-speed processors (20 Mhz or better), and use of network adapter card high-speed data interface.

Support For Nondedicated File Servers

Does the network operating system run on nonproprietary servers, such as IBM-compatible 80386 and 80286 machines? What is the supported-user threshold for satisfactory response and throughput compared to a specified dedicated file server? What are the network addressable I/O port capabilities (printers and comm devices) compared to a specified dedicated file server? Does the nondedicated file server provide any significant advantages because of its having an open architecture?

Network Mass Storage Options

How many total megabytes of disk storage are supported? What is the maximum file size supported by the network operating system? Maximum partition size? Can hard drives be daisy-chained? If so, how many? List all the possible hard drive combinations with the resulting mass storage capacities.

Shared Printer Support

How many printers can be connected to the file server? Number of serial printers? Parallel printers? Do printers require a dedicated server or can they be located anywhere on the LAN? Can applications software print requests be immediately run without leaving the application? Can printers be set up to handle different form sizes and formatting options? How are network printers set up by the network administrator? Are print spooling queues controllable by the network administrator? What print spooling features are supported by the print service?

Other Shared Device Support

What other shared devices are supported by the network operating system? Modems? Facsimile? Telex? Plotters? High resolution and color laser printers? Scanners and imagers? CD-ROMs and other image-storage devices? Hardware and software support requirements for specific brands and model numbers should be ascertained.

Network Naming Support

Does the network support a distributed-naming service? Is the naming service permanent or does it log off with the user or when the network node shuts down (e.g., NETBIOS)? Does the naming service support password-protected log ons by users? What network entities does the naming service recognize? How does the naming service support internetworking? Does the naming service recognize and map NETBIOS-compatible names?

Internetworking Schemes

What other networks may be attached to this one using either bridges or gateways? Does the file server support internal bridges? Are external (to the file server) bridges supported? If so, must the bridge work station be dedicated to communications? What communications gateways are available? APPC/LU6.2? IBM 3270/SNA? 3270/Bisynchronous? Remote Job Entry (RJE)? X.25 Packet-Switching? High-capacity T-1 links? Asynchronous? Is there support for stand-alone, remote PC dial-in? What protocol do servers use for internetworking connections?

File Locking Standards Supported

Does the network operating system support physical byte-range locking? Logical byte-range locking? Transaction activity? File locking? Is file locking automatic for single-user applications? Check what file and byte-range locking function calls are implemented, including those that extend MS-DOS or OS/2 lock service.

Host System Access Capabilities

Does the network support access to popular host-based systems? What main-frame or minicomputer operating systems, telecommunications access methods, control systems, and front-end processors are supported? What mainframe or min-icomputer applications may be executed through network gateway processors? Does the network support IBM's Advanced Program-to-Program Communications Protocol (APPC)? How many mainframe sessions can be active on the network at one time?

Network Performance Monitoring

What system, if any, is used to monitor network performance? Are statistics kept in real time and used to present graphic analysis of network performance? Can the moni-toring system be used in a reasonable fashion to predict performance bottlenecks? Can an experienced network administrator use the network monitoring system to plan hardware and software upgrades such as the need to add more servers? Will the monitoring system help in determination of server and other shared resource load balancing?

Access Control and Security

What safeguards prevent unauthorized users from entering the network and logging on to the file server(s)? What access-control method is used to protect directories, files, and other shared resources? What resources are protected by the security system? Does the network support encryption systems?

File Server Software

What type of operating system software does the file server employ? Is it a proprie-tary variant of MS-DOS? OS/2? UNIX or XENIX? Will it support several simultaneous requests for access to hard disk resources? By what method does it interact with network user stations? Can a user log on to the file server and gain access to network files through OS or DEBUG commands?

Fault-tolerant Design

Does the file server have a hot standby feature (mirrored servers)? Is it backed up by a battery or other uninterruptable power supply (UPS)? Is the UPS connected to a logical port on the file server for automatic shut-down features? Are disk directories and file allocation tables (FATs) mirrored on alternate disk platters? Are individual disk drives mirrored? Is disk drive duplexing supported? Does the network operating system have built-in support for transaction fault-tolerance such as transaction logging and transaction roll-forward and roll-back recovery?

Electronic Mail

What type of electronic mail system, if any, does the network software package support? Is is capable of internetworking? Does it gateway to commercial store-and-forward EMail services such as MCI Mail and CompuServe's InfoPLex? Are editor capabilities built in? Can external editors be used? What network server configuration is required to run electronic mail applications? Is Message Handling Service (MHS) supported? Is it scheduled to support international X.400 and X.500 E-Mail standards?

Backup and Archiving Capability

What streaming tape devices does the network operating system recognize? What other types of storage devices are supported for backing up the primary mass storage device? How many megabytes of tape storage are supported? What are capacities of other backup media? Can backups be made while the network is up and running? Are backup devices centralized on servers or distributed on the network? What logical directory units does the backup system handle? Can backups be set for time intervals, for clock times, or both?

Network Utilities

What other types of general software support are provided to the users and to the network administrator by the network operating system? Are utilities menu-driven, command-driven, or both? Is there some type of batch-processing facility or other customization technique? Do dedicated file servers use an external console for control? If so, what types are supported?

Memory Required on Work Stations and Servers

With the advent of new operating systems, a wide variety of expanded and extended memory managers and larger applications, the memory requirements for network operating systems have become much more critical. By the time one loads OS/2, LAN Manager, and one or two major applications, the memory requirements on work stations can easily exceed six to eight Mbytes. What are the minimum memory requirements of the network operating system on both work stations and servers and are there configuration options to reduce RAM requirements?

Protocol Options and Interoperability

What transport protocol and/or Interprocess Communications (IPC) APIs does the network operating system support? Can protocol be run in parallel or are they singularly selectable? What client-server protocol facilities are supported? What work station/file server protocol are supported? What work station host operating system, network operating system, and transport protocol combinations are interoperable on a single network? What file server combinations will support these work station combinations? List all the interoperable work station/file server combinations with required hardware and software configuration.

Summary

You will notice that none of the above questions are related to the clock speed of network media systems, to network topology considerations, to the type of media employed, nor to the hardware efficiency of network adapter cards. This is consistent with our treatment of hardware-independent network software architectures in this chapter. Every major network hardware implementation is supported by at least one of the systems reviewed in this chapter, and many are supported by more than one operating system.

We do not attach relative importance weights to the above factors since importance can only be related to the desired application and the needs of the organization. One commonly accepted method to arrive at a semiobjective ranking during an RFP evaluation process is to attach a criterion weighting and a scoring range to each factor being evaluated. The final score is then a weighted average of the factor scores.

In this chapter, we have reviewed the leading network operating systems for PC-based LANs. With each of these systems, some clear trends are discernable: greater support for interoperability within networks and between networks and increased standardization of core services. As LANs continue to proliferate and network software becomes even more sophisticated than the current generation, some of the more likely trends are:

- OS/2 improvements reflected in Version 1.2, incorporating a new high-performance file system that will lead to significantly enhanced network performance.
- Increased reliance on multitasking operating systems, providing standardization and higher performance for server-based operating systems and making proprietary DOS extensions unnecessary. Major competition for server-based operating systems will come from OS/2, UNIX, and NetWare.
- Improved network operating system support for host-based connectivity solutions, including application-level interoperability and the use of host-based systems as network resource servers.
- Increased acceptance of standard internetworking protocol, evolving from the need to build more sophisticated distributed applications that span multiple LANs and WANs. TCP/IP has become a dominant standard for this purpose, but OSI protocol will make increased inroads. Operating systems such as VINES, NetWare, and LAN Manager now support concurrent use of multiple logical transport protocol stacks.
- Increased development of distributed applications using the client-server model as typified by the Microsoft/Ashton-Tate SQL Server. This trend will lead to a new generation of LAN sophistication and to virtual parity with the minicomputer

world. Distributed applications will, in turn, drive the implementation of more sophisticated security and fault-tolerant features in LANs.

- Expanded development and automation of network management facilities, including the integrated management of local- and wide-area networks.

Appendix A

ASCII Character Set

What Morse Code was to the telegraph operator, computer communication codes and controls are to the IBM PC. They are a standard sequence of signals that can be translated into meaningful information by a recipient. Without standardization of these signals, however, significant incompatibilities between equipment made by different vendors would have developed. Fortunately for the IBM PC owner, there are standards for character codes and communication controls that have kept many of these potential problems from developing.

There are two predominant character codes currently in use in the United States. The *American Standard Code for Information Interchange, or ASCII* (pronounced as-key), is by far the most widely used character code throughout the world. The IBM-developed *Extended Binary Coded Decimal Interchange Code, or EBCDIC* (pronounced ebb-see-dick), is the other major code and is used for communication between and with all IBM mini and mainframe computer equipment. There is also a third code in use on older communications equipment called the *Baudot code*. The characteristics and applications of each of these codes are discussed in this appendix and in Appendices B, C, and D. Because of the predominant use of the ASCII code in communications, that code is explored in detail in this appendix and in Appendix B, Communication Controls.

The ASCII character set is the most universally used convention for the encoding of alphanumeric characters and is a new twist for IBM equipment. Before the introduction of the IBM line of personal computers, all IBM equipment except the System/34 minicomputer used the IBM-developed EBCDIC character set as a standard interchange code.

IBM and Microsoft originally selected ASCII for the IBM PC because of its international acceptance. The first 128 characters of the IBM PC ASCII character set are

Table A.1 Standard ASCII character set.

7	6	5	4	3	2	1	0 0 0	0 0 1	0 1 0	0 1 1	1 0 0	1 0 1	1 1 0	1 1 1
x	x	x	0	0	0	0	NUL	DLE	SP	0	@	P	`	p
x	x	x	0	0	0	1	SOH	DC1	!	1	A	Q	a	q
x	x	x	0	0	1	0	STX	DC2	''	2	B	R	b	r
x	x	x	0	0	1	1	ETX	DC3	#	3	C	S	c	s
x	x	x	0	1	0	0	EOT	DC4	$	4	D	T	d	t
x	x	x	0	1	0	1	ENQ	NAK	%	5	E	U	e	u
x	x	x	0	1	1	0	ACK	SYN	&	6	F	V	f	v
x	x	x	0	1	1	1	BEL	ETB	'	7	G	W	g	w
x	x	x	1	0	0	0	BS	CAN	(	8	H	X	h	x
x	x	x	1	0	0	1	HT	EM	)	9	I	Y	i	y
x	x	x	1	0	1	0	LF	SUB	*	:	J	Z	j	z
x	x	x	1	0	1	1	VT	ESC	+	;	K	[	k	{
x	x	x	1	1	0	0	FF	FS	,	<	L	\	l		
x	x	x	1	1	0	1	CR	GS	–	=	M	]	m	}
x	x	x	1	1	1	0	SO	RS	.	>	N	^	n	~
x	x	x	1	1	1	1	SI	US	/	?	O	_	o	DEL

defined by the ANSI *X3.4-1977 (Revised 1983), Code for Information Interchange.* Two other world standards organizations have published almost identical character codes, further ensuring ASCII as an international standard for communications between computers from different vendors. The other two standards are: *Alphabet Number 5* of the *International Consultive Committee for Telephone and Telegraph (CCITT)*; and *Standard Number 646, 7-Bit Coded Character Set for Information Processing* of the *International Standards Organization (ISO)*.

Almost all American computer hardware companies and many foreign hardware producers support this ASCII code, which places the PC in an excellent community of standardized communications hardware and software. Participation in communication networks using commercially available hardware and software is assured because of this use of a standardized code.

A translation table showing the binary coding of the standard 7-bit ASCII character set is shown in Table A-1. The characters included in this set are 26 uppercase letters, 26 lowercase letters, 10 numbers, and other special text characters found on most typewriter keyboards. A set of standard communication *control codes* is also provided and is discussed in detail in Appendix B.

Table A.2 Hierarchy of ASCII characters.

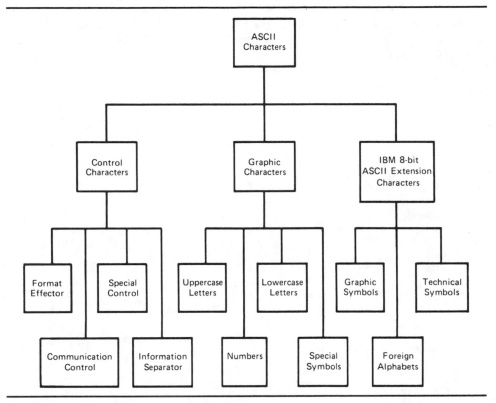

The standard ASCII characters shown in Table A-1 can be represented by seven data bits, but the special ASCII *extension* characters developed by IBM and Microsoft for the IBM PC require eight data bits. Seven data bits give you the ability to combine two things (either a 1 or a 0) seven at a time, resulting in a number of possible unique combinations equal to 2 to the seventh power. If you perform that computation, you will find that the result is 128. This value equals the number of standard ASCII characters (0-127). If you do the same computation by taking two things eight at a time, you will find that the result is 256, which equals the total number of ASCII characters shown at the end of this appendix. This simply means that IBM and Microsoft ASCII characters with values greater than 127 can only be represented with eight data bits. This is the case whether the character is being stored in an ASCII file or transmitted long distance to another microcomputer.

The ANSI standard for ASCII characters divides them into two major categories according to their function. Characters used to generate readable text are labeled *graphic characters* and characters used to achieve action are labeled *control characters*. The former of these categories is somewhat misleading because the standard ASCII graphic characters are actually normal text characters. The term graphic would better apply to the *special extension characters* provided by IBM and Microsoft in the PC character set. The special characters and symbols with values of 176 through 223 are useful in the creation of graphic images while in the text display mode. Table A.2 shows the hierarchy of ASCII characters based on the ANSI standard, and includes the special extension characters.

Appendix B

Communication Controls

$\mathbf{A}$s noted in Appendix A, the first 128 characters of the IBM PC character set are defined by the *American National Standards Institute* (*ANSI*) in the *American Standard Code for Information Interchange* (*ASCII*). This ASCII code (pronounced as-key) is used in almost all computers made in America with the notable exception of IBM mini and mainframe computers. Such standardization has contributed significantly to the development of computer technology and the standardization of computer communications.

The ANSI-standard character set, along with the extended IBM PC ASCII character set, are discussed in general in Appendix A. This appendix provides a detailed description of a subset of the ANSI-standard characters that were originally designed to provide communications and printer controls. These *control characters*, the first 32 ASCII characters, are shown in Table B-1. This table also provides a brief description of each control character and the control group that it falls within. Refer to the diagram of the hierarchy of ASCII characters shown in Appendix A, Table A-2 to get a better feel for the relationship between these control characters and other ASCII characters.

Although the control characters are represented by seven digital bits, just as the other ANSI-defined characters, they produce more than printable results when received by certain devices. These "characters" act as *signals* to control specific operations of printing, display, and communications devices. The entire group of ASCII control characters is sometimes called *non-printing control characters*, but the label does not apply to personal computers that operate under PC- or MS-DOS. All but one of these characters has been assigned a graphic representation by IBM and Microsoft, as you can see in Appendix A, Table A-1. Unfortunately, this dual role of control and graphic character depiction does cause some confusion for PC users who wish to display or print these images.

Most of the first 32 IBM PC characters can be displayed on the PC screen, but getting them onto the screen may take some imagination. Using DOS commands such

Table B.1 ASCII control characters.

ASCII Value	Mnemonic Character	ASCII Character	IBM Function	Group	Communication Usage
000	^@	NUL	null	CC	Null character—filler
001	^A	SOH		CC	Start of heading
002	^B	STX		CC	Start of text
003	^C	ETX		CC	End of text
004	^D	EOT		CC	End of transmission
005	^E	ENQ		CC	Enquiry
006	^F	ACK		CC	Acknowledge affirmative
007	^G	BEL	beep	SC	Audible alarm
008	^H	BS	backspace	FE	Backspace one position
009	^I	HT	tab	FE	Physical horizonal tab
010	^J	LF	line feed	FE	Line feed
011	^K	VT	home	FE	Physical vertical tab
012	^L	FF	form feed	FE	Form feed
013	^M	CR	carriage return	FE	Carriage return
014	^N	SO		SC	Shift out
015	^O	SI		SC	Shift in
016	^P	DLE		CC	Data link escape
017	^Q	DC1		SC	XON or resume
018	^R	DC2		SC	Device control 2
019	^S	DC3		SC	XOFF or pause
020	^T	DC4		SC	Device control 4
021	^U	NAK		CC	Negative acknowledgement
022	^V	SYN		CC	Synchronous idle
023	^W	ETB		CC	End of transmission block
024	^X	CAN		SC	Cancel
025	^Y	EM		SC	End of medium
026	^Z	SUB		SC	Substitute
027	^[	ESC		SC	Escape
028	^/	FS	cursor right	IS	File separator
029	^]	GS	cursor left	IS	Group separator
030	^^	RS	cursor up	IS	Record separator
031	^–	US	cursor down	IS	Unit separator
127		DEL		SC	Delete

as TYPE to send a file containing these characters to the screen may produce different results than sending them to the screen from within a software application, such as a communications software package. DOS, and the BASIC language that uses DOS services to display characters, will react to the control aspects of these characters, whereas software written in other languages such as C or assembly can send these images directly to the display buffer in memory, thereby bypassing their control side effects.

Another aspect of control characters that may cause confusion is the way they are listed in tables or in text. The 32 control characters are often depicted as a caret followed by a letter or symbol, which implies that they can be formed by the combination of two non-control ASCII characters. The confusion comes from the use of the *caret* to represent the *Ctrl key* on the PC keyboard that can be used in combination with a letter or symbol to create a control character. When the Ctrl key is held down and a letter or symbol key is pressed, a control character is generated, but DOS displays the results for many of these characters as the caret followed by the letter or symbol. For example, the Ctrl-C keystroke combination used to abnormally terminate a DOS task also produces a C on the display.

The caret-symbol depiction of control characters should be viewed as a *convention* that allows authors to show or discuss control characters in text without using lengthy titles for them. This convention has evolved over many years and is not likely to change with the IBM PC, even though these characters are now assigned special graphic symbols. One reason the graphic symbols are not likely to become an accepted method of depicting control characters is that word processors and text editors normally translate these characters into the caret-symbol format automatically so they can be printed on standard printers. If the actual control characters were to be sent to the printer, they would not print as graphic symbols—they would produce the results discussed in the following paragraphs.

Control Character Groups

The ANSI standard breaks the ASCII control-character group down into three functional subgroups. These groups are *communication controls, format effectors*, and *information separators*. There is a fourth group not categorized by the ANSI standard that performs special functions; these characters are labelled *special control characters*, for later reference. Table B-1 shows the control group associated with each of the 32 control characters.

To eliminate ambiguity and establish specific guidelines for the use of communication control characters, the ANSI has given each character a unique definition. These definitions and the specific use the IBM PC makes of these characters are discussed next. References to applications of these characters as printer controls are generalized and may not apply to all printers used with the PC. Refer to the manual that comes with a printer to determine its specific use of control characters.

Logical Communication Control

The ANSI definition of a *communication control* (*CC*) character is a character that controls or facilitates data transmission over a communications network. Several of these characters are illustrated in the discussion of bisync protocol in Chapter 2 and file transfer protocols in Chapter 6. These logical communication control characters are typically used in both asynchronous and synchronous serial protocols for data transfer handshaking. They tell the receiving device what to expect as data; they indicate a transition in type of data being transmitted; or they are used to verify proper transmission and receipt.

SOH

The *Start of Heading* (*SOH*) is used in bisync data streams to denote the start of a message heading data block. Stations in a network check the data that follow this character to determine whether they are to be recipients of the data that will follow the heading. In essence, it is a "listen to see if your name is called" signal for stations in a network.

The SOH character is sometimes used in asynchronous communications to transfer a series of files without handling each file as a separate communication. The SOH character is used during the transfer of multiple files to signal the beginning of the filename of each file before transfer of the file begins. In asynchronous communications, there is only one receiver monitoring the communication line, so there is no need for a destination device address to follow the SOH character; only the filename of each file is needed. This type of file transfer is often limited to communications between microcomputers using the same communications software, because it is not a standardized file-transfer protocol.

The SOH is also used with the Xmodem file-transfer protocol to signal the start of a 128-byte data block transfer. This character is followed by two block number bytes used to ensure that blocks are transferred properly.

STX

The *Start of Text* (*STX*) control character is also used in the bisync protocol. It signals the end of heading data and the beginning of information data.

ETX

The *End of Text* (*ETX*) control character is a bisync protocol signal that tells a receiver that all information data have been transmitted. This character can also be used to signal the beginning of block check characters used to detect communication errors.

EOT

The *End of Transmission* (*EOT*) control character is used to indicate the end of transmission of all data associated with a message sent to a particular device. This character also tells other devices in a network to check further transmissions for the presence of messages directed to them. The EOT character is the end frame for a message that is initiated by an SOH character. It is also used in the Xmodem protocol to indicate the end of a file transfer.

ETB

The *End of Transmission Block* (*ETB*) control character indicates the end of a particular block of transmitted data. The bisync protocol uses this character instead of an ETX character when data are transmitted in two or more blocks instead of a single continuous block.

ENQ

The *Enquiry* (*ENQ*) control character is used to request a response from a communication receiving station. It may be used to obtain the identification of a device or to determine the status of transmitted data. Some IBM PC asynchronous communication packages use this character in protocol file transfers. In response to the receipt of the ENQ character, a receiving device may be required to respond with the number of the last block successfully received. This nonstandard application of ENQ facilitates the retransmission of data blocks that were not properly received by the destination device.

ACK

The *Acknowledge* (*ACK*) control character is used to verify proper communication between a transmitter and receiver. One application of ACK is in detecting errors in transmitted data. After receiving a block of data, a receiver may be required to send the transmitter an ACK character indicating that the error-check character or characters show no transmission error. The transmitter may be required to receive the ACK before more data can be transmitted.

DLE

The *Data Link Escape* (*DLE*) control character is used to modify the meaning of a limited number of subsequent characters. It is used in the bisync protocol along with other control characters to signal the start and end of data field transmission in the transparent mode.

NAK

The *Negative Acknowledge* (*NAK*) control character is used to indicate improper communication between a transmitter and a receiver. This character is generally transmitted by a receiver to initiate a retransmission of data when an error-check indicates the presence of data transmission errors. The ENQ, ACK, and NAK characters are often used together for protocol data transmission that does not involve user interaction. These signals take place between two communication software packages and, when they are being properly executed, are transparent to the user. The NAK is also used in the Xmodem protocol to tell the transmitting computer that the receiving computer is ready to start a file transfer.

SYN

The *Synchronous Idle* (*SYN*) control character is used in the bisync protocol to initiate or maintain communication synchronization when no data are being transmitted. This character performs a function similar to the stop bit in asynchronous communication— it maintains a known signal on the data line when no data are being transferred. The interruption of a series of SYN characters is an indication of heading or data information to follow.

PHYSICAL COMMUNICATION CONTROL

This group of communication controls are used with physical devices such as printers, displays, and other computers.

NUL

The *NUL character* is, as its name implies, a *null entity*. It is often used as a non-printing *time delay* or *filler character* and is especially useful for communicating with printing devices that need a finite amount of time for positioning the print head. Communication terminals that print hard copy often require at least two NUL characters following each carriage return to give the print head sufficient time to return to the left margin before receiving the next character. Some host system software packages allow you to specify a certain number of nulls to be transmitted to your computer after each carriage return.

DEL

The *Delete* (*DEL*) character is not actually a character but is used to erase or obliterate characters. The IBM PC BASIC editor uses this signal to remove characters positioned above the cursor. The character also causes the IBM Graphics Printer and Proprinter to delete the last received character. Other applications of the DEL character are comparable to the time delay application of the NUL character. The DEL can affect information layout or equipment control, however, which necessitates careful placement of the character.

CAN

Cancel (*CAN*) has many different applications, depending on the vendor, but it is generally used to denote an error in data transfer. The character is an indication that the data received should be disregarded.

EM

The *End of Medium* (*EM*) control character is used to indicate either the physical end of a data medium (data storage, representation of communication material) or the end of a portion of data medium containing desired data.

SUB

The *Substitute* (*SUB*) control character is used for controlling the accuracy of data communication. It replaces a character that is determined to be in error, invalid, or impossible for the receiving device to display or print.

FORMAT EFFECTORS

The *format effector* (*FE*) characters are used to control the position of characters being printed or displayed. Sending these characters to the IBM printer either directly or as a BASIC CHR$(n) string allows you to produce text formatting. Wordprocessing packages use these control characters in the control of text layout.

BS

The *Backspace* (*BS*) control character is used to control the active print position for both the visual display monitor and the printer. This character moves the IBM PC cursor to the left one position, assuming the cursor is not in column one when the character is executed and removes any character displayed in the position vacated. The key that produces this character is sometimes called the backspace delete key because of the action it produces. This character can be transmitted as data just as any other character is transmitted, but it is normally used only when data are transmitted in the conversation mode. Properly designed communication software will perform a backspace when the character is received instead of printing a new character.

HT

The *Horizontal Tabulation* (*HT*) control character causes the active printing device to move to the next predetermined position before printing the next character. The HT character is executed on the PC keyboard by using special tab stop keys and can be executed on IBM printers by performing a BASIC LPRINT CHR$(9).

LF

The *Line Feed* (*LF*) control character causes the active printing position to advance to the same column position in the next line. The results produced by this character are often confused with that of the carriage return (CR) discussed next. The line feed does not advance the cursor or print head to the first column of the next line unless it is preceded by a CR. Most business-oriented communications packages do not send line feeds with CRs unless specifically instructed to do so, and a file received without line feeds cannot be properly listed on an IBM PC monitor until they are added. Using the DOS TYPE command to display such a file results in a stream of text that moves rapidly across the screen in a single line. Appendix B contains a listing of a BASIC program that will add line feeds after each CR contained in a file so that a user can list or edit the file.

VT

The *Vertical Tabulation* (*VT*) control character causes the active printing or display position to advance to the same column a predetermined number of lines down from the present line being printed or displayed. Some conventions use the VT to move the cursor or print head to the first column of the new line. Transmitting a VT character to an IBM printer produces the same result as a single line feed—the print head moves down one line, but the column position remains the same.

FF

The *Form Feed* (*FF*) control character clears the IBM PC display and places the cursor at the upper left-hand corner of the screen. This is often used by bulletin board and host systems to clear the display before starting a new function. If the communication session is being captured to a printer as it is displayed on the PC monitor, the FF character used to clear the display can result in a lot of wasted paper. As the FF clears the screen, it is also received at the printer where it will advance the printer head to the next logical top of form or to a predetermined line on the next form or page.

If the print head is at the top of a page when the printer is turned on, transmitting an FF character to an IBM printer while in the "On Line" mode will cause the printer to advance the print form to the top of a new page, regardless of the number of lines already printed on the page. If the print head is not at the top of a page when it is turned on, an FF will cause the paper to advance but not to the top of a new page. The logical top of form that will be advanced to on receipt of an FF is the line position on a new page that matches the line position of the print head when the printer was powered up.

CR

The *Carriage Return* (CR) control character advances the active print or display position to the first column of the same line. Unless the carriage return is followed by a line feed, the characters that follow the carriage return will overstrike characters already printed on the line. This will often be the case when printing or displaying files that were received electronically from host or bulletin board systems because those systems normally do not send line feeds after each carriage return. The carriage return is also used to initiate the printing of a line when used with an IBM PC printer. The printer captures all characters it receives in an area of its memory called a print buffer, then sends those characters to the print head when it receives a carriage return or an LF, or when the print buffer has received enough for one full print line.

INFORMATION SEPARATORS

Information separator (IS) characters are used to control the separation of logical divisions of information as the information is transmitted over communication channels. These characters are not generally used in communications and will not be reviewed in detail in this text.

FS

The *File Separator* (FS) control character is used to mark a logical boundary between files being transferred.

GS

The *Group Separator* (GS) control character is used to mark logical boundaries between groups of transmitted data.

RS

The *Record Separator* (RS) control character is used to mark the boundaries between records in data transmission.

US

The *Unit Separator* (US) is the final information-separator control character, and it is used to mark the logical boundaries between distinct units of data.

SPECIAL CONTROL

The *special control* (SC) characters are used for printer control, data transmission speed-matching, or special data transmission error signaling. Some of these characters, such as ESC, perform communication control functions, but they are not included in that category by the ANSI standard.

BEL

The *Bell* (*BEL*) is a special ASCII control character that performs a function in keeping with its name. This character may be included in a text file or it may be transmitted between devices to signal the need for human attention. When transmitted in the conversation mode, which can be done by pressing the CTRL and G keys simultaneously, the character will cause a speaker connected to the PC to emit an attention-getting beep.

SO

The *Shift Out* (*SO*) is a special ASCII control character that serves to extend the standard graphics character set. The receipt of this character turns on the double-width printing mode of the IBM printer for the remainder of the line of text or until a DC4 control character is received. This same character is used by other printers to extend the character set to special graphic symbols used in math and engineering.

SI

The *Shift In* (*SI*) control character may be used to reset the receiving device to the Standard ASCII character set. It is also used by some printers to reset the print mode initialized by the Shift Out character. IBM printers do not use this convention, however. They use the DC4 character to frame or terminate the printing of double-width characters and use the SI character to initiate compressed mode printing. The compressed mode is retained until the printer receives a DC2 character.

DC1

The *Device Control 1* (*DC1*) control character is an electronic toggle switch. Its function may be different for different vendor-supplied equipment, but it is generally used to control communications data flow. For local display of files, this character (a *Ctrl-Q*) will reinitiate the listing of a file that was temporarily halted by a DC3 character (a *Ctrl-S*). In data communications, this character is often designated as *XON* and is used to reinitiate the transfer of data that was temporarily halted by the transmission of an *XOFF* character. The IBM PC may or may not use this handshake convention, depending on the communication software being used. Many communication programs written in the BASIC language are capable of transmitting the XON to a host but are incapable of recognizing the receipt of either XON or XOFF characters because of the limited data-handling speed of the BASIC interpreter.

DC2

The *Device Control 2* (*DC2*) control character is also a toggle switch control character, and its role varies with vendor applications. The DC2 character is used with the IBM Graphics Printer and Proprinter to turn off the compressed printing mode and empty the print buffer.

DC3

The *Device Control 3* (*DC3*) control character is another ASCII toggle switch, and it is often used with the DC1 character for data transfer speed-matching. The DC3 character is an *XOFF*, and it is used to temporarily halt the transmission of data. When a receiving device has received all the data it can handle, it may send the host an XOFF to stop the flow of data. When the device has printed or saved all the data received before the XOFF was transmitted, it will send an XON character to the host to re-initiate data transmission.

As indicated with the DC1 character, many BASIC communication programs are capable of sending XOFFs but cannot recognize XOFFs received from other microcomputer or host systems. To recognize and act on received XOFF characters, a BASIC program would have to compare every character bit pattern received to the XOFF bit pattern as other characters are being received and displayed, printed, or saved. This comparison technique would slow down data handling and result in longer file transfers. Assembly-language communication programs, on the other hand, often use an interrupt design that reacts quickly to XOFF characters, thereby making them excellent programs for transferring large files. This character is also used to temporarily halt the local listing of a file. It can be invoked by holding down the Ctrl key then pressing either the S key or Num Lock key.

DC4

The *Device Control 4* (*DC4*) control character is the fourth and last electronic toggle-switch used in the ASCII character code, and like the other four toggle characters, its role often varies depending on the vendor. This character turns off the IBM printer double-width print mode that is initiated by the Shift Out character.

ESC

The *Escape* (*ESC*) control character is used extensively for communications with printers and to produce color and graphics on an IBM PC monitor. It is normally transmitted just before the transmission of other characters or numbers to provide character code extensions or control code extensions. The sets of characters used to control printers vary from one printer design to another. The IBM printers are capable of accepting escape code sequences to perform such functions as underlining and predetermining the values for horizontal and vertical tabs. Other dot-matrix printers are designed to accept over 30 escape codes to perform these same functions, plus many other advanced features such as dot-addressable graphics control. The key to proper use of this character is the compatibility of software and hardware combinations.

Appendix C

EBCDIC Character Set

ASCII Binary Code	EBCDIC Binary Code	Character
1 0 0 0 0 0 0	0 1 1 1 1 1 0 0	@
1 0 0 0 0 0 1	1 1 0 0 0 0 0 1	A
1 0 0 0 0 1 0	1 1 0 0 0 0 1 0	B
1 0 0 0 0 1 1	1 1 0 0 0 0 1 1	C
1 0 0 0 1 0 0	1 1 0 0 0 1 0 0	D
1 0 0 0 1 0 1	1 1 0 0 0 1 0 1	E
1 0 0 0 1 1 0	1 1 0 0 0 1 1 0	F
1 0 0 0 1 1 1	1 1 0 0 0 1 1 1	G
1 0 0 1 0 0 0	1 1 0 0 1 0 0 0	H
1 0 0 1 0 0 1	1 1 0 0 1 0 0 1	I
1 0 0 1 0 1 0	1 1 0 1 0 0 0 1	J
1 0 0 1 0 1 1	1 1 0 1 0 0 1 0	K
1 0 0 1 1 0 0	1 1 0 1 0 0 1 1	L
1 0 0 1 1 0 1	1 1 0 1 0 1 0 0	M
1 0 0 1 1 1 0	1 1 0 1 0 1 0 1	N
1 0 0 1 1 1 1	1 1 0 1 0 1 1 0	O
1 0 1 0 0 0 0	1 1 0 1 1 0 0 0	P
1 0 1 0 0 0 1	1 1 0 1 1 0 0 0	Q
1 0 1 0 0 1 0	1 1 0 1 1 0 0 1	R
1 1 0 0 1 0 1	1 1 1 0 0 0 1 0	S
1 0 1 0 1 0 0	1 1 1 0 0 0 1 1	T
1 0 1 0 1 0 1	1 1 1 0 0 1 0 0	U
1 0 1 0 1 1 0	1 1 1 0 0 1 0 1	V
1 0 1 0 1 1 1	1 1 1 0 0 1 1 0	W
1 0 1 1 0 0 0	1 1 1 0 0 1 1 1	X
1 0 1 1 0 0 1	1 1 0 1 1 0 0 0	Y
1 0 1 1 0 1 0	1 1 0 1 1 0 0 1	Z
1 0 1 1 0 1 1		[(left bracket)
1 0 1 1 1 0 0		/ (left slash)
1 0 1 1 1 0 1		] (right bracket)
1 0 1 1 1 1 0		∧ (caret or up arrow)
1 0 1 1 1 1 1	0 1 1 0 1 1 0 1	___
1 1 0 0 0 0 0	0 1 1 1 1 1 0 1	'
1 1 0 0 0 0 1	1 0 0 0 0 0 0 1	a
1 1 0 0 0 1 0	1 0 0 0 0 0 1 0	b
1 1 0 0 0 1 1	1 0 0 0 0 0 1 1	c
1 1 0 0 1 0 0	1 0 0 0 0 1 0 0	d
1 1 0 0 1 0 1	1 0 0 0 0 1 0 1	e
1 1 0 0 1 1 0	1 0 0 0 0 1 1 0	f
1 1 0 0 1 1 1	1 0 0 0 0 1 1 1	g

ASCII Binary Code	EBCDIC Binary Code	Character
1 1 0 1 0 0 0	1 0 0 0 1 0 0 0	h
1 1 0 1 0 0 1	1 0 0 0 1 0 0 1	i
1 1 0 1 0 1 0	1 0 0 1 0 0 0 1	j
1 1 0 1 0 1 1	1 0 0 1 0 0 1 0	k
1 1 0 1 1 0 0	1 0 0 1 0 0 1 1	l
1 1 0 1 1 0 1	1 0 0 1 0 1 0 0	m
1 1 0 1 1 1 0	1 0 0 1 0 1 0 1	n
1 1 0 1 1 1 1	1 0 0 1 0 1 1 0	o
1 1 1 0 0 0 0	1 0 0 1 0 1 1 1	p
1 1 1 0 0 0 1	1 0 0 1 1 0 0 0	q
1 1 1 0 0 1 1	1 0 0 1 1 0 0 1	r
1 1 1 0 0 1 1	1 0 1 0 0 0 1 0	s
1 1 1 0 1 0 0	1 0 1 0 0 0 1 1	t
1 1 1 0 1 0 1	1 0 1 0 0 1 0 0	u
1 1 1 0 1 1 0	1 0 1 0 0 1 0 1	v
1 1 1 0 1 1 1	1 0 1 0 0 1 1 0	w
1 1 1 1 0 0 0	1 0 1 0 0 1 1 1	x
1 1 1 1 0 0 1	1 0 1 0 1 0 0 0	y
1 1 1 1 0 1 0	1 0 1 0 1 0 0 1	z
1 1 1 1 0 1 1		{
1 1 1 1 1 0 0	0 1 1 0 1 0 1 0	¦
1 1 1 1 1 0 1		}
1 1 1 1 1 1 0		~
1 1 1 1 1 1 1		DEL
0 0 0 0 0 0 0	0 0 0 0 0 0 0 0	NUL
0 0 0 0 0 0 1	0 0 0 0 0 0 0 1	SOH
0 0 0 0 0 1 0	0 0 0 0 0 0 1 0	STX
0 0 0 0 0 1 1	0 0 0 0 0 0 1 1	ETX
0 0 0 0 1 0 0		EOT
0 0 0 0 1 0 1	0 0 1 0 1 1 0 1	ENQ
0 0 0 0 1 1 0		ACK
0 0 0 0 1 1 1		BEL
0 0 0 1 0 0 0		BS
0 0 0 1 0 0 1		HT
0 0 0 1 0 1 0		LF
0 0 0 1 0 1 1		VT
0 0 0 1 1 0 0	0 0 0 0 1 1 0 0	FF
0 0 0 1 1 0 1		CR
0 0 0 1 1 1 0		SO
0 0 0 1 1 1 1		SI
0 0 1 0 0 0 0		DLE
0 0 1 0 0 0 1		DC1
0 0 1 0 0 1 0		DC2
0 0 1 0 0 1 1		DC3
0 0 1 0 1 0 0		DC4
0 0 1 0 1 0 1		NAK
0 0 1 0 1 1 0	0 0 1 1 0 0 1 0	SYN
0 0 1 0 1 1 1	0 0 1 0 0 1 1 0	ETB
0 0 1 1 0 0 0		CAN
0 0 1 1 0 0 1	0 0 0 1 1 0 0 1	EM
0 0 1 1 0 0 1	0 0 1 1 1 1 1 1	SUB
0 0 1 1 0 1 1	0 0 0 1 0 1 1 1	ESC
0 0 1 1 1 0 0		FS
0 0 1 1 1 0 1		GS
0 0 1 1 1 1 0		RS
0 0 1 1 1 1 1		US
0 1 0 0 0 0 0	0 1 0 0 0 0 0 0	SP
0 1 0 0 0 0 1	0 1 0 1 1 0 1 0	!
0 1 0 0 0 1 0	0 1 1 1 1 1 1 1	"
0 1 0 0 0 1 1		#
0 1 0 0 1 0 0	0 1 0 1 1 0 1 1	$

ASCII Binary Code	EBCDIC Binary Code	Character
0 1 0 0 1 0 1	0 1 1 0 1 1 0 0	%
0 1 0 0 1 1 0	0 1 0 1 0 0 0 0	&
0 1 0 0 1 1 1	0 1 1 1 1 1 0 1	'
0 1 0 1 0 0 0	0 1 0 0 1 1 0 1	(
0 1 0 1 0 0 1	0 1 0 1 1 1 0 1	)
0 1 0 1 0 1 0		*
0 1 0 1 0 1 1	0 1 0 0 1 1 1 0	+
0 1 0 1 1 0 0	0 1 1 0 1 0 1 1	'
0 1 0 1 1 0 1	0 1 1 0 0 0 0 0	-
0 1 0 1 1 1 0	0 0 1 0 0 1 0 0	.
0 1 0 1 1 1 1	0 1 1 0 0 0 0 1	/
0 1 1 0 0 0 0	1 1 1 1 0 0 0 0	0
0 1 1 0 0 0 1	1 1 1 1 0 0 0 1	1
0 1 1 0 0 1 0	1 1 1 1 0 0 1 0	2
0 1 1 1 1 0 0	1 1 1 1 0 0 1 1	3
0 1 1 0 1 0 0	1 1 1 1 0 1 0 0	4
0 1 1 0 1 0 1	1 1 1 1 0 1 0 1	5
0 1 1 0 1 1 0	1 1 1 1 0 1 1 0	6
0 1 1 0 1 1 1	1 1 1 1 0 1 1 1	7
0 1 1 1 0 0 0	1 1 1 1 1 0 0 0	8
0 1 1 1 0 0 1	1 1 1 1 1 0 0 1	9
0 1 1 1 0 1 0	0 1 1 1 1 0 1 0	:
0 1 1 1 0 1 1	0 1 0 1 1 1 1 0	;
0 1 1 1 1 0 0	0 1 0 0 1 1 0 0	<
0 1 1 1 1 0 1	0 1 1 1 1 0 1 1	=
0 1 1 1 1 1 0	0 1 1 0 1 1 1 0	>
0 1 1 1 1 1 1	0 1 1 0 1 1 1 1	?

Appendix D

Baudot Character Set

Baudot Code					Lowercase	Uppercase
1	1	0	0	0	A	-
1	0	0	1	1	B	?
0	1	1	1	0	C	:
1	0	0	1	0	D	$
1	0	0	0	0	E	3
1	0	1	1	0	F	'
0	1	0	1	1	G	&
0	0	1	0	1	H	British Pound
0	1	1	0	0	I	8
1	1	0	1	0	J	'
1	1	1	1	0	K	(
0	1	0	0	1	L	)
0	0	1	1	1	M	
0	0	1	1	0	N	.
0	0	0	1	1	O	9
0	1	1	0	1	P	0
1	1	1	0	1	Q	1
0	1	0	1	0	R	
1	0	1	0	0	S	Bell
0	0	0	0	1	T	5
1	1	1	0	0	U	7
0	1	1	1	1	V	;
1	1	0	0	1	W	2
1	0	1	1	1	X	/
1	0	1	0	1	Y	6
1	0	0	0	1	Z	"
1	1	1	1	1	LETTERS (Shift to Lowercase)	
1	1	0	1	1	FIGURES (Shift to Uppercase)	
0	0	1	0	0	SPACE	
0	0	0	1	0	CARRIAGE RETURN	
0	1	0	0	0	LINE FEED	
0	0	0	0	0	BLANK	

INDEX

About the Authors

Larry Jordan has a BS degree in Nuclear Engineering from North Carolina State University and an MBA from The George Washington University. He has worked in engineering and computer science for 20 years.

Larry has worked with the IBM family of Personal Computers since 1981. Two of his first PC projects have contributed significantly to the popularity of communications with the PC. Larry worked with Andrew Fluegelman to enhance the interpreter and compiled versions of his PC-TALK smart terminal software. Larry also completed the conversion of the popular RBBS-PC bulletin board system from CP/M BASIC to IBM PC BASIC. He worked with the members of the Capital PC User Group to enhance the software for several years.

Larry's areas of greatest interest are communications, networking and systems integration with the PC and PS/2. Larry has written many articles on these subjects for national magazines and user groups. As a part of his education in communications and networking, Larry coauthored a commercial communications system in the C language. He also wrote a similar system in FORTRAN.

Larry works for IBM Corporation where he manages the integration of micro-, mini- and mainframe computers for utilities and other commercial customers.

Bruce Churchill is a retired Naval Aviator and has a BS from the US Naval Academy and an MS in Operations Research from the US Naval Postgraduate School. Bruce has over 20 years experience in local area networking, radio and data communications, and teaches an MBA course in Communications Systems Planning at a local university. He has also lectured on the subject of LANs at the annual Navy Microcomputer Conference. Bruce co-authored the first and second editions of *Communications and Networking for the IBM PC and Compatibles* and has written several magazine articles covering the local area networking field.

Bruce is currently the Deputy Vice President for Western Operations for TECHPLAN Corporation in San Diego, California, and is the Project Manager for several public safety and law enforcement projects throughout California.